Praise for

Lincoln and Douglas

"Surprisingly rip-roaring. . . . You can watch Lincoln evolve before your eyes into the great man he had yet to become."

—Lev Grossman, *Time*

"Guelzo's feat is that he does more than just resist the romanticized view of the event. He takes on with equal relish the counterclaim, widely accepted by academics, that the Lincoln-Douglas encounters were simply the trashy 'political theater' of a pre-wired age. . . . Guelzo gives the debates their popular due. . . . Stirring."

—David Greenberg, Slate

"The deepest, most instructive study yet of how on-the-ground politics actually worked just before the Civil War and how ordinary people involved themsleves with the nation's most fateful political question, the future of slavery."

—*The Atlantic Monthly*

"Guelzo is an astute analyst, not only of the candidates' words, but also of their speaking styles, the settings for the debates, the campaigns of which they were a part. . . . Guelzo's dramatic account of the debates gives one a sense of what it was like to have been there."

—Myron A. Marty, *St. Louis Post-Dispatch*

"Guelzo's book is an ambitious narrative that shows how and why the Lincoln-Douglas debates mattered at the time, why they still matter, and why Lincoln's words still speak to us more than a century later."
—Terry Golway, *The Star-Ledger* (Newark, NJ)

"A brilliant new analysis . . . Guelzo's magnificent study of the debates with its sparkling prose is a major contribution to Lincolniana"
—*The Journal of American History*

"A rowsing narrative, academically researched, embracingly informative, and deeply thoughtful. . . . This book is a real winner."
—*Library Journal* (starred review)

"In this layered reconstruction of Illinois' senatorial contest of 1858, Civil War historian Guelzo embeds the famed debates in the razzmatazz of the campaign. . . . This Lincoln-Douglas rendition will engage every interest in Civil War and black history."
—Gilbert Taylor, *Booklist* (starred review)

"An astute, gracefully written account of the celebrated Lincoln-Douglas debates of 1858. . . . Guelzo's smoothly narrated history of this segment of Lincoln's career, packed full of illustrative quotes from primary sources, will become a standard."
—*Publishers Weekly*

"A powerful story, deftly told. Guelzo's prose has an old-fashioned urbanity. . . . He has a keen ear for the telling anecdote and he knows how to step back and let the quotations make his point. The book exudes a cosmopolitan awareness of the distortions and corruptions of everyday politics, but Guelzo never lapses into cynicism. He knows that beneath all the hoopla serious issues were in play."
—James Oakes, *The New York Review of Books*

ALSO BY ALLEN C. GUELZO

The New England Theology, 1750–1850 (with Douglas R. Sweeney)

Lincoln's Emancipation Proclamation: The End of Slavery in America

Abraham Lincoln: Redeemer President

*Edwards in Our Time: Jonathan Edwards and the Shaping of
American Religion (with Sang Hyun Lee)*

Holland's Life of Abraham Lincoln (editor)

*The Crisis of the American Republic:
A New History of the Civil War and Reconstruction*

*For the Union of Evangelical Christendom:
The Irony of the Reformed Episcopalians, 1873–1930*

From Fort Henry to Corinth, by Manning Ferguson Force (editor)

*Edwards on the Will: A Century of American
Philosophical Debate, 1750–1850*

ALLEN C. GUELZO

LINCOLN

≈AND≈

DOUGLAS

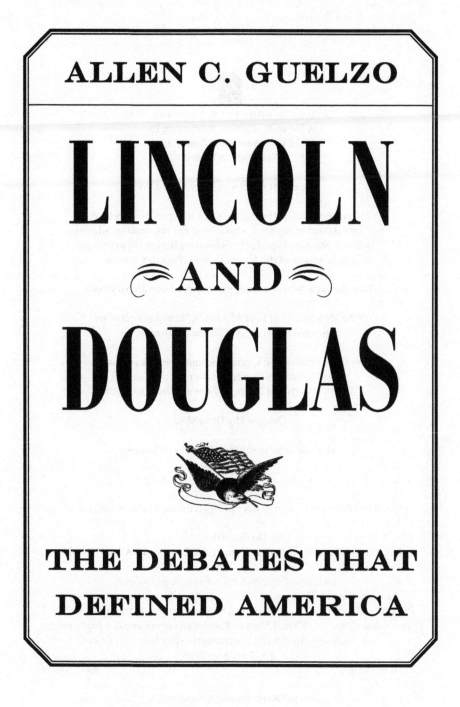

THE DEBATES THAT
DEFINED AMERICA

SIMON & SCHUSTER PAPERBACKS

NEW YORK   LONDON   TORONTO   SYDNEY

SIMON & SCHUSTER PAPERBACKS
A Division of Simon & Schuster, Inc.
1230 Avenue of the Americans
New York, NY 10020

First Simon & Schuster trade paperback edition January 2009

SIMON & SCHUSTER PAPERBACKS and colophon are
registered trademarks of Simon & Schuster, Inc.

For information about special discounts for bulk purchases,
please contact Simon & Schuster Special Sales at
1-800-456-6798 or business@simonandschuster.com.

Designed by Dana Sloan

Manufactured in the United States of America

1   3   5   7   9   10   8   6   4   2

The Library of Congress has cataloged the hardcover as follows:

Guelzo, Allen C.
Lincoln and Douglas : the debates that defined America / Allen C. Guelzo.
p.   cm.
Includes bibliographical references and index.
1. Lincoln-Douglas Debates, Ill., 1858.   2. Lincoln, Abraham, 1809–1865—
Political and social views.   3. Douglas, Stephen Arnold, 1813–1861—Political
and social views.   4. United States—Politics and government—1857–1861.
5. Illinois—Politics and government—To 1865.   I. Title.
E457.4.G84   2008
973.6'8—dc22   2007044254

ISBN-13: 978-0-7432-7320-6
ISBN-10:   0-7432-7320-6
ISBN-13: 978-0-7432-7321-3 (pbk)
ISBN-10:   0-7432-7321-4 (pbk)

For Janet R. Hirt

CONTENTS

INTRODUCTION:
From Lincoln and Douglas to Nixon and Kennedy   xi

1   The Least Man I Ever Saw   1

2   Take Care of Your Old Whigs   41

3   A David Greater Than Goliath   89

4   For God's Sake, Linder, Come Up   131

5   In the Face of the Nation   183

6   The Same Tyrannical Principle   235

EPILOGUE: One Supreme Issue   281

NOTES   315

ACKNOWLEDGMENTS   365

INDEX   369

ILLUSTRATION CREDITS   383

FROM LINCOLN AND DOUGLAS
TO NIXON AND KENNEDY

T<small>HE YEAR</small> 1858 began badly for the state of Illinois. A sudden and
sharp economic recession deflated land values, brought railroad
construction to a halt on the Illinois Central and Michigan Central
railroads, and reduced the money supply of banknotes from $215 mil-
lion to $155 million. In Chicago alone, 117 businesses failed, wiping
out $6.6 million in investments. "We went through a financial crisis
which swept over the country like a whirlwind," recalled Carl Schurz, a
German immigrant. "Money grew suddenly so scarce with us that a
man possessing ten dollars in coin or in notes of a solvent bank might
call himself a capitalist." National imports fell by 24 percent, and Horace Greeley, the editor of the country's most influential newspaper,
the *New-York Tribune*, was fearful that Illinois farmers "are generally
in debt, out of money and almost out of credit, and are making a final
stand against the sheriff." As the winter yielded to spring in 1858, a
great rush of religious revival took fire, and "additions to the membership of the churches [were] unprecedented." Nothing since "what was
known as the 'Great Awakening'" was "equal to what [was] now passing." Torrential rains sent the Ohio River up to forty-one feet at
Cincinnati, soaking the waist-high grass of the prairies into a swamp

and flooding the southern-tip Illinois city of Cairo. The Mississippi River steamer *Pennsylvania* blew up on June 13, killing 200 of the 450 aboard.[1] The veteran Missouri Democrat Thomas Hart Benton died on April 10, followed by Commodore Matthew Perry, the opener of Japan; the Yale theologian Nathaniel William Taylor; and the Mexican War heroes Persifor Smith and John A. Quitman. Benito Juarez proclaimed a new revolutionary republic in Mexico, the native troops of the Honorable East India Company rose in revolt against their British rulers, the transatlantic telegraph cable carried its first message and then promptly broke, and Donati's comet, with two brilliant tails easily visible to the naked eye, arched through the summer sky.

But of all these omens, not one took the attention of Illinois and the nation like the election campaigns which were carried on across Illinois in the late summer and autumn of 1858 by Abraham Lincoln and Stephen A. Douglas. In Dallas, the Lincoln-Douglas campaigns were termed "one of the most exciting political contests that has ever occurred." In Richmond, "W.A.S." wrote for the *Richmond South* that "seldom has a local election been looked forward to with such interest, seldom have politicians in so many different localities taken sides so strenuously, and expressed themselves so decidedly in favor of one or the other candidates." The Speaker of the House, James Orr of South Carolina, took time in a testimonial speech in his hometown to endorse Douglas, while William Lloyd Garrison's *Liberator* reported that "Illinois is all in a blaze just now. Lincoln and Douglas, candidates for the United States Senate, are canvassing the State." Henry Villard, another German immigrant who went to Illinois to represent the *New-Yorker Staats-Zeitung*, thought that "the eyes of the whole country were fixed" on Lincoln and Douglas. "Illinois has been the battle-ground of the Union," Judge Anson Miller told Lincoln. "The prairies seemed animated with political fervor and discussions," and by August, one Indiana editor wrote that "the canvass now going on in Illinois is probably the most exciting and earnest that ever preceded a State election in the Union." At least "for the time being," one Washington newspaper remarked, "Illinois becomes, as it were, the Union."[2] Whatever else Illinois and the nation had to think about in 1858, they thought with a peculiar passion about Lincoln and Douglas.

And in the blood-thickened years of the great Civil War that began in 1861, Americans would look back to the campaigns of Lincoln and Douglas and see in them the ultimate omen in that season of omens. Because the campaigns brought Abraham Lincoln his first national attention, and because the crucial presidential election of 1860 pitted Lincoln and Douglas against each other again, this time as candidates for the presidency, the campaigns of 1858 took on the role of overture to a violent opera, as though they had been designed that way from the first. Lincoln's rise to the presidency sent curious readers in search of the texts of the debates to find clues about Candidate Lincoln's politics, and two editions of the debates were published before he was elected; after the Civil War and Lincoln's death, still others went hunting for the debates to find historical patterns that explained the coming of the war, and between 1894 and 1908, eight separate editions or versions of the debates had been published.

But commentary on the debates in the years afterward remained as divided as it had been in the heart of the 1858 senatorial election. The first biographies of Lincoln were usually written by his associates and admirers, and they unreservedly gave the palm of victory in the debates to Lincoln. "The world has pronounced Mr. Lincoln the victor," Isaac Arnold confidently announced in *The History of Abraham Lincoln and the Overthrow of Slavery* in 1866; even though "Douglas was returned to the Senate," Joseph Barrett insisted that "there was a general presentiment that a juster verdict ... [was] yet to be had, and that Mr. Lincoln and his cause would be ultimately vindicated before the people." As late as 1900, Ida Tarbell's great *Life of Abraham Lincoln*, written from the sources and based on the last interviews held with those who had known Lincoln, portrayed the debates not only as a technical knockout for Lincoln but as the single event which "attracted the attention of all the thinking men of the country."[3]

The seven face-to-face debates Lincoln and Douglas conducted in the midst of their campaigns were read and reread like a code which would have warned Americans of the whirlwind about to descend on them, if only they had known how to read them rightly. "There could not be a more admirable text-book of the great antebellum conflict" than the Lincoln-Douglas debates, wrote one celebrator of the Lincoln centennial in 1909. They were "a dramatic and titanic struggle between the two contemporary men best fitted . . . to defend their respective sides in a popular discussion." In novels and stories, Lincoln and Douglas came to resemble David and Goliath, battling alone for the future of the nation, or as *retiarus* and *secutor*, solitary in the gladiatorial ring, as though the world around them had dissolved into transparency.

But the ultimate comment on the shadow cast by Lincoln and Douglas was not uttered until the evening of September 26, 1960, when John F. Kennedy and Richard M. Nixon began, by television, a series of four debates for the upcoming presidential election which looked like nothing so much as a reenactment of Lincoln and Douglas. Coming as they did only two years after the centennial of the Lincoln-Douglas debates, the Kennedy-Nixon debates had no better example to follow, and like Lincoln-Douglas, the 1960 debates featured an opening statement, followed by a reply, and then (instead of a rejoinder from the first debater) questions from a panel of four journalists. Even more oddly, two of the Kennedy-Nixon debates would fall on the same days—October 7 and October 13—as the fifth and sixth of the Lincoln-Douglas debates. And in another eerie resemblance to the 1858 debates, the performance of the front runner—Nixon—was upstaged by his challenger. The Lincoln-Douglas debates had outgrown their role as portents of the Civil War; they had become, in the words of the chairman of the Civil War centennial's national steering committee, "one of the most striking instances in our history of an appeal to the voice of democracy."* And the pattern set in 1858/1960 became the established pattern for presidential debates thereafter.

Looked at more archly, however, Nixon-Kennedy might appear more like a diminishment of Lincoln-Douglas than a continuation. The opening statements of each candidate were limited to eight minutes, and responses to the journalists' questions to two and a half minutes, so that few issues or questions could be handled with anything more than packaged banalities. And the medium was not a series of open-air meetings but television, where the kind of consecutive, logical thought which animated Lincoln and Douglas was reduced to staging, presentation, and entertainment. The distance between Lincoln-Douglas and Nixon-Kennedy, complained Neil Postman, was the distance between the Age of Exposition and the Age of Show Business, and the one was definitely the inferior of the other.[5] The Lincoln-Douglas debates were not only "the preeminent examples of political discourse in the mid-nineteenth century," they were a demonstration of "a kind of oratory that may be described as literary," which Postman defined as having "a semantic, paraphrasable, propositional content." This universe of "typographical" discourse was permanently shattered by the technological innovation of advertising, which relied on illustrations, photographs, and "non-propositional" slogans, and the advent of television, which "speaks in only one persistent voice—the voice of entertainment."[6]

But was Lincoln-Douglas really free from all taint of the Age of Show Business? After all, could an off-year election on the Illinois prairies really bear the weight Lincoln's admirers attributed to it? Did we focus on Lincoln and Douglas in 1858 only because we knew that Abraham Lincoln would later advance to center stage in 1860 and in the Civil War? After 1865, almost everything Lincoln touched assumed a quasi-religious aura, although a sober second thought would remind people that even the life of Abraham Lincoln had to be lived through the midst of the humdrum and irrelevant. But there was a more sour skepticism at work about the 1858 campaigns, especially by the 1920s, when the hoopla of the Lincoln centennial had died, the last of the Civil War veterans were fading away, and a deep and corrosive cynicism about the possibilities of American democracy had settled into the bloodstreams of American thinkers. The Progressive Republican senator from Indiana, Albert Beveridge, turned in disgust from politics to the writing of history, and to a massive biography of Lincoln as the last genuinely heroic American politician. But the more closely he studied Lincoln, the less admirable and heroic his subject seemed to be. And as the stature of the candidates sank, so did the debates. Beveridge concluded, "Solely on their merits, the debates themselves deserve little notice. For the most part, each speaker merely repeated what he had said before." Instead of a contest of giants, the generation that had passed through the Versailles debacle and the presidency of Warren Harding wondered if there was any real difference between Lincoln and Douglas after all. The judgment of the Mississippi Valley Historical Association (which would emerge as the Organization of American Historians) in 1920 was that "the joint debates of 1858 did not reveal them as men who were poles apart, but, on the contrary, they were brought nearer to each other during that memorable canvass." If anything, the hero of the debates was Douglas rather than Lincoln. Douglas, as the onetime Progressive James Garfield Randall believed, may not have been on the right side of history as far as slavery was concerned, but at least he was trying to pour the oil of reason, compromise, and larger national purpose onto the slavery question. Between 1902 and 1924, Douglas became the subject of seven major biographies, and from them his reputation rose reborn as a practical and hardheaded statesman trying to stave off the radicals and showboaters on both sides of the slavery question and preserve the national peace.[7]

If the Progressives, sunk in the disenchantment of the 1920s, wondered whether democracy had really been served so grandly by the great debates, the university-based historians who came to dominate American history writing from the 1930s onward, embittered by the Depression and the Cold War, wondered whether there was any real democracy for the debates to serve. As the attention of historians drifted from the politics of Lincoln and Douglas, the one thing of value which seemed salvageable from the wreckage was the enthusiasm and passion with which the people participated in the campaign. George Beatty, a merchant living in Ottawa, Illinois, recalled the rallies, speeches, and debates of 1858 as "something very different than . . . idling about, listening to the speakers for a half hour or so" and finally concluding "what's the use of listening to that chap! I can get his speech in tomorrow's paper." When the first of the Lincoln-Douglas debates came to Ottawa in August 1858, Beatty remembered that "it did not take long for this crowd of farmers to realize that the question that was before them was one that demanded sober, solemn decision, if they were to vote rightly . . . I tell you that debate set folks to thinking on these important questions in way[s] they hadn't dreamed of."[8] One veteran of Illinois politics recalled the 1850s as an era of political mania in the state: "Political clubs were formed at all the little towns throughout the State. Those of us who lived there at that time had never known the like before. Public speaking was held before these nearly every week in the daytime and after night. Men went to these in buggies, wagons, and on horseback." It could have as easily been P. T. Barnum, rather than Lincoln and Douglas, who was on the hustings.[9]

But the crowds and hubbub might just as easily mean that it *was* Barnum—or at least entertainment—which was at the heart of democratic politics in the 1850s. In the 1960s, as American society fractured along racial, class, and gender lines fully as much as political ones, a "new political history," whose chief practitioners were Lee Benson, Richard McCormick, and Ronald Formisano, dismissed the massive voter turnouts, the flag-waving, the crowds at the courthouse steps as misleading indicators of genuine participatory democracy. Real political loyalties lined up along patterns of "machine" organizations, kinship, religion, language, and ethnicity rather than political ideas. The apex of this devaluation of politics came with Glenn Altschuler and Stuart Blumin's *Rude Republic: Americans and Their Politics in the Nineteenth-Century*, which insisted that American politics before the

Civil War was little more than an amusing spectacle, put on by party wire pullers who controlled the proceedings from the sidelines, while the people good-naturedly enjoyed the show but declined to take the politicking seriously. The bing and bang of the campaigns was an expression not of the people's engagement with politics but of the efforts party organizers had to mount to get the people to show up at all. "Nearly always, crowds at major campaign events were swollen by the carefully arranged importation of party workers from nearby towns and counties," Blumin and Altschuler concluded; nearly always, the nominating conventions were carefully scripted, the debates subject to "close management, and voter turnout the product of generous treating with free food and drink."[10]

Inside this skepticism about how democratic nineteenth-century American democracy really was lurked what Mark Neely diagnosed as a collapse of faith in the very nature of liberal democracy itself. For the last half century, an increasing chorus of economists and political theorists has treated the democratic voter as a kind of licensed juvenile, driven by irrational and irreconcilable desires for low taxation and more government spending, for free markets and more government economic regulation, for free trade and higher protective tariffs. Voters in a democracy are not just ignorant or disengaged; they vote by whim and they do so because in a political system so vast as the American democracy they feel at liberty to vote for privileges and exceptions as "free riders." Because they cannot see how just one vote based on selfish impulse can really harm a process so enormous, their voting is impulsive, unstudied, and prey to the propaganda of special interests.[11]

Driven by suspicions of this sort, it has been increasingly easy to turn back to Lincoln and Douglas and conclude that the great debates of 1858 might have been good political theater but not more than that. Even a magisterial historian like David Potter, in his 1976 valedictory survey of the prewar years, *The Impending Crisis*, did not want entirely to dismiss the campaigns, but he did want to deconstruct the way the debates had "become a symbol of democracy at the grass-roots level."

The moment generally cast as the most dramatic of the entire contest—the second public debate at Freeport, when Lincoln posed his famous "Freeport Question" to Douglas—appeared particularly to Potter as "one of the great nonevents of American history." And in the most recent overview of the Lincoln-Douglas debates, David Zarefsky finds the best evidence of the debates' limited impact in their odd omission from *The American Almanac*, one of the key reference annuals of the 1850s, which didn't even bother to mention the debates in its listing of the two hundred most important events of 1858.[12]

And yet the mute, inherited sense that the Illinois senatorial race of 1858 really did represent a prologue to the Civil War, and a symbolic high mark in American politics, refused to die. At almost the same time that J. G. Randall was reinventing Stephen A. Douglas as a coolheaded pragmatist swimming in a sea of immature and reckless partisans, Allan Nevins's vast, eight-volume survey of the Civil War era energetically denounced Douglas as an amoral political fixer whose demagoguery and moral obtuseness exposed a fundamental betrayal of democracy and jeopardized the ethical core of American popular government. "Never in our history have orators stood in more dramatic contrast," declared Nevins, and never did Douglas offer more than "labored," "torturous," and "chocolate-covered" excuses for a hideous dereliction from democratic principles. Don E. Fehrenbacher, in a brilliant series of essays on Lincoln's career in the 1850s, admitted that certain aspects of the campaigns—especially the Freeport Question—had probably been blown out of proportion, but he still warned against "the fashion . . . to belittle the actual content of the Lincoln-Douglas debates."

But the heaviest reply to the skeptics came not from a historian but from a political scientist, Harry V. Jaffa, in 1959, in *Crisis of the House Divided*. As a student of the émigré political philosopher Leo Strauss, Jaffa shared his mentor's anxiety that democracy had lost any moral imperative in the eyes of modern intellectuals and become merely a strategy to permit the unhindered accumulation of material wealth.

Beside the baleful but alluring passions of Nazism and Communism, democracy had come to seem purposeless, greedy, and spineless, generating endless permissions for indulgence and deep cover for bourgeois "imperialism." Strauss turned back to a close reading of the classical texts of Western politics—especially to Plato and Aristotle—and from them he taught that democracy, to survive, had to be linked to the cultivation of the classical virtues, whether philosophical or religious. And following Strauss's lead, Jaffa turned to the Lincoln-Douglas debates as the closest American equivalent he could imagine to the *Symposium.*

Unlike the earlier admirers of Lincoln, Jaffa did not dismiss Douglas as a simple political sharpie. Instead, he found in Lincoln and Douglas two ideas of democracy struggling within the womb of the Republic for supremacy. On the one hand stood Douglas, whose notion of democracy entitled majorities to decide all questions, purely on the grounds of being majorities and without respect to theories of political right or wrong. Such theories, Douglas believed, were the sort that never find final answers and only end up paralyzing prosperity. Lincoln, however, thought of politics as a moral pursuit. He was not a moral absolutist and he did not doubt that popular majorities were the essence of free government. But there were certain moral lines even majorities could not cross, certain transcendent and foundational truths which no vote could repeal, and some preferences which no amount of Romantic passion could justify. Lincoln thus transformed the debates into a moral reply to liberalism's preoccupation with process and unencumbered individualism, without indulging the bathos of religion. Lincoln, admits one biographer of Douglas, "not only entered a plea for morality, he made his kind of morality palatable to a large number of Americans." [19]

The advance of Straussian neoconservatives into positions of policy-making influence in the 1990s, and the corresponding erosion of confidence, even among political liberals, in a democracy without a moral core, clothed these warring interpretations of the Lincoln-

Douglas debates with more than the usual academic rancor. Michael Sandel, who parted company with New Deal liberalism to espouse a politics of communitarian republicanism, fastened onto the debates in *Democracy's Discontent: America in Search of a Public Philosophy* as the key example in American history of the conflict between responsibility and selfishness. Douglas, for Sandel, was the paragon of a "thin" notion of democracy, in which a preoccupation with personal rights trumps all notions of advancing a common good, and the citizen degenerates into an "unencumbered self" whose politics is moved—when it is moved at all—by sentimentality.

Sandel's Lincoln, by contrast, saw politics as moved by a universal and shared morality, and opposed slavery as a violation of that morality. Douglas argued that the people ought to be allowed to make up their own minds about slavery—this was the essence of his doctrine of "popular sovereignty"—and that all that mattered was whether the process of making up those minds was open-ended and uncoerced; Lincoln argued that minds which could not see that slavery was an abomination were operating on the wrong principles. The catastrophe of 9/11 only made the need for a morally informed notion of democracy all the more urgent, and it soon enough led Paul Berman, in *Terror and Liberalism*, to single out Lincoln as the best defender of democracy precisely because Lincoln based his justification of democracy on an "absolute commitment to solidarity" and not just a desire for individual satisfactions.[14]

The campaigns of 1858 have been served by a number of workmanlike historical narratives over the years, but not necessarily served very well. The earliest of these narratives were embedded in the biographical literature on Lincoln and reached their high mark in Beveridge's unfinished *Abraham Lincoln, 1809–1858* (1928); the first freestanding narrative appeared from Richard Heckman only in 1967 in his *Lincoln vs. Douglas.* Heckman was soon followed by an amateur historian, Saul Sigelschiffer, who spent ten years writing a five-hundred-page survey of Lincoln and Douglas and published it under the Jaffaesque title *The American Conscience: The Drama of the Lincoln-Douglas Debates* in 1973. David Zarefsky, a rhetorician, took his turn at Lincoln and Douglas in 1990 with *Lincoln, Douglas and Slavery: In the Crucible of Public Debate.* But Zarefsky's book was really a technical rhetorical analysis of the debates rather than a narrative history of the campaigns, just as Jaffa's *Crisis of the House Divided* was a work of political theory rather than a history of 1858.

All of these efforts suffered in varying degrees from the temptation to focus on the Lincoln-Douglas *debates* while allowing the Lincoln-Douglas *campaigns* to fall off the table. The debates, after all, were seven moments out of campaigns that stretched over four months. Far more Illinoisans heard Lincoln and Douglas on courthouse steps, from railroad platforms, from hastily hammered-together stands at county fairs, and from the flatbeds of wagons than heard them in face-to-face debate. Nor were the strategies of either campaign exactly built around the debates. Both Lincoln and Douglas knew that the election of 1858 would be decided by swing voters in central Illinois counties where only three of the seven debates were held. The debates were, yes, a central feature of the campaigns of 1858, but in the narratives, they have come completely to eclipse the campaigns.

That is, in large measure, the accident of print. It is one mark of the national stake in the 1858 Illinois senatorial contest that the rival Chicago newspapers—the *Chicago Press & Tribune* and the *Chicago Times*—hired stenographers trained in shorthand to take down every word of the debates as uttered, then used the state's rail network to speed the debate transcripts into the newspapers' copy rooms and so have them in print (and available to the new national wire service, the Associated Press) within forty-eight hours. This was an expensive and labor-intensive proposition, and neither newspaper was in a position to extend that kind of coverage to the balance of the candidates' individual speaking stops. So the debates, simply on the basis of their availability, rapidly overshadowed the other speeches made by Lincoln and

Douglas throughout the campaign, and when Lincoln assembled a scrapbook of newspaper cuttings from the campaign for publication in 1860, it was the texts of the debates, rather than any of the other speeches, which made up most of the book.

In turn, Lincoln's biographers shaped their accounts of the campaign around the published text of the debates. Curiously, when Edwin Earle Sparks produced the first scholarly edition of the debates, in 1908, for the *Collections of the Illinois State Historical Library*, he took the trouble to interleave the debate texts with a running account of the campaign as well as extracts of reports of the debates from an extraordinary sampling of faded Illinois newspapers, rather than just the *Tribune* and the *Times*. But the result was simply sharpened concentration on the debates, since the contemporary newspaper extracts Sparks so meticulously included were only those concerned with the debates, actually reinforcing the impression that they were the only matter of consequence in the campaigns. Only when Roy P. Basler and the Abraham Lincoln Association set about the mammoth task of constructing the eight-volume *Collected Works of Abraham Lincoln* (1953) were the texts of Lincoln's speech, delivered out on the campaign and apart from Douglas, unearthed from even deeper in the Illinois newspaper morgues. But these, of course, were only Lincoln's speeches, and even then, mostly paraphrases, written down days or weeks after the fact and sometimes larded with hostile editorial asides.

No wonder that almost all of the attempts to reconstruct the story of Lincoln and Douglas in 1858 have ended up with so much color drained out of them. Not *all* color, since the debates pack plenty of power on their own, as Jaffa's and Zarefsky's books both testify. But taken solely on their own, the debate texts are like Shakespeare without a stage. The campaigns, however, tell us that Lincoln and Douglas also had to struggle with the issue of rivals—that Lincoln earned his nomination for the Senate race in 1858 as the collection of a political debt, and not a debt that some of his own political allies thought it was right to pay him, and that Douglas has been disowned by his party and had to fight off destruction from within his own ranks as well as Lincoln from the outside.

The campaigns also bring out of the shadows the multitudes who shaped both the campaigns and the debates, especially the state party committees, who were responsible for the management of the overall contest and its final results. Neither Lincoln nor Douglas was in charge of his own political world in Illinois, and the people who were, were often as much at odds with the candidates and each other as with their opposition. The campaigns are thus an important corrective to the prevailing skepticism about the participatory quality of nineteenth-century democracy, since it was not in the debates (where the presence of the shorthand reporters imposed a measure of decorum) but in the campaigns and the election itself that the hecklers, the paraders, the brass bands, the trains overflowing with excursion-rate meeting goers, the teakettle river steamers draped in banners, the speech-making for hours into the night, the fistfights and racial slurs, the hawkers and pickpockets working the crowds, the anxious reports by letter from the field that one begins to feel the wide open spigot of the American passion for politics. "In our country," wrote one reviewer of the "memorable contest in Illinois" between Lincoln and Douglas, "every thing is swept into the gulf of politics." [15]

There are also a number of nagging questions, even about the debates, which none of the writers on the 1858 contest have ever quite settled. For instance: was Lincoln's "House Divided" speech, which he delivered as his acceptance speech at the convention which nominated him in June 1858, and which became one of the accepted gems of American political rhetoric, really a mistake which cost him the election at the very beginning? Why did Lincoln pose the Freeport Question, and was it really an example of a remarkable clairvoyance that allowed him to see that his opponent's answer would deny Douglas the presidency and give it to him instead? Was the election a blowout defeat for Lincoln, or was it a "near run thing" in which he came narrowly close to upsetting Douglas and driving him out of politics forever? Finally, did the campaigns and the debates reveal Lincoln to be a racist whose only concern about slavery was containing it in the Southern slave states, so that the western territories could be held open for free, and white, settlers? What has now become one of the most famous utterances in the debates—Lincoln's promise at the opening of the fourth debate at Charleston, Illinois, that "I am not, nor ever have been, in favor of bringing about in any way the social and political equality of the white and black races; that I am not, nor ever have been, in favor of making voters or jurors of negroes, nor of qualifying them to hold office, nor to intermarry with white people"—has been taken as the undeniable testimony of a bigot whose only real difference from Douglas was his belief that *enslaving* blacks as opposed to disenfranchising and deporting them was just pushing things too far. But was this a settled conviction on Lincoln's part? Or was it a careless (and off-the-cuff) response to Douglas's nonstop race-baiting? Or a directive from a state central committee which was growing nervous about the applause Douglas's race-baiting was getting from the voters? "There is a natural disgust in the minds of nearly all white people, to the idea of an indiscriminate amalgamation of the white and black races," Lincoln said in 1857. But he left open the question whether this disgust "accords with justice and sound judgment." What he did know, however, was that "Judge Douglas evidently is basing his chief hope, upon the chances of being able to appropriate the benefit of this disgust to himself," and it is against that debasement that Lincoln's words have to be measured.[16]

With questions of this sort looming over the year 1858, it has seemed to me that understanding the significance of Lincoln and Douglas in 1858 can be served only by reconstructing the intricate political geography of the debates *and* the larger campaigns, which the Civil War—and the deaths of both Lincoln and Douglas within seven years of the debates—swept away. For not only were these contests about each man's eligibility for a national office and about their contrasting views on the expansion of slavery but they were also about the intricacies of Illinois politics, the boundaries of political life in mid-nineteenth-century America, the futility of a victory, and the spectacular success of a defeat. And in the end, the campaigns and the great debates would accomplish two things. First, they would introduce Abraham Lincoln, who had no political visibility beyond the horizons of Illinois, to the front rank of national politics. Two years later, the struggle of 1858 became the basis for the critical invitation he received to come to New York City and deliver at the Cooper Institute, as if it was his national political tryout, the speech that allowed him to become the dark-horse presidential nominee of the Republican party in May 1860.

Second, the year 1858 would indeed see Lincoln and Douglas articulate not just two different positions on a policy questions but two radically different notions of what democratic politics really is. For Douglas, as Michael Sandel warned, the essence of democracy was process. Democracy was a means for creating a happy, free, and prosperous society, and what the people as a whole desired in the way of happiness, freedom, and prosperity was what democracy should enable them to get. For Lincoln, the essence of democracy was principle. Democracy was a virtuous end in itself, a summum bonum (so to speak), which was the expression, in political life, of the natural ends for which men were made.[17]

But, as the experience of civil war demonstrated only too well, principle can also introduce rigidity into democratic deliberations, a rigidity which either ensures defeat by alienating all but the purists or ensures catastrophe by blinding its adherents to their own mistakes and excusing their crimes. The Civil War years which followed would demonstrate to some people that Lincoln was a man of inflexible purpose and uprightness who cleansed the soiled "republican robe" of America of a great evil, even at the cost of his own life. It would demonstrate to others that Lincoln was a crusader, looking for only one answer rather than allowing for a diversity of them, heaping violence upon violence because violence is what men of principle resort to when their principles are challenged. No wonder, then, in the turn-of-the-century era of pragmatism—of William James, Oliver Wendell Holmes, and John Dewey—that Stephen A. Douglas could be resurrected as a focus of biographical admiration. What had seemed in 1858 to be a lack of moral perception now looked like flexibility and a determination to defuse antagonism.

In the largest sense, the 1858 campaigns and debates of Lincoln and Douglas were only one round in a struggle between the two men that ended only with Douglas's death in 1861. Lincoln kept pursuing Douglas into 1859, when he and Douglas were on the stump on behalf of party candidates in Ohio, and Lincoln's great Cooper Institute speech of February 1860 was actually an extended reply to a large-scale article Douglas published in *Harper's New Monthly Magazine* for September 1859, titled "The Dividing Line Between Federal and Local Authority: Popular Sovereignty in the Territories." But if we conceive of the struggle between Lincoln and Douglas as one which asks whether process or principle should be the polestar of a democracy, then the Lincoln-Douglas debate has never actually ended. As a nation we have continued to lunge to one side and then the other—the First World War asked us to make the world safe for democracy, and the postwar disillusion asked whether democracy was safe for us; World War II, the Cold War, and the civil rights struggle of the 1950s and 1960s asked us to work on behalf, sometimes in explicitly religious terms, of the creation of a "beloved community"; and when the Cold War ended, the voice of pragmatic process once again began to sing. And is it too much to say that Lincoln and Douglas still face each other across the length of the National Mall in Washington—that at one end we have built a memorial to Abraham Lincoln, solitary in his righteousness, while at the other end we have built a far larger one, vast in ambiguity and self-seeking, to Stephen A. Douglas?

LINCOLN

AND

DOUGLAS

CHAPTER 1

THE LEAST MAN I EVER SAW

Upon our platform there will stand
Clad in judicial toga
With clinking hand-cuffs in his hand
An old pro-slavery fogy,
And first beside him on the box
In attitude defiant
Like frog that tried t'outswell the ox
There stands our Little Giant.

And these two worthies shall engage
In a vehement tustle
Each other from the platform's edge
By lawful right to hustle
Displaying thus before our sight
The right to drive away there
What has itself an equal right
By the same law to stay there.

H. P. H. Bromwell Papers,
Library of Congress

The Honorable Senator from Illinois, Stephen Arnold Douglas, began digging his political grave with the first item of business before the Senate of the United States on Wednesday, January 4, 1854. For a man approaching the height of his political powers, Senator Douglas did not look particularly uneasy, nor did the instrument he had in hand appear all that lethal. It was simply a "bill to organize the Territory of Nebraska," which Douglas was reporting out of the Senate Committee on Territories and laying before the entire Senate for its action. But it would be the undoing of Douglas all the same, and of the peace of the American Republic.[1]

Ever since 1803, when Thomas Jefferson shrewdly bought up half the American West in the great Louisiana Purchase, Congress had been slowly organizing the immense landmass of "Louisiana" and setting up provisional governments there as territories—Missouri in 1812, Arkansas in 1819, Iowa in 1838, Oregon in 1848, Minnesota in 1849. A *territory* was a legal halfway house between the moment when lands like the Louisiana Purchase were acquired by the United States, and the moment they could be admitted to the Union as full-fledged states. Under Article IV of the Constitution, Congress was responsible for setting up temporary governments in newly acquired lands, subdividing or fixing their boundaries, recognizing each of the new units as an incorporated territory, appointing territorial governors and supervising the creation of territorial legislatures and constitutions, and eventually, if territorial organization was successful, guiding a territory's application for statehood. This process stabilized the rule of law, allowed the people living there a measure of self-government, and created a test period before the territory was fully admitted to the Union as a state. Without it, land titles, law enforcement, incorporation, investment, and development would all hang fire.

The territorial process, however, was not necessarily rapid. By the time Minnesota was organized as a territory, in 1849, most of the immense bulk of the Louisiana Purchase, from the northern Rockies to the vast plains west of Nebraska, was still without territorial government. And then, in 1848, another expansion-minded president, James Knox Polk, used the Mexican War to acquire the great southwestern triangle of the continent, from the Rio Grande west to California and from Texas northwest to the Great Salt Lake. If the pace of territorial organization in the old Purchase lands was any indication, organizing the huge new American West could take another century.

No one felt the burden of pushing territorial organization in the West more urgently than Stephen A. Douglas, whose life up to this point read like a primer in the opportunities of western development. Douglas's forebears arrived in Rhode Island as early as the 1640s, but they gradually drifted north and west in search of new land, finally setting up on four hundred acres of land near Brandon, Vermont, in the 1790s. The Douglases acquired enough wealth and standing in Vermont to send Douglas's father to Middlebury College to become a physician, and the elder Douglas soon settled down to marriage and medicine in Brandon in 1811, followed by the birth of Stephen Arnold in 1813. Then, the bliss of the Douglas family abruptly stopped. In 1815, the doctor suffered a fatal heart attack. "I was only about two months old, and of course I cannot recollect him," Douglas wrote years afterward. But "I have often been told he was holding me in his arms when he departed this world." With the death of the senior Douglas died any prospect of Stephen following his father into a lucrative and respectable profession. Despite his "taste for reading"—his favorite works were "those telling of the triumphs of Napoleon, the conquests of Alexander, and the wars of Caesar"—and spending "night and Sundays in reading and study," the young Stephen Douglas was apprenticed to a cabinetmaker.[2]

It was typical of Douglas that he at once began looking for a new way upward. He wheedled permission from his master to attend the Brandon Academy, and when his mother remarried in 1830 and moved to New York, young Stephen was given leave to enter the Canandaigua Academy and then, in 1833, to begin reading law with two local lawyers. But his stepfamily's money began to run dry, and the process of examination and admission to the bar in New York was long and expensive. In mid-1833, he embarked on yet another Douglas move westward, to Cleveland. "When shall we expect you to come home to visit us, my son?" pleaded his mother. "On my way to Congress, Mother," he replied.[3]

The way to Congress appeared to be no easier for Douglas than the way to law. Cleveland was a professional dead end. Douglas hoped to find work in St. Louis, but St. Louis was already overstocked with lawyers, as were the Illinois towns on the other side of the Mississippi River. It was not until he walked into the middle of a public auction at Winchester, Illinois, in the fall of 1833 and volunteered his services to an auctioneer who needed somebody literate enough to keep track of sales that Douglas finally found himself earning two dollars a day—as a clerk. This bounty gave him the bright idea of opening a school for clerks. In short order, Douglas had forty pupils and (at the end of the school quarter in March 1834) enough money to support him in a year's law study. Before the end of the year, Douglas was licensed to practice in Illinois and was the proprietor of his own one-man law practice. He was all of twenty-one years old.[4]

Lawyering followed a short path to politics in Illinois, and never more so than in the volatile year of 1834. The President of the United States, the white-haired but iron-tempered hero of the Battle of New Orleans, Andrew Jackson, had thrown every ounce of his energies against the sucking of the American economy into the maw of the Industrial Revolution. Jackson was a devout old Jeffersonian Democrat—which is to say that he saw American life in much the same terms as Thomas Jefferson had when Jefferson wrote that God's only chosen people were farmers on their own land. Democrats from Jefferson to Jackson looked uneasily on men who worked in shops for wages, since mere wage earners became dependent on the goodwill of wage payers and were vulnerable to political manipulation by their employers. They looked even more coldly on those who traded in bonds and securities (these were examples of imaginary wealth, whose value could be driven up and down without warning) or who made their living in merchandise and commerce (since they traded in fancy goods which no upstanding farmer really needed but which could trap him in a punitive cycle of debt and dependence). No man who did not own his own land, or who could not live from that land, could ever be truly free and independent.[5]

This hostility led to political war in 1834 between Jackson and the Second Bank of the United States, the pumping station of the national financial system created by Alexander Hamilton in the 1790s. Andrew Jackson was one of the few real heroes Americans could boast of in the disastrous War of 1812, and he had not defeated one enemy in scarlet coats only to concede to another in silver and gold. The Second Bank became, for Jackson and his allies, a monster with financial tentacles, seeking to reach into every corner of the Republic and entrap its virtuous farmers in paper chains of debt. When in 1834 the bank's president, Nicholas Biddle, challenged Jackson by seeking an early renewal of the bank's charter by Congress, Jackson vetoed the renewal legislation with all the vehemence with which he had bestowed gusts of grapeshot on the British.

All this should have been of little consequence to a novice lawyer in central Illinois in 1834. But when an attorney from Jacksonville stood up before a local club to which Stephen Douglas belonged and denounced Jackson's veto of the bank as tyrannical and treasonous, Douglas was furious at hearing America's premier military hero flogged verbally like a common bandit. "I could not remain silent when the old hero's character, public and private, was traduced, and his measures misrepresented and denounced," he recalled later, and in a trice, Douglas was on his feet making a speech of his own. A week later, an Illinois Democratic newspaper printed Douglas's speech in "two entire columns" and "for two or three successive weeks," and suddenly Douglas was a political celebrity. He was elected state's attorney for the First Judicial Circuit and then, in August 1836, won a seat in the state legislature. Seven months later, Andrew Jackson's successor in the presidency, Martin Van Buren, rewarded Douglas's faithful party service by appointing him register of the lucrative federal land office in

Springfield. In 1838, Douglas ran for Congress on a platform which denounced corporate charters for "railroads, canals, insurance companies, hotel companies, steam mill companies &c., &c." as "unjust, impolitic, and unwise"—and lost by a squeaker to John Todd Stuart. But in 1840, Douglas was back on the upward spiral when he was appointed by the Democratic governor Thomas Carlin to the Illinois Supreme Court.

Finally, in 1843, Douglas won the congressional seat he craved in a special election, defeating the formidable lawyer from the Mississippi River town of Quincy, Orville Hickman Browning. After he won re-election in 1846, the Illinois legislature's Democratic majority (operating under the then-current constitutional rule that U.S. senators were elected by state legislatures rather than by a direct vote of the people) elected Douglas to Illinois's junior U.S. Senate seat. At thirty-three, he only just met the Constitution's age qualification for U.S. senators.[6]

Douglas was, from his start in Congress, an ardent antibanking, antitariff Jacksonian Democrat. "In this country," he declared in 1837, "there are two opposing parties." One was the Democrats, the "advocates of the rights of the people," and the other was "the advocates of the privileges of Property." By *property*, he meant "the principles of 'consolidation,' 'monopoly,' and 'property privilege.'" And the weapon which would keep these dragons at bay was "a strict observance of every provision of our constitutions—state and national." But the dragons of privilege were still formidable, and they included banks, corporations, and protective tariffs for manufacturing. And alongside the privileged marched rank upon rank of white-tied clergymen trying to use government power to impose Christian moral codes in defiance of the Jeffersonian separation of church and state, and appealing over the head of the people and the Constitution to God. "We should all recognize, respect, and revere the divine law," Douglas agreed, but only as individuals, and only on questions of private moral virtue. The Bible "has not furnished us with a Constitution," nor has it laid down "the form of government under which we shall live, and the character of our political and civil institutions." But the voice of the people had. "The great fundamental principle" of government was that "every people ought to possess the right of forming and regulating their own internal concerns and domestic institutions in their own way."[7]

And yet, for all of Douglas's brass-lunged endorsement of the Democratic line, he was not a one-note party ideologue. Far from it. Douglas "neither felt nor thought deeply on any question." He, for instance, "during his entire political life" criticized programs of government-financed public works (or "internal improvements") on the grounds that these only favored the moneyed interests. But the moment it became clear that his Illinois constituents were lusting quite happily for the cornucopia of goods which "internal improvements" poured before them, Douglas suddenly discerned a difference "between those works which were essential to the protection of commerce" and those "asked for by parties having local interests to serve," and he threw his votes behind federal appropriations to dredge the sandbars at the mouth of the Chicago River, federal land grants to the proposed Illinois Central Railroad, and the completion of the Illinois River canal.[8]

"He showed always a certain curious gift of alertness," George Murray McConnell recalled—although it was never entirely clear whether that alertness was an attentiveness simply to his constituents' needs or to the next main chance that would promote his own fortunes. People who thought that Douglas's chief problem was his lack of height (like Missouri senator Thomas Hart Benton, who growled that "his legs are too short, sir. That part of his body, sir, which men wish to kick, is too near the ground!") missed Douglas's real shortcoming, that morally speaking, he had no chest. It was no accident that, once the authorization for the Illinois Central land grants had passed through Congress, Douglas placed an order with Washington banker W. W. Corcoran for Illinois state bonds. Once he had been elected to the Senate, Douglas moved his law practice to Chicago and began speculating in lakefront real estate (which he then sold to the Illinois Central for ten times the purchase price). He bought a large house at New Jersey and I Streets in Washington, where he entertained on imported china, smoked Havana cigars, poured Madeira by the cask—and shrewdly invested in District real estate by buying two blocks of rental housing in 1851. He married Martha Martin, whose plantation-owning father bestowed on Douglas the title to a 2,500-acre Mississippi plantation; and when Martha Douglas died in 1853, Douglas married Adele Cutts, a Washington socialite and "a Southern lady of good family" with "the air of a queen, with perfect features as if carved in marble, white and smooth as marble, too, with clear liquid eyes and shadowy lashes."[9] If ever a man had done well by doing for the common good, it was Stephen A. Douglas.

Douglas took as his pet project in Congress the creation of a railroad to connect Chicago (and the entire Mississippi valley) with the newly acquired lands of the Pacific coast, funded in part or in whole by federal tax dollars. This was, he frankly admitted, a retreat from the usual Democratic opposition "to the doctrine of internal improvements by the Federal Government within the different States of the Union." But if Americans wanted "to make the great ports of the world tributary to our wealth," then "we must penetrate the Pacific, its islands, and its continent, where the great mass of the human family reside," and a Pacific railroad was the means to do it. If this raised eyebrows among the Democratic faithful, then that only showed that it was time for "a statesman who can bring young blood, young ideas, and young hearts to the councils of the Republic"—not to mention the Democratic party—and by 1852 a Douglas-for-president boom was in the works.[10]

What shielded Douglas from the suspicions of old-guard Democrats was the sheer sparkle of his charisma. Although standing only five foot four on legs which were three inches shorter than average, Douglas "had a large head, surmounted by an abundant mane" of brown hair, which gave him the "appearance of a lion prepared to roar or crush his prey" or a "short, thick-set . . . bulldog." Even in his youth, his chip-on-the-shoulder willingness to take on a fight earned him the nickname "The Little Giant." But he could just as readily beam with "real geniality, and wholesome grace, and forceful dignity." He was a "perfect 'steam engine in breeches,'" and "to see him threading the glittering crowd with a pleasant smile or a kind word for every body, one would have taken him for a trained courtier." His voice was "deep and strong . . . melodious and sympathetic," and he had the knack of drawing people into his circle of attention and flattering them with the thought that they were Stephen A. Douglas's sole concern in the universe. "He would say, 'I can tell *you*'; 'I know that I can say *to you*'; 'I have no hesitation in confiding *in you*'; 'I want *you* to know,' etc." He never lost an opportunity to cultivate "a popularity." Hezekiah Wead (who, like Douglas, was born in Vermont but emigrated to Illinois to practice law) remembered that, in court, Douglas would "go round among the listeners & spectators, sit upon their knees and chat and laugh & joke with them," even "while the counsel were arguing to the Jury." Onboard a train, "scarcely a man, woman, or child in the cars escaped his attention, or passed by unspoken to." His joy was "to stand in the centre of a listening throng, while he told some Western story or defended some public measure; to exchange jokes with a political adversary; or, ascending the rostrum, to hold thousands spellbound for hours." The Illinois politician Shelby Cullom wrote that Douglas "was a wonderful man with the people. . . . When he came through the State, the whole Democratic party was alive and ready to rally to his support."[11]

But Illinois only gave Stephen Douglas a platform; it could not give him the nation. And his charisma could only protect him; it could not promote him in the upper echelons of the party, where his departures from party orthodoxy were seen more dimly. In Illinois, Douglas was able to build a formidable political machine across the state, constructed of federal patronage appointments that he oversaw and major corporations (like the Illinois Central Railroad) whose interests he was in a position to favor, regardless of Jacksonian orthodoxy. By the

1850s, Douglas ruled the Illinois Democratic party as "absolutely supreme . . . and his supremacy was a despotism." But his allies failed to get a Douglas-for-president nomination past the national party convention in 1852, which instead nominated the handsome, heroic, and (as it turned out) talentless Franklin Pierce. A second, more serious Douglas-for-president campaign died a lingering death at the party convention in Cincinnati in 1856. And James Buchanan, who got the nomination instead, saw no reason to extend to Douglas more than polite formality. Buchanan's chief advisers would be Jesse Bright of Indiana and John Slidell of Louisiana, both of whom preferred that Douglas get only the crumbs from Buchanan's patronage table.[12]

There was, however, an obstacle to Douglas's ascension to the very top of Democratic party leadership more forbidding than just resentment at his political opportunism, and that had to do with the Southern Democrats, who held the numbers, the money, and the balance of power within the party. And that, in turn, had everything to do with slavery.

Slavery was a legal institution in fourteen states in the Union. It was a repulsive system, but it was also powerful. The fact that the slave states were all contiguous, and lay south of the Mason-Dixon Line and the Ohio River, together with the fact that slave labor in these states produced the single most valuable agricultural commodity on the planet—cotton—gave them a sense of shared regional defensiveness and an enormous political heft in the federal Congress. Likewise, the fact that Southern slavery was based on racial supremacy—of white slaveowners over enslaved blacks—provided a brutal reinforcement to Southern suspicions of the free states of the North. Since slavery's power grew from the seeds of an agricultural commodity, the slave states' instinctive party loyalty was pledged to the Democrats. From Thomas Jefferson to James Buchanan, Southern Democrats either led the party and dominated the presidency or else picked for president Northern Democrats who were securely buttoned to Southern interests. Northerners who criticized slavery and called for its abolition were easily marginalized by Southern plays to economic self-interest or white racial terrors.

Stephen A. Douglas might have been a Democrat, and a successful one, but he was still a Northerner from a free state, and that made Southern Democratic brows crinkle with apprehension. Of course, calling Douglas's Illinois a "free" state meant only that slavery was illegal there. It did not mean that Illinois Democrats were interested in freeing slaves anyplace else, or in welcoming blacks of any description, free or slave, into the state to compete with them for land. When Douglas arrived in Illinois, in the 1830s, the state population stood at 269,974—of these, only 2,261 were free blacks. Another 488 blacks were deemed "apprentices" by various legal subterfuges and were, for all practical purposes, slaves on "free" soil. Twenty years later, the population of Illinois had bulged to over 850,000, but the laws only became more draconian. In 1853, the state legislature banned "any negro or mulatto, bond or free" from settling in Illinois on pain of a fifty-dollar fine or the threat of being sold "at public auction" into forced labor to "serve out" the fine.[13]

There is no record that Douglas felt any deep pangs of conflict over the toleration of slavery in a republic of liberty. While antislavery Northerners struggled to overcome the "gag rule" that prevented antislavery petitions from being introduced onto the floor of the House of Representatives, Douglas cheerfully voted to uphold it. The abolition of slavery was merely a British connivance, Douglas explained, "for the purpose of operating upon the peculiar institutions of some of the States of this Confederacy, and thus render the Union itself insecure." Just as no church had the privilege of imposing its creed upon any American citizens, and no "consolidated" government in Washington had the power to force a program of publicly funded commercial development on the states, so no one had the authority to compel the slave states to abolish slavery. Or, he added in 1853, the authority to compel the free states to take in freed blacks: "Our people are a white people; our State is a white State," Douglas declared. "We do not believe in the

equality of the negro, socially or politically, with the white man." In
Illinois, "we mean to preserve the race pure, without any mixture with
the negro." [14]

The real question, however, was not whether Douglas could be
trusted to keep Northern hands off slavery in the South but whether
he would be willing to give the South what, in the 1850s, it really
wanted, which was a free ticket to legalize slavery in the western territories. No matter how indifferent Douglas might be to the Andes of
suffering inflicted by slavery, white Illinoisans not only wanted blacks
kept out of Illinois but also wanted them kept out of the territories,
since the territories were the next stop in the white farmers' incessant
rush for land. Yet white Southerners were just as convinced that slavery, in order to remain prosperous and healthy, needed constantly to
expand its borders. This determination had created serious collisions
in Congress as far back as 1819, when the Missouri Territory peti-
tioned for admission to the Union as a state with a constitution that
legalized slavery. Northerners (and they included an ominous number
of Northern Democrats) saw no good sign for the future when the
first new state to be organized out of the Louisiana Purchase wanted
to legalize slavery. To the relief of the country in general, the greatest
political compromise builder of the day, Kentucky's Henry Clay, stage-
rigged a formula for all future territorial admissions in the Missouri
Compromise of 1820. Clay simply took the southern boundary of Missouri, drew it straight through the Purchase, and decreed that hereafter only lands *south* of that line could be organized as slave territories
and admitted to the Union as slave states. And with that neat partition,
everyone could, presumably, be happy.

Happy, that is, until the great blowup over Texas.

At the time of the Missouri Compromise, Texas was a sparsely settled
province of Mexico. The Mexicans were only just tearing themselves
loose from the colonial dominion of Spain and setting up as a republic
of their own, and they were happy to accept American immigrants as a

way to settle Texas on the cheap. But in the intervening years, immigration from the United States turned into an uncontrollable flood, a very large part of it contemptuous of Mexican law and Mexican government, and much of it led by slave owners. Too late, the Mexican government tried to seal the border and bridle the Americans in Texas. That only provoked Texas into open revolt and a declaration of independence as a republic of its own. In due time, Texas turned to the United States as an applicant for statehood—bypassing territorial organization, which it scarcely needed—as a slave state.

Mexico never recognized the legitimacy of the Texan republic in the first place, and it was alarmed at the prospect of the rebel province attaching itself to the United States. When Texas was finally annexed by the United States, in 1845, the annexation triggered war between the United States and Mexico, and the war led to a humiliating defeat for Mexico and the cession of its remaining northernmost provinces to the United States. The shooting part of the war had not even stopped before a round of pompous and hysterical charades over slavery even more violent than the one in 1819 began, complete with threats of secession from the Union by the Southern states and demands for the complete exclusion of slavery from the Mexican Cession by Northerners. It took all the compromising skills of the aged Henry Clay to fashion a new compromise, and even then, the actual formula for that compromise—as well as the strategy for recruiting enough votes for it—would fall to a younger man, Stephen A. Douglas.[15]

The formula was called "popular sovereignty," and it was first devised not by Douglas but by an old Democratic party wheelhorse, Lewis Cass of Michigan. But it was seized by Douglas as the banner under which he saw himself marching into the White House. In the largest sense, popular sovereignty was simply another form of Jacksonian Democracy's first article of belief, that "the voice of the people" in a democracy was the ultimate and only rule. And it rang the changes on the Democracy's second article, which was the preference for local decision-making over policies made at the national level. No one but the people of each territory itself—not Northerners in the free states, not Southerners in the slave states, not the president in Washington, not even compromisers in Congress—ought to decide whether slavery should be legal in their territory or not.

"The principle of self-government," explained Douglas, "is, that each community shall settle this question for itself . . . and we have no right to complain, either in the North or the South, whichever they do." For Stephen A. Douglas, this view had the added advantage of re-locating the entire debate over slavery's future in the territories to the territories themselves, and out of the halls of Congress, where the issue was paralyzing all other initiatives for western development. And so while Henry Clay brought every ounce of his fading powers of eloquence to the fashioning of a new compromise, it was Douglas who cobbled together the actual components of the compromise and navi-gated them to adoption.[16] The nation heaved a collective sign of relief, and when Clay died, in 1852, the laurels for statesmanship, compro-mise, and levelheadedness descended upon Stephen A. Douglas.

No one, least of all Douglas, could have suspected that this was, in fact, as far as his tide would carry him. This was partly because, by this point, Southern slaveholders had painted themselves for so long as the victims of Northern perfidy that nothing less than an absolute federal guarantee for legalized slavery in the West would satisfy them. But the other factor which proved Douglas's undoing was his simple inability to rest on those laurels. Almost as if the success of popular sovereignty in 1850 had convinced him that it was the answer to every question, Douglas now proposed to organize the balance of the West—the old Louisiana Purchase lands still governed by the Compromise of 1820s ban on slavery—under the same doctrine.[17]

Precisely because Nebraska was reserved by the Missouri Compro-mise for free settlement only, Southerners in Congress truculently re-fused to support territorial organization there, leaving both the settlers' and Douglas's hopes for what he called "a continuous line of settlement from the Mississippi Valley to the Pacific Ocean" in a legal limbo. But under the terms of Douglas's Nebraska bill, Congress would junk the Missouri Compromise, substitute for it "the principles and model of the compromise measures of 1850," and allow Nebraska to be organized as a territory whose people would make their own decision about slavery. Southerners would no longer have any logical reason to oppose the organization of Nebraska, and in order to make that explicit, Douglas added a provision to the bill which expressly declared the Missouri Compromise to have been "superseded by the principles of 1850":

> *The act preparatory to the admission of Missouri into the Union . . . being inconsistent with the principle of non-intervention by Congress with slavery in the states and territories, as recognized by the legislation of eighteen hundred and fifty, commonly called the compromise measures, is hereby declared inoperative and void; it being the true intent and meaning of this act not to legislate slavery into any territory or state, nor to exclude it therefrom, but to leave the people thereof perfectly free to form and regulate their domestic institutions in their own way, subject only to the Constitution of the United States.*[18]

It was that long, dangling sentence which threw Congress, and the nation, into a tumult.

Douglas was fully aware that the Northerners whom he persuaded to allow popular sovereignty to rule the Mexican Cession did so only with the mental reservation that most of the Cession was useless desert anyway and unlikely to offer much attraction to settlement by slave owners. They never dreamt that Douglas would expect them, four years later, to apply it with equal force to the old Purchase lands, where the opportunities for slave-based agriculture were considerably more substantial. If Southerners sulked because popular sovereignty gave them no more than a mere chance to have slavery legalized in Nebraska, Northerners were horrified to discover that slavery would be given a chance at all, much less a fifty-fifty one. The Missouri Compromise, which had stood for thirty years as the fire door banning slavery from the Louisiana Purchase, now hung off its hinges. New York senator William Henry Seward wrote to his constituents that "we who thought only . . . of securing some portion at least of the shore of the Gulf of Mexico and all of the Pacific coast to the institutions of freedom, will be, before 1859, brought to a doubtful struggle to prevent the extension of slavery to the shores of the great lakes, and thence westward to Puget's sound."[19]

The gasp of horror soon found a national tongue. Ohio senator Salmon P. Chase, a onetime Jacksonian but now turned abolitionist, published "An Appeal of the Independent Democrats" on January 24 in the *National Era,* Washington's main antislavery newspaper, denouncing the Nebraska bill as a "gross violation of a sacred pledge; as a criminal betrayal of precious rights; as part and parcel of an atrocious plot to exclude from a vast unoccupied region immigrants from the Old World and free laborers from our own States, and convert it into a dreary region of despotism, inhabited by masters and slaves." And Chase's "Appeal" (which was signed by yet another senator, Charles Sumner, and four representatives) was only the beginning. "No pretext was urged for the repeal of the Missouri restriction, that it was asked for by the people of the Territory," raged Michigan governor Kinsley Bingham; Douglas had only one purpose, and that was "to appease the inexorable demand of the slave interest for dominion" and bring "the Democratic party of the North . . . under the perfect subjugation to the interests of slavery." Or perhaps he had another purpose: to solicit the favor of the slaveholding South as the last deal he had to make for the presidency. "To him," wrote John Minor Botts of Virginia, "was the glittering prize of a nomination held up as a reward," and Mississippi governor Henry Stuart Foote believed that Douglas had been bribed with a promise from President Pierce that he would endorse a Douglas presidential nomination for 1856. "He has sold the freemen of the North for office," fumed one Illinoisan, "which Heaven grant he may never be able to reach."[20]

Just what induced Douglas to swat at the Nebraska wasps' nest has always been a mystery, to both his admirers and his detractors. Apart from gaining the thanks of the Nebraska settlers, it was hard to know what game Douglas was about, or even if there was a game. "The whole country, which by the previous adjustment of 1850 had settled down in peace, was suddenly taken by surprise," wrote Anna Ella Carroll. "No one dreamed of the compromise being disturbed, and that the triumph of Mr. Clay, and the tranquility happily secured by him over the country, were soon to come to an end."[21] So why the Nebraska bill? Because at bottom, Stephen A. Douglas had the temperament neither of a statesman nor of a demagogue but of a gambler. He was, said the shrewd old Ohio senator Thomas Ewing, "inconsiderate and reckless." He stayed away from cards and horses, but in every other respect, no one loved a risk more than Douglas. Hezekiah Wead remembered that Douglas's decisions as a judge on the bench were often a matter of "guess," supported by "his quickness of apprehension, his amiable manners and his general urbanity." His speculations in land were another game of risk, and even his reputation as a "formidable parliamentary pugilist" was a gamble he took with the fact that he was far from being physically "formidable." Despite the commanding presence and the leonine posturing, the Little Giant was actually fragile of health. Chronic illness had disabled him early in his wanderings between Vermont and Illinois. He was constantly prey to colds and upper respiratory infections, and his climactic speeches seemed always to come when he "was at the time ill in bed" and had to drag himself to the floor of the Senate to speak. But he could not deny himself the thrill of combat, the always-upped stakes over more and more dramatic issues. The greatest risk he would take, however, would be the Nebraska territorial bill. It would, he predicted, "raise the hell of a storm." And into that storm he sailed, smiling.[22]

The only concession Douglas made to the uproar over the Nebraska bill was to permit the division of the enormous Nebraska domain into two territories, Kansas and Nebraska. Otherwise, rather than simply defend the bill as a useful piece of pragmatic politics, he bounded into the congressional arena as the lion, asserting that popular sovereignty was not a means only but a worthwhile end in itself. The question at stake in the organization of Kansas and Nebraska (he declared on March 3, 1854) was whether the people truly had the sole right to govern themselves as they saw fit, "whether the people shall be allowed to regulate their domestic institutions in their own way, according to the provisions of this bill, or whether the opposite doctrine of Congressional interference is to prevail." [23]

Douglas's discovery that popular sovereignty embodied a form of eternal political truth, and not just political sloganeering, "is not an afterthought with me, seized upon this session for the first time, as my calumniators have so frequently and boldly charged." No, the principle of popular sovereignty is the embodiment of popular liberty, "the great fundamental principle of self-government," leaving "the people entirely free to form and regulate their domestic institutions and internal concerns in their own way." It also, incidentally, got the slavery controversy out of the halls of Congress, because "the attempt on the part of Congress to interfere with the question of slavery" always produced deadlock and acrimony. But "whenever that cause had been removed" by letting the people decide for themselves, "the agitation has ceased." When a petition from three thousand New England clergy protesting the repeal of the Missouri Compromise was introduced into the Senate by the venerable Edward Everett, Douglas's reaction was to suggest pretty bluntly that they mind their own religious business and stop trying "to establish a theocracy to take charge of our politics and our legislation." When the vote finally came in the Senate, Douglas carried the day for the Kansas-Nebraska bill—and popular sovereignty—with thirty-seven senators in favor and only fourteen opposed; on May 22, 1854, it squeezed through the House of Representatives as well, 113 to 100. President Pierce signed it four days later—the day of a near-total eclipse of the sun. [24]

But popular sovereignty only cried about "peace"; it did not bring it, either to Kansas or to Stephen A. Douglas. Of the Northern Democrats in the House, over half had voted against Douglas; resolutions attacking the Kansas-Nebraska bill were issued by five Northern state legislatures; and in the fall elections, Democrats who had voted for Kansas-Nebraska fell in heaps, with only seven of the forty-two House Democrats who voted for the bill surviving. When Douglas tried to speak in defense of Kansas-Nebraska on September 1 on his home ground in Chicago, he was hissed, booed, and taunted for two hours until he finally gave up and stamped off the platform. The Illinois elections two months later had an even more dangerous message: in the nine congressional districts, five of the Democrats elected were opponents of the Kansas-Nebraska bill, while the other four (including two Douglas loyalists, Thomas Harris and William Richardson) only narrowly avoided defeat. Douglas-sponsored Democrats clung to only forty-three of the one hundred seats in the state house and senate, and the anti-Douglas majority looked as though they were perfectly capable of taking down another Douglas ally, James Shields, whose U.S. Senate seat was up for reelection by the new legislature when it would meet after the turn of the new year.[25]

In Kansas, popular sovereignty, instead of bringing peace, brought on a minor civil war. The chant of popular sovereignty as "the true principle" and "the only way to restore peace" was so entrancing that it barely passed notice that the Kansas-Nebraska bill had not specified the point in a territory's development when the populace would exercise its sovereignty and decide for or against slavery.[26] Should the decision be held at the very outset of territorial organization? If so, wouldn't a negative decision make it impossible for any slave owners to move there, and infuriate Southerners, who would denounce "popular sovereignty" and its champion as frauds? Or should it come at the end of the process, when the territory wrote its proposed state constitution and asked Congress for admission to the Union? If so, and the new constitution banned slavery, were slave owners to be forcibly expelled?

And who would police the decision-making process? If enough proslavery settlers—or antislavery settlers—could be rushed into Kansas to create a temporary majority, then that majority might declare that the moment for deciding had arrived and announce the results before the next wagon trains from Missouri or Illinois could create a new majority. So began a frantic outfitting of wild-eyed emigrants—New England abolitionists with Bibles, "border ruffians" from Missouri with slaves—to seize control of the territorial process.

Those who, in addition to Bibles or slaves, brought rifles with them to Kansas soon discovered that subtraction by murder was as effective for making majorities as addition by immigration, and so Kansas quickly degenerated into a maelstrom of guerrilla violence, lynch law, and assassination. What popular sovereignty finally produced in Kansas was two hundred murdered settlers, along with two rival territorial legislatures, one proslavery and the other antislavery, each claiming to be the legitimate voice of the people, and two rival state capitals, at Lecompton (for the proslavery legislature) and Topeka (for the antislavery legislature). From them came two rival demands for the authority to apply for statehood and to write a state constitution. At which point, the Kansas imbroglio would be deposited on the doorstep of Congress to settle, and Douglas's promise that popular sovereignty would clear the slavery problem out of Washington would fall over like a hollow tree in a windstorm.

Assuming that Congress had long since illustrated its incapacity to resolve the slavery question, it would not be long before the other branches of the federal government decided that it was up to them to bring about a final settlement. The first turn was taken by the chief justice of the United States, Roger Brooke Taney, an old-line Jacksonian and onetime slaveholder from Maryland, who imagined that he could defuse the issue by simple judicial fiat. The origins of this fiat stretched back to 1846, when a Missouri-born slave, Dred Scott, sued in the Missouri courts for his freedom on the grounds that his former master, John Emerson, an army surgeon, had taken him on post while

Emerson was stationed at Fort Snelling in the Minnesota territory in the 1830s. Since the Minnesota territory was part of the Louisiana Purchase, it had been organized, under the terms of the Missouri Compromise, as a free territory; hence, Scott insisted that his residence there with Emerson made him a free man.[27] The case wound its way up through the state and the federal courts, attracting attention and support at every new level, until it was appealed to the U.S. Supreme Court in 1856. Chief Justice Taney announced the court's decision on March 6, 1857, and it was bad news for both Dred Scott and Stephen A. Douglas. Scott, simply by virtue of being black and a slave, had no civil standing in a federal court, and therefore Taney wrote in the court's majority opinion, his appeal was denied; but even if Scott *had* civil standing, a plea for freedom based on the Missouri Compromise was invalid because Congress had no authority to forbid slave owners, who were citizens entitled to due process, from carrying their slave "property" with them into any of the federal territories. And, Taney added with a twist of the knife, if Congress had no authority to ban slaves from being taken into the territories, neither did the people of the territories, since territorial governments were creations of Congress. So much for popular sovereignty.[28]

It was bad enough that Taney and *Dred Scott* made constitutional hash of popular sovereignty. What was worse was the way Douglas's critics raged that "popular sovereignty" had been a pro-Southern play all along, and that Douglas, eager to curry Southern Democratic favor, had lured Northerners into replacing the Missouri Compromise with "popular sovereignty" so that Taney could slap it down and open the gate to slave expansion. From the perspective of *Dred Scott*, it was easy to conclude that the Kansas-Nebraska bill was simply the second act of an opera whose first act was the Compromise of 1850 (opening the Mexican Cession to the possibility of slavery by popular sovereignty) and whose third act was *Dred Scott* (making it impossible to keep slavery out, whether by popular sovereignty or by any other means).

But Douglas was nothing if not resourceful, and in a major speech in the Illinois statehouse on June 12, he insisted that, far from destroying popular sovereignty, the *Dred Scott* decision had actually left it as the only legal weapon for resisting slavery. It may be true, Douglas conceded, that slave owners' property rights cannot be extinguished by an act of Congress or a territorial legislature, popular or not. But what is also true is that slavery, in order to function, requires the enactment of a battery of local codes and enforcement statutes. If the people of a territory, exercising their sovereignty, decide not to enact those regulations, they have made slavery just as impossible in that territory as though it had been banned by Congress. The *right* to slave ownership remains intact, but it "necessarily remains a barren and a worthless right, unless sustained, protected and enforced by appropriate police regulations and local legislation." [29]

This formula might have allowed Douglas to dodge Taney's dagger had it not been for James Buchanan. The veteran Pennsylvania Democrat liked to advertise himself as "a Northern man with Southern principles," but he might as well have left the Northern part out. Elected president in 1856, after Douglas grudgingly gave up the fight for the nomination, Buchanan chose a cabinet and advisers who were Southerners, and he regarded *Dred Scott* as the golden key he would use to unlock national peace. Buchanan was also personally suspicious of Stephen Douglas, whom he rightly regarded as his principal rival for party leadership and for "re-election as President," and he felt no sorrow at seeing Douglas's pet doctrine of popular sovereignty so severely damaged by *Dred Scott*. Douglas wrote a friend that he'd quickly found that "at present, I am an outsider. My advice is not coveted nor will my wishes probably be regarded." Nor was Buchanan any less indulgent when the proslavery Lecompton legislature in Kansas, taking the last step toward admission to the Union as a state, staged a referendum on a proslavery constitution in December 1857, which garnered a suspiciously resounding majority of 6,243 to 569. When the Thirty-fifth Congress opened for business in that same month, Buchanan was ready with a presidential message which recommended the admission of Kansas as a state under the Lecompton constitution. Douglas could either fall in line behind Buchanan and set a match to any hope that Northern Democrats would ever forgive him *or* go into open rebellion against Buchanan, in which case the president would manipulate every lever of party power and influence to wreck Douglas's reelection in 1858.[30]

It took Douglas no long time to make up his mind. He arrived in Washington on December 2 for the opening of Congress and went at once to see Buchanan at the White House. The interview was polite but frosty. "Mr. Douglas, I desire you to remember that no Democrat ever differed from the Administration . . . without being crushed," the president warned him. Such, at least had been the fate of earlier Democrats who challenged Andrew Jackson. "Mr. President," Douglas icily replied, "I wish you to remember that Gen. Jackson is dead, sir." The day after Buchanan's message was read to both houses of Congress, Douglas rose to accuse the president of "a fundamental error" in endorsing the Lecompton constitution. "Did we not come before the country and say that we repealed the Missouri restriction for the purpose of substituting and carrying out as a general rule the great principle of self-government, which left the people of each State and each Territory free to form and regulate their domestic institutions in their own way?" Douglas asked with mounting passion. But the Lecompton legislature was a "pretense" of a legislature instead of an expression of popular sovereignty. The referendum behind the Lecompton constitution was "the act and will of a small minority, who have attempted to cheat & defraud the majority by trickery & juggling," and Buchanan's attempt to cram Lecompton down congressional throats was an act of blinding executive dictation, which Douglas intended to dispute to the last yard.

It was not slavery or an anxiety to shore up his standing with Northern voters, Douglas insisted, which drove him to this conclusion. "If Kansas wants a slave-State constitution she has a right to it. . . . I do not care whether it is voted down or voted up." It was the principle of the people's right to self-government which made his heart beat, and which now drove him into opposition to the president and his own party, and he played upon his own impending political martyrdom as the reward political virtue must expect from political vice. "I should regret any social or political estrangement, even temporarily, but if it must be, if I cannot act with you and preserve my faith and honor, I will stand on the great principle of popular sovereignty."[31]

On February 4, 1858, Douglas broke openly with the administration and called for the Senate to reject the Lecompton constitution, and in March, as the constitution finally came to a vote, Douglas rose to address a Senate chamber so packed with spectators that even the corridors outside were jammed. "Is there a man within the hearing of my voice who believes that the Lecompton Constitution does embody the will of a majority of the *bona fides* inhabitants of Kansas?" he asked angrily, and over the course of three hours, he attacked the legitimacy of the Lecompton constitution and rebuked James Buchanan for trying to "prescribe" artificial "tests" for party loyalty.[32]

The problem, as Douglas knew all too well, was that, because he was head of the Democratic party, prescribing "tests" was exactly what Buchanan could do very effectively. In the political era of the 1850s, before civil service reform professionalized the federal bureaucracy, every federal office was an executive appointment. And patronage appointments, from the cabinet down to the smallest post office, were the lifeblood of national politics. They were the principal means of rewarding the party faithful; they were the practical device that ensured a lucrative salary and modest responsibilities to a party's newspaper editors; and at election time, patronage appointees turned into the party's foot soldiers and contributed to the party's coffers from their salaries. Buchanan, who had spent a lifetime within the federal patronage system, was not shy about using it to "prescribe tests," and he cheerfully did so now. Only two Democratic senators joined Douglas in voting against Lecompton.[33]

In the House, Buchanan's floor managers were distracted by in-
sults and fistfights between members, and by the substitution of an
amendment from Indiana congressman William English, which required the Lecompton constitution to be resubmitted to Kansas voters
in a second—and this time federally supervised—referendum. Otherwise, Kansas would have to agree to make no new application for statehood. After hesitating because of the referendum provision, Douglas
finally came out in opposition to both Lecompton and the English
amendment. The House then voted to endorse Lecompton, but only
with English's amendment and only by a margin of 112 to 103. The
Senate backed the House version, with Douglas and his two last allies,
David Broderick of California and Charles Stuart of Michigan, standing out to the end. When the Senate closed its session on June 14,
Douglas seemed to have lost the fight over Lecompton and now had to
look ahead to Illinois, to a campaign for reelection, and to the possibility that a triumphant James Buchanan would move heaven and earth—
and every patronage appointment in them—to see him defeated.[34]

Abraham Lincoln first encountered Stephen A. Douglas in the winter
of 1834, when the tall, stilt-legged store clerk turned surveyor, with
"his gaunt but intellectual face" and "negligent dress," arrived by
stagecoach in the Illinois capital of Vandalia to sit for the first time as a
state legislator.[35] Both men were immigrants to Illinois (Lincoln was
born in Kentucky in 1809, moved with his parents to Indiana in 1816,
and thence to Illinois in 1830), both of them had lost a parent early in
life (in Lincoln's case, his mother, in 1818), both turned to law as a profession but to politics as a vocation. Thereafter, all similarities ended,
for Lincoln's model statesman was not Andrew Jackson but the man
who emerged as Jackson's great political nemesis in the 1830s, the
great compromise builder, Henry Clay.

In earlier days, Clay had been a devoted Democrat in Congress, de-
spising banks and lauding the virtues of the agrarian life. But the near
catastrophe of the War of 1812, in which a virtuous agricultural re-

public ruled by Democratic agrarians was nearly snuffed out because it could not raise the cash to pay its soldiers or rely on a vast base of manufacturing to arm them, taught Clay how unlikely it was for virtue to triumph unless virtue was self-sufficient. For the next twenty years, he tirelessly promoted an "American System" of domestic manufacturing, a system protected by high tariffs against foreign manufacturers, supported by the government-sponsored "internal improvements" the Jacksonians despised, and undergirded by a national bank that used the proceeds from the tariffs and the sale of federal land in the West to provide the start-up funding for ambitious new corporations. What looked to Andrew Jackson like pandering to the "moneyed interests"—or worse, a plot to enmesh the American farmer in the tentacles of consumerism, debt, and British-style industrial capitalism—looked to Clay like an investment in a robust economy, the first line of resistance to hostile monarchies. Anyone who could not endorse that "must be for reducing us either to a dependence on . . . foreign nations, or to be clothed in skins."[36] Certainly, the leadership of the Democracy had no business complaining about "moneyed interests" when so many of them, beginning with Jackson himself, owned vast plantations, worked by battalions of black slaves. If anything, a thriving and diverse manufacturing economy offered to the poor and middling sorts an openness to talent, ingenuity, and self-transformation which made the agrarian Eden of the Jacksonians smell stale and pigeonholed.

Unlike Douglas, Lincoln had experienced firsthand all he cared to experience of the pleasures of the agrarian life growing up in Indiana. "I was raised to farm work," he recalled in 1859; he had "an axe put into his hands" almost as early as he could walk "and from that till within his twentythird year, he was almost constantly handling that most useful instrument." His father, Thomas, was a textbook illustration of the independent farmer who subsisted cheerfully on what he could grow or make from his own land, without the need for banks or for the baubles of the marketplace, and without the slightest prickling of ambition for anything better. Thomas Lincoln "was satisfied to live in the good old fashioned way," raising just "a Nuf for his own use" and with no interest in marketing "any produce to any other place Mor than Bought his Shugar and Coffee and Such Like." He was also a test case for the dark side of agrarianism—brutal, abusive, ignorant, semiliterate, and suspicious of the "uncommon natural talents" his son was already displaying at an early age. The boy "was a constant and . . . Stubborn reader," but the only appreciation Thomas Lincoln showed was "to slash him for neglecting his work by reading." Years later, Abraham Lincoln would retaliate by remembering his father as a man who "never did more in the way of writing than to bunglingly sign his own name."[37]

By the 1830s, neither Abraham Lincoln nor Henry Clay could live under such roofs any longer. Clay organized an anti-Jacksonian "National Republican" faction within the Democratic party, and when that failed to halt Jackson's relentless drive to the presidency, he bolted from the Democratic ranks entirely and raised the banner of what he christened the Whig party—*Whig* after the venerable old name applied in England to the party of resistance to royal despotism and military power. "A Whig," insisted one of Clay's Virginia admirers, "means one who prefers liberty to tyranny—who supports . . . the rights and immunities of the people . . . against the predominance of the Crown, or executive power"—meaning, especially, Andrew Jackson. But Clay's Whigs evolved quickly from a hate-Jackson movement into an entire political culture of their own, built around the upwardly mobile aspirations of the American middle class. They were predominantly urban rather than agrarian, wedded to commerce and industry rather than agriculture, and they took the whole nation—not just their local parts of the Union—as the basis of their political identity, as befitted a party determined to link the various states and regions of the Union into a single, efficient national market. "The Whig party is a National party . . . and not to be disturbed by all the local questions of policy that may arise."[38]

Whigs worshiped at the shrine of social mobility and self-improvement, something which laid the basis for the Whigs' alliance with the multitude of evangelical Protestant churches in America. This alliance did not require Whigs to become converts. Abraham Lincoln, who drank in the religious skepticism of Tom Paine and Robert Burns with his earliest reading, never joined a church. But he also insisted that he could not "be brought to support a man for office, whom I knew to be an open enemy of, and scoffer at, religion." Transforming the self was as much a goal of the Whigs as it was of the evangelical revivalists, and their shared confidence in the possibilities of personal transformation marked the merchants and the preachers as men of seriousness and dividends, and set them off decisively from the obsession with class and racial stability and the violent defense of personal honor that characterized the Jacksonians, and Andrew Jackson himself. "Every manufactory known to me, is in the hands of enterprising and self-made men, who have acquired whatever wealth they possess by patient and diligent labor," wrote Clay. "Is there more tendency to aristocracy in manufactory, supporting hundreds of freemen, or in a cotton plantation, with its not less than numerous slaves?"[39]

Just as Clay left the Jacksonians, so did Lincoln leave his father's farm for the upward-looking possibilities of wage-labor and commerce. Once the Lincolns moved to Illinois, in 1830, and Lincoln turned twenty-one, he left his father's two-room cabin and never looked back. "His father taught him to work" on the farm, Lincoln wisecracked, "but never learned him to love it," and in years to come, Lincoln would equate the way his father hired him out as a farm laborer with slavery. Unlike Douglas, "he said he had no capacity whatever for speculation" in land "and never attempted it." Instead, he plunged into the market economy as a store owner and then finally, in 1837, as a member of the first rank of capitalism's enforcers, a lawyer. And when he arrived in Vandalia as a freshman state legislator, he was already armed as a Whig, ready to battle for state-funded "internal improvements," turnpikes and canals, and a state bank. "He was as stiff as a man could be in his Whig doctrines," remarked Stephen A. Logan, who took Lincoln into law partnership in the early 1840s. "In this he made no concession of principle whatsoever." Henry Clay was Lincoln's "beau ideal of a statesman," and he was so "deeply imbued with the Principles of Henry Clay" that decades later he would still describe himself as "always . . . an old-line Henry Clay Whig." And as a Whig, he voted at the end of the legislative session in February 1835 against the Democratic candidate for state's attorney for the First District, Stephen A. Douglas.[40]

Lincoln had not liked Douglas then—he referred to the five-foot-four-inch Douglas as "the least man I ever saw"—and the impression did not improve with time. The two had publicly crossed political swords as early as 1838, when Lincoln took the stump on behalf of his law partner, John Todd Stuart, in Stuart's race against Douglas for a seat in Congress. They shared an election platform again during the 1840 presidential race, when Lincoln became a "travelling missionary" across Illinois for the Whig candidate, William Henry Harrison. Despite Lincoln's sharp suggestion that it would be better "never to speak of Douglas at all" (since that was "the best mode of treating so small a matter"), both men went "all around the Circuit . . . & spoke." (In 1858, Lincoln would remark at the Tazewell county courthouse that "he had often met with Douglas upon the very steps upon which he was speaking, before as now to oppose his political doctrines.") A partisan himself, Lincoln had a partisan's contempt for an opposing partisan. That distaste was not softened by the tattletales who smirked that Douglas had been Lincoln's chief rival for the hand of Mary Todd, whom Lincoln married in 1842. Douglas was exactly the risk taker Lincoln was not, a man who "will tell a lie to ten thousand people one day, even though he knows he may have to deny it to five thousand the next." "Of all men he has ever seen," Lincoln bitterly remarked, Douglas "has the most audacity in maintaining an untenable position."[41]

But by that audacity, Douglas had "bamboozled thousands into believing him," and the result was that Douglas had scampered to the top of the ladder of American politics while Lincoln had languished in honest obscurity, with only his personal integrity to console him. "Douglas had got to be a great man, & [be]strode the earth," Lincoln complained sarcastically in 1852. "Time was when I was in his way some; but he has outgrown me & [be]strides the world; & such small men as I am, can hardly be considered worthy of his notice; & I may have to dodge and get between his legs." In Lincoln's eyes, Douglas was the Democratic golden boy who had everything in politics handed to him effortlessly, while Lincoln was left to struggle and lose, unappreciated and unsupported. "Twenty-two years ago Judge Douglas and I first became acquainted," Lincoln wrote in 1856. "With me, the race of ambition has been a failure—a flat failure; with him it has been one of splendid success. His name fills the nation; and is not unknown, even, in foreign lands." Lincoln was not normally one to hold grudges. But Douglas was an exception. "He was intensely jealous of him," remembered Ward Hill Lamon, one of Lincoln's favorites. He "longed to pull him down, or outstrip him in the race for popular favor, which they united in considering 'the chief end of man.'"[42]

In the shadow of his self-pity, Lincoln forgot that, once elected to the Illinois legislature, he, too, had moved quickly to the forefront of the Whig caucus and successfully pushed to adoption bills for massive "internal improvements" projects across Illinois, and a state bank to fund them. He forgot also that he was the principal force behind moving the state capital from Vandalia to Springfield, where he practiced law with Stuart and Logan, two highly placed Whigs; that he had boosted himself into the top layer of Springfield's Whig ascendancy by marrying Mary Todd; that he had converted the visibility he earned in the legislature and the courts into election to Congress in 1846; and that, by the 1850s, he had established his own law firm with a very handsome income from civil litigation in the Illinois appeals courts and state supreme court. "At that time," recalled Shelby Cullom over fifty years later, "Abraham Lincoln and Stephen T. Logan and Stuart and [Ninian] Edwards [Lincoln's brother-in-law] were the four ablest lawyers in the capital city."[43]

The problem was that these successes were not the successes he craved. Lincoln was a man of "great ambition" who as "early as 1830 began to dream of a destiny." But by 1850 few of his accomplishments looked much like a "destiny." Springfield and its surrounding counties in central Illinois formed a comfortable belt of Whig loyalty which ran horizontally across the state, but it was easily dwarfed by Democratic majorities everywhere else in the state, which kept the state legislature, the governor's mansion, and all the Illinois congressional districts (except Lincoln's own Seventh) locked in Democratic hands. Behind his back, friends whispered that his marriage "was a policy Match all around," and his third law partner, William Henry Herndon, went so far as to describe the Lincoln home as an "ice cave" that offered Lincoln nothing but "domestic *hell*." Above all, Lincoln's term in Congress was marked by a bid to earn standing for himself as a Whig by criticizing the war with Mexico, a gesture which turned out to be a colossal political blunder. Only two weeks into his first congressional session, Lincoln rose to attack President James Knox Polk through a series of eight questions, demanding to know whether Polk had deliberately provoked a clash with Mexico by ordering American troops into a disputed boundary zone where they were ambushed by the Mexican army. Lincoln wanted to know "whether the spot on which the blood of our citizens was shed" was really American soil—as though nice points in international law meant anything now that a full-blown war was in progress. This hectoring drew guffaws and denunciations from Democrats in Congress and only embarrassed Illinois Whigs, who had no desire to look like they were giving aid and comfort to the Mexicans.[44]

Lincoln worked hard to elect a Whig president, Zachary Taylor, in 1848, but unlike Douglas's, his hopes for a reward in the form of some high-profile federal office were dashed when all the Taylor administration offered him was the governorship of the Oregon Territory. Lincoln buried his disappointments behind a wall "of quite infinite silences . . . thoroughly and deeply secretive, uncommunicative, and close-minded as to his plans, wishes, hopes and fears." And once his order of William Lloyd Garrison or Frederick Douglass. On the long spectrum of opinions that constituted opposition to slavery, abolition was only the most radical, because it stood for an immediate end to slavery, without gradual timetables or financial compensation to slave owners. Abolition was a radicalism fueled by a heady blend of Romantic ethics and renegade evangelicalism, which explains why it was so uncompromising and so passionate in its demands, since in the calculations of Romantic fervor, half measures are generally worse than none. But Lincoln was neither a Romantic nor an evangelical. His guiding star was reason, "cold, calculating, unimpassioned reason" rather than the "fury" of the moralists. When the abolitionists insisted that they must "do their duty and leave the consequences to God," that struck Lincoln as little better than "an excuse for taking a course that they were not able to maintain by a fair and full argument." Reason told him that this world was "a world of compensations" rather than absolutes, where prudence and caution were the best cures for evil, and that the best solution to evils like slavery was to allow reason to be "moulded into *general intelligence, sound morality* and, in particular, *a reverence for the constitution and laws.*"[47]

As clear as it was in Lincoln's mind that the Founders would never have talked about equality if they had not seen slavery as a "great and crying injustice," it was equally clear that the Founders tolerated slavery's existence in the new Republic because that was the only way they could get the Southern states to ratify the Constitution. The states, in the judgment of good Whigs, "came into the Union in good faith, and with a full and perfect understanding, that the powers of the Union should not extend to the compulsory reform of their domestic institutions." But it was only a temporary toleration. Once cemented together in a national Union, Americans would start from a new baseline of equality, which would permit no new growth of slavery and would encourage slavery in the old states to die out on its own. "No man has the right to keep his fellow man in bondage, be he black or white," Lincoln assured the Hungarian exile Julian Kune, "and the time

will come, and must come, when there will not be a single slave within
the borders of this country." But so long as the Constitution spread
that temporary sanction over slavery, "it is our duty to wait."[48]

Kansas-Nebraska, however, was not what Lincoln thought he was
waiting for. "The repeal of the Missouri compromise aroused him as he
had never been before," Lincoln wrote years later; it "took us by surprise—astounded us," and "raised such an excitement . . . throughout
the country as never before was heard of in this Union." Kansas-
Nebraska was not "a *law*" but an act of "*violence* from the beginning,"
first crammed down the throat of Congress and now clamped like a
vise on Kansas. Popular sovereignty was not a mechanism for promoting peaceful democratic choice in the territories; it was a political
sham, devised as a clever strategy of "the slaveholding power" for tearing down the antislavery barrier erected by earlier generations to the
vast stretches of the West. No one, Lincoln explained, better "appreci-
ated . . . the sacred right of self-government, rightly understood . . .
than himself." And if popular sovereignty meant only that "individuals
held the right to regulate their own family affairs; communities might
arrange their own internal matter to suit themselves; States might
make their own statutes, subject only to the Constitution of the United
States;—no one disagreed with this doctrine." But if popular sovereignty meant the freedom of one man to plunge another into the
"moral, social and political evil of slavery," then they were talking no
longer about popular sovereignty in the territories but about popular
tyranny. "Any man who has the sense to be the controller of his own
property, has too much sense to misunderstand the outrageous character of this whole Nebraska business."[49]

And not only the territories. If there was no legitimacy to banning
slavery in the territories, then, by the same logic, there should be no legitimacy to opposing slavery at all. On those terms, slavery was not an
evil to be eclipsed but merely another economic arrangement to be
processed under the equal—and indifferent—protection of the laws.
To see no difference "between freedom and slavery—that both are

equal with us—that we yield our territories as readily to one as to the other" was "practically legislating for slavery, recognizing it, endorsing it, propagating it, extending it." What argument, then, could possibly be offered to sustain the bans on slavery in the free states? "This thing is spreading like wild fire over the Country," Lincoln warned Joseph Gillespie, his old Whig political ally. "In a few years we will be ready to accept the institution in Illinois and the whole country will adopt it." And standing behind it, fully expecting to reap the highest reward for his service, stood Stephen A. Douglas—"Our Senator." And so, even though "we were thunderstruck and stunned . . . we rose each fighting, grasping whatever he could first reach" to strike a blow at Kansas-Nebraska—and Douglas.[50]

Lincoln could not, in 1854, directly challenge Douglas at the polls, since Douglas's seat as Illinois's senior senator would not come up for reelection until 1858. But he could certainly begin undermining Douglas in Douglas's own Illinois heartland, and to that end, Lincoln threw himself into the fall state legislative campaigns in order to promote the election of Whig candidates. They, in turn, would be casting votes, come the new year, for the junior senator's seat, which was held at that moment by one of Douglas's lieutenants, James Shields. (Lincoln had no personal love for Shields, either, having once nearly fought a duel with him over a series of insulting newspaper articles Lincoln ghostwrote).[51]

So when Douglas returned to Illinois in September to campaign "with a furor" on Shields's behalf, Lincoln began showing up at Douglas's rallies and following up Douglas's speeches in defense of Kansas-Nebraska and popular sovereignty with sharply tuned rebuttals "until he run him into his hole or made him holler." Between September and November, Lincoln averaged one major campaign speech a week, hanging on Douglas's coattails and, on October 4 in Springfield, speaking so soon after Douglas that the event almost looked like a debate. Over and over again, Lincoln drilled home his questions: What was popular sovereignty? It was a "lullaby" which put to sleep the

original love of liberty inherited from "our revolutionary fathers."
What was slavery? It was a "total violation" of the real doctrine of self-
government, that "no man is good enough to govern another man,
without that man's consent," and "a gross outrage on the law of nature." What was the solution? "The Missouri Compromise ought to be
restored" and slavery put back behind the barriers within which it
must eventually die. These speeches, remembered one veteran Whig,
were "the occasion of his becoming a great antislavery leader," and he
"rallied the Whig Party of Central Illinois almost to a man against
[the] Nebraska Bill."[52]

However, Lincoln understood that he would accomplish little simply by rallying Illinois Whigs. The Whigs were themselves bitterly divided over Kansas-Nebraska, both in Illinois and across the country,
since large numbers of Whigs who distrusted Kansas-Nebraska were
even more distrustful of the abolitionists and anti-Nebraska Democrats who were opposing Douglas. Lincoln tried to cajole them in Illinois by asking whether they would "allow me as an old whig to tell
them good-humoredly, that I think this is very silly? Stand with anybody that stands RIGHT." And that fall, in Michigan and Wisconsin, a
new "fusion" party of anti-Nebraska Democrats and antislavery
Whigs took the name Republican, swept all its nominees to victory in
Michigan, and left only one Democratic congressman standing in
Wisconsin. In Ohio, anti-Nebraska Democrats and old Whigs joined
hands under the banner of the "People's Ticket" and swamped regular
Democrats in all but nine counties. And in Illinois, the Democratic
leadership in Chicago—Norman Buel Judd, John Wentworth, and
Burton C. Cook—together with the downstaters John M. Palmer and
Lyman Trumbull, deserted Douglas to run as anti-Nebraska Demo-
crats for the state legislature. "Douglas can no more control Illinois
than a Hottentot Chief can," crowed Lincoln's law partner, William
Herndon.[53]

The success of the anti-Douglas candidates led Lincoln to begin
toying with a more ambitious goal than simply denying the junior Sen-

ate seat to James Shields. "It may come round that a whig may, by possibility, be elected to the U.S. Senate," he wrote frankly to a newly
elected member of the Illinois House, "and I want the chance of being
the man." Although in normal times a Whig was no more likely to be
elected to the Senate by the legislature's Democratic majorities than an
abolitionist, these were not normal times, and anti-Nebraska Democrats were certainly not going to reelect a Douglas puppet. And if a
Whig could promote himself as more anti-Nebraska than Whig, he
might just win by default. "I would rather have a full term in the Senate" than any other office, Lincoln explained, because it was "a place in
which I would feel more consciously able to discharge the duties required and where there was more chance to make reputation and less
danger of losing it"—not to mention the satisfaction of finally pulling
even with Stephen A. Douglas. "I have really got it into my head to try
to be United States Senator," Lincoln wrote to Joseph Gillespie on December 1, and as he tallied the numbers, he counted twenty-eight
Whigs and fourteen anti-Nebraska Democrats in the state House, and
fourteen more in the state Senate. Fifty-six, which should be more than
enough to elect him to the Senate.[54]

What he did not expect was that, much as he might want to "fuse"
with the anti-Douglas Democrats, they might decline to "fuse" with
him. By the middle of December, Lincoln was already worried that
"there must be something wrong about U.S. Senator, at Chicago," since
he could tease no commitments from Judd, Cook, or Wentworth. And
when the legislature met, in the wake of a blinding snowstorm, to cast
ballots for senator, Lincoln received only forty-five votes—minus the
Chicago delegation and six short of a majority—while Shields still had
forty-one and a downstate anti-Nebraska Democrat, Lyman Trumbull, had five. It was apparent that Stephen A. Douglas had not been
idle, either. Douglas hoped that Shields would be reelected by "accla-
mation" and "in that event let every paper in the State put Shields name
at the head of its columns for Senator." (Anything, including a deadlock, "would be better than the election of Lincoln," Douglas added.)

But Shields only continued to lose ground, and on orders from Douglas's ally Thomas L. Harris, the Douglasites substituted the popular former governor Joel Matteson as the Democratic nominee. Matteson had taken no public stand on Kansas-Nebraska and even tried "to privately impress them with the belief that he was as good Anti-Nebraska as any one else." As relieved Democrats began swinging to Matteson, Lincoln decided that it would be far better to elect Trumbull, even at his own expense, than a man whose leading-strings would be in Douglas's hands. "I could not . . . let the whole political result go to ruin, on a point merely personal to myself," he wrote, no matter how "ambitious" he was. So Lincoln "urged his friends to vote for Trumbull," and on the tenth ballot Trumbull was elected. (It is an indication of how embarrassing this loss really was for Douglas that Douglas tried—and failed—to have Trumbull's admission to the Senate blocked on a technicality.) [55]

The biggest loser, however, was neither Lincoln nor Douglas but the Whig party. Fusion had scored some impressive successes in the western states, but it had failed to generate much energy in the East, and it had signally failed to elect Lincoln in Illinois. Fusion also had no long-term future. Whig loyalists might temporarily bury a few hatchets in order to defeat Douglas, but that did nothing for the Whigs in the long run, and it even implied that the Whig party had become so feeble that it no longer had any hope of electing candidates purely on its own strength. "The Whig party is dead," complained a longtime Whig lawyer, Usher F. Linder, "and I am left a widower." Some turned to the American party (or "Know-Nothings"), a rapidly emerging party organized around hostility to immigration. Others turned to the Republicans, and in northern Illinois, Republican and "Peoples" conventions assembled at Rockford, Aurora, and Bloomington to adopt openly abolitionist platforms. Lincoln might have joined them at that moment—he declared himself ready to "fuse with anyone who would unite with him to oppose the slave power"—but he was as yet still enough of a Whig, and still too uncertain that affiliation with the "abolitionist" Republicans would advance him anywhere. Still, the days of Whig loyalty were numbered, as in fact were the days of Democratic loyalty in Illinois. Soon enough, the major anti-Nebraska Democrats—Trumbull, Cook, Judd, Wentworth—all broke their ties to the Democratic party and joined the Republicans.[56]

And in the spring of 1856, as the shrinking circle of the Whig party nominated Millard Fillmore for president and sagged toward an alliance with the Know-Nothings, Lincoln made his move, too. In February, he accepted an invitation from key Republican leaders in Illinois to a state organizing meeting in Decatur, where they "concluded by toasting Mr. Abram Lincoln as the warm and consistent friend of Illinois, and our next candidate for the U.S. Senate." He agreed to address the Republican state convention in Bloomington in May and brought down the house with what John M. Palmer thought was "the greatest speech of his life." It now remained only for Lincoln to grasp the opportunity to confront Douglas—and the "slaveholding power"—directly, when the senior Illinois seat came vacant in 1858.[57]

CHAPTER 2

TAKE CARE OF YOUR OLD WHIGS

Illinois! The pivot on which turns the scale
Of Liberty's blessing or Slavery's bale.
The eyes of a continent rest on the fight—
The hearts of the world are warm for the right!
. . . But mindful the cause of the poor and oppressed,
Most safely shall rest in Abraham's breast.
So take a link off from the slave-chain, anon,
And to Liberty's livery add a Lincoln!

"THE TOCSIN," ILLINOIS STATE JOURNAL,
JULY 12, 1858

"THE WHIGS ARE all dead," complained one longtime Whig politician in the fall of 1856; or, if not exactly dead, "they call themselves the *Republican party*—which means negro worshippers." This, of course, was not true. The Republican party was a far cry from being merely a rollover of the Whigs, much less "negro worshippers," and no one knew that better than those Whigs who had stepped off the sinking deck of the Whig party that year to join the Republicans. Although antislavery Northern Whigs eventually made up more than half the overall rank and file of the new Republican organization, they had to share the table with anti-Nebraska Democrats who had been read out of their old party, with the immigrant haters who were disappointed that the Know-Nothings refused to take an antislavery stand, and with abolitionists who hoped to see the Republicans grow beyond simple opposition to the extension of slavery. And the balance within this coalition differed from state to state, and from election to election. In 1856, the Republicans had accumulated enough political mass to hold a national nominating convention in Pittsburgh and ran the celebrity adventurer John Charles Frémont as their presidential candidate. But the dying rump of the Whig party insisted on nominating a candidate of its own, Millard Fillmore, who also got the endorsement of the Know-Nothings, and Fillmore drew more than enough votes from old Whig loyalists and Whigs-turned-Know-Nothings to guarantee the election of James Buchanan. "The Republican party," David Davis warned Lincoln, "is a confederated—not a consolidated party." [1] Under pressure, its Whig pieces could fly off into the air.

No one was in a better position to appreciate the wobbliness of the Republican coalition than the Republicans of Illinois. Once the Republicans had formally organized themselves as a distinct political body at the Bloomington convention, there were no shortage of ex-Whig faces on the party ticket for the fall elections: Jesse Dubois (who had been elected as a first-timer and a Whig to the state legislature in the same year as Lincoln) was nominated for state auditor, Ozias Mather Hatch (who had also sat in the state legislature as a Whig) was to run for secretary of state, and Orville Hickman Browning, the frowning Whig giant from Quincy, chaired the program committee. But the Bloomington convention chose for its president John M. Palmer, one of the anti-Nebraska Democrats who had denied Lincoln the senatorship less than a year and a half before; nominated another anti-Nebraska Democrat, William Bissell, for governor; and awarded the chairmanship of the newly appointed state central committee to another of Lincoln's naysayers from 1855, Norman Judd of Chicago. And platform speeches were assigned to Owen Lovejoy, northern Illinois's most colorful abolitionist; Leonard Swett, a conservative ex-Whig from Bloomington; and to "Long John" Wentworth, who had followed his own eccentric political path, from four-term Democratic congressman and mayor of Chicago to sworn enemy of Stephen A. Douglas. "The Republican party here is composed of five Whigs to three Democrats," wrote one of Lincoln's correspondents. In this wild mix, only two things held the Illinois Republicans together: opposition to the extension of slavery and a mortal loathing of Stephen A. Douglas. "Moral principle," Lincoln admitted, and not patronage or "pecuniary interest" or tariffs, "is all, or nearly all, that unites us."[2]

"Moral principle" might not be enough. For the moment, Lincoln's position within the Illinois Republican party seemed politically enviable. The old Whigs "for a long time felt sore over the defeat of Mr. Lincoln and the forcing of" Lyman Trumbull on them in 1855, and they were set to demand Republican support for a second Lincoln bid for the Senate in 1858 as a reward for their continued cooperation. At the same time, Norman Judd and the ex-Democrats understood very clearly that they had to make peace with Lincoln, as well as reward him for falling so loyally on his own spear and permitting Trumbull's election. They, too, would rally solidly behind a Lincoln-for-Senate bid in 1858—especially if it meant defeat for Douglas. Trumbull's "election . . . under the circumstances, created a moral obligation upon us which there was no wish to evade." The rewards, in fact, started coming in as early as the Bloomington convention, when Lincoln was selected as a delegate to the national Republican convention in Pittsburgh and even garnered a favorite-son nomination from the Illinois delegation as Frémont's vice president. (Lincoln did not, in the end, attend the convention, and the vice presidential nomination ultimately went to the former New Jersey Whig William L. Dayton.) "I take it that it is a foregone conclusion," wrote Charles H. Ray, the new coeditor of the *Chicago Tribune*, "that Abraham Lincoln will be the next Republican candidate for Mr. Douglas' seat."[3]

But if Lincoln wanted not just the nomination but the Senate seat itself, it would take more than the enthusiasm of his new Republican colleagues to pull it off. In 1856, Frémont defied every expectation by carrying eleven Northern states, including Ohio, Wisconsin, Iowa, Michigan, New York, and all of New England, while Republicans captured the state senates in Indiana and Pennsylvania, and the entire legislatures in Wisconsin, Iowa, and New England. But in Illinois, they failed to dislodge the Douglas Democrats from their hold on both the state senate and the state house, and though they captured the state offices (from governor on down to state treasurer), the presidential vote went 105,348 for Buchanan, 96,189 for Frémont, and a telltale 37,444 for Fillmore.

One reason the Republicans failed to seize control of the legislature had to do with the reapportionment of the state's districts. A new apportionment plan had been approved by the legislature in 1854, but by 1856, it was already falling behind the realities of immigration into Illinois. "The apportionment of the State, which, being that of 1854 gives the Southern and mostly Democratic counties a larger representation in the Legislature," complained the *Chicago Tribune*.[4]

The three southernmost districts (the first, second, and third) each sent one representative to the state house, representing approximately 19,000 people in the first, 16,000 in the second, and 21,000 in the third. At the other end of the state, the fiftieth, fifty-second, and fifty-third districts also sent just one representative each to the legislature, but they represented 25,000 in the fifty-second, 24,000 in the fifty-third, and 22,000 in the fiftieth. In effect, southern districts with only two-thirds of the population of northern districts still got the same representation in the legislature. And the southern districts were heavily and routinely Democratic. Efforts to mend these inequities by granting larger districts multiple representation only ended up replicating the same uneven pattern: with a population of 25,000, the eighth district, smack in the heart of southern Illinois, was allowed to send two representatives to the legislature (even though the fifty-second, with the same population, still was sending just one), as was the fourteenth district, which had 31,000. But in the north, Cook County, which was divided into two districts, the fifty-sixth and fifty-seventh, which each sent two representatives to the legislature, had a population of 144,000. The fifty-sixth and fifty-seventh districts each had double the number of people living in it as did the eighth or fourteenth, yet all of these districts elected just two representatives apiece. As Joseph Medill later complained, in "Republican districts it requires on average a population of 19,635 inhabitants to elect a representative . . . while in the Democratic districts" it requires only "15,675 for a Representative." If Lincoln was to have any hope of winning, he could not rely solely on the Republican districts, no matter how strongly populated, to carry him through.[5]

But a more ominous reason for Republicans' failure in 1856 was their lack of success in teasing old Illinois Whigs out of the dead shell of Whiggism, even when it was clear that Fillmore's last-stand nomination was a forlorn hope. Lincoln campaigned vigorously for Frémont, despite his premonition that the choice of the erratic but well-known explorer would send "a good many whigs, of conservative feelings" away. He stumped northern and central Illinois, wrote editorials to soothe immigrant voters who worried about the Know-Nothing influence in the Republican party, and pleaded with longtime Whig associates and friends to see that "every vote taken from Frémont and given to Fillmore, is just so much in favor of Buchanan." But he could not budge them. In the central Illinois Whig strongholds "in Edgar county . . . in Coles and Shelby counties," Lincoln found "our whole trouble there has been & is Fillmoreism." Lincoln might have been (as the *Jacksonville Sentinel* grudgingly conceded) "the ablest black republican that has taken the stump . . . during the canvass." But the Whigs went for Fillmore. In Bond County, one of Lincoln's allies reported that "the Fillmore & Frémont men unite and elected their Ticket for County Officers," but not for the presidential voting. (Bond gave Fillmore 657 votes, Buchanan 605, and Frémont only 153; Madison County, another Whig citadel, gave Fillmore 1,658, Buchanan 1,451, and Frémont 1,111.)⁶ If he was to have a clear shot at Douglas's Senate seat, Lincoln and the Republicans would have to be sure that no Whiggish third-party distractions surfaced to siphon old-guard Whig voters away and no inside-party squabbling between ex-Whigs and ex-Democrats divided the Republicans.

So long as coalition-building in Illinois seemed to be the order of the day, Lincoln was content to take only occasional notice of the ongoing civil war in Kansas between the free-staters and the proslavery Lecomptonites. Likewise, the *Dred Scott* decision in March 1857 surprised him not at all. In January, he worked up a memorandum on the probable outcome of the case and predicted (correctly, as it turned out) that the "broader scope" of the decision would mean an attempt to make slavery legitimate—if not actually legal—everywhere in the nation, so that "the whole community must decide that not only *Dred Scott*, but that *all* persons in like condition, are rightfully slaves." Slavery began by begging the Founders' pardon for existing. It progressed through the Missouri Compromise to demanding toleration in the South, and the popular sovereignty dogma had given it opportunity to spread into the West. Now, slavery was not merely to be tolerated or given chances; it was deemed *right* by the Supreme Court, and it would take only one more challenge of the *Dred Scott* sort to force the free states to recognize it as right on their soil, too.

But for the moment, Lincoln regarded *Dred Scott* as merely a decision, not a constitutional dictum, "not having yet quite established a settled doctrine for the country." Its chief interest for him was the way the decision cut the ground out from under Douglas and popular sovereignty, since not even the people of the territories could now enact a ban on slavery. Lincoln was even less ruffled by Douglas's desperate insistence that popular sovereignty (in its indirect form) was in fact the

only way to keep slavery out of the territories. And when President
Buchanan slapped Douglas down by demanding approval of the
Lecompton constitution, Lincoln merely advised Lyman Trumbull
that "the Republicans should stand clear of it" because "both the President and Douglas are wrong."[7]

One month later, Lincoln realized he had made the first great mistake of his campaign.

However much Douglas's anti-Lecompton stand might have infuriated
President Buchanan, it had (on the logic of the-enemy-of-my-enemy-is
my-friend) charmed the East Coast leadership of the Republican party.
"The unexpected course of Douglas has taken us all somewhat by surprise," Trumbull wrote to Lincoln uneasily from Washington. Worse
than surprised, they were beginning to act like "fools in running after
& flattering Douglas." Leading this bizarre courting game were Henry
Wilson (former Whig and now Massachusetts senator), William
Henry Seward (New York senator and the most prominent of the
Whigs to turn Republican), and the frenzied abolitionist editor of the
best-read American newspaper (with 220,000 copies of its daily and
weekly editions in circulation), the *New-York Tribune's* Horace Greeley. These were men who would have cheerfully strangled Stephen A.
Douglas over Kansas-Nebraska in 1854. Greeley, who had briefly
served in Congress with Lincoln in 1848 (the New Yorker was elected
to serve out the term of a congressman who had died in midsession),
actually called Douglas "a criminal."

But in 1858, Kansas-Nebraska was the past; the Lecompton constitution, and Douglas's stand against it, was now the talk of the politicos,
and the talk could afford to be indulgent toward the Little Giant's past
sins. Wilson, Seward, and Greeley did not have to live cheek by jowl
with Douglas and his all-powerful machine in Illinois, and they lacked
the fiery animus that inspired the hatred of both the ex-Whigs and the
ex-Democrats of the Illinois Republican party. Besides, the Republicans had done so well with running Frémont for president that it was

almost beyond joy to dream of a ticket on which Douglas would unite all the antislavery votes under a Republican banner and lead them to a victory in 1860, which the other Republican paladins could use as platforms for their own presidential hopes in 1864 and 1868. Morton McMichael of the *Philadelphia North American* cooed that Douglas "deserves the honor of a rude honesty of purpose," while Samuel Bowles of the *Springfield Republican* was convinced that "Douglas and his associates . . . have crossed the Rubicon" and will soon adopt "new associations and new principles." Of course, this strategy would lose all value if Douglas lost his bid for reelection to the Senate in 1858; and the losing would be all the more painful if Republicans in Illinois spoiled this new détente by trying deliberately to unseat Douglas. So Greeley now began turning up "in the parlor of Judge Douglas," appealing to his readers "to read and say whether Mr. Douglas does not speak the words of common sense as well as patriotism," and "planning and scheming, the election of Judge Douglas to the Senate of the United States from Illinois." If Illinoisans only understood how "profoundly obnoxious to Buchanan and the Slavery-extending oligarchy" Douglas had become, then "nothing" could prevent his reelection. Greeley urged Indiana Republican congressman Schuyler Colfax to "form a party of young men to call on Douglas every week or so" to prod him toward the light, and sent Illinois congressman Elihu Washburne back to his home state with the message to the state Republican committee that if Illinois Republicans stood down in 1858, Douglas would cut his last ties to the Democratic party and join the Republicans.[8]

In some versions, Douglas had actually offered to withdraw from the Senate race and run for the House of Representatives from his home district in Chicago if the Republicans would allow him to do so unopposed; in others, he was leading "the Douglas Democrats" into a "union" with the Republicans and Know-Nothings, "thro' the influence of Seward." In December 1857, Greeley and Colfax paid a call on Douglas in Washington, and Douglas reciprocated. Douglas "invites such men as Wilson, Seward . . . to come & confer with him & they seem wonderfully pleased to go," Trumbull warned Lincoln. Frederick Douglass, the black abolitionist, was dumbfounded that "during the last Congress . . . [Douglas] managed to produce the impression on the country that he was about to abandon his old slaveholding policy," and in the spring of 1858, even Joseph Medill, Charles Ray's partner in producing the *Chicago Tribune*, had been persuaded, after an interview with Douglas, that he had burned too many bridges to the Democratic party and "will gradually drift toward our side and finally be compelled to act with us in 1860."

In January, the Republican state committee's treasurer, Ozias Mather Hatch, was teasingly urged to visit Washington, so that "you can welcome Douglas into the Republican party. He certainly is an acquisition." Illinois Republican congressman William Pitt Kellogg heard the stories about meetings between Douglas and the Republican leadership and implored Jesse Dubois in Illinois to tell him "what was the kind of proposition" made "about an arrangement with Douglas . . . in Chicago and Springfield?" And William Henry Herndon, Lincoln's law partner, also picked up hints about a meeting "by accident or otherwise" in Chicago between Seward and Douglas to swap support for Douglas's reelection in return for Douglas's support of Seward's run for the presidency in 1860. One important Republican organizer frankly argued that it would be just as well for the Illinois Republicans to endorse Douglas, since a Republican attempt to contest Douglas's reelection would leave the Republicans "in this state as dead as herrings. . . . The majority of the democrats who have joined the Republicans will return to his support," and the Whigs "will join him too & justify themselves by the Republican endorsements Douglas has received."[9]

Douglas, for his part, did nothing to discourage these rumors, and considering his position, it may have been more merely than rumor. In March 1858, Douglas dispatched James W. Sheahan, who managed his Chicago organ, the *Chicago Times*, with an offer to back out of the Senate race "and take his chances by and by" if the Republicans would not oppose the election of Douglas's candidates for the House of Representatives. The next month, he sent another emissary to Ebenezer Peck, a Cook County Republican state representative, again offering to step aside from the Senate race if, Peck wrote to Lyman Trumbull, "we should consent to run Douglas as our candidate for the House of Reps from this District." When Herndon traveled to Washington in the spring of 1858, he met with Douglas and bluntly asked him what his intentions were. Douglas replied obliquely that he was not out to oppose Lincoln and instructed Herndon to "tell him I have crossed the river and burned my boat"—whatever that meant. Even one of Douglas's backers in the state legislature, John W. Singleton, anxiously wrote Douglas to ask whether he had actually "declined being a candidate for re-election to the U.S. Senate? If you have not it is proper you should advise your friends at once." The Buchananites heard the same mutterings. "A Union was effected at the last session of Congress," Iowa senator George W. Jones told Illinois judge Sidney Breese, "by which it was stipulated & agreed that Douglas was to be re-elected Senator next winter . . . ; that Seward is to be made their candidate for Prest in 1860 . . . & that Douglas is to follow for the Presidency in 1864." [10]

"God forbid Are our friends crazy," erupted Jesse Dubois when Herndon reported on his interview with Douglas. To Illinois Republicans, the idea of striking a deal with Stephen A. Douglas strained belief. "Many of our people are greatly alarmed here that we shall be obliged to receive Douglas into the Republican party," Charles Ray wrote to Lyman Trumbull. If they did, Dubois grumbled, the party would be "scattered and disbanded in Ill." All that Douglas had ever done, complained a conference of Peoria Republicans in February, was "to maintain some kind of notoriety," and he was neither "so deep or sincere as to entitle him to the full confidence of any portion of the Republican party."

But to no one was a Douglas endorsement more incredible than to Abraham Lincoln. He had spent the past year focused on shoring up support for his senatorial bid in Illinois, only to find, without any more justification than convenience, that the East Coast leadership of the party expected him to abandon it all and leave Douglas alone. "What does the New-York Tribune mean by it's constant eulogizing, and admiring, and magnifying of Douglas?" Lincoln demanded. "Have they concluded that the republican cause, generally, can be best promoted by sacrificing us here in Illinois? . . . If the Tribune continues to din his praises into the ears of it's five or ten thousand Republican readers in Illinois, it is more than can be hoped that all will stand firm." [11]

Lincoln now had two fires to tend—wooing the uncommitted Whigs *and* convincing the Republicans that Douglas was no more a friend in 1858 than he had been in 1854—and if he took too vigorous a stand against the latter, he might end up convincing the former that his anti-Douglas vigor was really abolition radicalism. "There remains all the difference there ever was between Judge Douglas & the Republicans," Lincoln insisted. The Republican position had always been that "Congress shall" forbid the extension of slavery into the territories, and if that meant repealing Kansas-Nebraska and waiting for some new judicial wind to blow down *Dred Scott*, it would be worth the work and the wait. Douglas's position had always been that "congress shall not keep slavery out of the territories" but would stand idly by while incompetent presidents and kangaroo federal courts in the pay of the "slave power" forced slavery in, all the while twaddling about "popular sovereignty." But who was listening to Lincoln? Trumbull warned Lincoln that Douglas's opposition to Lecompton "was so unexpected to many & was looked upon as such a God send that they could not refrain from giving him more credit than he deserves." The gloom now settled in over Lincoln again. "I have believed . . . that Greeley . . . would be rather pleased to see Douglas re-elected over me or . . . any one of our better undistinguished pure republicans." [12]

The best way to reply to Greeley, as well as to make that reply the united voice of the Illinois Republicans, was through a state Republican convention. "There is no safe way but a convention," Lincoln wrote

Ward Hill Lamon, "which all are willing to stand upon."[13] Not that
conventions were a novelty. (Illinois Democrats held their first conventions in the 1830s, and the Whigs held their first national nominating convention in 1839.) In fact, the entire electoral system in Illinois
and elsewhere looked like a pyramid of conventions, called for the purpose of identifying candidates, endorsing issues, and dispatching delegates to the next level of conventions. Party newspapers issued calls
for "mass meetings" in towns, villages, and cities, and the meetings
elected "seven or nine persons" as delegates to county conventions;
they in turn sent delegates to district conventions, who finally dispatched yet more delegates to statewide conventions. Not only did
these conventions parallel each other but they frequently overlapped,
since district conventions had to be called for both state legislative districts and federal congressional districts, with the result that conven-
tioneering could begin in the late spring of an election year and still be
going in August. In all, Illinois had nine federal congressional districts, fifty-eight state house districts (several of which elected multiple candidates), twenty-five state senate districts, and exactly one
hundred counties; and all but the four-year seats of the state senate
had to go through the entire electoral process of nominating, "canvassing," and electing candidates every two years. It was a wearing, seemingly endless process, as the high turnover rate in state legislative
candidates testified.

There was also no guarantee that the process would be easily controlled. Normally, the primary purpose served by a convention was the
enforcement of party discipline, either in nominating candidates or in
recommending policies. Douglas wrote that he was confident that "by
producing a perfect organization . . . you can have any man you please
nominated for the Legislature & can in all probability elect him." But
that purpose could easily be reversed, as insurgent conventions and
factions of "bolters" who organized rival conventions could easily
demonstrate. The convention system could veer unpredictably between stage-managed control and democratic uproar. "Our republican

institutions offer nothing so splendid," proclaimed the *Democratic Review* in 1852, and "nothing so well calculated to inspire the American with a firmer belief in the eternity and justice of democracy, as these voluntary and periodical assemblages of the people."[14]

In no case that anyone could remember, however, had a convention done what Lincoln and the Illinois Republican state committee now proposed. Since United States senators were elected by the state legislatures (and would be until 1913 and the Seventeenth Amendment to the Constitution), there was no direct sense in which anyone actually ran a campaign for the U.S. Senate. It would have done no good, since there was no direct vote on any popular ballot for people to cast; and it seemed pointless for any senatorial hopeful to announce his intentions until the composition of the state legislature was certain. Hence, in 1854, Lincoln waited until after the regular legislative elections to begin promoting himself; and since there was no popular campaign to run, no conventions were called to nominate senatorial candidates. At best, an incumbent senator might have a resolution "sustaining his conduct" adopted as an indicator of a convention's preferences when the time came for the new legislature to vote. But in early April 1858, "the leading Republicans of Illinois" met in Chicago, and the state central committee "spontaneously and heartily agreed" that every county convention should endorse Lincoln as "the first, last, and only chance for the vacancy soon to occur in the United States Senate," and that a state convention should meet in June to nominate Lincoln as the one Republican choice for the Senate "and fight this matter out squarely with Mr. Douglas."[15]

The call was issued through the Republican newspapers across the state, over the signature of Norman Judd and the state central committee, and the response was everything a disciplined and well-managed party organization could have wished for. "It seems to be understood on all hands," reported the *Cincinnati Weekly Gazette*, that the Illinois Republicans "will select a tried and true friend of the their cause . . .

Hon. Abram Lincoln, formerly of the House of Representatives." Within six weeks, ninety-five local Republican conventions came together to select delegates to the June state convention and bind them to endorse Lincoln as "the natural and expected remonstrance against outside intermeddling." The McLean County convention came together on May 5; in Lincoln's home county, Sangamon, the convention assembled on the eighth, as did the Will County Republicans on May 20 and the Brown County Republicans on May 29; in Schuyler County, "notwithstanding the state of the weather, quite a respectable crowd were in attendance" for the county convention on June 5, followed by Jasper County on June 7 and Clinton County on June 8; in Bureau County, the convention did not assemble until June 12, only four days before the state convention was due to open in Springfield.

"We will not sell out to Douglas," wrote Jackson Grimshaw from Adams County. "We are not content merely with the defeat of Lecompton, we are opposed to the extension of slavery & believe Douglas & the leaders of the Illinois Democracy are responsible for affording the South the opportunity of carrying slavery into Kansas." In Jasper County, a member of the county convention confidently predicted that "there is not a Republican in the County . . . who is for Douglas in preference to Lincoln." And in McLean County, Lincoln's old Whig friend Jesse Fell rose to pledge the convention to Lincoln, "and that despite all influences at home or abroad, domestic or foreign, the Republicans of Illinois, as with the voice of one man, are unalterably so resolved; to the end that we may have a big man, with a big mind, and a big heart, to represent our state."[16]

It helped, too, that Norman Judd, "a sly, crafty, shrewd politician," had some personal fish to fry. The leadership of the Republicans in Judd's own Chicago was almost entirely composed of former anti-Nebraska Democrats, and they brought over into the Republican party all the old animosities which had divided them as city politicians. That was especially true of the hatred that roiled the waters between Judd and Chicago's mayor, the ever-ambitious schemer "Long John" Wentworth. "The height of Mr. Wentworth's ambition," warned Joseph Medill, "is the seat Douglas holds in the U.S. Senate." Charles Wilson, one of Judd's allies and the editor of the Republican *Chicago Journal,* also warned Lincoln that Wentworth "still has some yearnings for the Senatorship," and Springfield's Douglasite newspaper, the *Illinois State Register,* chortled over the rumor that Wentworth was plotting to throw his weight behind Douglas for the presidency in 1860 if Douglas would allow Wentworth to stand unopposed for the Senate in 1858. Lining the state convention up behind Lincoln would, if it did nothing else, put a stop to what Lincoln called the "everlasting croaking about Wentworth." But the ultimate target of a Lincoln nomination was not Wentworth but Greeley and the East Coast Republicans. "Abram Lincoln is our choice for the seat in the United States Senate, now occupied by Stephen A. Douglas," resolved the Bureau County convention, and they would elect him (as Wilson's *Chicago Journal* added) without "interference from outsiders." [17]

"I think our prospects gradually, and steadily, grow better," Lincoln decided in mid-May, as the county convention endorsements began to pile up. Only "the weather" (which the Schuyler County convention had complained about) failed to cooperate. At the end of May, a vast cold front swept across the state, spawning tornadoes in northern Illinois that killed four people in Chicago, followed by rains that carried away houses on the Rock River and sent the Missouri and Mississippi rivers up three feet in a matter of hours. This was followed on June 9 by even heavier rains that lasted for five days, inundating New England and the Midwest, and carrying away roads and bridges. At Cairo (at the southernmost tip of the state, where the Ohio River flows into the Mississippi), the river waters flowed over the levees and submerged the streets in water so deep "that a steamer might float without rubbing the bottom." [18]

But none of it seemed to hinder the 578 delegates to the state convention who now swarmed into Springfield from all parts of the state, and (along with fifteen hundred spectators) jammed the capitol's lobbies and the upstairs meeting hall of the state house. The rain stopped, and by the opening of the convention, the floodwaters of the Mississippi had crested and begun to fall. And almost as if on cue from the weather, the convention was, from the first gavel on the morning of June 16, an unsullied triumph for Norman Judd's organizing skills. It was Judd who called the convention to order, Judd who managed the certification of delegate credentials, and it was Judd's thirty-eight-member Cook County delegation which interrupted the morning session's business by parading a "white cotton banner" through the hall, "with the inscription COOK COUNTY FOR ABRAHAM LINCOLN" emblazoned on it and planted it to the left of the chairman's rostrum. After a break for lunch, the afternoon session moved smoothly ahead to nominate candidates for the two statewide offices which would be open in the fall, James Miller for state treasurer and Newton Bateman for state superintendent of public instruction.[19]

The only moment when the reins nearly slipped from Judd's hands was the Bateman nomination, since an unanticipated number of competing nominations were made from the floor, and it took three ballots to get Bateman "duly nominated." But from then onward, all the sailing was breezy. Orville Hickman Browning brought in a series of policy resolutions "which were unanimously and enthusiastically adopted," followed by a motion "sustaining" Lyman Trumbull for his "distinguished ability and fidelity." And in the midst of the voting, an enthusiastic delegate jumped up with "a white cotton rag" on which he had written ILLINOIS in "large lampblack letters" and asked permission to "amend the banner" by pinning ILLINOIS over COOK COUNTY, so that the banner now read ILLINOIS FOR ABRAHAM LINCOLN. That was the signal. Once the balloting on Bateman was over, Charles Wilson (from Judd's own Cook County delegation) rose to nominate Lincoln as "the first and only choice of the Republicans of Illinois for the U.S. Senate, as the successor of Stephen A. Douglas." Everything on the agenda—everything, in fact, under Judd's direction for the last six weeks—had been aimed at this moment, and the timing was perfect. The hall erupted in a blizzard of "shouts" and "applause," and the resolution was adopted without a single dissent.[20]

Lincoln had also been preparing for this moment. "This nomination was anticipated, and Mr. Lincoln had prepared a speech," recalled Shelby Cullom, and William Pitt Kellogg added that Lincoln "had evidently written the speech with great care and deliberation . . . as if he had weighed every word." Once the convention had adjourned for dinner, and then reassembled at eight o'clock in the Hall of Representatives, Lincoln rose behind the rostrum and proceeded to deliver not a routine acceptance speech or even a policy statement but an apocalyptic denunciation of Stephen A. Douglas, which he hoped would drive the stake of truth once and for all into the heart of any suggestion that Douglas would be, or should be, welcomed by the Republicans. Lincoln began, suggesting at the very start that people did not know where they really were or where they were really going:

> If we could first know where we are, and whither we are tending, we could then better judge what to do, and how to do it.
>
> We are now far into the fifth year, since a policy was initiated, with the avowed object, and confident promise, of putting an end to slavery agitation.
>
> Under the operation of that policy, that agitation has not only, not ceased, but has constantly augmented.
>
> In my opinion, it will not cease, until a crisis shall have been reached, and passed.
>
> "A house divided against itself cannot stand."
>
> I believe this government cannot endure, permanently half slave and half free.

For four and a half years—and a little quick subtraction put Lincoln's hearers at 1854 and the Kansas-Nebraska Act—the nation had been acting on a policy which it had been assured would put an end to the "agitation" over slavery. This "policy" was the doctrine of popular sovereignty, which Douglas had promised so confidently would get the slavery controversy out of the halls of Congress, out of the newspapers and legislatures, and into the hands of the people, where it would fizzle away in the free air of democratic choice. Well, said Lincoln, "under the operation of that policy," the exact opposite had occurred, and the civil strife in Kansas, the impotence of two presidents, Pierce and Buchanan, and the *Dred Scott* decision were more than enough evidence of that.[21]

Nor was this merely because, as Douglas complained, popular sovereignty had not been given enough chance, what with armed bands, meddling justices, and the heavy hand of James Buchanan behind the Lecompton constitution. In Lincoln's opinion, the "agitation" had no prospect of ever being quieted by popular sovereignty, because popular sovereignty, however superficially charming it sounded to American ears, contained within it a tendency toward self-destruction. Popular government could accommodate differences in religion; it could even tolerate differences on policies and presidents and still remain intact. But the one thing it could not survive was a fundamental disagreement on the definition of freedom itself, and the national division over slavery was nothing if not that. It was a maxim of the Gospels (to whose authority, Lincoln knew, a Protestant and evangelical culture would grant automatic deference) that a house divided against itself cannot stand. In just the same way, Lincoln did not believe that a government of the people could be divided on slavery, "permanently half slave and half free," and still endure. The result would be that either the house stops being a house and falls down or it stops being divided and becomes a single, unified house again, this time under the aegis of either slavery or freedom.

The vivid imagery of *a house divided against itself,* based on Jesus' rebuke to the Pharisees in Matthew 12:25 (where he is rebutting the accusation that he is serving Beelzebub rather than God—if that were true, why is he able to cast out devils, who are presumably Beelzebub's servants?), was not new to Lincoln. In 1843, ghostwriting a circular to

Whig campaign workers, he had used the statement *a house divided against itself cannot stand* to exhort his fellow Whigs to greater cooperation; and in 1855, he posed the question *Can we, as a nation, continue together permanently—forever—half slave, and half free?* in a letter to the prominent Kentucky lawyer George Robertson. He had even unwrapped the warning that *a house divided against itself cannot stand* and attached it to what was clearly a test run of the state convention speech at the Madison County Republican meeting at Edwardsville only a month before. Even the opening declaration, about first knowing *where we are*, was a paraphrase of the great Whig orator Daniel Webster and his second reply to Robert Hayne in the Senate in January 1830.[22]

Lincoln was surprised, then, that the "eight or twelve friends" to whom he read the convention speech "a few days before . . . in the Library Room in the State House," were horrified at his use of the *house divided* image. He thought he had made it clear that he expected the house would stop being divided, not that it would fall or that the divisions would begin fighting each other. "I do not expect the Union to be dissolved," he added to the opening sentences. "I do not expect the house to fall—but I do expect it will cease to be divided. It will become all one thing, or all the other." That, at least, was the logic of Matthew 12.

But the "friends" to whom he read the speech that night—and they included Herndon, Jesse Dubois, and James Cook Conkling (a Springfield attorney and member of the state central committee)—heard the overtones of a related parable, this time in Matthew 7, about the "foolish man" who built his house on the sand, only to have it fall when the wind and the rain beat on it. *And great was the fall of it.* What they heard Lincoln conjuring with was not a problem in logic but a prophesy that civil war and collapse were unavoidable, and sooner rather than later. And that would be just the formula to send the "Fillmore men" and "old line Whigs" scampering for the safety of Stephen A. Douglas. "Every man among them Condemned the speech in Substance & Spirit and especially that section quoted above," recalled one of the group twelve years later. Only Herndon urged Lincoln to change nothing in the speech and "deliver it just as it reads," and even he asked Lincoln privately whether the *house divided* imagery was wise. Lincoln refused to budge. "I want to use some universally known figure, expressed in simple language as universally known," he said. He dismissed the others' worries as a bad case of the jitters.[23]

Besides, what he was about to launch into next seemed infinitely more provocative than parables about divided houses. Assuming that the house reestablished its unity, on what principle would that unity take place? On the slave principle, or the free principle? Certainly "it will become all one thing or all the other." And it was more than possible that it would be the slave principle which would win, "till it shall become alike lawful in all the States, old as well as new—North as well as South." Why? Because a deep and terrible conspiracy was at work to push the conclusion in the direction of slavery becoming "alike lawful in all the States."

Look at the events of the last four years: first had come Kansas-Nebraska, opening all the national territory to slavery; then came *Dred Scott* (which "the reputed author of the Nebraska bill finds an occasion to make a speech at this capitol indorsing"), backed by both the outgoing president, Franklin Pierce, and the incoming one, James Buchanan. Does this not look as though it was all worked out beforehand? If Pierce and Buchanan, together with Stephen Douglas and Roger Taney, had shaped "a lot of framed timbers with all the tenons and mortices exactly fitting," the normal observer would assume that they all worked upon "a common plan or draft drawn up before the first lick was struck." Should the normal observer conclude that the joinery of "Stephen and Franklin and Roger and James" in creating Kansas-Nebraska, *Dred Scott*, and Lecompton was any less the evidence of complicity than "the frame of a house or a mill"? True, a squabble had arisen between Buchanan and Douglas over Lecompton. But that was on a mere technicality, whether the referendum on the Lecompton constitution represented "a fair vote for the people" of Kansas. The larger goal of legalizing slavery in Kansas was never in question, since (and Lincoln was delighted to take the words right out of Douglas's mouth) "he cares not whether slavery be voted down or voted up."[24]

This much established "exactly where we now are"; it remained, as Lincoln had promised at the opening, to see "whither we are tending," because the trajectory of this conspiracy was by no means spent. If it was to be granted, thanks to Kansas-Nebraska, that no legislative mechanism any longer existed to ban slavery from the territories, nor (thanks to *Dred Scott*) that any constitutional mechanism could ban slavery in the West, would it take anything more than another Supreme Court decision from the pen of Roger Taney, this time striking down the antislavery statutes of the Northern states? And would it not be easy enough to do it on the same grounds he had struck down the antislavery restrictions on the territories, that slaves were property which their owners could not be deprived of without due process? And if there was enough effort exerted "to educate and mould public opinion, at least Northern public opinion, to not care whether slavery is voted down or voted up," in the fashion of Stephen A. Douglas, then who would be left to object?[25]

What, then, was to be done? Some people, Lincoln suggested, tell us that "Senator Douglas is the aptest instrument there is" to oppose slavery's extension. Are they absurd? "How can he oppose the advances of slavery?" Lincoln demanded. "He don't care anything about it." No, Douglas "is not now with us—he does not pretend to be—he does not promise to ever be," and the best course for Republicans to adopt is to put "our cause," and our votes, "into the hands of those whose hands are free, whose hearts are in the work—who do care for the result." And that, of course, would mean the Republican candidates for the state legislature who would dump the almighty trickster Douglas from his Senate seat—and install Abraham Lincoln in his place. Lincoln sat down amid a "shriek for freedom," and after more speeches from Norman Judd, Isaac Arnold, "and others," the convention adjourned.[26]

Publicly, the party faithful joined in rejoicing over the House Divided speech. Certainly, it was true that Greeley and the eastern Republican leadership had been pretty forcibly instructed in the impossibility of looking on Stephen A. Douglas as Republican party material. Greeley, in fact, got the message all too clearly, and irritably wrote Joseph Medill at the *Chicago Tribune* that Lincoln's nomination by the Illinois Republicans had now "thrown a load upon us that may probably break us down." Medill and the Illinois Republicans knew perfectly well "what was the almost unanimous desire of the Republicans of other states," Greeley told him, "and you spurned and insulted them." Right up to the meeting of the state convention, Samuel Bowles and the *Springfield Republican* criticized the "bitterness of spirit" among "the papers and leaders" of the Illinois Republicans against Douglas, and two days after the convention, Bowles expressed happy indifference to whether "Abraham Lincoln, an old Whig and a devoted Republican, or Mr. Douglas, will represent Illinois . . . to neither of them do we have a word of objection to offer."

To Greeley, it seemed "not only magnanimity, but policy" that "the Republicans of Illinois . . . should promptly and heartily tender their support to Mr. Douglas and thus ensure his re-election," and when Greeley finally editorialized for the *New-York Tribune* on the Illinois race, it was only to agree with Bowles. Other observers were piqued by the unusual tactic of designating a senatorial candidate so far in advance of the state legislative elections. "It's the first time that history Records A candidate canvassing for a Seat in the Senate before the Legislature is chose that appoints," one of Douglas's allies wrote warily to the Little Giant. "Instead of going before the people on a clearly defined platform," complained the *Illinois State Register*, "for the first time in the history of our state politics, they nominate a candidate for U.S. senator!" [27]

But instead of congratulating Lincoln for rebuking Greeley and catching the Douglasites off-guard, the reactions of the Illinois Republican leadership to the House Divided speech ranged from unease to irritation. Yes, Lincoln had certainly painted Douglas in the most dire proslavery colors, and that would keep the faint-hearts and celebrity-struck "sisters" from running after the Little Giant with their caps in hand. But he had forgotten that Douglas and the eastern Republicans were only one of his problems, and the House Divided speech sounded so much like an abolition tract that the critical Whig moderates Lincoln was counting on would turn away in disgust, even from a former Whig. Norman Judd, who had not been consulted in advance about the speech, told Lincoln that "had I seen that Speech I would have made you Strike out that house divided part." Leonard Swett believed "these words were hastily and inconsiderately uttered" and "wholly inappropriate." One visitor to Lincoln's office in Springfield told him plainly that "Lincoln, that foolish speech of yours will kill you—will defeat you in this Contest—and probably for all offices for all time to come." And less than a week after the convention, John Locke Scripps, yet another friendly Chicago newspaper editor, informed Lincoln that Whigs "who want to be Republicans but who are afraid we are not sufficiently conservative" were convinced that talk about dividing houses "is an implied pledge on behalf of the Republican party to make war" on the South and destroy the Union. Had he now made a second mistake, before the campaigning even started?[28]

Lincoln stood briskly to his own defense. He had merely told the truth: "If I had to draw a pen across and erase my whole life from Existence & all I did," he replied aggressively, "and I had one poor gift or choice left, as to what I should save from the wreck, I should choose that speech and leave it to the world unerased." Less aggressively, however, he explained to Scripps that people had misinterpreted the speech. He had no desire to divide the Union, only to awaken the free states to the likelihood that an already-divided Union would not stay divided forever, and that it was up to them to make sure that its restoration was on the free rather than the slave basis. And he had no notion of using "the General Government, nor any other power outside of the slave states" to march an army of liberation into the South

workers and salary kickbacks he would need to provide hands and funds for his campaign. "The treachery of that Judas in the Senate," wrote one Buchananite in April, "should now be taught a lesson of remembrance.... Let every Douglas ... man be made to walk the plank." Douglas's loyal Springfield editor, Charles Lanphier, was warned at the beginning of 1858 that his *Illinois State Register* would probably get the current post office printing contract, "but it is the last you'll get." In central Illinois, the word was out that "every post Master—great and small—and every other Federal office-holder who fails to do the work of the Administration is to be removed." And every replacement postmaster might further paralyze the Douglas machinery by delaying the delivery of Douglasite newspapers, losing bundles of campaign mail accidentally-on-purpose, and even opening and reading the Senator's personal mail.[30]

Whether Buchanan actually turned so viciously on Douglas has been questioned over the years—by Roy F. Nichols, David Meerse, and Philip G. Auchampaugh—since most of the accounts which refer to the "removals" are anecdotal and revolve around a handful of high-visibility federal patronage appointments. The key Illinois patronage job—the postmaster of Chicago, who administered the entire network of post office appointments in Illinois—went to an anti-Douglasite, Isaac Cook, in February; in March, the collector of the Port of Chicago, Jacob Fry, lost his position (and control of its $1.5 million in revenues), after four decades of party service, to Philip Conley. But whether Buchanan's influence in Illinois extended any deeper has never really been explored. One Buchananite wrote despairingly to the president in June 1858 that "our enemies hold nearly all the offices ... the Route agents and Post Masters refuse to distribute other than Douglas documents," and Isaac Cook "has not a single deputy in the State who is not an avowed Douglas man and many of them *speak of the President in terms too coarse to bear repetition.*" If anything, Douglas's friends urged *him* to use the loyalty he had built up among patronage appointees to repel any effort by Buchanan to meddle in the Illinois election. "I would declare war or repel aggression to the 'knife,'" advised John Pearson. "What democrat has any confidence any more in James Buchanan, a man that . . . never was any great leader of things in any party." [31]

But the evidence that Buchanan was willing and able to wreck the Democratic party in Illinois, if that was what it took to wreck Stephen A. Douglas, is actually quite substantial. Of the twenty-six Illinois postmaster appointments with the most lucrative incomes (over $1,000 per annum), twelve were replaced over the course of 1858, largely in two suspicious heaps in July and October, at the height of the Lincoln-Douglas campaigns. Peter Sweat, the postmaster in Peoria (whose post office generated the largest net proceeds in the state after Chicago), was removed for "malfeasance in office," which was a polite way of saying that "he lets Douglas documents pass through his office without destroying them." Not only was James Davidson (the U.S. marshal for the Illinois Northern District) fired and replaced by "a Lecompton Democrat" but so were the U.S. marshal for the Southern District and the federal district attorneys for both Northern and Southern districts. Likewise, half of the twelve Treasury appointees in Illinois—including the surveyors at Peoria, Quincy, and Alton—were bounced. (The surveyor at Quincy, Austin S. Brooks, also held the Quincy postmastership and edited the Douglasite *Quincy Herald* and was "publicly asked about his position, concerning the current situation of the parties, and he had freely answered that he . . . was willing to support the Administration in every respect, except in the Kansas issue." That was not enough to save either his surveyorship or his postmastership.)

Rewards and punishments for joining the attack on Douglas even went beyond Illinois. Richard B. Carpenter, who had been fired as "disbursing agent" in the Chicago customshouse at Douglas's prompting in 1857, was reappointed by Isaac Cook and promised "the Commissionership to China" by Buchanan if he "canvassed Illinois against Mr. Douglas." The Buchanan administration, howled Philadelphia's Democratic editor John W. Forney, has become "one wide reign of terror," and even Douglas croaked in dismay that Buchanan was "removing all my friends from office & requiring pledges of hostility to me from all persons appointed to office."[32]

Buchanan's other tactic was to disrupt the state Democratic convention, either by pulling the patronage strings to deny a "sustaining" resolution to Douglas or, if necessary, by sponsoring a rival state convention, which would nominate its own legislative candidates, and forcing patronage appointees to support the Buchanan convention. The Democratic state committee was Douglas's own pick of political favorites, including the chairman, John Moore, and his two most energetic newspaper editors, James Sheahan of the *Chicago Times* and Charles Lanphier of the *Illinois State Register*. And its machinery was sufficiently well-oiled that the Sangamon County Democrats had their convention meeting as early as January. When the state convention was called to meet in the state capitol in Springfield on April 20, ninety-seven counties were represented by a turnout of 520 delegates from across the state. But the convention was, for the first time in the twenty-odd years of Douglas's ascendancy, in turmoil from the moment it was called to order. Much as Douglas had ruled Illinois as his private political fiefdom, he had made enemies in the process, and that, together with the squeeze Buchanan's demand for loyalty was exerting, offered an unanticipated number of recruits to the Buchanan banner. "Mr. Douglas will find that he does not carry the state of Illinois in his breeches pocket," snarled one Democratic editor who had been slighted by the senator and who now rose to the opportunity for revenge. "However much the people may have esteemed him, they will not bear always with his vagaries and inconsistencies." The "old leaders," especially, who had been nudged aside by the rise of Douglas, "were discovered working for Mr. Buchanan," and one old party hand jubilantly crowed, "Down with this damnable *oligarchy* is the watch word." As soon as the call for the convention went out, Buchanan's wire-puller in Chicago, Isaac Cook, instructed as many Buchananite officeholders as possible to obtain seats as delegates. Without Douglas on site, the delegates offered up warm endorsements of Douglas but tactfully pulled shy of condemning Buchanan. It did no good. "A squad of about forty or fifty persons, summoned here by the postmaster of Chicago," withdrew from the convention, set up a rump meeting in the Illinois senate chamber, and issued a call for a new convention "in order to have a full expression of the Democracy of Illinois," on June 9.[33]

The rattled Douglasites pulled themselves together sufficiently to pass "sustaining" resolutions for Douglas and for Illinois's five Democratic congressmen, and to nominate William B. Fondey and Augustus C. French for state treasurer and state superintendent of public instruction. But on June 9, Isaac Cook, by diligently "levying contributions" from officeholders on pain of dismissal, and "re-quiring their co-operation," assembled a rival state convention in Springfield, with 263 delegates representing forty-two Illinois counties, which "rejects and condemns the course of Senator Douglas" and "characterizes the course of Senator Douglas in his opposition to the Administration as overweening conceit." They did not put up a rival senatorial candidate—that would come later—but they did nominate two of the "old leaders," John Dougherty and former governor John Reynolds, for treasurer and superintendent. Douglas now faced not only a Republican opponent but an aggressive rebellion within the ranks of his own Illinois Democratic party. "It is my conviction that in six weeks time, Douglas will not have one thousand followers in Chicago, if he can boast even of half that number," predicted Charles H. Ray of the *Tribune.* "They are going over in crowds to Lecompton."[34] In the largest sense, Douglas's most serious opponent for his reelection to the Senate looked to be not Abraham Lincoln but James Buchanan.

From afar, Douglas observed the plotting with mounting irritation, to the point where he could not keep it from welling up in his speeches in the Senate. "I tell you the evidence is complete," he roared on the next-to-last day of the Senate's session, of a "coalition to break down the Democracy of Illinois." He particularly fingered Isaac Cook, Richard B. Carpenter, and Cook's chief enforcer, Charles Leib, as "confederates" in a plot to sell the Illinois Democratic party to the Republicans. But instead of confrontation, Douglas's friends begged him to seek some form of détente with Buchanan, lest a division of the Illinois Democracy into Douglas and Buchanan factions make for a house very much likely to fall. "The true friends of democracy including yourself should feel bound to make some sacrifice of personal pride now to save the good old democratic party from the obvious impending serious danger," pleaded one Illinois backer on June 21. "Let pride go to hell where it belongs." But it was not pride which stiffened Douglas's resolve to fight the "Buchaneer" challenge so much as it was his insatiable love of the gamble against all odds. "It is a melancholy spectacle to see the party . . . so totally disorganized and demoralized," but he was willing to "let the consequences take care of themselves."[35]

To the Republicans, however, the split in the Illinois Democratic party was the source of unhallowed delight. "We are to have *funny* times this year in *Suckerdom,*" wrote Mark Delahay to Lyman Trumbull, and William Pitt Kellogg rejoiced to Jesse Dubois that, with "the various kinds of democrats . . . cutting off all approach to one position by the Rank & file of Dug's friends," there was no "doubt of the ultimate overthrow of the Douglas party." A contingent of Republicans— including Lincoln, Norman Judd, and Charles H. Ray—sat as observers at the Douglas convention in April and trooped downstairs in the capitol after the Democrats broke down in "squalls" and "had a good time" drawing up the plans for their own state convention.

In fact, as Douglas soon learned, a number of Illinois Republican operatives were not above supplying the Buchananites with advice and incitements. Charles Leib, for instance, had been in touch with the Republican leadership as early as December 1857, even to the point of offering advice of his own about possible Republican patronage appointments after the election, and Lincoln came away from a meeting with John Dougherty (the "Buchaneer" candidate for state treasurer), telling Dougherty that if the Buchananites really managed to run a "National Democrat for each and every office," then "the thing is

settled—the battle is fought," and the Republicans would be victori-
ous. But Lincoln would have nothing to do with Leib or any other
cloak-and-dagger agents. Herndon told Lyman Trumbull that Lincoln
"does not know the details of how we get along. . . . That kind of thing
does not suit his tastes." Nor did Norman Judd put much faith in Leib
and his "confederates"—or for that matter, since he knew them all
well, in the entire Buchanan movement. "The Buchanan arrangement
for Illinois is a failure with its present leaders," he wrote to Trumbull
just before the Douglas convention in Springfield. "They have not the
brains to take in the whole field of operations, nor the character to give
them position." [36]

Both Lincoln and Judd understood that the strategy most likely to win
the legislative elections—and then the Senate vote—would be found
not in dividing the Democrats so much as in coaxing the Whigs. Stubborn Illinois Whigs wanted nothing to do with what they supposed
was abolitionism; what was surprising was that they had been so little
charmed by James Buchanan's stance as a "northern man with Southern principles" that they preferred throwing away their votes on Fillmore. What was even more significant for the 1858 Senate race,
John Frémont had carried twenty state house districts (and won counties in three others) and eight senate districts (and counties in five others), while Fillmore had carried only two house districts. But the
combined Fillmore and Frémont vote won majorities in fourteen more
house districts and sizable blocs of counties in four others, while the
state senate races gave two districts to Fillmore as well as controlling
portions of six others.

What this promised the Republican state central committee in
1858 was, if they could win the twenty-nine state house seats and the
eight state senate seats from the Frémont districts (who were clearly
not going to go for *any* Democrat, Buchanan or otherwise), and com-
bine them with the nineteen house seats and five senate seats where
the Frémont and Fillmore vote had outpolled Buchanan, they could

wind up with a grand total of forty-eight Republican state representatives and thirteen Republican senators—more than enough, in a legislature of one hundred members, to elect Lincoln in January. (Twelve of the twenty-five senatorial districts were not up for reelection, but of those, five were held by Republicans.) Lincoln, ever the cautious calculator, held the possible gains in the state senate to the "certain" districts, which he pegged at nine, and he warned Lyman Trumbull that "with the advantages they have of us, we shall be very hard run to carry the Legislature." But even Lincoln believed that it was not impossible to win the forty-eight state representatives whose districts had gone for Frémont or Fillmore or both. Add those to the five Republican incumbents already in the state senate, and Lincoln was satisfied that "the skies are bright and the prospects good." [37]

Geography simplified the task of reaching these voters. The counties and districts which went most strongly for Frémont were ranged across the northern tier of Illinois, above a line that could be drawn from Monmouth and Galesburg in the west to Urbana and Danville in the east; there, the voters varied from strongly antislavery Whigs, who would vote Republican because their opposition to slavery overcame any other hesitations, to outright abolitionists, who would vote Republican because no other party came so close to their own principles or to success. This northern tier was the last major region of Illinois to be pioneered, and it had drawn heavily from a great New England diaspora that populated northern Ohio, lower Michigan, and Wisconsin with Congregational churches and white clapboard farmhouses. In reverse, the southern cone of Illinois was first settled from the upper South, and it retained Southern sympathies that had no particular interest in either promoting or eliminating slavery. This was the region which had voted most consistently for Buchanan, below a line which slanted from Chester on the Mississippi River upward to Marshall and the Wabash River, and little that Lincoln and the Republicans had to say would ever sound to them like anything but rank abolitionism.

It was in the middle tier of counties, a Whig belt extending from

Edgar County in the east to Pike County on the Mississippi, and then up the Illinois River to Peoria, that the "old-line Whigs" held the balance. These were the counties settled by emigrants from the border states, filled with the loyal Whigs who had sent Lincoln on his lone term to Congress, who ruled the social roost in Springfield, and who voted in vain for Henry Clay and "Fillmore the Wise." It was to those counties that both Lincoln and Douglas would be told to devote almost all of their campaigning attention. "Let me advise you to Commence at once," Douglas was urged a week after Lincoln's nomination, but "for Gods sake don't spend time in the North part of the State where all is lost . . . but attend to the doubtful districts, such as Sangamon, Madison and Marshall, and Jo Daviess & Peoria Senatorial Districts." Gustave Koerner gave Lincoln the same advice: "If we can carry Morgan, Macoupin, St. Clair, Peoria, Randolph McDonough & one or two more, I think all is safe"—and Norman Judd seconded it: "If Lincoln expects to be Senator, he must make a personal canvass for it in the center of the State."[38]

It would all be for nothing, however, if Lincoln kept on talking about houses dividing, or if the long history of political distrust between the former anti-Nebraska Democrats and the former antislavery Whigs was aggravated by either Douglasite propaganda or simple irritability within the Republican ranks. In the Third Congressional District, all but one of the fourteen counties had gone for Frémont in 1856 and elected the archabolitionist Owen Lovejoy, a New School Presbyterian preacher with a fiery humorlessness burning in each eye. Lovejoy was the brother of the abolitionist martyr Elijah Lovejoy, whose murder by a mob at Alton, Illinois, in 1837 had been a watershed event for abolitionists nationwide, and Owen Lovejoy had every bit of his brother's talent for inflammatory abolitionist rhetoric. Lovejoy grated most sharply on the nerves of the sizable contingent of ex-Whigs in the Third District, whose principal spokesman was the puffy and dour David Davis. Convinced that "the Whig part of the Republican party" was being ignored by Judd and his ex-Democrats on the state committee, and shouldered aside by Lovejoy and "his long-haired abolitionists," Davis grumbled that "if it were not for saving Lincoln for the United States Senate a pretty great outbreak would follow." Anything that suggested that Lovejoy was the tail that was wagging Abraham Lincoln would make Lincoln candidates unelectable in middle Illinois.

Lincoln was as dicey as any other old Whig about Lovejoy, and it "turned me blind" when Lovejoy won an upset victory over Lincoln's friend Leonard Swett at the district nominating convention in 1856. But Lincoln was willing to "let it stand." Davis was not, and that was where Lincoln and Davis parted company, because Lincoln was no more eager to alienate the Lovejoy abolitionists than the Davis Whigs. In March, Lincoln felt constrained to warn Lovejoy that the Democrats "would wheedle some republican to run against you," and indeed, unbeknownst to Lincoln, Davis was quietly orchestrating a dump-Lovejoy movement which would nominate Davis instead. Lincoln gently pressured Davis to back down, and Lovejoy was duly nominated.[39]

Unhappily, Lincoln needed to do more than just dampen the disgruntlements of ex-Whig Republicans. David Davis and every other ex-Whig like him might agree grudgingly to let the Lovejoys of the Republican party capture nominations, but then go off and sulk in their tents. Orville Hickman Browning, who had befriended Lincoln from his first days as a Whig state representative in the 1830s, admired Lincoln as "one of the most conscientious men I have ever known." Conscientious, though, was not the same as qualified, and Browning said that he had "never been able to persuade myself that [Lincoln] was big enough for his position." Only four days before the state convention nominated Lincoln, Browning allowed his own name to go forward from the McDonough County Republican convention for "the place now filled by S. A. Douglas in the Senate." This yielded Browning nothing; and perhaps for that very reason, he made no appearances for Lincoln during the campaign. Douglas's chief lieutenant, William Richardson, happily confirmed that Browning "will not labor very hard to help Lincoln to a vote"; Browning even took a pass on serving with the arrangements committee that was to welcome Lincoln to Browning's hometown of Quincy, sending his law partner, Nehemiah Bushnell, instead. Browning allowed Lincoln to use his house as a local headquarters during the visit, but Browning himself managed to be out of town, campaigning instead for the local Republican congressional candidate, Jackson Grimshaw.

Whether Lincoln, as a former Whig, would be able to keep the Whig converts steady in the Republican ranks, and recruit undecided Whig voters to the Republican banner, would become the most significant strategic question of the campaign. "The republicans from the old Democratic ranks, constantly say to me, 'Take care of your old whigs, and have no fear for us.'"[40]

For the moment, Lincoln seemed to have no strategy at all. He made a handful of appearances at the county conventions running up to the state convention in June. But he begged off other appearances—partly because it was "too early" to start campaigning ("when I once begin making political speeches I shall have no respite till November," he said), partly because he had cases to try and his law practice was his only source of income (in the ten days after the state convention, he had six cases to appear for in the federal circuit court in Springfield), and partly because he was waiting on Douglas. His instinct, based on the experience of campaigning around Douglas in 1854 and 1856, was to follow his opponent from place to place, letting Douglas be the crowd-getter, and arrange to make a speech of his own after Douglas had finished. "My recent experience shows that speaking at the same place the next day after D. is the very thing," Lincoln explained. Doing so would give him the last word on all issues, and the last word in the hearing of the voters—"it is, in fact, a concluding speech on him." This approach also cost nothing, since the expenses for printing broadsides and flyers, and gathering and entertaining a crowd, would all be borne by the Douglasites. The Republicans, as the outsiders in Illinois and national politics, had no patronage appointees to tap for funds, and Judd, who faced the task of running the campaign "upon the most economical plan," had to appoint a "guarantor" for each county to recruit "by subscription, the sum assessed to the said County." Lincoln, who had what Herndon called "the avarice of the keep," was notoriously reluctant to put out much of his own money for his campaign. He "was altogether too poor" in his own estimate and had already "lost nearly the working part of last year, giving my time to the canvass."[41]

But Douglas was not in a much better position. He greeted the news of Lincoln's nomination with grim resignation. "I shall have my hands full," he told John W. Forney. "He is the strong man of his party,—full of wit, facts, dates,—and the best stump speaker, with his droll ways and dry jokes, in the West. He is as honest as he is shrewd; and if I beat him my victory will be hardly won." And years later, he remarked that "though he often met his fellow-Senators in debate none of them had ever proved so hard a match" as Lincoln. Douglas could not count on his usual fund-raising sources because of the heavy threat of Buchanan hanging over the heads of Illinois's Democratic patronage appointees—which was why Douglas was taking so long, after the adjournment of Congress, to return to Illinois. Instead, he betook himself to New York to raise fifty thousand dollars from Cornelius Vanderbilt and other New York Democrats with grievances against Buchanan. This was not going to be nearly enough to finance the kind of campaign a presumably triumphant incumbent should be seen undertaking, with "a general hurrah and big mass meetings," surrounded "by a retinue of followers and enjoying all the luxuries of the period," and Douglas ended up mortgaging his own Chicago real estate holdings to the tune of eighty thousand dollars.

On July 2, he and Adele boarded a train for upstate New York (where he spent the Fourth of July with his mother's family), then took the train again through Buffalo, Cleveland, and Toledo, "amid the plaudits of the lovers to freedom in all parties for his valiant fight for popular rights," the cheering of "three thousand citizens," and "the firing of cannon." He arrived in Chicago on July 9, as the Windy City greeted its most famous son with a 150-gun salute from Dearborn Park and a parade (led by the German Turnverein Band, the Emmet Guards, and the Montgomery Guards) which marched from the Illinois Central's city depot up Lake Street, over Wabash Avenue to Washington Street, and then down Dearborn to Lake and the venerable Tremont Hotel.[42]

Douglas had not planned to begin his campaign here. That would have to wait until he met with the Democratic state committee, which was due to assemble in Springfield on the seventeenth to plot campaign strategy and issue a list of Douglas's "appointments" throughout the state. But as he stepped out onto the north balcony of the Tremont at eight o'clock that evening to behold, by the light of torches and a set of portable gas jets, the "vast sea of human faces" in the street below (which Henry Villard estimated "cannot have been less than 20,000"), the spirit of the gambler rose within him and he began to speak. "If there is any principle dearer and more sacred than all others in free governments," Douglas began, "it is that which asserts the right of every people to form and adopt their own fundamental laws, and to manage and regulate their own internal affairs and domestic institutions." He had pledged to fight for that principle over the Nebraska bill in 1854, "when it was assailed by Free-Soilers," and he pledged to fight for it by opposing the "fraud" of Lecompton "during this Congress . . . when it was attempted to be violated by a united South." And he now asked "my fellow citizens . . . whether I have not redeemed that pledge in good faith?" Had he not done everything which deserved the reward of reelection?[43]

Instead, he was faced with a Republican party which "not only laid down a platform, but nominated a candidate for the U.S. Senate, as my successor." He had nothing against Lincoln personally—"I have known him personally and intimately, for about a quarter of a century" and "regard him as a kind, amiable, intelligent gentleman, and an honorable opponent." But Lincoln had made "two distinct propositions" about the nature of "free governments" which were utter mistakes.

First was the image of the "house divided" and the inevitability that it would become "all one thing or all the other." Lincoln and the Republicans could quote Scripture all they liked, but "the fathers of the Revolution, and sages who made the constitution" were the authorities on which the American government had been founded, and they had not the slightest problem with the house being divided, or subdivided. "The framers of our government never contemplated uniformity in their internal concerns," Douglas declared. If anything, their anxiety had been to create a government in which each locality, each region, each state, and each individual could live their own lives as they deemed fit. Hence, no one was required to own slaves, and no one should be forced not to. The same logic applied to the states and territories. "Our complex system of State and Federal Government contemplated diversity and dissimilarity in the local institutions of each and every State then in the Union."[44]

Lincoln's other error grew out of the real reason why Douglas's old foe had flourished his attack on "diversity, dissimilarity, variety in all our local and domestic institutions," and that was a bizarre and perverted obsession with "an inferior race." Lincoln had thrown himself against Douglas, and against the Supreme Court in *Dred Scott*, and against slavery, "because it deprives the negro of the privileges, immunities and rights of citizenship which pertain . . . only to the white man." Douglas had nothing in particular against the Negro: "I would give him every right and every privilege which his capacity would enable him to enjoy." But that "capacity" was far below that of the white man, and "I am free to say to you, that . . . this government of ours is founded on the white basis." For a white man to enslave a white man was a violation of the other white man's claim to freedom under the Constitution. But "a negro, an Indian, or any other man of an inferior race" belonged to an entirely different category; *they* could be enslaved without any violation of "free governments" because the American free government had never intended to include them. No "negro, descended from African parents" had moral, natural, or legal standing to plead for the protections the Constitution gave white people, any more than a horse, a cow, or a pig. It was Lincoln's mistake to think that "the negro" required "an equality with the white race," because it was from that point that he descended to the conclusion that Negroes should not be slaves. That, the South would resist, and the result would be "a war of the sections—a war of the North against the South—of the free States against the slave States—a war of extermination . . . until . . . all the States shall either become free or become slave."[45]

The crowd, up till this point, had been unusually tepid. There had been several bursts of applause and three or four "cheers." But there had also been catcalls: *Talk more to the crowd!* and even *Three cheers for the administration.* And almost as if he needed to whip up a whirlwind to satisfy himself, Douglas now declared that he had returned to Illinois to face down the "unholy and unnatural alliance" which he had complained of in the last days of the congressional session, between "the republican leaders" and "a portion of unscrupulous office-holders." Striking a Napoleonic pose—and forgetting the restrained compliment he had paid Lincoln and the Republicans a half hour before—Douglas launched into a histrionic portrayal of himself as the commander of the Russian fortress of Sevastopol, hurling shot and shell at the English, French, and Turkish allies. (The siege of Sevastopol was the centerpiece of the Crimean War of 1854–56, pitting an unequally yoked army of British, French, and Turks against the Russians.) Like the Russians, who did not "stop to inquire when they fired a broadside, whether it hit an Englishman, a Frenchman, or a Turk," so Douglas would not "stop to inquire . . . whether my blows shall hit these republican leaders, or their allies who are holding the federal offices."[46]

The Douglas Democratic newspapers loved it. A hastily worked-up transcript was published the next day in James Sheahan's *Chicago Times* and, four days later, downstate in Charles Lanphier's *State Register* (and even cross-country in Greeley's *New-York Tribune*). Buchanan's in-house newspaper, the *Washington Union*, was correspondingly skeptical. "Mr. Douglas, we fear, has mistaken a demon-stration in his behalf in two or three cities for popular support and con-fidence by the whole country." But the most skeptical member of Douglas's audience that night was Abraham Lincoln. Like Douglas, Lincoln had no thought of launching a campaign from Chicago. But since he had to be in Chicago anyway to defend a case in the federal District Court for Northern Illinois, he turned up at the Tremont Hotel that evening, and Douglas recognized him and even invited him to take a seat just inside Douglas's hotel balcony while the Little Giant spoke. This vantage point would give Lincoln an earful of the pet argu-ments Douglas had been developing for the campaign, and it would provide Lincoln an opportunity to begin his own strategy of "conclud-ing speeches," because the next morning the *Chicago Tribune* carried an announcement on its front page that Lincoln would speak that evening from the same balcony at the Tremont.[47]

For an event with so little preparation time, Lincoln still managed to draw upward of nine thousand people, and Charles Wilson of the *Chicago Journal*, who had put Lincoln's name into nomination at the state convention three weeks before, delivered the introduction. Lin-coln stood up amid "a perfect storm of cheers," with clippings from the *Chicago Times* of Douglas's speech from the previous night in his hand. He began with what "I deem of somewhat less importance" than the other parts of Douglas's speech: the charge of conspiracy, which Lincoln found amusing if Lincoln really was the "poor, kind, amiable, intelligent"—by now, he was mugging up with every word and trig-gering outbursts of laughter—"gentleman" Douglas had said he was. Once the hilarity died down, Lincoln denied that there was any "al-liance" between the Buchananites and the Republicans, if by *alliance* Douglas meant a "contribution of money or sacrifice of principle on the one side or the other." Of course, it was true that Republicans would be only too glad "to see the other great party to which they are opposed divided among themselves." But there was no *alliance* in the works be-yond the satisfaction both Republicans and Buchananites would get from "putting him where he will trouble us no more." And they would, if the analogy to Sevastopol meant anything. Somewhere in the mix of his rodomontade, Douglas had forgotten that, after a year of siege, Sevastopol had been abandoned and surrendered to the other alliance.

Nor was there any more substance to Douglas's paean to "everlasting popular sovereignty!" Look at it closely, Lincoln said, and the whole concept evaporates, especially in light of the *Dred Scott* decision. The Supreme Court had decided "that the people of a territory have no right to exclude Slavery" and "that if any one man chooses to take slaves into a territory, all the rest of the people have no right to keep them out." So what could popular sovereignty do about slavery? Nothing (and a voice from the crowd called out, *It has all gone*). What good did popular sovereignty do the people of a territory if their legislature had no way to keep slavery out before writing a state constitution? Did anyone imagine that, by the time a territorial convention was called to write a state constitution, they were really going to enact a free-state constitution and then expel every slaveholder who had settled there? "All that space of time that runs from the beginning of the settlement of a Territory until there is sufficiency of people to make a State Constitution—all that portion of time popular sovereignty is given up," Lincoln said. So what did Douglas's plea to let popular sovereignty settle the territories amount to? Nothing except a free pass for slaveholders, who (thanks to Roger Taney) could not be kept out until it was far too late to push them out.

This finally brought Lincoln to the House Divided speech. It was ridiculous, he declared, to claim that he was in "favor of inviting . . . the South to a war upon the North." He had only made "a prediction" about where things were "tending"—although it measured how deeply the complaints of Judd, Swett, and the others had cut that Lincoln conceded that "it may have been a foolish one"—that the nation would become "all one thing or all the other." He was perfectly well aware, and needed no history lessons from Douglas, that the Founders had sanctioned slavery and that the nation had been living with that division in its house ever since the Revolution. And at the end of the day, "no man believed more than I in the principle of self-government." But where Douglas was wrong was in believing that the Founders *loved* division in the house, whereas everything Lincoln knew about the Founders showed that they had only *tolerated* division over slavery in order to finish building the house in the first place. From the moment the house was finished, they expected the division to diminish, and slavery to be "in course of ultimate extinction."

Working behind that expectation was the Founders' understanding that slavery was an utter and damning contradiction of popular government itself. Douglas waved away slavery "as an exceedingly little thing," but in truth, it was "a matter of keeping one-sixth of the population of the whole nation in a state of oppression and tyranny unequalled in the world." The people who opposed it did so not because they were puritanical fanatics trying to fasten "uniformity" around American necks but because it was "a vast moral evil," and it could be shown "by the writings of those who gave us the blessings of liberty . . . that they so looked upon it," too.

But what made slavery so heinous, so much a "moral evil"? The fact that it faced so utterly in the other direction from the natural law reflected in the Declaration of Independence, "that all men are created equal." This equality was a foundational maxim of human existence, and the proof of it was in the experience every man—"German, Irish, French, and Scandinavian"—who read that premise and yielded up an automatic and resistless assent. "Then they feel that that moral sentiment taught in that day evidences their relation to those men, that it is the father of all moral principle in them, and that they have a right to claim it as though they were blood of the blood, and flesh of the flesh of the men who wrote that Declaration." (By now, the crowd was roaring with "loud and continued applause.")

However, the moment we begin creating classes of exceptions—

that "you Germans are not connected with it," for instance—we have set foot on a slippery slope that, "if confirmed and endorsed," will "tend to rub out the sentiment of liberty in the country." The same was true with the Negro. "If one man says" the Declaration "does not mean a negro, why does not another say it does not mean some other man," and so on until we have "transformed this Government into a government of some other form?" Call the negro *inferior*, and he is still a *man*. Try to say that he is not a *man*, and what argument have you made except "the arguments that kings have made for enslaving the people in all ages of the world." Every argument which justified slavery was "the same old serpent that says you work and I eat, you toil and I will enjoy the fruits of it." It made no difference "whether it come from the mouth of a King, as excuse for enslaving the people of his country, or from the mouth of men of one race as a reason for enslaving the men of another race" (or perhaps, from a father auctioning off the labor of his son) "it is all the same old serpent."

Lincoln might have stopped there, and if the state central committee could have known what was coming next, they surely would have caught his elbow. But Lincoln was approaching the summit of his speech, and he was not turning back. "Let us discard all this quibbling about this man and the other man," as though there were no differences between men big enough to negate their natural equality. Let us even discard all the blathering about "this race and that race and the other race being inferior, and therefore they must be placed in an inferior position." Instead, let us "unite as one people throughout this land, until we shall once more stand up declaring that all men are created equal."[48]

There was, this time, a frozen burst of silence. And like a man who has heard the first crack of ice beneath his feet and stops still in the hope no more cracking will follow, Lincoln announced that he would end there "without launching off upon some new topic." (Only then did the applause come.) He had crossed a very dangerous line, not only be-

cause the Illinois of 1858 remained an undrained swamp of white su-
premacist thinking, but because only the most radical of the Republican abolitionists would "say the black man is, or shall be, the equal of
the white man." Lyman Trumbull thought it would be just as well to
oppose slavery extension and leave it at that, and "to have nothing to
do with either the free negro or the slave negro." Better still, he said, "I
would be glad to see this country relieved of them."[49]

Lincoln, however, was less apprehensive about speaking of black
and white equality because he understood that equality, like the Bible,
had more than one meaning, even in Illinois. When the Declaration of
Independence spoke of self-evident truths—*that all men are created
equal, that they are endowed by their Creator with certain unalienable Rights,
that among these are Life, Liberty and the pursuit of Happiness*—both Jefferson and Lincoln understood these rights to be *natural* rights, something akin to the natural law that the moral philosophers of the
nineteenth century saw giving an underlying order to the moral and
natural worlds. They were *unalienable*, because they were hardwired
into human nature *by their Creator*, and *self-evident*, so that even the
most superficial self-inspection would reveal an unforced longing for
them in everyone. On this point, Lincoln differed in the most forcible
way from Douglas, and from almost all of his contemporaries in Illinois, because he believed blacks and whites shared a common humanity, and shared all the natural rights which went with it. "No sane
man," Lincoln would say that summer, "will attempt to deny that the
African upon his soil has all the natural rights which" the Declaration
"vouchsafes to all mankind."[50]

But that was the hinge on which the argument about *rights* turned.
The "African" in Illinois was *not* upon his own soil; instead, he was in
the midst of an overwhelmingly white, European-descended population, which, for its own unlovely reasons, decided not to grant him
equal *civil* rights. Civil rights—eligibility to vote, to serve on juries, in
militias, and the like—were different from natural rights in that they

were local, shifting, and sometimes even arbitrary. But in a democracy, majorities had the privilege of determining the distribution of civil rights. The Declaration "does not declare that all men are equal in their attainments or social position," said Lincoln, nor was he going to insist that Illinois had to make blacks "politically and socially our equals." But that did not diminish the essential humanity of black people any more than imposing liquor laws or setting minimum voting ages somehow dehumanized children. Slavery, however, because it was a violation of the natural right to liberty, was in a different category altogether. Voting was a *civil* right which could come or go, and Lincoln would go with whatever the majority dictated; but liberty was a *natural* right, and slavery was its unnatural violation, and it was everywhere and at all times "a moral evil." [51]

The distinction between natural rights and civil rights was classical enough that Lincoln was betraying no disingenuity in using it. Yet he must have expected that it would also be a convenient device for explaining why, on the one hand, the containment and "extinction" of slavery was morally nonnegotiable and, on the other, this would not be a threat to white racial supremacy. If so, it did him no good, for Douglas seemed to have no particular notion of either rights or equality, apart from popular sovereignty, and the Douglas papers lost no opportunity in pressing fine distinctions between natural and civil equality into the ugly motto of *negro equality*. "Mr. Lincoln cannot be permitted to play 'fast and loose' in this manner," declared Charles Lanphier in the *State Register*. "He must be either for or against placing the negro upon an equality with the whites." Lincoln was not addressing an abolition lyceum, Lanphier snorted. "The white men of the prairie state—who deal in facts, and take the world as it is, will never submit to the amalgamation theories which the black republican aspirant for senator bases upon his construction of the declaration of independence—that the negro is the white man's equal—that he is entitled to political privileges with the white man." The *Freeport Weekly Bulletin* wanted to know, "if the extracts from his Chicago speech be true," why "the negro in this state ought not only to be allowed to vote, but even to be a candidate for the Senate."[52]

Douglas had no objection to turning this "natural equality" doctrine into another misstep for Lincoln, on top of the House Divided speech. The senator was due in Springfield for the Democratic state committee meeting on the seventeenth, but he took his time getting there, chuffing down the Illinois Central, stopping to speak in Joliet and Bloomington, and luridly playing up Lincoln and "Negro Equality." Along the tracks, "all the stations were crowded to see Douglas." At Bridgeport, immigrant Irish track workers "quit their work to cheer the senator as the train swept by," and in Bloomington, he stopped to wave the race card in a speech on the steps of the McLean county courthouse to two thousand people. It was mostly a rerun of his Chicago speech, in which Douglas "declared himself the champion of popular sovereignty" and "indorsed . . . the Dred Scott decision." But he now also "harped upon 'Amalgamation,' 'Negro Equality,' 'a war of the sections'" for two and three-quarter hours. By the time he arrived in Springfield (in the middle of another of that summer's drenching rains), he was unblushingly fondling every white racist prejudice he could summon and gleefully painting the bull's-eye of "Negro equality" all over Lincoln's back.[53]

Lincoln followed Douglas's train down to Springfield, and even as Douglas spoke there, Lincoln was planning a follow-up speech for that evening. As in Chicago, he patiently laid out the emptiness of popular sovereignty and the impossibility of reconciling it with the Supreme Court's determination in *Dred Scott* that "forbids the people of a territory to exclude slavery." Much as Douglas had done right to oppose Lecompton, he had been one of only three Democrats in the Senate to oppose it, and the heat of the battle against Lecompton had actually been borne by the Republicans. Why then did Douglas pose "in majestic dignity" as the only hero of the Lecompton fight? But it was noticeable that Lincoln devoted far more of his Springfield speech to defending himself than to refuting Douglas—defending the House Divided speech, denying that he was preaching "consolidation and uniformity" in wanting to see slavery "placed in the course of ultimate extinction," denying that he was inciting the North "to disturb or resist" the *Dred Scott* decision, denying (at the end) that he wanted "to make negroes perfectly equal with white men in social and political relations."[54]

This was the kind of rhetorical posture that befitted a civil lawyer whose long suit was the logical analysis of torts and trespasses. But Lincoln was not in front of a jury now, and he was not facing a man for whom the fine points of consistency weighed much against the thrill of accusation. As in war, so in politics: the victory more often went not to those who conducted good defenses but to those willing to risk, to seize the initiative, and to hold it by any means necessary. On those terms, his follow-up on Douglas's strategy was not working, and people were starting to tell him so. John Mathers, a brick manufacturer in Jacksonville, was a total stranger to Lincoln; yet even he wrote Lincoln that "if Douglass can only succeed in keeping you *defending* yourself all the time he will have accomplished his object. . . . Would it not be better . . . to *cease* to *defend*, & occupy the side of the *assailant*, and keep this *position* until the close of the fight." Worse still, the following-up plan was beginning to become a strategic as well as a tactical embarrassment. On July 20, the Democratic state committee published a list of Douglas's "appointments" through the month of August; Lincoln published nothing. "Mr. Lincoln goes from place to place where Mr. Douglas goes," jeered the *State Register*, "and avails himself of the opportunities afforded by the assembling of the people, or by the excitement created on these occasions, to make his speeches." And that, in the long run, would be fatal. Lincoln was the junior partner in this contest. Douglas's speeches were published word for word in *The New York Times* and the *Washington Union*, while Lincoln's replies were curtly acknowledged with a four- or five-line summary. (Out-of-state editors persistently misspelled his name as Abram, and the *New York Sun* bestowed on him a nonexistent middle name by identifying him as "Abraham R. Lincoln.)" Unless he found some dramatic new way to cast his own shadow rather than standing in Douglas's, the campaign would be as good as over.[55]

Which is why, on July 21, Lincoln was back on the Illinois Central, on the way to Chicago. Norman Judd and the Republican state committee had summoned him, and they were going to tell him that he must be ready for a momentous shift in plans.[56]

★ CHAPTER 3 ★

A DAVID GREATER
THAN GOLIATH

Sing ho! Those spirited debates,
Bereft of all restrictions!
When statesmen carried on their hips
The strength of their convictions!

STEPHEN VINCENT BENÉT,
THE DEVIL AND DANIEL WEBSTER

Why don't you take the papers?
They're the life of my delights;
Except about election time,
And then I read for spite.

N. F. WILLIS, "TAKE THE PAPERS,"
CAIRO WEEKLY TIMES & DELTA, MAY 12, 1858

"IT REALLY is a pity that Douglas and Lincoln do not participate jointly in debates in every county of Illinois," wrote the German-born journalist Henry Villard, who had been sent out to cover the campaigns by the German-language *New-Yorker Staats-Zeitung* and who made no effort to conceal his ardent pro-Douglas opinions. Let the two debate, Villard added venomously, and "the cure for the Republican fever would come surprisingly swift." Anyone who challenged the Little Giant to an open-air exchange would certainly be stripped of every argument and every defense, and sent howling back to the woods. Who could hope to trump Stephen A. Douglas on the same platform?

But open-air debate was exactly what was in the mind of Norman Judd and the Republican state committee when they summoned Lincoln to meet with them in Chicago on July 22. The campaign was only two weeks old, and Judd's listening posts across the state were already reporting Lincoln lagging behind Douglas. Worse than that, he was beginning to look ridiculous, "trailing" Douglas from place to place. The cure, then, would be in squaring Lincoln and Douglas against each other on the same stand. Horace Greeley actually broached the idea in the *New-York Tribune* on July 12, just after Douglas's Tremont House speech and Lincoln's next-evening reply to it. "We trust Messrs. Lincoln and Douglas will speak together at some fifteen or twenty of the most important and widely accessible points throughout the State," Greeley urged, "and that the controversy will be prosecuted through the rival candidates for the Lower House at every county seat and considerable town."

Judd and the state committee appear to have settled the matter before Lincoln even arrived in Chicago, since the *Chicago Tribune* ran its own "suggestion" on the twenty-second that "Mr. Douglas and Mr. Lincoln agree to canvass the State together." Lincoln, who had been perfectly content with the follow-around strategy, was not thrilled with the suggestion. Douglas, he argued, "was the idol of his party," and in front of crowds which Douglas might pack to his own advantage, it was likely that "the imperious and emphatic style of his oratory" would allow *Judge Douglas said so* to clinch a debate and be written up in the newspapers as a Douglas triumph. But Judd had had

enough of following Douglas and was determined that the state committee keep Lincoln firmly under its "intellectual guardianship," evalu-
ating "every word, every thought, every argument he utters." Lincoln
was counting too heavily and too passively on the division of the
Douglasites and Buchananites to hand him the election. Besides, the
anti-Nebraska men on the state committee, who had lived most of their
lives as Democrats in Douglas's shadow, thirsted for something more
from Lincoln than second-fiddle appearances in towns Douglas had
just left "with a sort of Napoleon air." And so, however reluctantly, Lincoln wrote to Douglas on July 24 to ask him "to make an arrangement
for you and myself to divide time, and address the same audiences during the present canvass." Judd, taking no chances, insisted on delivering the letter personally.[1]

This was harder to do than Judd thought. Douglas was already
preparing for his first major campaign tour into the vital midsection of
the state, and it took three days for Judd to catch up with Douglas and
present the letter to him. The Little Giant's first response was a contemptuous refusal. "What do you come to me with such a thing as this
for?" he blazed at Judd, "and indulged in other equally ill-tempered remarks." And James Sheahan's *Chicago Times* echoed Douglas's annoy-
ance by running an editorial asking Judd why he didn't look up the
managers of the "two very good circuses and menageries traveling
through the State" and persuade them, rather than Douglas, "to include a speech from Lincoln in their performances." When Douglas finally responded to Lincoln, he sounded very much like refusing
outright: he had already announced his speaking schedule through August 21 and could not create a new one to accommodate Lincoln, nor
could he ask Douglasite legislative candidates, who had invited him to
speak in their districts, to allow Lincoln to barge onto the already
scheduled campaign events, and anyway, Lincoln was probably scheming with the Buchananites to bring an as-yet-unnamed "Administration" Senate candidate onto the platform, "so that you and he might be
able to take the opening and closing speech in every case." Privately, he

was also wary of the outcome. "I have seen men make appointments for joint discussions," Douglas said, "and the moment their man has been heard, try to interrupt and prevent a fair hearing of the other side." Even if he trounced Lincoln on the platform, what would he gain by it? "The whole country knows me," Douglas remarked, while "Lincoln, as regards myself, is comparatively unknown." But if Lincoln "gets the best of this debate . . . I shall lose everything." Just by appearing with Lincoln, Douglas was already conceding a measure of equal standing. No, Douglas argued, "I do not want to go into a debate with Lincoln."[2]

And yet he did. Perhaps he was nettled by the Republican papers' indelicate chirping that Douglas was showing "the white feather," skulking "behind the appointments of the immaculate Democratic State Central Committee." Perhaps, at the end of the day, he simply could not resist the lure of one more risk. Whatever the reason, when Douglas responded to Lincoln's challenge, he recited the full list of his objections—and then, at the end, proposed an alternative. They would debate, but not by sharing the platforms at places around the state where Douglas had already scheduled "appointments." They would appear together for just seven debates, and they would do so "at one prominent point in each Congressional district in the state." (There were nine congressional districts, but since Lincoln and Douglas had already spoken in Chicago, in the Second District, and in Springfield, in the Sixth, Douglas deleted those two.) And Douglas would do the picking of each "prominent point": Freeport (in the First District, where the Republican Elihu Washburne was the front runner), Ottawa (in Owen Lovejoy's Third District), Galesburg (in the Fourth District, where the Republican William Kellogg was the incumbent), Quincy (in the Fifth), Charleston (in the Seventh), Alton (in the Eighth), and Jonesboro (in the Ninth). "The mode of conducting the debate" would have to be agreed upon later; the dates and the hours would be determined by Douglas's schedule and, he went on, "at any of these places I must insist upon your meeting me at the time specified." Lincoln could take it or leave it.[3]

He took it. Not that Lincoln had any choice, since Judd, who sent
Lincoln Douglas's reply on July 29, told Lincoln frankly that he and
Orville Hickman Browning had looked over it and concluded "you
should accept his proposition as to the places named." Lincoln bridled
at Douglas's "insinuations of attempted unfairness on my part," but he
agreed, grudgingly, "for us to speak at the seven places you have
named." His acceptance letter found Douglas at once (this time with
Lincoln tracking down Douglas outside Bement and pulling it from
his pocket on the roadside), and on July 30, Douglas responded with
the full schedule: he would meet Lincoln at Ottawa on August 21 and
Freeport on the twenty-seventh, take a two-week hiatus and meet
again at Jonesboro on September 15 and Charleston on September 18,
then take another pause and finish the series at Galesburg on October
7, Quincy on the thirteenth, and Alton on the fifteenth.

As for the "mode," Douglas's proposal was simple: he would speak
for an hour at Ottawa, Lincoln would reply for an hour and a half, and
Douglas would conclude with a half-hour rebuttal. They would switch
the order of speaking at each place, so that Lincoln would lead off at
Freeport, Douglas at Jonesboro, and so forth. The next day, Lincoln
agreed to both Douglas's "mode" and his schedule, and on the following Monday (August 2), Lincoln had an announcement of the debates
duly inserted into the two rival Springfield newspapers, Charles Lanphier's *State Register* and Edward Baker's *State Journal.*[4]

Behind Judd's proposal for debate between Lincoln and Douglas was a
long history of parliamentary debating, stretching back to the seventeenth century, and reinforced in the American Republic by the great
debates of Daniel Webster and Robert Hayne in 1830. Debating between congressional candidates was in play as early as 1813, when a
Federalist candidate, John H. Thomas, began following William
Pinkney's campaign tour in Maryland and ended up taking turns on
the platform with Pinkney. Nor was the debating habit confined to politics. Abolitionists and slaveholders debated each other, as Jonathan

Blanchard did against Nathan L. Rice for four days in October 1845, "upon the question: Is slaveholding in itself sinful, and the relation between master and slave, a sinful relation?" Alexander Campbell, founder of the Disciples of Christ, challenged the freethinker Robert Owen to a public debate in Cincinnati in 1829 and Archbishop Jean Baptiste Purcell to a debate on Roman Catholicism in 1837, and conducted a twelve-day debate on baptism in Lexington, Kentucky, in 1843, presided over by no one less than Henry Clay. Even in Lincoln's Springfield, the Scottish-born pastor of the First Presbyterian Church, James Smith, purchased national attention for himself by challenging Charles Olmsted, "the champion of Deism," to an eighteen-day-long debate that saw Olmsted and Smith exchanging hour-long arguments followed by half-hour rebuttals. Even Lincoln and Douglas had debated each other as far back as 1839, and in 1854, when Lincoln came out of political retirement to challenge the Kansas-Nebraska bill, Jesse Fell had tried to talk Douglas into "a joint debate."[5]

What was peculiar about these debates was that they were not, in the strictest sense, debates at all. They were sequences of speeches, with only the most meager nod in the direction of interaction between speakers. The debate manuals of the nineteenth century—for example, James McElligott's *American Debater* of 1855—separated debating into two overall categories, one of them for "deliberative assemblies" (which was little more than a guide to parliamentary rules of order) and the other for "debating societies" (which featured scholastic-style statements of a question which participants addressed, both affirmative and negative, in a highly stylized rotation). Joseph Bartlett Burleigh's *Legislative Guide* of 1856 also gave rules for "Order in Debate," which were really only directions for keeping order on the debate platform. The best-known debates of the American nineteenth century were sequential-speech events, "at the same places on the same day," which was "the usual, almost universal western style of conducting a political campaign."

This meant, in practical terms, that debating was less an event for intelligent persuasion than it was a forum for political declamation. (Increase Cooke's *American Orator* of 1819, in fact, listed "reading, recitation, declamation, oratory, and acting," but not actual *debate*, as the "general objects of public speaking," and Caleb Bingham's much-reprinted *Columbian Orator* promised examples of "Orations, Addresses, Exhortation from the Pulpit, Pleadings at the Bar, Sublime Description, Debates" but actually delivered neither examples of debate nor instruction in debate proceedings.) And the event itself took on the trappings of a carnival, with "each candidate having a sort of triumphal entry, at the head of his followers, into the towns and neighborhoods where they meet." This, as one Richmond newspaper sniffed, was an invitation for things "to pass from words to blows," because "the passions of the populace so frequently override the law." [6]

If there was any clear goal in view with sequential-speech debates, it seemed principally to be getting transcribed and reported in newspapers or published afterward as books. Either way, debate was more often an affirmation of print, rather than a triumph of voice. Alexander Campbell conducted his debates with a hired stenographer on hand, taking down Campbell's words in a primitive shorthand. Newspapers thus extended the range of debate *and* confirmed the dominance of sequential-speech-style debating, since this format translated easily into lively political reading matter (which scholastic debate, with its elaborate structure of alternating affirmatives and negatives, does not).

And politics were what made the world of the newspapers go round. Although American newspapers began as organs of commercial news, they lost little time after the Revolution in transforming themselves into partisan political sheets, and by the 1850 census, only 5 percent of American newspapers could claim independence from some form of political party affiliation or control. By the 1820s, it was becoming customary for incoming presidents to establish a new Washington paper as their national political mouthpieces, and the lucrative printing contracts the federal government awarded to these "house organs" for publishing official documents and bulletins turned into yet another form of administration patronage. In the hinterland, editors of newspapers became the equivalent of national (and state, county, and municipal) party secretaries, using their papers as the vehicles for publishing party news, drawing the party line, and printing the party ballot. And sometimes not just secretaries: in the 1840s, seven onetime editors sat in the U.S. Senate, having risen through the ranks from editors to patronage appointees to candidates.[7]

What gave the newspapers added heft in the political process was the introduction in the 1830s of the Napier steam-powered press (which could press five thousand print pages an hour) and, in 1846, of Robert Hoe's rotary-cylinder "Lightning Press" which allowed the volume of print pages to rise to twenty thousand an hour. A single large sheet of newsprint could, by these means, be printed, folded twice, and cut, yielding a four-page single-sheet daily newspaper which cost only a penny a day (or three dollars a year) to purchase. As production costs fell, a whole new market for newspapers opened up. By the 1850s, New York City alone had a daily newspaper circulation of 153,000 (for 500,000 residents), and newspapers made up anywhere from half to 95 percent of the mail in any given year between 1820 and 1860. In 1858, the Chicago post office handled 5.2 million newspapers (and 5.6 million letters) over just three months' time. Each of these copies had a pass-around readership of seven to twenty more people, and George Beatty, a twenty-ish farmer living south of Ottawa, recalled that "a newspaper was loaned about from house to house and read over until it was worn to tatters ... then the farmers, in turn, discussed it among themselves."[8] This ad hoc circulation was greased by the indulgent rates charged for circulating newspapers in the U.S. mail, which guaranteed that 20 percent of them went out free of charge. "The Newspaper Press," complained one critic of the newsprint free-for-all, "controls the state and the church; it directs the family, the legislator, the magistrate and the minister. None rise above its influence, none sink below its authority."[9]

While the steam press expanded the newspapers' power of circulation, the invention of the electrical telegraph in 1844 permitted next-to-immediate communication of events at one end of the country with newspapers at the other. Within fifteen years, there were upwards of fifty thousand miles of telegraph line strung like webs across the United States and over 5 million messages sent per year. A substantial number of these messages were newspaper traffic. As early as 1849, the sheer volume of newspaper communications on the telegraph lines was so great that the principal New York papers—including Horace Greeley's *Tribune* and James Gordon Bennett's *Herald*—created the Associated Press to lease a single telegraph line to Halifax, Nova Scotia, so that New York readers could get commercial news of ships before they docked in New York without each paper bottlenecking the available lines. What worked for commerce worked for politics, too. Reporters could be hired at great distances to telegraph special "exclusive" reports—or transcripts of speeches and debates taken down by a stenographer. George Prescott's *History, Theory and Practice of the Electric Telegraph* boasted that a New York governor's speech of five thousand words, delivered in Albany, would be set in type and ready to print two hours later in a New York City newspaper.[10]

Illinois had its own atmosphere of newspapers to breathe. One Peoria editor estimated than anyone in the state who could borrow or raise three hundred dollars could set up a print shop and begin issuing a newspaper and, with less than a thousand subscribers, still turn a profit: "Every Tyro, who can raise enough money to pay for three cases of type, and impudence and brass enough to get trusted for paper, rent and labor" can "start a new paper, devoted to certain new principles . . . and thus rigged out . . . abuse with his crude thoughts every one he, in his wisdom, thinks fit." So, from only 5 newspapers in the state in 1824, there were 161 by 1853, and the number would continue to rise over the following decade. Of these, 74 were Democratic papers, and they ranged from Douglas's two principal mouthpieces, the *Chicago Times* and the *Illinois State Register* (both of whom fattened on the federal printing contracts the senator steered their way), to the

clusters of rural weeklies (the *Weekly Madison Press* out of Edwardsville, the *Fox River Expositor* in Batavia, the *Wabash Sentinel*, the
Toulon Prairie Advocate, the *Cairo Weekly Times & Delta*) that dotted the
downstate districts. Only ten failed to remain staunchly loyal to Douglas in 1858; the principal exceptions were Isaac Cook's own *Chicago
Union* and George Raney's *Chicago Democratic Union*, which gratefully
took over the federal printing contracts in 1858.

The chief of the Republican papers were Edward Baker's *Illinois
State Journal* (whose founder, Simeon Francis, had played matchmaker
to Abraham and Mary Lincoln and opened his editorial columns for
Lincoln to write political journalism) and the *Chicago Press & Tribune*,
owned and edited by Joseph Medill and Charles Ray. The thirty-five-
year-old Medill was born in Canada, had worked for a rural newspaper
in Ohio, and arrived in Chicago to become editor of the failing *Tribune*
in 1855; Ray, just two years older than Medill, inherited a small family
fortune, bought into the *Tribune* in order to acquire a platform for denouncing Douglas and the Kansas-Nebraska bill, and merged it with
John Locke Scripps's *Chicago Press* and William "Deacon" Bross's
Prairie Herald in 1858. Together, Medill and Ray proved a formidable
team, with Ray writing the editorial columns and Medill managing the
paper's day-to-day operations. Ray also proved to be a natural ally of
Norman Judd and Lyman Trumbull, and soon became an enthusiastic
promoter of Abraham Lincoln. None of them made the slightest pretense to anything less than utter and complete party loyalty. "The day
of neutral papers has passed away," editorialized the *Weekly Madison
Press* that summer. "In this age of stern realities, it is imperative that
the public journalist shall be . . . a fit director of that public opinion he
seeks to lead."[11]

Despite the electrical conduit between debates and newsprint, the
debates were still speech events. Speaking and speeches were heard *and*
seen, and their effect depended on the cumulative impact of both.
They would not only be transcribed and published for newspaper sub-

scribers (and their circles of friends and borrowers) but also be reported upon in the same newspapers, and that kept more than enough pressure on Lincoln and Douglas to perform as speakers as well as the authors of words bound for print. Only a few years before, George William Curtis, the associate editor of *Putnam's Magazine,* had wondered whether the steam-powered press would force "oral instruction . . . to yield the palm, without dispute, to written lecture." Instead, the two had grown up "side by side . . . governed by similar circumstances, and tending alike to the elevation of the masses." The poet Henry Wadsworth Longfellow regretted that Americans saw literature as "effeminate" compared with the "huge, two-fisted sway" of popular speaking, and the easiest proof of that was the outsize popularity of Josiah Holbrook's lyceums. Holbrook, who established the lyceum circuit for popular lecturing in the 1820s, saw the number of lyceums grow to over one thousand within a decade and four thousand a decade after that, and celebrity orators were rewarded with assemblies of fifteen hundred to three thousand people, depending on their star power.[12]

And two more different speakers, in both style and appearance, could scarcely have been imagined than Stephen A. Douglas and Abraham Lincoln. "I have never seen any other two public men appearing on the same platform so unlike in stature," remembered one onlooker decades later. Lincoln towered over Douglas by a foot, and even that foot seemed exaggerated, since Douglas's stumpy legs and paunchy torso made him look like Humpty Dumpty in a toupee, while Lincoln's height was entirely in his legs and gave audiences the impression of a scarecrow come to life. He was "crooked-legged, stoop-shouldered . . . and anything but handsome in the face," wrote one Illinois editor who saw Lincoln speak for the first time in 1856, and Henry Villard's original impression of him was that he was "a man of some years already—I assume he is in his sixties." (Lincoln was actually forty-nine years old in 1858.) William L. Gross, a telegrapher who listened to Lincoln speak at Mount Sterling in October 1858, wrote in his journal that "as

far as Lincoln is concerned I am prepared to testify that his phiz *is*
truly awful." Nor did he find Lincoln much of a textbook on elocution:
"His pronunciation is bad, his manners uncouth and his general appearance anything *but* prepossessing."[13] Seymour Thompson, who
watched Lincoln speaking at Freeport in 1858, thought that he appeared sluggish when beginning to speak: "His mouth was weak" and
"his eyes . . . seemed wholly dead, snake-like." Even his old Whig
friend Joseph Gillespie admitted that "Mr Lincoln had the appearance
of being a slow thinker." But "as soon as he had fairly entered upon his
theme, his stooping posture ceased. . . ." George Beatty, who watched
Lincoln in action at Ottawa, thought his "gestures were awfully awkward but, at the same time, weighty."[14]

> *He elongated himself to his full height and delivered himself awkwardly, it is*
> *true, but with the greatest animation and with one single gesture delivered*
> *with his right forefinger . . . in fact that forefinger seemed to be continually*
> *scratching away out in front of the speaker. If I recall it rightly, he wore one of*
> *those old-fashioned satin stocks or chokers, and it was warm and evidently*
> *impeded full use of his organs of speech, for he pulled it off and threw it down.*
> *A few moments later, with nervous impatience he pulled off his shirt collar,*
> *tearing loose the buttons and throwing it to the winds, and continued his*
> *speech minus both necktie and collar; and the old farmers cheered and howled.*

William Herndon also remembered Lincoln's habit of "sometimes
shooting out that long bony forefinger of his to dot an idea or to express a thought, resting his thumb on his middle finger." And less frequently, when "he was moved in some indignant and half-mad moment
against slavery," he would extend his "arms out . . . above his head at
an angle of about fifty degrees, hands open or clenched according to
his feeling and ideas," which resulted in what Henry Villard described
as an "almost absurd, up-and-down and sidewise" movement. Beyond
that degree of animation, however, Lincoln rarely ventured. Most of
the time, he rose to speak with his hands locked behind him ("the back

part of his left hand resting in the palm of his right hand," according to Herndon), and then moved his still-locked hands "to the front of his person," slowly "running one thumb around the other" and sometimes grasping the "left lapel of his coat . . . with his left hand, his left thumb erect." Herndon recalled that Lincoln "never moved much about on the stand or the platform when speaking," and William Pitt Kellogg only occasionally saw him, "as he reached some climax in his arguments," move "to the front of the platform . . . and with a peculiar gesture hurl the point, so to speak, at his audience," and then "walk slowly backward" and "again resume his speech."[15]

Douglas, by contrast, was a hurricane of passion. One observer at the Alton debate in 1858 thought he spoke "in a very blustering manner, and so to speak, 'frothed at the mouth' when he became excited." When Douglas first arrived in Congress, John Quincy Adams irritably described him as "ranting out his hour in abusive invective, his face convulsed, his gesticulation frantic," and Harriet Beecher Stowe, watching Douglas in action in the Senate in 1856, described him as charging into floor debate "horse and foot." He had "a quick, jerky, fiery way" and would emphasize his points "by shaking his head and seeming to dart forward . . . like the spring of a panther," rather than merely extending a Lincolnesque finger. He was "impetuous" and "denunciatory," and paced "the platform to and fro, very seldom stopping, and standing in one place to address the people." George Beatty remembered that "Douglas's favorite gesture when he wanted to especially emphasize some point was to raise his hand diagonally up toward the Heavens," with his fist closed, and "he made this movement with such force that it never failed to add in driving in his idea."[16]

On the other hand, in an age when too many congressmen "stammer and boggle through a speech, finishing one half of the sentences improperly, and leaving a good portion of the other half not finished at all," Douglas was also a model of verbal precision and power. Carl Schurz reluctantly admitted that Douglas's "sentences were well put together, his points strongly accentuated, his argumentation seem-

ingly clear and plausible." And "he had the voice, not of a little giant
but of a big one," with an "orotund quality, like the roar of a lion." Lincoln thought that in debate "it is impossible to get the advantage of
him" because "even if he is worsted, he so bears himself that the people
are bewildered and uncertain as to who has the better of it." His sentences were also short, and since "his bass voice was incapable of great
speed," he tended to speak at a rate of about 120 to 125 words a minute,
with generous pauses between words or phrases. The *National Era*
described him deliberately speaking "each word as follows: " '*I—
disagreed—and—Mr.—Buchanan—told—me—if—I—did—not—go—
with—him—die.'* " [17]

Lincoln's voice was a high, piercing tenor, pitched almost to shrill-
ness, with a distinct border-state twang which lengthened an *a* to an *e*
(*chair* to *cheer*) and shortened diphthongs from *ai* to *i* (*again* to *agin*).
He spoke more slowly than Douglas, at about 100 words a minute, and
tended to bunch "several words with great rapidity," then come to a
word or phrase he wished to emphasize "and let his voice linger and
bear hard on that," then "rush to the end of the sentence like lightning." He repeated himself and sometimes broke into his own train of
speech with an additional explanation or qualification. "Exactness in
the statement of things was a peculiarity with him," recalled one
Springfield neighbor. "When he was asked a question and gave an answer it was always characteristic, brief, pointed, a propos, out of the
common way and manner, and yet exactly suited to the time place and
thing."

Herndon tried to persuade him to speak more swiftly and evenly,
but Lincoln demurred: "I am compelled by nature to speak slowly, but
when I do throw off a thought . . . it has force enough to cut its own
way and travel at a greater distance." And much as his voice had the
tonal quality of a steam whistle, it was also penetrating and could be
heard at unusual distances without any extra effort on his part.
Charles Zane asked him if speaking for an hour at a time exhausted
him. "No," Lincoln replied, "I can speak three or four hours at a time

without feeling weary." Mary Cunningham Logan thought that Douglas "won your personal support by the magnetism of his personality," but Lincoln "seemed able to brush away all irrelevant matters of discussion, and to be earnestly and simply logical." Give them each five minutes, and Douglas "would make the greater impression." Give them an hour, "and the contrary would be true." As David Davis remarked, "Lincoln is the best stump speaker in the State." He may show "the want of an early education, but [he] has great powers as a speaker." [18]

It would be charming to think of these different speaking styles as some form of untutored revelation of the opponents' different characters. But both were learned styles, something which can be seen on the pages of the popular rhetoric textbooks. The *Columbian Orator* dictated that, to "express admiration, and addresses to Heaven," the arms "must be elevated, but never raised above the eyes" (in just the fashion of Lincoln's "fifty degrees" of angle), while in "expressions of compunction and anger," the hands should be closed (as Lincoln's were "according to his feeling or ideas"). Like Lincoln again, the *Columbian* urged speaking slowly at the beginning because this "has the appearance of modesty, and is best for the voice." The *American Orator* and William Scott's *Lectures on Elocution* diagrammed no fewer than fifteen positions for the arms alone (along with four "plates" of gestures), and both the *American Orator* and Epes Sargent's *Standard Speaker* encouraged speaking with both arms "projected forward in authority" or "spread extended in admiration." But it was the right arm and hand which were the most "natural" source of authority in Hugh Blair's *Lectures on Rhetoric*, and it was "to be employed more frequently than the left." And "direct periods, commencing with participles of the present and past tense," must have a "long pause and rising inflection" inserted between them. Such pauses, as Douglas discovered, "excite uncommon attention, and consequently raise expectation." [19]

But more than just the textbooks, it was the political cultures of Douglas's Democratic party and Lincoln's Whig Republicans which dictated the elements of each debater's style. The Whigs, as the party of the middle class, placed an enormous premium on "reasonableness, costiveness, correctness, and frost." Like the Second Bank of the United States, they calculated profit and loss, politically and economically, in rational terms. Daniel Webster, the greatest of the Whig orators, displayed "nothing dazzling or brilliant" in speaking, but instead aimed for what is "elevated, severe, sober and argumentative." And it was Henry Clay's claim that Whigs appeal not to "the feelings and passions of our Countrymen," but "to their reasons and their judgment." By contrast, Andrew Jackson was the model of the Romantic democrat, full of "terrible" passions against the seemingly plausible rationalizations of the "moneyed interests." And those who paid Jackson the kind of homage Douglas paid, followed it by speaking as Jackson spoke, full of "unhemmed latitude, coarseness, directness, live epithets, expletives, words or opprobrium, resistance" in which "the neck is stretched out, the head forward, often nodding and shaken in a menacing manner against the object of the passion." The moment Lincoln and Douglas crossed the first debate platform, they would be carrying with them not just their own ideas and arguments but thick skeins of ideas on speech and print, on newspapers and politics, and on passion and reason. They would become what Ralph Waldo Emerson called "representative men," and they would drag the whole of American culture up onto the platform with them.[20]

Douglas came away from the Democratic state committee's deliberations in Springfield like a thoroughbred out of the gate. And with a full month before the first debate would take place, the Little Giant turned at once to the belt of old Whig counties in central Illinois, speaking at Clinton (in De Witt County) on July 27 and in Monticello (the county seat of Piatt County) two days later. Already Douglas was laboring to establish that he was the only candidate worth considering for the Senate: the state committee was underwriting the printing of eighty thousand copies of the speech he had given in Chicago and Bloomington for

MAP 1: FIRST PHASE OF THE LINCOLN-DOUGLAS CAMPAIGNS, JULY 27–AUGUST 21

free distribution by hand and through loyal postmasters and legislative candidates "across the entire State by districts."

Campaigning in the grand style was, of course, going to eat up money. The great reception in Chicago had cost over fifteen hundred dollars, and Charles Wilson's *Chicago Journal* observed sardonically that Chicago Democrats "have been begging and scraping together all the spare dollars, shillings, dimes and sixpences that could be obtained" to pay the bills. Every stop on Douglas's list of "appointments" would cost at least four hundred dollars for banners, accommodations, ground rents, and so on; in the twenty-eighth house district, the printer's bill for campaign materials—posters for convention, fifty posters for the polling places, 8,500 Douglas tickets—alone amounted to fifty-two dollars (which translates into something close to six thousand dollars in modern equivalents), not to mention the money which had to be shelled out hiring, and paying the expenses of, campaign workers whose places would normally have been filled by patronage employees. (Henry Villard, who was supposed to be filing exclusive reports for the *New-Yorker Staats-Zeitung*, was moonlighting as a Douglas campaign worker, delivering "speeches in thirteen different locations" for the candidate, and receiving nothing by way of remuneration except "in a few of the visited places [where] the Democrats paid my hotel bill.)" And to show the flag properly, Douglas leased the Illinois Central Railroad directors' "palace-car" for himself, Adele, two stenographers, a Chicago sculptor named Leonard Volk (who was working on a bust of Douglas), and Douglas's two loyal editors, James Sheahan of the *Chicago Times* and Charles Lanphier of the *Illinois State Register*. Strung along the side of the baggage car was a banner, S. A. DOUGLAS, THE CHAMPION OF POPULAR SOVEREIGNTY, and attached to Douglas's car was a flatbed with a baby brass howitzer nicknamed "Little Doug" and two gunners, in red militia shirts and "wearing cavalry sabers," to "awaken the natives along the route" to his arrival.[21]

But in Clinton on July 27, Douglas showed no sign of worries over money. Clinton was the county seat of De Witt County, in the thirty-sixth state house district, laying almost dead center in the state and in the Whig Belt. This was, despite the speeches Douglas had made in Chicago, Bloomington, and Springfield two weeks before, the real beginning of his campaign. "For the past ten or a dozen days," posters had been battened all over the county announcing Douglas's arrival in Clinton, and a brass band and a crowd of "two or three hundred" Douglasites were posted at the train station to meet him. Unfortunately, Douglas's train did not show up until four in the afternoon. But once there, he was bundled into a "close-bodied hack" and driven in a procession two miles long to the county fairgrounds, "where it was arranged he should speak" to a crowd of "at least five thousand people." By now, Douglas had sharpened his message to three barbed points: first, he had fought the good fight in Congress against Lecompton and for popular sovereignty, and was utterly innocent of the Pierce-Buchanan-Taney conspiracy Lincoln had hung around his neck in the House Divided speech. Second: if anyone was guilty of conspiracy, it was Lincoln, who had become a shill for abolitionism. "There was no difference between the position of his opponent and that of the Garrisonian abolitionists." Give Lincoln and the Republicans control of the legislature, and "it will be six months ere they will be urged . . . to proscribe white men of foreign birth" and "thousands of negroes will drift into this state" to be enlisted by the "black republicans" as the basis of a new Illinois political dictatorship. (And, especially for the benefit of old Whigs in the district, it should be understood that Lincoln had made a devil's bargain with Douglas's "abolition enemies" to recruit his onetime Whig friends in the Whig Belt, through "shallow maneuvering," to the Republicans.) Third, Lincoln had set himself up in defiance of the Supreme Court, as though he thought abolition ought to be above the law. "Beware the advocates of Negro equality," Douglas cried, with one more flourish of the race card. "Fight and overthrow the black-republican party!"[22]

From Clinton, Douglas spiraled southwest to Monticello (where the final agreement for the debates was exchanged), Mattoon, and Paris in the twenty-fourth and twenty-fifth state house districts, and then curved eastward through the Whig Belt to Hillsboro, which he had not visited since 1848, in the twentieth state house district on August 2. The local Douglasite "committee of arrangements" had more than made up for his ten-year absence—a semicircle of seating for a crowd of five to six thousand was installed at the county fairgrounds, crowned with "several banners . . . constructed for the occasion," including a banner at the gate which read on one side (in contradiction of the House Divided speech) THE UNION CAN EXIST HALF SLAVE AND HALF FREE and on the other, DOUGLAS THE CHAMPION OF POPULAR SOVEREIGNTY.

The weather had turned hot and dry ("The weather is awfully hot!" complained Governor William Bissell to Joseph Gillespie. "What do those poor fellows do who are canvassing politically nowadays?"), and the brass band which led Douglas's parade to the fairgrounds stamped up so much dust that the air became "nearly suffocating." He was introduced to the crowd by James Davis, the Douglas candidate for the legislature in the twentieth state house district, and being in the heart of the Whig Belt, he took the opportunity to declare "his great love and esteem for Whigs." (With him on the platform, as living proof of this claim, was John Todd Stuart, Lincoln's onetime law partner.) From that point, Douglas launched into his standard chart of grievances with Lincoln: "He charged Lincoln with a desire to abolish slavery, and of favoring amalgamation" and defying the Supreme Court.[23]

Over the balance of that week, Douglas continued his curve westward through Madison County (fourteenth district, which had gone for Fillmore in 1856 and was entitled to two representatives in the legislature) and northward to Pike County (twenty-eighth state house district, which also would elect two representatives and which had split its votes between Frémont and Fillmore in 1856), where he spoke to between three and five thousand in Pittsfield on August 9. It had become a stock speech: he would "ever maintain the principle of popular sovereignty," he would flay Lincoln for resisting a decision of the Supreme Court, and he would deny that blacks enjoyed any equality with whites, or at least none that necessarily exempted them from slavery or allowed them "to be classed as citizens." From there, Douglas left behind his palace car and brass cannon and boarded an Illinois River steamer for stops along the river counties and districts, until by August 20 he was in Ottawa (twenty miles above the Illinois River's great eastward bend toward Chicago) and ready for the first of his debates with Lincoln.

This first great loop of Douglas's campaign had all been in onetime Whig territory, through the Whig Belt and up the Illinois River, and he had done remarkably well. Winchester, his "old home" in Illinois, gave him a tumultuous welcome on August 7, with "a band of music and a long procession of people in carriages, wagons and on horseback." "At least *five thousand* people" crowded into a park west of the town, where he spoke for "an hour and fifty minutes." When he stopped at Beardstown on August 11, he rang the changes on everything designed to spark unease in Whig minds—"Negro Equality, Amalgamation, the Great Principle of the Nebraska Bill, and sighs for the lost merits of Henry Clay." And he was rewarded for his efforts on August 9, when Theophilus Lyle Dickey, "an old line Henry Clay Whig" formally endorsed Douglas.[24]

Like Lincoln, T. Lyle Dickey was Kentucky born, moved to Illinois (in 1834), and began practicing law. He met Lincoln for the first time in 1836, Dickey recounted, "and our co-operation in political matters (we were both Whigs) and our intercourse socially increased and continued." Dickey recruited a company of volunteers for the First Illinois in the Mexican War and served for three years as circuit judge of the Ninth Judicial Circuit, but it was not until 1856 that he plunged directly into political life, and then it was to run as a spoiler in the Third Congressional District in a failed bid to deny the Republican nomination to Owen Lovejoy. Like other Illinois Whigs, Dickey "*wants to have . . . Douglass defeated*, but stands opposed to Abolitionism, & is afraid of Separating the Union through any means & fancies the Republican movements are likely to do it."

Dickey had warned Lincoln repeatedly about allowing himself to be shanghaied by the abolitionists, or promoting the "opinion that our Government Could not last—part slave & part free." When Lincoln did exactly that in the House Divided speech, "Dickey avowed himself to be anti-Lincoln," and on August 9, he wrote a public letter for Sheahan's *Chicago Times* announcing that since "the Republican party of Illinois, unfortunately, has passed under the control of the revolutionary element of the old Abolition party," he was throwing his support to Douglas. This was an ill wind for Lincoln, not only for the signal it sent to the voters of the Whig Belt but also, as Lincoln would eventually learn to his sorrow, because of Dickey's connections to old-line Whigs across the nation.[25]

In contrast with Douglas's energetic sprint into the Whig Belt, Lincoln seemed almost slothful. After following up Douglas in Chicago, Bloomington, and Springfield, and then again in Clinton and Monticello, he was back in Springfield and stayed until August 10. Much of what he was doing was taking care of campaign correspondence, dunning a client for money due, arranging for the printing of seven thousand copies of his Chicago speech, and in large measure, trying to tie down the loose ends of the law practice he depended upon for a living. Through the month of July, Lincoln had coming to trial a divorce case, four suits over nonpayment of debts, an expensive breach-of-contract suit over the sale of land in Sangamon County, a minor inheritance suit, two promissory-note suits, and a routine debt collection from the Great Western Railroad. Unlike Douglas, he was not free to turn off his practice and give himself over at once to the campaign. He was not back on the trail in earnest until August 12, when he arrived in the Illinois River town of Beardstown on the riverboat *Sam Gaty* to make the real beginning of his campaign. Lincoln had been in Beardstown as recently as May, when he defended Duff Armstrong in what is surely his most famous case, the "Almanac Trial," and for this first stride onto the field, the local "committee of reception" had labored to turn out a reception as colorful as any Douglas had enjoyed. Two militia companies were drawn up to welcome him at the wharf, a cannon banged out a salute, and a parade with "a number of flags and banners" and the Rushville Band escorted Lincoln to the "beautiful grove of the town square" for a two o'clock rally.[26]

It is a measure of how deeply Lincoln had inflicted his own wound in the House Divided speech that his first comments were an attempt to explain why it wasn't intended to sound the way it did, or the way

Douglas made it sound in "old-Line" Whig ears. "I made a speech in June last, in which I pointed out . . . a series of public measures leading directly to the nationalization of slavery," to which Douglas had been party. Nothing more than that. No houses dividing or all one thing or all the other. Rather than explaining why he had signed on to these "measures," Douglas had chosen to rant "against our tendencies to negro equality and amalgamation." And how unfortunate, because "Douglas had no foundation for charging him with being favorable to negro equality." Lincoln said nothing about his call in Chicago to "discard all this quibbling about this . . . race and that race and the other race being inferior." Both he and the Republican state committee had seen all they wanted to see of Douglas using this to enlist racial bigotry. Charles Wilson of the *Chicago Journal* feared that "the doctrine of negro equality" was a "rock more dangerous than any other in the pathway of the Republican party," and Lincoln had been begged before leaving Springfield to make it clear that "the Republicans are not in favor of making Blacks socially and politically equal with the Whites."

So Lincoln now explained himself as simply a conventional white Illinoisan who opposed slavery extension precisely because "where slavery existed, the white race was mixed with the black to an alarming degree." There was no attempt at theoretical distinctions between natural and civil equality, no careful denial that using natural equality to oppose slavery constituted a mandate for requiring civil equality. Two days later, the riverboat *Editor*, sporting a banner on its pilothouse reading, *For Senator*, ABRAHAM LINCOLN, brought Lincoln to the river town of Havana (the seat of Mason County and the thirty-fifth state house district), and once again Lincoln did his best to dissociate himself from "negro equality and amalgamation" and brand Douglas as the author of a "conspiracy to Africanize the American continent." Whether it was Judd and the state committee, or simply his own anxieties for the damage Douglas could do on the race issue, Lincoln had chosen to take the low road and to reposition himself as interested in the effects of slavery extension more on whites than on the slaves.[27]

Yet five days later, as he moved up the Illinois River on the steamboat *Senator*, Lincoln climbed back out onto the race limb. At Lewistown, where he was greeted with a thirty-two-gun salute and the braying of the Canton Brass Band to escort him to the town square, Lincoln insisted that the Declaration of Independence "said to the whole world of men: 'We hold these truths to be self evident: that all men are created equal; that they are endowed by their Creator with certain unalienable rights; that among these are life, liberty and the pursuit of happiness.'" That, said Lincoln, was the Founding Fathers' description of "the economy of the Universe," and it extended to "the whole great family of man." The Founders knew enough of human depravity to anticipate that "in the distant future," somebody would attempt to "set up the doctrine that none but rich men, or none but white men, were entitled to life, liberty and the pursuit of happiness." But so long as that promise of equality was embedded in the Declaration, there would always be a weapon there to resist such a "doctrine" and save "the great principles on which the temple of liberty was being built." This fell some way short of Lincoln's attack in Chicago against "quibbling" about race, but it also made it impossible to square the idea of a universal human right to liberty and equality with the deliberate degradation of any one race to slavery.[28]

All this mattered little enough to Douglas, who knew how difficult it would be for Lincoln to splice the difference between a natural equality of blacks and whites that forbade the enslavement of blacks and the "principle of perfect and entire equality of rights and privileges between the negro and white man" over which white Illinoisans would foam hotly at the mouth. "I hold this Government was established by white men of the continent," Douglas told a delegation of German immigrants, "men of European birth or European descent" and "for the benefit of white men, to be administered by white men, on the white basis." Forget this airy talk of a "great family of man." The practical experience "of the world proves that there is such a thing as superior and inferior races," and the black race is indisputably in the latter category, "incapable of self-government" and therefore naturally fit to be enslaved. "Can the white men of Illinois fail to see," asked Charles Lanphier in the *State Register*, "the tendency of black republican policy ... in favor of the equality of the races?" And to add an extra layer of contempt, Douglas persistently refused to use anything but the epithet *nigger*. And he would use it again, in Ottawa.[29]

Ottawa had been the seat of La Salle County since the first courthouse was built there in 1837, and once upon a time it had been a Methodist missionary station. Politically, it lay within the forty-third state house district (and along with Livingston County, it elected two representatives to the state house), the seventh state senate district (where Norman Judd's ally Burton C. Cook was the senator), and the Third Congressional District, which had just renominated Owen Lovejoy for Congress on June 30. This was, in other words, territory Lincoln could presume to be his for the asking: La Salle County had gone for Frémont and for Republican legislative candidates in 1856 by 58 percent. But it was only just above the boundary of the Whig Belt—across the district line, in the forty-second state house district, the Republican legislative candidate had won by a mere sixty votes in 1856—and Lincoln and Douglas could be sure that their audience would be full of the old-Whig David Davis sort from neighboring districts who would require more convincing than La Salle County might.

Ottawa sat at the confluence of the Fox and Illinois rivers— Ottawa, in fact, was almost as far north as the Illinois was navigable to ordinary river steamboats—and was linked the rest of the way to Lake Michigan and Chicago by the Illinois and Michigan Canal. The Chicago and Rock Island Railroad station in Ottawa was a little less than four hours' time from Chicago, and the C & RI's managers had already arranged a half-fare excursion to bring in spectators from Chicago and Joliet. By the morning of the debate, twelve thousand people were streaming into Ottawa, more than twice the number of the forty-third district's total voting population. "The bare announcement that the two candidates were to meet in open debate," reported John W. Forney's *Philadelphia Press*, "was sufficient to bring together an immense crowd."

But they were not necessarily coming to hear Lincoln. Lincoln was a down-stater, and faced a visibility problem in the north of the state. "One trouble in talking Lincoln to the people is that people haven't seen him—don't know him," wrote one Republican loyalist from De Kalb County (just above Ottawa), and in the antislavery north of the state "a great many of the anti-slavery men think he is a little tinctured with pro-slaveryism, because he was born in a slave state." In Ottawa, "Nobody who was anybody was for Lincoln," recalled one Ottawan, "and by 'anybody'" was meant "especially those who owned property." Of the nineteen marshals recruited by the Republican arrangements committee to head the parade greeting Lincoln's arrival in Ottawa, three were farmers, one was a carpenter, one a bookkeeper, one a twenty-three-year-old relative of Burton Cook's, one a ferryman, and one a twenty-eight-year-old German butcher—only one of them, Dr. Azro Putnam, a physician, held political office (he was a town alderman)—which did not look much like northern Illinois's elite.[30]

By stipulating that he would have the opening speech, Douglas hoped to take control of the Ottawa debate, and he pushed that control to the point of refusing "a joint reception" alongside Lincoln in Ottawa. Instead, he would step off the riverboat at Buffalo Rock, four miles below Ottawa, and allow his own reception committee to form up a triumphal parade to "escort him with carriages" into the town and his hotel rooms at the Geiger House. The local Republican arrangements committee countered this by instructing Lincoln to leave the Illinois River at Peoria and intercept the Chicago & Rock Island excursion at Morris, so that he could arrive at Ottawa in the company of seventeen passenger cars full of Republican banner wavers, including Owen Lovejoy. He would be met a mile out of town by a band, a carriage, and "one of the longest processions of horsemen probably ever seen in the State," each horse flaunting a badge "bearing the letters A.L." [31]

The town began filling up fully a day before the debates, and by early afternoon of the twentieth, George Beatty (who lived outside Ottawa and described the scene to Ida Tarbell forty years later) had "never seen such a crowd in Ottawa." The "streets were crowded with people," until the "few hotels, the livery stables, and private houses were crowded and there were no accommodations left." The latecomers camped out along the bluffs and bottomlands of the Illinois River, and "that night the campfires that spread up and down the valley for a mile made it look as if an army was gathered about us." The next morning, "every road was filled with horses and wagons." [32]

Horace White, a Beloit College graduate and, at twenty-four, already a veteran reporter for the *Chicago Journal*, the Associated Press, and now the *Chicago Tribune*, joined the Lincoln campaign at Beardstown, and early on the morning of the twenty-first, he set himself up "on elevated ground overlooking" Ottawa and the "surrounding country" to see what he fully expected would look like nothing so much as a page out of the *Canterbury Tales*. He was not disappointed. With the "very dry" weather, "dust rose at every slight movement" over the ground, and long before he could actually see anything on the roads, "clouds of dust began to rise on the horizon . . . from all points of the compass," and by eight o'clock, "the town resembled a vast smoke house." The clouds soon resolved themselves into trains of "large four-horse" wagons, filled with raucous political clubs and canvas banners "indicating their habitation and their political belonging." The debate was scheduled for two o'clock on Washington Square, but long before that time, the roads, and then the streets of Ottawa, became "densely packed with human beings," and the rail fence which ran around the square had given up "every inch of space" to "wagons, buggies," and "teams of all sorts." [33]

A central platform, facing southward, was already in place, with a

wooden awning to shield the speakers. (The awning soon was fes-
tooned with a half dozen "clowns" whose weight broke through several
of the boards before the debate began.) Onto the platform marched the
moderator, Mayor Joseph Glover, the members of the two arrangements committees, and finally the debaters. There was no hand shaking or backslapping between Lincoln and Douglas: "Their demeanor
on the platform," wrote Horace White, "was that of rather cool polite-
ness. There was nothing like comradeship between them." There were
also chairs for White, for Chester P. Dewey (who was representing
William Cullen Bryant's *New York Evening Post* and had to spend the
evening before on a sofa in the Geiger House because no other rooms
were available), for Henry Villard, and most unusual of all, for two
shorthand reporters whose job would be to take down every word of
Lincoln and Douglas verbatim.[34]

The development of a rapid-transcription English alphabet for
recording speech as delivered was actually as old as the sixteenth century, when pious Puritans sought to invent ways of "taking down" ser-
mons as they heard them. Successive systems were devised in the
eighteenth century, but the most popular, a phonetic or "phono-
graphic" shorthand, was invented by Isaac Pitman in 1837 and introduced to the United States by Pitman's brother, Benn, in 1843. One of
these shorthand reporters, James B. Sheridan, had been lent by John
W. Forney, the Douglasite editor of the *Philadelphia Press,* to Douglas
for the 1858 campaign, probably out of anxiety that Illinois Democratic editors squirming under Buchanan's thumb could not be trusted
to print accurate accounts of Douglas's speeches.

But Medill and Ray's *Chicago Tribune* also had on retainer a shorthand reporter, twenty-four-year-old Robert R. Hitt, who had taught
himself shorthand to make an easier job of taking lecture notes as a
college student and thereafter became the "pioneer" of "verbatim reporting" in Chicago. Hitt had distinguished himself already in the
campaign by transcribing Douglas's and Lincoln's Chicago speeches
for the *Tribune,* and when Lincoln noticed Sheridan in the crowd at

Beardstown, taking down his speech for Douglas to review, the *Tribune* hired Hitt to provide shorthand transcripts of Lincoln in the debates.

Hitt's procedure was to fill up page after page with transcriptions of both Lincoln and Douglas, right up to the moment when the "first train they could get" from a debate site was ready to leave for Chicago; then a galloper named Larminie from Montreal, grasping Hitt's notebook, would run for the train, convert Hitt's notes into text en route, and have part of the debates ready for typesetting that evening in Chicago. As soon as the debate was complete, Hitt, with the balance of his transcripts, would take the next train to Chicago, turning his shorthand squiggles into text as he went, and have the balance of the debates ready to add to the portion already typeset, and the whole text done for the next morning edition. Douglas, with the same idea in mind, also hired a second reporter, a twenty-five-year-old Cockney with a self-developed shorthand system, named Henry Binmore, to assist Sheridan for the *Times.* In this way, the full texts of both Lincoln and Douglas were, for the first time imaginable, ready for publication in Chicago thirty-six hours after delivery, and in New York in three days.[55]

The crush of the crowd in the streets around Washington Square was such that the Lincoln and Douglas parades were half an hour late, and it was not until two thirty that Douglas was able to step "to the edge of the platform," bow "gracefully to the cheering multitudes," and begin speaking. "Prior to 1854 this country was divided into two great political parties, known as the Whig and Democratic parties," he said, and while they had their disagreements on many issues, "they agreed on the great slavery question," and that it should not divide the Union.

But within the last four years, Abraham Lincoln and Lyman Trumbull had struck an unholy deal, "each with his respective friends," Lincoln to break up the Illinois Whigs and Trumbull to break up the Illinois Democrats, and to draw "members of both into an Abolition party under the name and disguise of a Republican party." Their program was everything the abolitionists had promised, short of an actual war on the slave states—to abolish slavery in the District of Columbia, to "prohibit the admission of any more slave States into the Union," and to exclude slavery from the territories, whether they were already under federal control or to be acquired in the future—and Lincoln had already showed in the House Divided speech that war would be coming next. The proof of this sensational assertion? "I have the resolutions of their State Convention"—the first Republican state convention in 1854, held in Springfield—"and I will read a part . . . of this Abolition platform." With a flourish, Douglas opened up a notebook and read aloud:

> The Republican party [is] . . . pledged to the accomplishment of the following purposes . . . to restore Nebraska and Kansas to the position of Free Territories . . . to repeal and entirely abrogate the Fugitive-Slave law . . . to abolish slavery in the District of Columbia . . . to exclude slavery from all the Territories over which the General Government has exclusive jurisdiction; and to resist the acquirement of any more Territories, unless the practice of slavery therein forever shall have been abolished.

A smattering of cheers actually ran through the crowd as Douglas read the "resolutions." But that only gave him the opportunity he wanted. "Your Black Republicans have cheered every one of those propositions," he roared. Now, would Lincoln endorse them? If Lincoln hesitated, the solid Republican vote of the northern Illinois districts should desert him; if he endorsed them, as he should, he would make every Union-loving and peace-loving old Whig run for refuge. And if Lincoln endorsed them here in Ottawa, where it was relatively safe, would he also endorse them a month hence, when the debates moved to Jonesboro, in the heart of the downstate Democratic districts? "When I trot him down to lower Egypt," Douglas boasted, "I may put the same questions to him" and see if he tries to change his abolitionist tune in front of a far less forgiving, and far more Democratic, audience. If not, he would be exposed as a hypocrite, and worthy of neither Whig nor Republican votes.[36]

So what did Lincoln think of his party's "abolition" platform, Douglas asked:

- Do you advocate "the unconditional repeal of the Fugitive Slave Law"? . . . *so that runaway slaves can flood into Illinois without fear of capture?*
- Will you vote against the admission of any further territories to the Union as slave states? . . . *so that you can isolate and demonize the South?*
- Will you oppose the admission of a slave state to the Union, even if the people want slavery in their state constitution? . . . *so that the right of the people to determine their own destinies means nothing to you?*
- Will you vote to abolish slavery in the District of Columbia? . . . *as the first step to abolishing it everywhere else?*
- Will you vote to prohibit the interstate slave trade? . . . *and drive the first wedge of civil war between North and South?*
- Will you vote to ban slavery in all the western territories, above or below the Missouri Compromise line? . . . *so that no matter what you say about admiring Henry Clay, that great Whig champion was wrong in permitting slave states to enter the Union in 1820 and 1850?*
- Will you vote against any more territorial annexations (like the Mexican Cession) unless slavery is first banned from them? . . . *meaning that you would rather satisfy the self-righteous demands of your abolition ideology than permit the republic to grow, expand, and prosper from sea to sea?*

Mind you, Douglas paused, he had nothing personal against Lincoln in saying this. "Lincoln is one of those peculiar men who perform with admirable skill everything which they undertake," he conceded cheerfully—including selling whiskey in a saloon and getting himself elected to Congress, where (and here Douglas turned the knife swiftly) "he distinguished himself by his opposition to the Mexican war, taking the side of the common enemy against his own country." But Lincoln had made a great comeback from that disgrace, "having formed this new party for the benefit of deserters from Whiggery, and deserters from Democracy, and having laid down the Abolition platform which I have read." Listen to this "revolutionary and destructive" pronouncement of Lincoln's: *I believe this Government cannot endure Permanently half Slave and half Free. Well,* Douglas replied, *why not?* "Why can it not exist divided into free and slave States?" The Founders "made this Government divided into free States and slave States, and left each State perfectly free to do as it pleased on the subject of slavery," and the division had worked satisfactorily for seventy years. And there was no reason to suppose it couldn't keep on quite happily in that way, if only Lincoln and his radical abolition allies would give up their wretched plot to abolitionize the old Whigs into the Republican party and then abolitionize the country into "a sectional war between the free States and the slave States, in order that the one or the other may be driven to the wall."[37]

Do not be deceived by Lincoln's eloquent appeals to the Declaration of Independence, Douglas warned. Lincoln was just like "all the little Abolition orators" who tell you that "all men were created equal, and then asks how can you deprive a negro of that equality which God and the Declaration of Independence awards to him." Douglas believed that all the men who signed the Declaration were equal, but that did not include blacks. "I do not regard the negro as my equal, and positively deny that he is my brother or any kin to me whatever," he declared. But by pulling on the patriotic heartstrings of Illinois, Douglas complained, Lincoln was cleverly setting up a slippery slope which would allow blacks "to come into the State and settle with the white man," enable them "to vote on an equality with yourselves, and to make them eligible to office, to serve on juries, and to adjudge your rights."[38]

By now the Douglas supporters in the crowd were ecstatic (*Good for you* and *Douglas forever* some were heard to shout), and Douglas was ready to mingle their racial bile with the cause of popular sovereignty. "In relation to the policy to be pursued towards the free negroes, we [in Illinois] have said that they shall not vote. Maine, on the other hand, has said that they shall vote," and as much as Illinois may regard Maine as being out of its political mind in doing so, Stephen A. Douglas was not the man "to quarrel with Maine for differing from me in opinion." And then the punchline: "Let Maine take care of her own negroes and fix the qualifications of her own voters to suit herself, without interfering with Illinois, and Illinois will not interfere with Maine." The operation of popular sovereignty was what saved Illinois from black voters; grateful Illinoisans should recognize the power of that principle, and send back to the Senate the man who respected it and wanted to let it spread its blessings over the whole country. "If we will only act conscientiously and rigidly upon this great principle of popular sovereignty which guarantees to each State and Territory the right to do as it pleases on all things local and domestic instead of Congress interfering, we will continue at peace one with another." [39]

There it was, within the limits of one hour: Lincoln was an abolitionist conspirator, out to seduce the old Whigs into an abolition spider's nest. Lincoln was an unreliable politician who had voted against his country's interests in time of war. Lincoln, unlike the Founders, wanted to end the great American experiment in practical diversity. Lincoln wanted "black equality," which only popular sovereignty could save Illinois and the nation from. Douglas had not said one word about the failure of popular sovereignty in Kansas, not one word about the Lecompton constitution, not one word on how popular sovereignty was supposed to work in the territories in the face of the *Dred Scott* decision or how it would work in Illinois if a companion case to *Dred Scott* on slavery in the free states ever came within the grasp of Roger Taney. Instead, with "confidence and complete self-possession in his every movement" and "his remarkable fluency," Douglas had flung down a challenge to Lincoln's honesty, and as Douglas surely knew, Lincoln's anxiety over his resolute transparency of motive was, in lieu of the religion that was commonly supposed to be the real guarantor of sincerity, his softest spot. Lincoln might spend his hour and a half trying to deal with the challenges or he might spend it rising in a different direction.

Predictably, he chose the former. "This story that Judge Douglas tells of Trumbull bargaining to sell out the old Democratic party, and Lincoln agreeing to sell out the old Whig party," had "no substance to it whatever," Lincoln began. He had never signed on to abolitionist resolutions in Springfield in 1854, or at least none that he could remember, if only because he clearly recalled that, when the Republican state convention held its inaugural meeting that fall in the state capitol, he was attending "court in Tazewell County." (Something about this charge that the Republican state convention had adopted an abolitionist platform rested uneasily in Lincoln's memory, but he had no time then to work through it.) Nor had he ever called upon the North to fall on the South with blazing sword to extirpate slavery, nor had he ever talked about black equality—or at least black *civil* equality. "I have no purpose directly or indirectly to interfere with the institution of slavery in the States where it exists," and "I have no purpose to introduce political and social equality between the white and the black races," he declared. There was, Lincoln tried to explain, a "physical difference between the two" races—what it was, he did not say—and that "difference" would "probably forever forbid their living together upon the footing of perfect equality" anyway. In that case, it was simply a matter of self-interest to assign his own race "the superior position." But this was a functional, not an inherent, superiority; it in no way suggested that the black man was not a *man*. And if a man, "there is no reason in the world why the negro is not entitled to all the natural rights enumerated in the Declaration of Independence, the right to life, liberty and the pursuit of happiness," and not to be enslaved. Even if the black man was not "my equal in many respects," it was also true that a great many white people were not each other's equals "in many respects."

But you did not enslave *them*. So long as the black man is a man, he has a natural "right to eat the bread, without leave of anybody else, which his own hand earns." And in that respect, "he is my equal and the equal of Judge Douglas, and the equal of every living man." This time, and for the first time, Lincoln was interrupted by "Great applause," and by shouts of *All right* and *Bully for you*.[40]

But Lincoln was not finished defending himself. He had never been a saloonkeeper, although he might admit to having worked "the latter part of the winter in a little still-house, up at the head of a hollow"— which produced, as he had hoped, "roars of laughter." And he had never used his time in Congress during the Mexican War to vote against supplying the soldiers—only against the attempt of the Democrats "to get me to vote that the war had been righteously begun by the President." That, he was happy to underscore, was what every "old Whig" in Congress had done, too—just so that the "old Whigs" now packed into the town square could remember who had been one of their champions years back. There was no sense in which his warning against a "house divided" over slavery meant that it was the task of Congress to wipe out all variation and diversity across the Republic. But measured against all the ways in which "local institutions in the States" and "differences in the face of the country" served as "bonds of the union," slavery was the one such "institution" which served as "an apple of discord and an element of division in the house." This was why the Founders had originally adopted legislation to restrict it "from the new territories" in 1787 and cut off the African slave trade.[41]

Douglas—and it was becoming noticeable that Lincoln had stopped calling him *Senator* and now rather referred to him as *Judge* Douglas, his old state title—claimed that popular sovereignty was the best means for maintaining the status quo. No, it was not: it was the best method for promoting "the *perpetuity and nationalization of slavery*." Especially after *Dred Scott*, all that popular sovereignty allowed the people in a territory to do was vote to legalize slavery if they wanted it; it forbade them from banning it if they didn't want it. In fact, Lincoln closed in, at the time of the Kansas-Nebraska bill, in 1854, Douglas had explicitly voted against an amendment proposed by Salmon Chase, "expressly authorizing the people" of a territory "to exclude slavery." And he had worded the Kansas-Nebraska bill to state that its "true intent" was "not to legislate slavery into any Territory or *State.*" If Kansas-Nebraska was about organizing a territory, why was an allusion to *states* put in? Because, from the first, "Judge Douglas and those acting with him" had carefully paved the pathway in 1854, creating a "niche" for the *Dred Scott* decision to prevent people from excluding slavery "from a Territory" in 1857, and leaving another to be filled "if another Dred Scott decision shall come, holding that they cannot exclude it from a State."

True: Douglas had made himself a hero by opposing the Lecompton constitution. But his opposition was itself testimony to the existence of a relentless "design" by "the president and his Cabinet" to "make the institution of slavery national." Maybe, in the long run, Douglas was not an active member of a conspiracy "with Chief Justice Taney and the President before the Dred Scott decision was made." But he was certainly their dupe, and so long as he still defended *Dred Scott* as a *Thus saith the Lord*, he remained their dupe. It only remained for Lincoln to add that he stood at Ottawa as a living disciple of Henry Clay, "my beau ideal of a statesman, the man for whom I fought all my humble Life." Clay understood, even if Douglas did not, that "men who would repress all tendencies to liberty and ultimate emancipation" were "blowing out the moral lights around us." If Douglas succeeded in persuading people that choosing slavery was "a sacred right of self government," then it would require only a "second Dred Scott decision, which he endorses in advance, to make Slavery alike lawful in all the States."[42]

What was odd in Lincoln's reply was that he made no effort to respond to Douglas's seven questions. Lincoln never advertised himself as an off-the-cuff speaker, and in his cautious, lawyerly way, he was more inclined to wait until he had thought through the questions and the answers he wanted to give—something which the order of speaking decreed by Douglas at Ottawa was not going to give him. Nevertheless, his closing appeal to the Declaration and to Henry Clay, delivered with "vehemence and force," had clearly pulled the crowd with him. When Douglas rose to make his half-hour rebuttal, he was greeted with so much catcalling and heckling that Mayor Glover had to step forward and demand quiet.

Lincoln could deny as many things as he liked, Douglas began, but what he could not deny was that he had signed on to the Republicans' abolitionist platform in Springfield back in 1854. "My recollection is distinct," Douglas insisted, because he had been there when the abolitionist Ichabod Codding had announced the Republican meeting in the state capitol which adopted the abolitionist resolutions. (Lincoln was on his feet at once, "excitedly and angrily," striding to the front of the platform, trying to interrupt with a denial. But he got only half of his protest out before two members of the arrangements committee caught up with him and pulled him back to his seat for fear that the whole meeting might blow up.)

Not only, Douglas confidently continued, had the Illinois Republicans adopted an abolition platform but Lincoln had been selected "by the very men who made the Republican organization that day" as their spokesman, and on the same day Lincoln spoke publicly "in reply to me, preaching up the same doctrine of the Declaration of Independence that niggers were equal to white men." Lincoln could deny that all he liked, but Douglas would "yet bring him to his milk on this point," especially when Douglas "trotted" him "down to Egypt," as though Douglas was a dairy farmer with a stool, about to squeeze a reluctant cow's udder, or a horse breaker leading a reluctant yearling.[43]

Lincoln tells you that he believes in the "sacred right of self-government," but not popular sovereignty. But "if the people of the

Territory" were actually to decide to legalize slavery when they drafted their state constitution, would Lincoln vote to admit such a state, "as its own people might choose"? Evidently not: "He says that that kind of talk is blighting the glory of this country." What Lincoln means in practice is that "he is not in favor of each State doing as it pleased on the Slavery question," which included Illinois "doing as it pleased" in excluding blacks entirely. It might be that, in northern Illinois, where he had a sympathetic audience, Lincoln would take the plunge and answer clearly that he opposed the admission of a new slave state even if its people wanted slavery. But when the debates turned to the south of state, in Democratic "Egypt," it would be interesting to see whether Lincoln would sing the same song.[44]

It was now time for a little indignation. The charge of a conspiracy to "nationalize" slavery that included Douglas, Taney, Buchanan, and Pierce had been funny when Lincoln offered it up the first time; it was not funny now that he was repeating it as though it were fact. It was a lie to suggest that Douglas had snuck the word *State* into the Kansas-Nebraska bill to pave the way for more nationalizing of slavery. It was there to affirm that territories and states alike had full control over their own affairs and "the right of the people to do as they please." That doctrine was the only one which would secure "peace and harmony and fraternal feeling between all the States of this Union." Without it, there would "be sectional warfare agitating and distracting the country," leading to the "dissolution of the Union."[45]

Mayor Glover whispered that the half hour for his rejoinder was up, and Douglas stepped back amid "tremendous" shouts. He walked off the platform, headed for the Geiger House and then the railroad depot, leading a crowd of admirers and "swinging his hat to and fro" in salute. Lincoln tried to step off the platform, but he was rushed by "an immense crowd, numbering at least five thousand persons," half a dozen of whom hoisted him up on their shoulders and marched him around the square to Joseph Glover's house behind a brass band playing "Hail, Columbia!"

Firm, united let us be,
Rallying round our liberty,
As a band of brothers joined,
Peace and safety we shall find.

After dinner, the parades and processions reassembled, and fifteen hundred people marched Lincoln and Owen Lovejoy back to the square. There, by torchlight on the courthouse steps, Lovejoy "divested himself of his cravat and collar, opened his vest and shirt," and unlimbered "a telling speech—one of his characteristic sledgehammer efforts"—until "a late hour." [46]

"Every body here is delighted with the rencontre at Ottowa," exulted David Davis to Lincoln, and even Lyman Trumbull thought Lincoln's performance at Ottawa "ought to decide the contest with all intelligent men." Lincoln himself would later claim that "I was better pleased with myself at Ottawa than at any other place." It was hard to judge, however, whether these were precise measurements of success or merely statements of relief that Lincoln had done as well as he had against the Little Giant. Hiram Beckwith, a Danville lawyer whom Lincoln had sponsored before the state bar, recalled that even the stoutest Republicans had "looked forward to the debate between him and Senator Douglas with deep concern," and even "foreboding."

Douglas, by contrast, "had made elaborate preparations" for the Ottawa debate and was certain he had come through with flying colors. "Dug was highly pleased with the result," one of his confidants boasted to Henry Whitney, who in turn reported the conversation to Lincoln. "Dug had now got you where he wanted you—that you had dodged on the platform—that even if you replied to the platform query at Freeport &c. it would be too late." The newspapers made no effort to weigh the debate evenly. Sheahan's *Chicago Times*, Lanphier's *State Register*, and the other Douglasite newspapers around the state announced that "the triumph of Senator Douglas was complete" and "the excoriation of Lincoln was so severe that the Republicans hung their heads in shame." And when John W. Forney's *Philadelphia Press* reported on the Ottawa debate on August 26, it rejoiced that "Lincoln has killed himself by his ultra-Abolition-equality doctrine." With just as much energy and venom, Ray and Medill in the *Tribune* and Baker in the *State Journal* insisted "that Stephen A. Douglas is a used up man— that Lincoln, to use the expression of the crowd, 'chawed him up' completely." At moments, partisanship galloped so far ahead of reporting that it hardly seemed as though the papers were describing the same event. The *Tribune* had Douglas "livid with passion and excitement" in his reply to Lincoln, his face "distorted with rage" and "a maniac in language and argument." The *Chicago Times* had Lincoln so close to nervous collapse under Douglas's hammering that he could no longer stand up and had to be carried off the platform by his disheartened rescuers.[47]

Looked at from the distance of time, the Ottawa debate is much harder to call as a win-or-lose proposition. If the debate could be laid out on a grid, it would look something like this:

DOUGLAS	LINCOLN
Lincoln is an abolitionist radical	Denied
Lincoln and Trumbull are conspiring to abolitionize the old parties	Denied
Lincoln betrayed his country in the Mexican War	Denied
Lincoln opposes national diversity on slavery	Denied, except concerning legalization of slavery because of its divisiveness
Lincoln advocates racial equality	Denied, except in case of natural rights

DOUGLAS	LINCOLN
Popular sovereignty assures every state the right to self-determination	Popular sovereignty assures perpetuation and nationalization of slavery
Lincoln advocates dissolution of the Union	Denied
	Lincoln's position is the same as Clay
	Douglas's position conflicts with the morality of the Declaration

What leaps out at once from this view is how fragmentary and negative the Ottawa debate was. Douglas zigzagged from one inflammatory charge to another, with only the weakest transitions. He took for granted that people already understood popular sovereignty, and that he needed only to link popular sovereignty in their minds with political virtues no one really disputed—self-government, self-determination, national glory. He offered no defense of slavery, except to imply that it was an effective way of keeping blacks out of Illinois. Instead, he devoted almost all of his energies to associating Lincoln with radical notions he was confident longtime Illinois Whigs despised—negro equality, abolition, disloyalty, civil war—and carefully avoided the *Dred Scott* decision (as he had done before more dependable Democratic audiences in Bloomington and Springfield).

Lincoln was, if anything, even thinner in his arguments. His hour-and-a-half reply was a string of denials, as though he had thought out nothing of his own to say and had no better plan than merely reacting to whatever Douglas said. He repeated the conspiracy charge of the House Divided speech, and he refused to buckle completely to Douglas's racism. But he made no effort to take apart the popular sovereignty doctrine in detail, and his only significant attack on the evil of slavery itself came in the last five minutes of his reply. If people had come expecting to hear a reprise of Webster and Hayne, they could not have been more disappointed.[48]

But instead of disappointment, the prevailing mood seemed to be surprise. Although Douglas had carefully targetted his attacks by appealing to the worst fears of undecided Whigs, the remarkable fact of the day was how well Lincoln had done. "I can recall only one fact of the debates," one survivor of the audience said to Ida Tarbell four decades later, "that I felt so sorry for Lincoln while Douglas was speaking, and then to my surprise I felt *so* sorry for Douglas when Lincoln replied." Even Lincoln sounded a little taken aback. He wrote Joseph Cunningham, the editor of the *Urbana Union,* "Douglas and I . . . crossed swords here yesterday; the fire flew some, and I am glad to know I am yet alive." Robert Hitt remembered that the skeptics who "regarded the setting up of Lincoln" against the Little Giant as "farcical" were "confounded by the first debate" and by "the immense development of Lincoln's resources." And once Hitt's transcripts of the debate were published in the *Chicago Tribune,* and then reprinted across the country, letters began pouring in, asking "Who is this new man? . . . You have a David greater than the Democratic Goliath or any other I ever saw."[49]

1

2

ABRAHAM LINCOLN had sat for a photographer only four times in his life before a Chicago photographer made this daguerreotype of him on July 11, 1858. Just three weeks before, Lincoln had been nominated by the Illinois State Republican Convention for the U.S. Senate and would sit for eight more photographs during his campaign. The evening before this photograph was taken, Lincoln had made a major campaign speech from the balcony of the Tremont Hotel in Chicago in reply to Douglas's campaign-opening speech from the same balcony.

STEPHEN ARNOLD DOUGLAS scarcely needed publicity, as the author of the Kansas-Nebraska Act and the doctrine of "popular sovereignty." But he, too, would sit for a photograph in Washington, on May 7, 1858.

3

LINCOLN did not plan to debate Douglas as part of his campaign, but the Illinois State Republican Committee insisted on arranging the debates at the end of July 1858. Douglas agreed to seven open-air debates, with teams of stenographers representing the *Chicago Times* and the *Chicago Tribune* transcribing the entire series for publication.

4

CHARLES H. LANPHIER was one of Douglas's oldest and most loyal political friends and edited Springfield's *Illinois State Register*. Along with the *Chicago Times*, the *Register* was Douglas's most aggressive supporter among Illinois newspapers.

ORLANDO BELL FICKLIN was a prime example of a former Whig who had, unlike Lincoln, turned to the Democrats in the 1850s rather than to the Republicans. Douglas needed supporters like Ficklin to persuade other "old Whigs" to rally to him if he hoped to win re-election in 1858.

6

7

JAMES B. SHERIDAN covered the debates as a reporter for James Sheahan's pro-Douglas *Chicago Times*.

Accompanying Sheridan was English-born **HENRY BINMORE**, who was Sheahan's "phonographer" and took down Douglas's words in shorthand.

9

DAVID DAVIS of Bloomington was the presiding judge of Illinois's 8th Judicial Circuit, where Lincoln practiced law. A former Whig-turned-Republican like Lincoln, he was deeply suspicious of the abolitionists but remained firmly loyal to Lincoln throughout the 1858 campaign.

JOSEPH GILLESPIE was an "old line Whig" from Madison County and a fervent supporter of Lincoln. But even Gillespie had to soften the Republican antislavery message to appease key midstate voters.

11

HORACE WHITE *(left)* covered the debates as a reporter for the *Chicago Tribune*, in tandem with **ROBERT R. HITT** *(right)*, who served as the *Tribune*'s "phonographer." Hitt's shorthand transcriptions became the versions selected by Lincoln for publication in his 1860 edition of the debates.

12

Robert Marshall Root's 1918 reconstruction of the fourth debate at **CHARLESTON**, Illinois, on September 18, 1858. Orlando Ficklin is seated at the left front, beside Douglas. Just behind Lincoln's right arm is Robert Hitt, and under his left elbow is Henry Binmore.

KNOX COLLEGE.
GALESBURG, ILL.

13

The fifth debate took place on October 7, 1858, in **GALESBURG**, Illinois, where the debate platform was placed against the east wall of Knox College's "Old Main" building. The east wall is at the left.

14

LYMAN TRUMBULL was originally a Democrat, but turned
Republican after his election to the Senate in 1855. Although
Trumbull owed his election to Lincoln's decision to withdraw from
the 1855 voting, he was halfhearted in supporting Lincoln in 1858
and campaigned more *against* Douglas than *for* Lincoln.

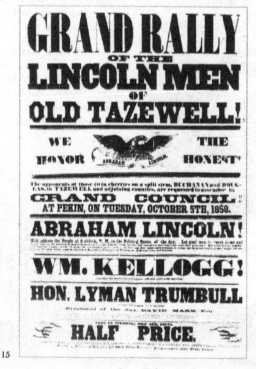

15

LINCOLN RALLY POSTER from Pekin, in the "Whig Belt" on
October 5, 1858. Notice that the poster calls for a meeting of "Lincoln
Men"—the term *Republican* is carefully avoided in order to disarm
"old Whig" suspicions of Republican abolitionists.

16

17

(Above) 5th Street and the east side of Washington Square, in QUINCY, the site of the sixth debate on October 13, 1858. Although located at the western point of the "Whig Belt," it had once been Douglas's home district. Still, Douglas's performance at Quincy was lackluster, and Horace White believed Douglas was "drinking himself to death."

(Left) ORVILLE HICKMAN BROWNING of Quincy was one of Lincoln's oldest political friends and another Whig who had gone into the Republican fold. But Browning was never convinced that Lincoln was an adequate candidate and made no effort to campaign for Lincoln.

18

ALTON CITY HALL, where the platform for the seventh and last debate was constructed. Lincoln seized the high ground here with his attack on slavery as no different in principle from "a king who seeks to bestride the people of his own nation and live by the fruit of their labor ... it is the same tyrannical principle."

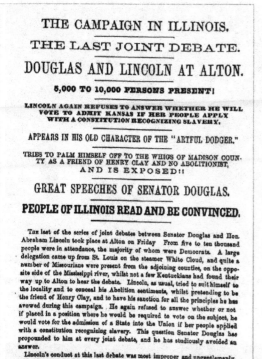

THE CAMPAIGN IN ILLINOIS.

THE LAST JOINT DEBATE.

DOUGLAS AND LINCOLN AT ALTON.

5,000 TO 10,000 PERSONS PRESENT!

LINCOLN AGAIN REFUSES TO ANSWER WHETHER HE WILL VOTE TO ADMIT KANSAS IF HER PEOPLE APPLY WITH A CONSTITUTION RECOGNIZING SLAVERY.

APPEARS IN HIS OLD CHARACTER OF THE "ARTFUL DODGER."

TRIES TO PALM HIMSELF OFF TO THE WHIGS OF MADISON COUNTY AS A FRIEND OF HENRY CLAY AND NO ABOLITIONIST, AND IS EXPOSED!!

GREAT SPEECHES OF SENATOR DOUGLAS.

PEOPLE OF ILLINOIS READ AND BE CONVINCED.

The last of the series of joint debates between Senator Douglas and Hon. Abraham Lincoln took place at Alton on Friday. From five to ten thousand people were in attendance, the majority of whom were Democrats. A large delegation came up from St. Louis on the steamer White Cloud, and quite a number of Missourians were present from the adjoining counties, on the opposite side of the Mississippi river, whilst not a few Kentuckians had found their way up to Alton to hear the debate. Lincoln, as usual, tried to suit himself to the locality and to conceal his Abolition sentiments, whilst pretending to be the friend of Henry Clay, and to have his sanction for all the principles he has avowed during this campaign. He again refused to answer whether or not if placed in a position where he would be required to vote on the subject, he would vote for the admission of a State into the Union if her people applied with a constitution recognizing slavery. This question Senator Douglas has propounded to him at every joint debate, and he has studiously avoided an answer.

Lincoln's conduct at this last debate was most improper and ungentlemanly. After he concluded his hour and a half speech, and Senator Douglas rose to reply, he seated himself where his motions could not be observed by the Senator, and, whenever a point was made against him, would shake his head at the crowd, intimating that it was not true, and that they should place no reliance on what was said. This course was in direct violation of the rules of the

19

20

AN ANTI-LINCOLN CIRCULAR, distributed in the two weeks between the last debate and Election Day, and aimed to convincing "old Whigs" that Lincoln was a closet abolitionist.

DOUGLAS SUSTAINED!

Lincoln's Comb is Out!

He is Brought to his Milk!

THE LITTLE GIANT HAS SPOTTED HIM!

DOUGLASITE NEWSPAPER, the Rock Island *Daily Islander & Argus,* crows over Douglas's victory on November 5, 1858. It had taken three days of counting and reporting before the results were finally apparent.

DOUGLAS responds to Charles Lanphier's notification of his formal re-election by the Illinois legislature on January 5, 1859: "Let the voice of the people rule!" Douglas mistakenly dated the telegram as 1858.

21

PRESIDENT THEODORE ROOSEVELT arrives at the dedication of the Freeport debates memorial in 1903. He was introduced by sixty-nine-year-old Robert Hitt, who had gone on to a lengthy career in politics and was representing the ninth Illinois district in Congress.

Although erecting monuments was the first impulse of those who wanted to memorialize the debates, other methods soon followed. The debates have been reenacted (at Freeport, for instance, in 1958, and for a televised series by C-SPAN in 1994), incorporated into movies (including a memorable scene in the 1940 RKO film, *Abe Lincoln in Illinois*), and painted by Victor Perard, Joseph Boggs Beale, Frank Schoonover, H. Charles McBarron, and Mort Künstler. The most recent memorialization, at the Abraham Lincoln Presidential Library and Museum in Springfield, shows a re-creation, in full-size silicone effigy, of the Galesburg debate.

CHAPTER 4

FOR GOD'S SAKE, LINDER, COME UP

> *This debate served as a sort of school for Mr. Lincoln, in which*
> *he studied, with the deepest intensity, those questions affecting*
> *human rights and the permanent welfare of the nation; and,*
> *while proving the capacity which he ever manifested to rise to*
> *every demand of the occasion, qualified him for the problems*
> *which he was called to face a few years later.*
>
> PAUL SELBY, *ANECDOTAL LINCOLN*

SOMETHING ABOUT DOUGLAS's reference to the "resolutions" of the 1854 Springfield Republican meeting gnawed at Robert Hitt as he sat on the train back to Chicago. The resolutions, as Douglas read them, made Illinois Republicanism sound like a Medusa of abolitionist radicalism. But Hitt could remember no such resolutions ever having been adopted by a Republican state convention. It had been Republican policy that "the less new resolutions our friends adopt, probably the best," and Lyman Trumbull judged it better for Republicans even "to say nothing about the admission or non-admission of any more slave states. It will be time enough to decide that question when it arises."

So in the process of transcribing the balance of the shorthand notes he had with him, Hitt decided to err on the side of caution rather than deadlines, and once in Chicago, he had the back files of the *Chicago Tribune* pulled so that he could compare Douglas's version of the Springfield resolutions with the printed version in the *Tribune.* John Locke Scripps found the 1854 Springfield resolutions and began reading them. "Hold on," interrupted Hitt. "That's not it at all." And it was not: the original meeting of the Illinois Republicans in Springfield in October 1854 had indeed adopted resolutions, but they were substantially milder in their antislavery tone and were clearly not the resolutions Douglas had read from his notebook. What had Douglas been reading then? "There followed a long search of the files," Hitt remembered, and "at length they were found." Douglas had been reading the resolutions of an obscure county meeting of abolitionists in Aurora, in the rock-ribbed northern forty-sixth district, not a state Republican platform.[1]

There is no evidence that this was anything other than an honest mistake on Douglas's part. Douglas had a vague recollection of a radical abolitionist platform of some sort being adopted by Republicans, although he knew of it only secondhand, from his loyal midstate lieutenant, Thomas Harris, who was running for Congress as a Douglasite from the Sixth Congressional District. As part of the "elaborate preparations" he made for the Ottawa debate, Douglas wrote on August 15 to Charles Lanphier of the *State Register,* asking if he remembered a speech given by Harris in 1856 about "a resolution, described as adopted at the first state Convention of the Black Republican party as a part of their platform." Lanphier dutifully looked up the speech and found that, indeed, Harris had cited the text of the resolutions from the Aurora meeting.

But Harris also claimed that the Aurora resolutions had been adopted by the state convention and every other Republican county convention in Illinois, and that was not true. It was not Douglas's fault that Harris had gotten the report wrong, or that Lanphier had passed it along without pressing more deeply for clarification. But on Monday the twenty-third (the first press day after the Ottawa debate), Charles Wilson's *Chicago Journal* ran a banner story on Stephen A. Douglas's "forgery," followed by a companion piece the next day in the *Chicago Tribune*, and from that moment, the Republican papers paraded the kind of indignation at Douglas's "BASE FORGERIES" which belonged to the commission of a felony. "What shall we say of the cause that needs support of such a desperate expedient as that which we have detected?" declaimed the *Tribune.* "What of the man, who, indebted to the people of Illinois for everything that he has been and is, attempts to delude and mislead them by a cheat?"[2]

Douglas was making a quick swing from Ottawa up to Galena to campaign for Hiram Bright, the Democrats' forlorn hope candidate for Congress in the First District, when the story broke. His first instinct was simply to admit that he had been misled: "In 1856, I heard Major Harris . . . read these resolutions and say they were adopted by the Republican Convention." His second, characteristically, was to bluff. Even if they turned out not to be the resolutions of the Republican state convention, weren't they what everyone had "abundant reason" to expect from the Republicans? "It matters not," added the Douglasite *Jacksonville Sentinel* on August 27, "at what place the Republicans adopted those resolutions. . . . *Mr. Lincoln dare not repudiate one of them.*" Still, it was a chip at Douglas's credibility, and one of Lincoln's central Illinois correspondents exulted that "these things well worked up and thoroughly brought before the people will give us 10,000 votes which otherwise are sure for Douglas."[3]

Douglas had another credibility problem looming at the same time, because just above the *Sentinel*'s so-what reply on the twenty-seventh, another article appeared that questioned the accuracy of the debate transcriptions from Ottawa published by Hitt in the *Tribune* and by Sheridan and Binmore in James Sheahan's *Chicago Times.*

Shorthand is not an exact science, and attempting to transcribe speeches given on the fly, and in the open air, with noise, interruptions, and the occasional gust of breeze to spin papers and ink across a table, did not make it any more exact. It did not help, either, that the bitter partisan spirit of the *Tribune* and the *Times* gave the reporters every encouragement to a perform a subtle rounding-up of the speaking of each papers' favorite and a corresponding carelessness in recording the words of the other. The variations that resulted were little more than a word or phrase here or there; as far as they affected the meaning of what Lincoln and Douglas were saying, they were inconsequential. But there were lots of them, and their triviality did nothing to prevent Sheahan from accusing the *Tribune* of prettifying Lincoln's "bad rhetoric and horrible jargon," or Medill and Ray from accusing the *Times* of deliberately garbling Lincoln. (The *Tribune* actually printed samples from both papers' reports in parallel columns to demonstrate the extent of "this infamous work.") The *Chicago Journal* chimed in on August 30 with the accusation that "the *Times* hugely garbles, interpolates and burlesques Mr. Lincoln's speech," and finally the *State Journal* concluded that this was all surely a deliberate plot on Douglas's part: "The fellow Benmore is assigned the task of reporting Lincoln's speeches . . . incorrectly, to leave out words and sentences, and otherwise to mutilate his arguments so as to destroy their force and effect on the minds of those who read the Douglas papers." This probably would have required more talent, or at least imagination, than Binmore, "a complete fop and a fool," actually possessed. But Hitt believed that the *Times,* if not Binmore himself, "treated Lincoln in a way . . . to make Lincoln ridiculous," and the result was to create "great sympathy for Lincoln" as the underdog.[*]

These efforts to cloud Douglas's credibility were matched by the sniping fire the senator continued to receive from Buchanan loyalists. The Republican state committee did "not anticipate much from" the Buchananites, but any votes they took away from Douglas were a gift to Lincoln, and so they had "been encouraging the Buchanan men as much as possible and stimulating them to organize." William Herndon's brother Elliott was high in the Buchanan counsels, and he became a back door through which encouragement, and sometimes money, was funneled to the Buchanan Democrats. "They make 'no bone' in telling me what they are going to do," Herndon reported with satisfaction, and that included nominating rival candidates to the Douglasites in five out of the nine congressional races, four out of the twelve state senate contests, and nine of the fifty-eight state house districts. In the southernmost districts, the Douglasites lost control of the nominating process altogether. Buchananites in the ninth state house district successfully deadlocked the nominating convention through three separate meetings and finally forced the nomination of John G. Powell, the county sheriff, for the state house. "They are all split to splinters," reported a gleeful Republican to Lincoln, and the losers walked away "swearing they would rather vote for the blackest Republican in Ills. The Lord keep & preserve them in their good intentions." A Buchanan convention in Springfield on September 7 featured ferocious attacks on Douglas and his followers as "bolters"—bolting, in other words, from loyalty to the national party—and ex-governor John Reynolds "mellowed the whole by . . . a solemn appeal to the faithful to stand by the regular organization, through thick and thin, until the Douglas Bolters were anxious to creep back and beg for re-admission." In other districts, Democratic nominees tried to sit on the fence. In the Fifth Congressional District (which took in the westernmost counties of the Whig Belt), Jacob Davis announced himself as a challenger to the Douglas candidate, Isaac Morris, but promised he would run as "a Democrat, not a Buchanan or a Douglass Democrat, but . . . for the party." No matter how much they owed Douglas, all but the most ardent Douglasites could not forget that an office "worth 10,000 a year" is "an object sufficiently large to enduse any Politician to play the mock friend of Buchanan—*$40,000 four years salary, Only think of it!!!*"[5]

The Buchananites did not stop there. Buchanan loyalists imitated Lincoln's follow-up strategy by following Douglas themselves from meeting place to meeting place to "feed the Senator with worm-wood." R. B. Carpenter pursued Douglas to Clinton two weeks after Douglas and Lincoln had spoken there, staged a meeting at the county fair-grounds "with musick banners Carriages & an old soldier marked 76," and spoke for two hours on why "property in slaves was recognized by the constitution, and that it was an unfair co-partnership if the South could not take her property into the territories as well as the north." Both Douglas's popular sovereignty and Lincoln's notion of congressional restriction were "dangerous to the welfare and perpetuity of the Union," Carpenter declared. Buchanan lent a hand personally by dispatching Louisiana senator John Slidell, a Buchanan loyalist and avowed enemy of Douglas, "as a secret top general," and Slidell suggested making political hay out of the Mississippi plantation Douglas held as a trustee for the sons of his first wife. It took no time at all for the Buchananites to make Douglas into an outright slave owner who starved his slaves and rented them out "like farm animals."

But their most direct challenge to Douglas came in the form of a rival nominee for the Senate, former U.S. senator and Illinois Supreme Court justice Sidney Breese. Born in New York, Breese had held almost every judicial and legislative seat Illinois had to offer—state legislature, circuit judge, supreme court, speaker of the state house—and was one of the prime movers in obtaining the land preemptions which funded the construction of the Illinois Central Railroad. But he had been bumped from prominence as Illinois's most influential Democrat by the ambitious climb of Stephen A. Douglas, and Breese had never forgiven the Little Giant for it. The Buchananites began tempting Breese to announce himself as a rival candidate to Douglas in late August, arguing that "your own popularity, in addition to our known advantage would render 'assurance doubly sure' and we would have the opportunity of teaching a lesson to the man who stole the glory from you." It was a temptation Breese could not resist, and on September 10, he announced himself as a candidate for the Senate and went to work in the Eighth Congressional District to get Philip B. Fouke, an Alton Democrat who resented Douglas's failure to endorse him, nominated by the Democratic district convention.[6]

These defections caused both personal and political pain to the Douglas campaign. "Things are in a bad way here," one Douglasite manager confided to Charles Lanphier, after a longtime Douglas loyalist, Rufus Miles, turned coat to Buchanan in order to get the Democratic nomination in the fifty-eighth state house district. "He has for twelve years been my best friend—& I have to fight him." The Democratic state committee struggled to shift front against the Buchananite eruptions, denouncing them as "Buchaneers" or "Danites" (after the shrine set up in I Kings 12 at Dan, to rival the shrine at Bethel in Israel—"And this thing became a sin: for the people went to worship the one even unto Dan") and recruiting Douglas candidates to take the stump against them. "The Danites held a convention at Monticello," reported one Douglas man to the Little Giant on August 30, but "I spoke for a few minutes after the Convention adjourned" and "knocked the wind out of their sails" by arguing that "the Common Enemy"—in this case, "Lincoln & his niggerisms"—required a united front.

But it proved difficult to spit into Buchanan's wind. The Democratic state committee was forced to throw rookie volunteers into the gap, recruiting young men of "gentle innocence of ability" and "maidenly timidity" to wade into "the saloon of some sturdy German" or "truculent Hibernian" and address them "with 'many holiday and lady terms.'" One party worker reported to Charles Lanphier that Vice President Breckinridge, Lazarus Powell, and Beriah Magoffin were all willing to campaign for Douglas. But when state committee chairman John Moore invited them, they only sent kindly endorsement letters, and Breckinridge denied that he had ever intended "to visit Illinois and address the people in the present canvass." By the end of August, Douglas was beginning to sweat. Although he assured Jacob Brown that "I have no such fears as you seem to entertain that it will not be possible for me to sustain my position," he still urged Brown to persuade his neighbor the ex-Whig lawyer Usher F. Linder "to take the stump immediately" and from "that time until the election." To Linder, Douglas was even more direct: "Lincoln and myself hold a joint discussion at Freeport on Friday the 27th of this month. . . . For God's sake, Linder, come up into the Northern part of the State and help me. Every *dog* in the State is let loose after me."[7]

It might have given Douglas a small consolation to know that Lincoln was having similar troubles. By endorsing him as "the first and only choice of the Republicans of Illinois for the U.S. Senate," the Republican state convention had banished any anxiety that Lincoln was going to be tossed aside in order to reward Douglas for opposing the Lecompton constitution. But this did not dispel his suspicion that he was being left to look out for himself without serious help or encouragement from the national party. Joseph Medill tried to solicit help from Thomas Corwin and Benjamin F. Wade of Ohio, and Caleb Blood Smith of Indiana, "but without success."

The state committee was more successful at persuading Owen Lovejoy, Richard Oglesby, John M. Palmer, a new Missouri convert to Republicanism, Frank P. Blair (whose brother Montgomery had been a member of Dred Scott's legal team), Carl Schurz of Wisconsin, Schuyler Colfax of Indiana, and the Ohio Republican governor, Salmon P. Chase, to take speaking tours across the prairie. But William Henry Seward, the party's presumptive presidential nominee in 1860, made no effort to speak publicly on Lincoln's behalf, nor did Lincoln's old friend Orville Hickman Browning. (Douglas's chief lieutenant, William Richardson, happily confirmed that Browning "will not labor very hard to help Lincoln to a vote.") "Long John" Wentworth spent the summer with his family in Troy, New York, and did not return to campaign for Lincoln until October; in the meanwhile, he was communicating privately with Isaac Cook and the Buchanan Democrats in the hope that, if the Buchananites elected enough legislators in November, Wentworth could come forward as a compromise candidate and finally overthrow Douglas himself.[8]

Politics is not so much the art of the possible as it is the art of the probable, and Republicans who believed that the national party was likely to win the 1860 presidential election, and who had heard "Judge

Douglas . . . bidding high for the nomination," would think twice about incurring the Little Giant's wrath by taking to the campaign trail against him, especially if he not only won the Senate in 1858 but became the party's figurehead later on. By the same token, too much of Lincoln's support in the state committee and the convention sounded like duty and obligation rather than confidence. "It was," recalled Carl Schurz, "well-known that Lincoln at the time did not have the sympathy and countenance of all Republicans in the country, nor even in his own state." He was respected; he was liked, even admired. But he had the reputation of being a loser, and it does not look well in politics to lay your money on a slow horse. "Mr. Lincoln . . . is a man of inflexible political integrity," wrote the *National Era*, but it may be that "he is too open, too honest, to succeed." The Democratic newspapers were less complimentary but just as calculating: "Hon. Abe Lincoln is undoubtedly the most unfortunate politician that has ever attempted to rise in Illinois. In everything he undertakes, politically, he seems doomed to failure." Another sneered that, in 1855, Lincoln "had been diddled out of the place of Senator by the friends of Judge TRUMBULL, and the same thing may happen to him again." [9]

The mention of Lyman Trumbull touched what was possibly the rawest nerve in Lincoln's campaign. Born in Connecticut in 1813, Trumbull was related to three governors of Connecticut, the great Revolutionary painter John Trumbull, and (on his mother's side) to the aristocracy of New England's clergy, back to Cotton Mather. Trumbull had been a Democrat. But he openly opposed Douglas's Kansas-Nebraska policy, and in the Senate, he turned into one of the sharpest thorns in Douglas's side. As the beneficiary of Lincoln's bow-out in 1855, Trumbull told John M. Palmer that "I certainly feel it a duty and shall take pleasure in standing by [Lincoln] to the utmost of my ability." Yet there were a good many Illinoisans, including Stephen A. Douglas, who were inclined to see Lincoln as little more than a proxy for Trumbull, conducting a statewide referendum on Douglas in anticipation of Trumbull's own upcoming reelection fight for the Senate in 1860. [10]

And despite his promises and his friendly letters of advice, Trumbull did not exactly rush to Lincoln's aid. The Senate adjourned on June 16, and Douglas opened his campaign on July 9 in Chicago, but Trumbull made no stir to come west until August. As he told his brother, John, "We are comfortably situated" in Washington, and "intend remaining here for some time." Those plans changed only after Norman Judd upbraided him: "You ought to come to Ills as soon as you can . . . and come by way of New York and straighten out the newspapers there." I *"suppose I must do so,"* Trumbull unenthusiastically admitted, but even then his principal motivation was not to help Lincoln but to hinder Douglas, "for it will never do to let him [Douglas] be re-elected, if we can help it," and he complained from Illinois to his wife that "it would be much more in accord with my feelings to come to you. . . . I am almost miserable with a desire to be with you."[11]

Once on the ground in Illinois, Trumbull proceeded to campaign as though Lincoln hardly existed. He told one Buchanan supporter that "he would never have consented to return from the east and go upon the stump had he not felt certain that Lincoln had no chance of success under any circumstances." And his first speech, at the Tremont House in Chicago on August 7, was a "fierce, malicious, vituperative, and scandalous" attack on Douglas, but without a single reference to Lincoln. "We are for leaving the question of slavery, where it exists in the States, to be regulated by the States as they think proper," Trumbull said, but "we are for keeping the Territories which belong to the United States free from the invasion of slavery"—and not a word about electing Lincoln. Or even agreeing with him: unlike Lincoln, who did not believe that the nation could "endure permanently half slave and half free," Trumbull was perfectly willing to have the territories, "when they become States . . . deal with their black population as they shall think best." Nor did he have anything to say about Lincoln in subsequent speeches.

Nonetheless, the state central committee ordered 25,000 copies of Trumbull's "crushing speech against the Pro-Slavery Party and the

'Artful Dodger.'" Trumbull's list of "appointments" appeared in the *Chicago Journal* alongside Lincoln's, as though they were running in tandem, and a Boston newspaper ran its report on the Illinois campaign under the headline ILLINOIS, TRUMBULL AND DOUGLAS, as though Lincoln were not running at all. Stephen Hurlbut, who was running as one of the paired Republican candidates in the fifty-fourth state house district, assured Trumbull that his district stood "firm" for Trumbull first, "Douglas next & Buchanan nowhere." As late as September, tale-bearers in the Douglas camp were whispering that Trumbull "considers [Lincoln] a dead dog, and therefore has no objection to appear as his disinterested friend and supporter, in order that he may reconcile himself with Lincoln's friends, who have cherished a bitter hatred for him ever since he cheated long Abe in 1856." He would need that reconciliation, too, because if Lincoln lost in 1858, Lincoln's "friends" would make a Trumbull renomination in 1860 exceedingly difficult. On the other hand, it was just as possible that Trumbull and Breese, both veteran Democrats, would come to "an understanding" and "in the event of their being able to control a majority in the Legislature, Lincoln is to be overthrown and Breese made United States Senator."[12] Unless Lincoln could somehow get out from under Trumbull's shadow, he might well end up as a spectator at his own political funeral.

But one beneficial thing Trumbull could do was make trouble for Douglas. "Mr. Trumbull was a political debater, scarcely, if at all, inferior to either Lincoln or Douglas," and he knew more about the turns and twists Douglas had performed in the Senate than any other Illinois Republican. One of the most damaging was a maneuver Trumbull had witnessed shortly after entering the Senate, in June 1856. It was the height of the fury over Kansas, with John Brown carving his murderous way along Pottawatomie Creek and a three-way civil war supperating among federal troops and proslavery and antislavery bands. Georgia senator Robert Toombs proposed a compromise bill to put an end to the horrors. It was one of several bills on the floor (including one by Trumbull, to terminate Kansas's territorial status and start

Trumbull had watched Douglas and the bill in the Senate, and he seized on "the record on the Toombs Bill" to show "the object of those who had broken down the barrier to slavery in the Territories." This stung Douglas past all point of restraint: "The miserable, craven-hearted wretch!" the senator exploded. "He would sooner have both his ears cut off, than to make the charge to my face." But the Republicans were delighted, and the Toombs bill now became a weapon for hecklers at Douglas's meetings. Trumbull "crowds his colleague very hard," wrote one, "harder, we think, than Mr. Lincoln has done in any of his published speeches." [14]

The revelation about the Toombs referendum gave Lincoln another proof of Douglas's insincerity; but the unflattering comparison to Trumbull was a reminder that Trumbull, not Lincoln, would get the credit for it, and that could hardly have pleased Lincoln. Already, his old ex-Whig allies, starting with Browning and David Davis, were grumbling at the way direction of the campaign had been taken over almost entirely by the Chicago ex-Democrats on the Republican state committee. "This campaign has not been managed right," Davis complained on August 18 to the committee's treasurer, Ozias Mather Hatch. It should have been "composed of men of intellect and accustomed to a political campaign" and headquartered "at Springfield"—in the Whig Belt, of course. But it was not, and now they would pay for it. Davis organized a Lincoln meeting at Tremont, in the Whig Belt's thirty-ninth state house district, on the afternoon of August 14, and "really not over 50 persons" apart from the townspeople attended. "No enthusiasm," Davis snarled, "& friends generally dispirited" until Samuel Parks "made a speech generally directed to the old Clay Whigs."

But the state committee had complaints of its own about the progress of Lincoln's campaign. Whatever the public hurrahs about Lincoln's performance in Ottawa, Judd and the other members of the committee were convinced that their candidate had to abandon his defensive postures and come out swinging at Douglas in the next debate.

"I have my view of the means to dispose of" Douglas, Lincoln insisted on August 23. But he yielded to Judd's anxieties enough to ask for a meeting with Judd on his way to the August 27 debate in Freeport. In the meantime, Lincoln spoke at rallies in Henry, Galesburg, Augusta (where he had to speak in "a beautiful grove near the town limits" in a drenching rain), and Macomb, in the western end of the Whig Belt, doing what irked Judd the most, "repelling the charges . . . that he was an 'Abolitionist,' in favor of 'negro equality,' and 'amalgamation,'" [15] and in general wiping Douglas's mud all over him rather than off him.

This was not what Judd and the committee wanted to see or hear, and when they met with Lincoln at Mendota, a junction stop on the Illinois Central line with the Chicago & Aurora rail line, they told him so. Judd, accompanied by Ebenezer Peck, had gone first to Freeport to meet Lincoln. Hearing that Lincoln had stopped in Mendota in order to allow the Republican arrangements committee to stage a triumphant entry into Freeport the next morning, they took the night train down and arrived at two in the morning. They woke Lincoln up at his hotel, "went up into his bed room, and had our talk with him there" while Lincoln sat on the "side of the bed in his short night shirt." Lincoln wanted to stand pat and make his answers to Douglas's seven Ottawa questions the substance of the debates; the committee wanted him to start asking questions of his own.

Joseph Medill and Charles Ray sent along letters in the same spirit: "Don't act on the *defensive* at all . . . be *bold, defiant* and *dogmatic* . . . in other words, give him hell." By all means, reply to Douglas's questions, but do it "briefly and quickly." Then, "put a few ugly questions at Douglas" of your own. A series of eight such "ugly" questions had already been drafted by Charles Wilson of the *Journal* (where Wilson published them on the twenty-fourth), and they included gems such as *Do you believe that the people of a Territory, whilst a Territory, and before the formation of a State Constitution, have the right to exclude slavery?* If so, how can that be reconciled with the Supreme Court's declaration that neither Congress nor a territorial legislature can ban slaveholders from taking slaves into federal territories? *Do you indorse and approve the doctrine of the Supreme Court in the Dred Scott case?* Then how, Stephen, are you different from James and Roger and all the other minions of the Slave Power? *Can slaves be lawfully excluded from the Territories?* Sure, Stephen, you can claim that the people of the territories, exercising their popular sovereignty, can refuse to pass the police codes legalized slavery requires, but is that *lawful* in the face of *Dred Scott?* Or is it just another hopeful wish that will turn out to mean nothing?

Medill had a few questions of his own for Lincoln to toss at Douglas: *Do you care whether slavery be voted up or down? What becomes of your vaunted popular sovereignty in Territories since the Dred Scott decision? will you stand by the English bill compromise* [guaranteeing a referendum on Lecompton]? *Having endorsed Dred Scott, will you endorse a similar Supreme Court decision which applies to the States?* Lincoln "listened very patiently to both Peck and myself," recalled Judd, "but he wouldn't budge an inch from his well studied formulas." [16] They would go back with him to Freeport on the morning train, but they had no reason to sleep the sleep of the saved.

The first phase of the campaigns, which ended at Ottawa, had lasted for nearly a month, from July 17 to August 21. The second phase would be significantly shorter, and the lead-in time to the second debate at Freeport was shorter still. Douglas made only one appearance before Freeport (on August 25 in Galena); Lincoln took his swing down to Galesburg, Augusta, and Macomb, but he had to double back northward quickly to make his date with Douglas in Freeport.

Freeport was the county seat of Stephenson County, which sat along the western end of the band of six counties bordering Wisconsin. It was difficult to get much farther north in Illinois than Freeport, and the town's politics showed it. This was the First Congressional District, where Elihu Washburne had reigned since 1852, first as a Whig, then as a Republican; John H. Addams (the father of the famous

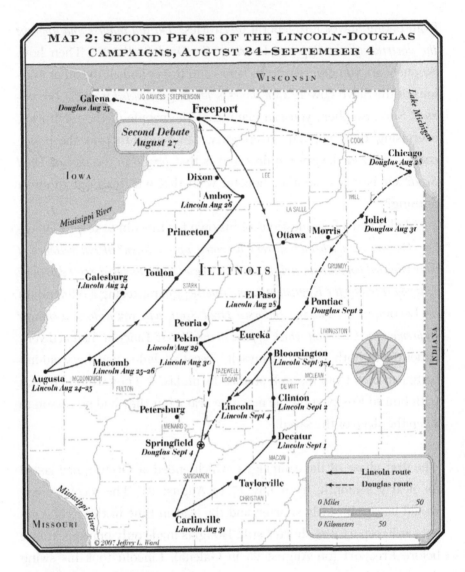

MAP 2: SECOND PHASE OF THE LINCOLN-DOUGLAS
CAMPAIGNS, AUGUST 24–SEPTEMBER 4

WISCONSIN

Galena
Douglas Aug 25

JO DAVIESS · STEPHENSON

Freeport

*Second Debate
August 27*

COOK

Chicago
Douglas Aug 28

Lake Michigan

IOWA

Dixon

LEE

Amboy
Lincoln Aug 26

WILL

LA SALLE

Joliet
Douglas Aug 31

Princeton

Ottawa   Morris

Mississippi River

Galesburg
Lincoln Aug 24

Toulon   ILLINOIS

STARK

GRUNDY

El Paso
Lincoln Aug 28

Pontiac
Douglas Sept 2

Peoria

Pekin
Lincoln Aug 29

Eureka

LIVINGSTON

INDIANA

Macomb
Lincoln Aug 25–26

MCDONOUGH

Lincoln Aug 30

Bloomington
Lincoln Sept 3–4

MCLEAN

Augusta
Lincoln Aug 24–25

TAZEWELL
LOGAN

DE WITT

Clinton
Lincoln Sept 2

FULTON

Petersburg

Lincoln
Lincoln Sept 4

MENARD

Springfield
Douglas Sept 4

Decatur
Lincoln Sept 1

MACON

SANGAMON

Taylorville

Lincoln route
Douglas route

CHRISTIAN

0 Miles   50

MISSOURI

Mississippi River

Carlinville
Lincoln Aug 31

0 Kilometers   50

© 2007 Jeffrey L. Ward

Chicago settlement-house reformer Jane Addams) sat for Freeport in
the state senate, and John A. Davis represented Stephenson County (as
the fifty-second state house district) in the statehouse. In 1856,
Stephenson County had given Frémont a whopping majority of 1,907
votes over Buchanan's 1,308, with only 50 votes for Fillmore; John A.
Davis did nearly as well, garnering 1,892 votes over his Democratic

rival's 1,450. It was, in other words, as safely Republican as any district could be.

The town's beginnings were in a solitary log cabin built in 1835, and by 1840, it numbered only 491 souls. But like much of the north part of the state, Freeport was undergoing a growth spurt in the 1850s, with an influx of immigrants from other northern states that doubled the settlement's population between 1855 and 1860. A good deal of that growth was Freeport's reward for sitting alongside the Galena & Chicago Union Railroad, which had a trackage agreement with the Illinois Central from Mendota to Galena, allowing the Illinois Central free use of the smaller line and direct access to Freeport. The town's 1857 business directory (which listed forty-eight dry-goods stores, seven shoe stores, five carriage makers, nine "commission merchants," three auction houses, and twelve hotels) was its own testimony to its embrace of the Whig, and now Republican, principles of small business, finance, and markets.[17]

Lincoln arrived at Freeport between nine and ten o'clock on a train "with twelve cars full" of supporters who had met him at Amboy and was met at the Illinois Central station (on the east side of Freeport) by the Republican arrangements committee, chaired by the town's mayor, Thomas J. Turner. A small cannon boomed a welcome, and Turner made a brief speech. From there, a parade marched Lincoln to the Brewster House, an impressive four-story hotel with iron balconies and a barbershop, opened by John K. Brewster only the year before. (Stephen and Adele Douglas were already in Freeport, having arrived the evening before; they rode to the Brewster in a "procession of 75 torches," and the Little Giant made "a short address from the Brewster House balcony.") Lincoln walked into the Brewster lobby "with one long, lank arm around a friend whom he had not seen for some time," shook hands through a crowd in the lobby, and went "with half-a-dozen friends" upstairs to his room, where he continued to hold court. "He was surrounded all the forenoon by sturdy Republicans, who had come long distances, not only to hear him speak, but to see him, and it was esteemed the greatest privilege to shake hands with 'Honest Old Abe.'"

The easy access to Freeport provided by the Illinois Central guaranteed another good crowd, and by eleven o'clock, "a train of eighteen passenger cars, filled as full as they could hold," arrived from Rockford, followed by another from Galena with "eight cars" and a sixteen-car special from Winnebago "with over one thousand persons!" Meanwhile, streams of local traffic were pouring into town, and "all the main streets, back streets, lanes and by-ways of Freeport, appeared to be literally alive with men." The town converted a corner of the courthouse square into a public barbecue, where "the carcasses of three beeves were being roasted over a ditch about six feet wide and six feet deep and free sandwiches were being served." The weather was not particularly cooperative: "chilly, cloudy, and lowering. Alterations of wind, rain and sunshine filled up the forenoon." But that did not prevent between ten and fifteen thousand people from squeezing into Freeport, and the free barbecue ensured that "whoever failed to obtain a good dinner, must have wanted the stomach to digest it."[18]

The arrangements committees had cleared a vacant lot one block north of the Brewster House for the debate and erected a three-foot-high square platform "of rough boards" with seats for the debaters, the two moderators (James Mitchell for the Democrats, Mayor Turner for the Republicans) and the arrangements committees, and the stenographers. Improvised benches had been nailed together for general seating, and by two o'clock "the place was jammed with humanity, and tugging and pulling and fighting to get up near the platform." Douglas dressed royally for the occasion—"a ruffled shirt, a dark blue coat with shiny buttons, light trousers, and well-polished shoes"—so, to draw a contrast between Douglas and the simplicity of Lincoln, Mayor Turner and his committee hired a plain, high-sided lumber wagon for five dollars from "an old drunken note-shaver and skinflint" to drive their candidate to the debate grounds. A plank had been set crosswise on the sides of the wagon for Lincoln to sit on and be seen, although what he looked like, perched on his plank seat, more nearly resembled "the skeleton of some greyhound" than a U.S. senator.

The crowd the wagon had to work through was a much rowdier one than in Ottawa. A "number of street and saloon fights" broke out. Chester Dewey complained in his report for the *New York Evening Post* that "the newspaper gentry have to fight a hand-to-hand conflict for even the meagerest chance for standing room," and the confines of the vacant lot were so tight that Robert Hitt, the stenographer, was having trouble elbowing his way to the platform. Thin-faced James Mitchell, the chair of the Democratic arrangements committee, demanded that the debate start promptly at two o'clock, and after a brief introduction from Mayor Turner, Lincoln had to spend his first two minutes offering a slow, long-winded opening—*Fellow . . . citizens . . . On . . . Saturday . . . last . . . Judge . . . Douglas . . . and . . . myself . . . first . . . met . . . in . . . public . . . discussion*—to give Hitt a chance to get himself in place.[19]

By the terms of their agreement, Lincoln was to speak first for an hour at Freeport, followed Douglas for an hour and a half, and then a half-hour reply from Lincoln. He came up to the apron of the platform "with his hands held clumsily behind his back," and when he announced "in a voice that nobody could hear" that he intended to reply to Douglas's "seven distinct interrogatories" at Ottawa, "a sense of disappointment" crackled through the crowd. He turned once to Douglas to ask if the Little Giant was interested in "saying 'yes' or 'no' right now." But Douglas made no response, so out came a small notebook, with the Ottawa "interrogatories" pasted in from the *Chicago Times*. It was a dreary recitation:

- *Do you advocate "the unconditional repeal of the Fugitive Slave Law"?* "I do not now, nor ever did, stand in favor of the unconditional repeal of the fugitive slave law."
- *Will you vote against the admission of any further territories to the*

Union as slave states? "I do not now, nor ever did, stand pledged" against territories which wanted slavery after they became states.

- *Will you oppose the admission of a slave state to the Union, even if the people want slavery in their state constitution?* "I do not stand pledged against the admission" of territories as slave states, if that is what comes out at the end of the territorial process.

- *Will you vote to abolish slavery in the District of Columbia?* "I do not stand to-day pledged" to abolishing slavery in the District.

- *Will you vote to prohibit the interstate slave trade?* "I do not stand pledged" to prohibit the interstate slave trade.

- *Will you vote to ban slavery in all the western territories, above or below the Missouri Compromise line?* "I am . . . pledged to a belief in the right and duty of Congress to prohibit slavery in all the United States Territories," a pledge which, whether anybody noticed it or not, rendered moot both the second and third questions, since a congressional ban on slavery in the territories would guarantee that no territories ever would develop as potential slave states.

- *Will you vote against any more territorial annexations* (like the Mexican Cession) *unless slavery is first banned from them?* "I am not generally opposed to honest acquisition of Territory."[20]

It looked odd for Lincoln to answer the second and third interrogatories in a way which sounded exactly like Douglas's popular sovereignty doctrine. But he hastened to add that saying he was "not pledged" to any of these measures was only to answer "the exact form" of Douglas's questions. If Congress acted first to ban slavery in the territories (which he *was* pledged to), then the second and third questions would never arise. Any territory which went slaveless through the territorial process and would then "do such an extraordinary thing as to adopt a Slave Constitution" might as well be allowed to, but Lincoln doubted whether this was likely to happen. He would not favor abolition of slavery in the District of Columbia, but he was perfectly willing to vote for emancipation there if the emancipation plan "should

be gradual . . . should be on a vote of the majority," and "that compensation should be made to unwilling owners." As for the interstate slave
trade, he was "not pledged" to its abolition simply because no one had
ever thought to ask him about it before.

It was a favorite strategy of Lincoln's, in the courtroom, to give
"away 6 points" in a case, then turn and hang the case and the opposing
counsel "on the 7th." The overconfident opposition would then see,
"when the whole thing is unravelled," that what Lincoln "was so
blandly giving away was simply what he couldnt get & Keep." Lincoln
"traded away every thing which would give him the least," and concentrated on the one point which would win him the case. But if this was
the strategy he was following at Freeport, then never had he seemed to
give away so much. The Fugitive Slave Law was a splinter in the eye of
every antislavery Northerner; but it was based on the Constitution's
provision for the return of "persons held to service," and so Lincoln
gave that away. He had once designed a bill to abolish slavery in the
District of Columbia, but not without a referendum in the District, and
so he gave that away. This was giving away so much that Henry Villard
sensed a "tumult among the 'republican' part of the audience," who believed that Lincoln had "repudiated the whole 'republican' gospel." But
they, and Villard, had missed the crucial sixth answer—the "right and
duty of Congress to prohibit slavery in all the United States Territories." This was the real keystone, the point on which Lincoln opposed
Dred Scott and popular sovereignty, and beside which all the others
were simple consequents. And what was more, he now had questions of
his own. Lincoln was about to go on the offensive at last.[21]

There is no record of when Lincoln decided to stop parrying
Douglas's blows and start landing a few himself. The fact that these
questions were scrawled in pencil on a slip of paper which he pulled
from his inner coat pocket, rather than his carefully stocked notebook
of clippings, suggests some degree of hasty improvisation. The four
questions he had written out were not even particularly novel, since all
were curiously similar to the questions which Charles Wilson had pub-

new slave states, new slave senators, and new slave representatives to Congress.[22]

Lincoln was now in free-swinging mode. One member of the crowd
remembered the characteristic "forking forward of his right forefinger . . . furrowing the air with that gesture," and "rising on his toes and
then jamming his heels down on the boards." He rounded on Douglas
over the Aurora resolutions "forgery," denying any association with or
responsibility for what had turned out to be the proceedings of an un-
connected caucus of abolitionists. In this case, Douglas had been not
merely wrong but deliberately, foolishly, and recklessly wrong. "Judge
Douglas did not make his statement upon that occasion as matters that
he believed to be true, but he stated them roundly as being true, in such
form as to pledge his veracity for their truth." If he could, after twelve
years in the Senate and "world-wide renown," show such carelessness,
what else could he be trusted to say? Douglas denied being part of a
conspiracy "to nationalize and spread slavery as being a good and
blessed thing." Was he careless about that, too? Douglas had still not
given an explanation of why he voted down the Chase amendment,
"that the people of the Territory should have the power to exclude
slavery if they saw fit." If Douglas was so devout a believer in popular
sovereignty, voting down the Chase amendment made no sense; but it
did make "perfectly rational and Intelligible" sense if Douglas "had it in
contemplation" that the Supreme Court would follow the Kansas-
Nebraska bill with the *Dred Scott* decision. "If it was done for a reason
different from this, he knows what that reason was, and can tell us what
it was. I tell him, also, it will be vastly more satisfactory to the country,
for him to give some other plausible, intelligible reason why it was
voted down than to stand upon his dignity and call people liars."[23]

This was not the Lincoln that Douglas had seen at Ottawa, nor
was the crowd as quiescent when Lincoln sat down and Douglas came
forward to reply. A small boy wiggled up onto the platform and un-

self-consciously hopped onto Douglas's lap, then traded places for Lincoln's lap when it was Douglas's turn to speak. (Half a century later, the boy, Thomas R. Marshall, would be the vice president of the United States.) Douglas crossed the stage and "was welcomed with . . . some hisses," and "some villain" shied a piece of melon at the Little Giant, which glanced off his shoulder. The catcalls and heckling were so fierce that Douglas had to stop and remind the crowd that "nothing is more honorable to any large mass of people assembled for the purpose of a fair discussion, than that kind and respectful attention that is yielded not only to your political friends, but to those who are opposed to you in politics."

When the hooting quieted down, Douglas congratulated Lincoln on finally cranking around to respond to the questions at Ottawa; he, however, would do better, and respond to Lincoln's four questions on the spot. First: if at any time Kansas wanted to reapply for admission to the Union with a freely chosen state constitution, Kansas should be able to do so. If it was a proslavery constitution, Douglas did not care, although he was quick to point out that he did not expect a freely chosen Kansas constitution to be proslavery. If Kansas "has population enough to constitute a slave State, she has people enough for a free State." Second: the strategy of "unfriendly legislation" *was* a lawful method to keep slavery out of a territory. "I answer emphatically, as Mr. Lincoln has heard me answer a hundred times from every stump in Illinois, that in my opinion the people of a territory can, by lawful means, exclude slavery from their limits prior to the formation of a State Constitution." Douglas did not understand why Lincoln was asking this question—Lyman Trumbull had asked Lincoln's question on the floor of the Senate in 1856, and Douglas had repeated his answer all through the Lecompton debates, won endorsements for it from Southern moderates, and reiterated it most recently in his whistle-stop in Bloomington a month before. "Mr. Lincoln knew that I had answered that question over and over again," and it puzzled Douglas what Lincoln was getting at.[24]

The wind was whipping up, making it difficult to hear Douglas, and that, in turn, only made the hecklers more restless. He interrupted his own chain of answers to deal with the Chase amendment, insisting that the Nebraska bill had already given "the full power and the full authority over the subject of slavery . . . to introduce it or exclude it," and Chase had only offered his amendment "for the identical purpose for which Mr. Lincoln is using it, to enable demagogues in the country to try and deceive the people." Then he came back to the third of Lincoln's questions: what would Douglas do if the Supreme Court hatched a new *Dred Scott* decision, this time preventing the free states from banning slavery? The question was ridiculous, Douglas pouted. "I am amazed that Lincoln should ask such a question." The Supreme Court would never dream of invading the sovereignty of the states. "It would be an act of moral treason that no man on the bench could ever descend to." (Seven weeks later, when Douglas made the same assertion in the final debate, at Alton, a voice would sing out of the crowd, *The same thing was said about the Dred Scott decision before it passed*, a voice which Harry Jaffa wrote "may well pass as the true voice of the muse of History.")

And so Douglas stalked past the third question and entered into the fourth: what about new accessions of territory? "I answer that whenever it becomes necessary, in our growth and progress to acquire more territory, that I am in favor of it, without reference to the question of slavery, and when we have acquired it, I will leave the people free to do as they please, either to make it slave or free territory, as they prefer"—a lovely restatement of popular sovereignty without any attention to the unpleasant fact that the most likely new additions to the American Union would be Cuba, where slavery was legal, and Central America, where it would be profitable.[25]

That took care of Lincoln's questions, and while Douglas was at it, wasn't it funny that his opponent could come up with only *four?* Perhaps Lincoln needed to consult with Lovejoy, or even with Frederick Douglass, to gather more—and that gave the Little Giant the opening he wanted to flaunt the race card again. "The last time I came here to make a speech," he said, recalling an incident from a speaking tour in northern Illinois in 1854, "I saw a carriage . . . drive up" in which "a beautiful young lady was sitting on the box seat, whilst Fred. Douglass and her mother reclined inside, and the owner of the carriage acted as driver." Imagine: a white man and white woman playing the roles of servants, while a black abolitionist and a white woman "reclined inside." If they liked this sort of arrangement, with "the nigger . . . on a social equality with your wives and daughters" or riding "in a carriage with your wife, whilst you drive the team," then they should vote for the "Black Republicans." This drove the crowd into a frenzy, some with "laughter, cheers," and others with cries of *Right, what have you to say against it, what of it?* [26]

Taunting the crowd energized Douglas; he "walked back and forth on the platform swinging his arms, shaking his head until his rather long hair fairly stood on end." So what if the Aurora resolutions had nothing to do with Lincoln? He was objecting to them only because they weren't "adopted on the right 'spot.'" And so out came Lincoln's Mexican War "spot" resolutions. "He declared the Mexican war to be unjust and infamous"—Douglas laughed—"because he said that American blood was not shed on American soil in the 'right spot.'" So here we go again with Lincoln: "He cannot answer the questions I put to him at Ottawa because the resolutions I read were not adopted at the 'right spot.'" Breezing straight past his own carelessness about the Aurora resolutions, Douglas conceded that "it may be possible that I was led into an error as to the spot on which the resolutions I then read were proclaimed." But identifying the "spot" was as irrelevant and pettifogging to this campaign as Lincoln's "spot" objections had been to the Mexican War. "I . . . am not in error as to the fact of their forming the basis of the creed of the Republican party when that party was first organized," Douglas asserted.

He was being more and more "frequently interrupted" as he baited the crowd—every time he used the phrase *Black Republican,* angry voices screamed *white, white*—and his hour and a half was running out, so Douglas turned finally to his mainmast argument: "Lincoln on the one hand and Trumbull on the other, being disappointed politicians . . . formed a scheme to abolitionize the two parties and lead the Old Line Whigs and Old Line Democrats captive, bound hand and foot into the Abolition camp." ("That's exactly what we want," roared a voice from the crowd, but Douglas only seemed to enjoy provoking his listeners and shook his fist at them, roaring back, "I know that the shoe is pinching you. I am clinching Lincoln now and you are scared to death for the result. . . . I have seen your mobs before, and defy your wrath.") Lincoln said he would not repudiate the Fugitive Slave Law, or vote down new slave states. But that was not the platform of Black Republicanism; Lincoln accused Buchanan, Pierce, and Taney of conspiracy, but Lincoln had cooked up an alliance between "his supporters and the federal office holders of this State, and Presidential aspirants out of it, to break me down at home." Lincoln said he didn't intend to provoke civil war between North and South; but what else did the talk of a "house divided" mean except the violent dissolution of the Union? Lincoln was a schemer who wanted "to divide the Democratic party, in order that he may defeat me and get to the Senate"—and in midstride, Douglas's time ran out "and he stopped on the moment." [27]

Lincoln stood up, unwrapped the green shawl he was wearing, and handing it to one of the arrangements committee members, said, "There, Father Brewster, hold my clothes while I stone Stephen." His first task, however, was to silence the hubbub Douglas had caused. "In regard to Judge Douglas' declaration about the 'vulgarity and black-guardism' in the audience—no such thing, as he says, was shown by any Democrat while I was speaking," and a Republican audience needed to find its manners. Once quiet prevailed, Lincoln asked whether it was not time for Douglas to put to bed the business of abolitionist resolutions and Lincoln's consistency with them. "It is true that many of these resolutions are at variance with the positions I have here assumed," he admitted. But why was that so newsworthy? In 1854, when Douglas introduced his Nebraska bill, it seemed like "a new era" was "being introduced in the history of the Republic, which tended to the spread and perpetuation of slavery." People rose up in opposition to the Nebraska bill, "but in our opposition to that measure we did not agree with one another in everything." It was not until the Bloomington convention in 1856 that "we at last met together" and the full-bore abolitionists agreed "to yield" their abolitionism to create a common front. Any Republicans in the fifty-second district who were unhappy with "my views" because they were only "partly coinciding with yours" were perfectly free to vote for . . . Douglas.[28]

Douglas complained that his Ottawa questions had not been answered. "If it can be pointed out to me how I can more fully and fairly answer him, I aver I have not the sense to see how it is to be done." Douglas complained that he had been unfairly linked to Buchanan, unfairly quoted, unfairly represented in the Buchanan newspapers. But that, Lincoln remarked, was only because "the Judge's eye is farther south now." A whoop of laughter went through the crowd, because they knew what Lincoln was getting at. Douglas's presidential ambitions, and only those ambitions, made him interested in playing up his opposition to Lecompton in front of Northerners. "His hope rested on the idea of visiting the great 'Black Republican' party" whereupon he would turn Republican and place himself at the head [of] our organization." But Republicans were wiser than that, and so Douglas was once again promising serene indifference to whether popular sovereignty resulted in slavery or freedom. "He is crawling back into his old camp, and you will find him eventually installed in full fellowship among those whom he was then battling, and with whom he now pretends to be at such fearful variance."[29]

The crowd wanted more, but, Lincoln concluded, "my time has expired." The debate broke up as noisily as it had assembled, and at the Brewster House, Owen Lovejoy stood at the top of the front steps and delivered "one of the most powerful speeches that has been made in this campaign." That evening, Lovejoy spoke again at a rally at the

Freeport courthouse (where the barbecue pit had been dug that morning), and by Henry Villard's unsympathetic lights, he "gave in front of a crowd of political fanatics one of the most excessive rhetorical gaffes I have ever had the questionable pleasure to listen to." [30]

And for Freeport, the grid looks thus:

LINCOLN	DOUGLAS
Responds to Douglas's Ottawa questions	
Poses four questions, including the Freeport Question (No. 2)	Answers Lincoln's questions: No. 2, that the people of a territory *can* exclude slavery, No. 4, that we should always encourage new territory, whether slave or free
Denies that Aurora resolutions are Republican platform—corollary: Douglas is deceitful	Lincoln is making much ado about nothing over the Aurora resolutions
Douglas's failure to accept Chase amendment to Kansas-Nebraska bill shows ulterior motive	Chase's amendment was unnecessary
	Lincoln endorses the *spirit* of the Aurora resolutions even if not endorsing the letter
	Lincoln advocates racial equality
	Lincoln betrayed his country in the Mexican War
	Lincoln and Trumbull are conspiring to abolitionize the old parties
Denied	The House Divided speech means the dissolution of the Union
	Lincoln falsely accuses two presidents and the Supreme Court of conspiracy

No part of the Lincoln-Douglas debates has entered more firmly into American legend than Lincoln's second Freeport question. Thirty-seven years afterward, Joseph Medill explained, in an article for the *Chicago Tribune*, that Lincoln was writing a far vaster script at Freeport than anyone had expected, and that the second question— *Can the people of the United States Territory, in any lawful way, against the wishes of any citizen of the United States, exclude slavery from it limits prior to the formation of a State Constitution?*—was part of a larger, secret strategy of Lincoln's to win the White House in 1860. If Douglas answered *no*, then his popular sovereignty doctrine would deflate like a shot balloon and it would be apparent to everyone that he had no real plan to stop the expansion of slavery into the territories; that would be fatal to his chances for reelection in Illinois in 1858. And if he could not be reelected there, his political career, and his ambitions for the presidency, were over.

But, Medill warned Lincoln, if Douglas answered *yes*, as his doctrine of popular sovereignty dictated, it would "open the door through which Senator Douglas will be enabled to escape from the tight place in which he finds himself on the slavery question in this State." True, Lincoln had conceded. But he would run that risk. An affirmation by Douglas that popular sovereignty could stop slavery in its tracks would cost the Senator every Democratic vote in the South, and that would extinguish once and for all his long-denied hopes for the presidency in 1860. Over the protests of Medill and the other members of the Republican state committee who met Lincoln before the Freeport debate, Lincoln sacrificed his own aspirations for the Senate in 1858 in order to head off Douglas's designs on the White House in 1860.

Douglas responded at Freeport as Medill had feared he would, with a *yes*. But Lincoln, according to Horace White's chapter on the debates in John Locke Scripps's campaign biography of 1860, waved the significance of this aside: that would get Douglas votes in Illinois in 1858, but not across the nation in 1860, and Lincoln claimed to be "killing larger game. The battle of 1860 is worth a hundred of this." By this means, Lincoln was shown to possess a Christ-like willingness to sacrifice himself for the sake of principle, just as he would for the nation seven years hence. But even more, he was showing a supernatural prescience not only about the senatorial election but of a presidential election, because *he* would be Douglas's opponent for the presidency in 1860, and the senatorial election he sacrificed in 1858 would lead to a victory over Douglas for the presidency in 1860. Norman Judd, who retailed a version of this story to William Herndon "soon after the assassination of Mr. Lincoln," was clear that *larger game* meant that Lincoln was covertly announcing, "I am a candidate for the Presidency of the U.S. of America. That is what I am fighting for."[31]

This was all too melodramatic to be believed. For one thing, Medill claimed that his discussion with Lincoln had taken place on the train "from Macomb to Freeport" on the morning of the Freeport debate. Lincoln's train, however, did not go from Macomb to Freeport: Judd and Ebenezer Peck met with Lincoln in *Mendota* the night before the Freeport debate. Mendota is ninety miles south of Freeport, which would give a steam-powered locomotive just enough time—at least three hours—to pull a twelve-car train to Freeport that morning and have Lincoln there at the time all accounts agree he arrived, between nine and ten o'clock. Macomb is 180 miles away, and even at top 1858 speeds, Lincoln would have had to begin a journey from Macomb to Freeport at two in the morning—which is when Judd and Peck were waking him up, according to Judd's 1876 reminiscence to John G. Nicolay. For another, Medill claimed that he had strongly advised Lincoln not to ask the second question and, once in Freeport, had enlisted Judd and Elihu Washburne in the same cause. But far from Medill trying to dissuade Lincoln from asking the Freeport Question, his letter to Lincoln just before the Freeport debate urged him to ask precisely that question: "What becomes of your vaunted popular Sovereignty in Territories since the Dred Scott decision?"[32]

More to the point, however, the Freeport Questions were not original with Lincoln, nor did he imagine he was damaging Douglas with

the Southern Democrats by asking them. From his own correspondence during the campaign, it was evident to Lincoln that Douglas's
obsession with popular sovereignty had already cost him any hope of
swaying the hardpan Southern Democrats. "He cares nothing for the
South he knows he is already dead there," Lincoln wrote to Henry Asbury on July 31. Ask him the question about the lawfulness of "unfriendly legislation," Lincoln (quite accurately) predicted, and "he will
instantly take ground that slavery can not actually exist in the territories, unless the people desire it, and so give it protective territorial legislation. If this offends the South he will let it offend them; as at all
events he means to hold on to his chances in Illinois." Nor was Douglas
surprised when the question was asked at Freeport. He had been
warned that "there is a determination on the part of the republicans to
ask you . . . whether, under the Dred Scott decision, in your opinion,
the territorial legislature would have power to prohibit slavery." [33]

But why, then, did Lincoln bother to ask the question at all? Clark
Carr, who debunked the Medill story in 1909, could only suggest
that Lincoln was simply trying "to make up and so plainly define the
issues of the campaign that they would be clear to everybody." Certainly, the Buchananites were delighted to have Lincoln show how
much Douglas had betrayed party doctrine. One Buchanan partisan
exulted to Sidney Breese, "We know that at Freeport he took ground
that a territorial legislature could exclude slavery whilst it is the position of our party that so long as it is in a territorial condition being the
'property' of all . . . the people of any state may go there with any kind
of property they may possess." And it is true, as David Donald remarks, that forcing Douglas to repeat this answer yet again, and in a
public forum where shorthand reporters were, for the first time, taking
down every word for the telegraph, sent Southerners into raging
tantrums, so that from that point on, regardless of whether Douglas
had articulated it before, his answer became "the Freeport doctrine." [34]

What does not go away so gently is the repeated claim that
Lincoln's eye, in asking this Freeport Question, was on the election of

1860, either denying the presidency to Douglas or gaining it for him-self. The first published version of the *larger game* story appeared as early as 1860 in John Locke Scripps's campaign biography of Lincoln, and again in 1866, in Isaac Arnold's *History of Abraham Lincoln and the Overthrow of Slavery*, based on what Arnold had been told "by a friend of Mr. Lincoln." This "friend" was probably Norman Judd, who gave much the same account to Herndon during the interviews Herndon conducted in 1865 and 1866 for a planned Lincoln biography. There is simply too much testimony—from Gustave Koerner, from Horace White, not to mention Herndon, Judd, and Arnold—that Lincoln re-ally did expect the second Freeport Question to deny Douglas the presidency, and that he was "fighting for bigger game." But unless we grant that Lincoln actually did possess some occult prevision, how can we reconcile his own statement that Douglas was already "dead" in 1858 with the need to kill him all over again at Freeport? And why should Lincoln have thought that deliberately taking a fall in 1858 would make him a suitable candidate for a Republican presidential nom-ination in 1860? Unless, of course, the presidency Lincoln thought he was denying Douglas was not a Democratic one but a Republican one.[35]

No political rumor took on more undeserved life between Doug-las's defiant anti-Lecompton speech in February and the beginning of the debates in Illinois than the anticipation "that Mr. Douglas was coming over to the republican party as fast as he could carry his fol-lowers with him, and that his extraordinary hold upon the masses of the democratic party at the North would enable him to bring to the re-publican ranks a reinforcement which would prove irresistible at the approaching presidential election." Irresistible, of course, to everyone but Abraham Lincoln, whose closing comment at Freeport gave vent to his irritation that Douglas had been planning to "turn Republican and place himself at the head of our organization." A Douglas presi-dential candidacy "supported by the Republicans" would, wrote one of Douglas's backers, garner Douglas "three-fourths if not more of all the Votes cast in this state" and would constitute a "complete 'coup

meeting. "About one half of his time was pleasantly . . . occupied in talking familiarly and often eloquently to his old Whig friends," especially about all the campaigning he had done as a Whig in the 1840s. He swung southward the next day to Carlinville, where the Macoupin County Republicans were having their convention, and spoke for two hours "in the grove just south of town." News of the debate at Freeport, and especially the Freeport Question, elated the Macoupin Republicans. "Douglas's answer to Lincoln's question amounts to nothing more or less than *Mob Law* to keep slavery out of the Territories." Lincoln himself was feeling confident enough at Carlinville to bring back his natural-equality argument against slavery. "Negroes have natural rights . . . as other men have," Lincoln declared, and on that basis alone, slavery was an assault on natural law that no appeal to popular sovereignty could justify. Blacks may not have the same *civil* rights as whites in Illinois, but civil rights come and go as communities change and develop; slavery, however, is a denial of the natural right to liberty guaranteed by the Declaration of Independence, and "no sane man will attempt to deny that the African upon his own soil has all the natural rights that instrument vouchsafes to all mankind." [38]

Macoupin County was not the only place where Lincoln's performance at Freeport had put a second wind into Republican lungs. "Everything is going on in first rate order here," Ozias Hatch chortled to John C. Bagby from Springfield. When Judd and the state committee met in Springfield to give directions "for the entire canvass of the State" to the nine Republican congressional candidates, they *"resolved to carry the State"* and asserted that "Lincoln's election can now be considered as certain." One of Hatch's correspondents, returning from the East Coast, said he had been led "to think that modern democracy was sweeping like a tornado all before it & that the Republicans were paralyzed & thunderstruck." But once he "got into Ill . . . the political horizons began to brighten." That Hatch's friend had been hearing about the Illinois senatorial election as far away as the East Coast was remarkable enough, but it was now becoming the talk of the continent.

The full texts of the Ottawa debate were in the East Coast papers by August 26, and they were making "every one East look with great anxiety to our Elections," Jackson Grimshaw informed Hatch. "The canvass now going on in Illinois is probably the most exciting and earnest that ever preceded a State election in the Union," remarked an Indianapolis newspaper three days after Freeport; five days later, the editor of the pro-Douglas *Boston Ledger* wrote privately to the Little Giant to tell him that "public interest in New England intensifies in the canvass now going on in Illinois." In Virginia, "great interest" in Douglas's reelection and "triumph over that Black Republican Lincoln . . . prevails all over the state." And the out-of-state "newspaper gentry" were astounded at the "tropical intensity" they found within Illinois.[39]

All over the state, the multiple layers of candidates and elections were fermenting madly. During the third week of August alone, two congressional districts and the twenty-fifth state house district held nominating conventions; and several of these contests were beginning to take their cue from the debate model being followed by Lincoln and Douglas. In the Ninth Congressional District, the Douglas Democrat, John A. Logan, and the Republican Benjamin Wiley had "agreed to stump the District together." Chester Dewey wrote that "it is astonishing how deep an interest in politics this people take."

> *Over long dreary miles of hot and dusty prairie, the processions of eager partisans come—on foot, on horseback, in wagons drawn by horses or mules; man, women, and children, old and young; the half-sick just out of the last "shake"; children in arms, infants at the maternal front, pushing on in clouds of dust and beneath a blazing sun; settling down at the town where the meeting is, with hardly a chance of sitting, and even less opportunity for eating, waiting in anxious groups for hours at the places of speaking, talking, discussing, litigious, vociferous, while the roar of artillery, the music of bands, the waving of banners, the huzzas of the crowds, as delegation after delegation appears . . . combine to render the occasion one scene of confusion and commotion.[40]*

Lincoln and Douglas arrived in Springfield on September 4, when both the Danite and Douglasite nominating conventions for Sangamon County were to meet. The campaigns were beginning to wear on both of them. The state committee was running Lincoln ragged with appointments and connections: "Get from Bloomington or Clinton to Monticello by private conveyance," read one directive. "Monday after noon after speaking, go to Bement take the night train to Tolono. The morning train will take you to Mattoon. There you will have to remain until one oclock, when you can get to Paris so as to arrive at half past 2 oclock, a little late it is true, but time enough, if they know you are coming— By this plan, you will be at Mattoon from 6 oclock A. M to one oclock." He caught sleep between events by stretching out on train seats and wrapping his cloak around him "till his long legs and arms were no longer in view."

By the time he spoke to a rally at Pekin on August 29, Lincoln looked "jaded and worn down." By September, he told Julian Sturtevant that "if it were not" for knowing "that if Mr. Douglas's doctrine prevails, it will not be fifteen years before Illinois itself will be a slave state . . . I would retire from the contest." Douglas traveled easier "in his private car . . . enjoying all the luxuries of the period," but he had far less physical stamina. He was railing at stop after stop about "niggers, nigger equality, and amalgamation," and he began reinforcing himself with brandy. (One observer at Freeport thought he "had evidently been drinking very strongly . . . during the day of this great debate.") Both candidates needed the weekend to recover, but both also needed to set off on the following Monday, September 6, for what was going to become the third phase of the campaigns.[41]

The third debate in the series had been scheduled for Jonesboro, which meant that the campaigns' third phase would feature an enormous loop southward to the first state house district, the southernmost district in all of Illinois and one of the state's most staunchly Democratic preserves, and then a swift jump backward to the Whig Belt for the fourth debate, at Charleston. With nine days before the meeting in Jonesboro, both Lincoln and Douglas worked their way through the Whig Belt, Douglas splitting eastward and Lincoln westward. On Monday Lincoln spoke at Monticello, where three to four thousand turned out with two brass bands and "banners almost innumerable":

DON'T LEAVE ME BUCK!—ABE WANTS *MY PLACE.*
I'M FOR THE ENGLISH BILL NOW!

DOUGLAS'S POLITICAL HISTORY IN THREE SHORT WORDS:
"HURRAH FOR *ME!*"

Two days later, Lincoln was in Paris, in the twenty-fourth state house district, where he "spoke for two hours with unusual power and effect." But then he crossed westward over the Whig Belt to Edwardsville, in the fourteenth district, where he was welcomed by his old Whig ally Joseph Gillespie, along with the Madison Guards and the Edwardsville Band. This was Lincoln's first campaign stop in the district, and here he was in the deepest trench of old Whig stubbornness. Some of the Whig holdouts were organizing under the forlorn banner of the Know-Nothings, and Gillespie was sufficiently nervous about the tar of abolition being painted on the Republican party that he advised the district's Republicans to organize under the title of "People's Party." Anxious to play up his Whig credentials, Lincoln "commenced his speech by referring to his former connection with the old Whig party; a connection of twenty years."[42] But not even for Gillespie would he hide his antislavery light under a bushel: "he don't propose to make the black the equal of the white," but he still believed that "the Declaration of Independence" should apply "to the black as well as white, and should be received as a political axiom." Whatever was done or not done about civil equality, fastening "the chains of bondage" on black people only meant that "you have lost the genius of your own inde-

MAP 3: THIRD PHASE OF THE LINCOLN-DOUGLAS
CAMPAIGNS, SEPTEMBER 4–SEPTEMBER 23

pendence and become the fit subjects of the first cunning tyrant who rises among you."[43]

Meanwhile, Douglas was spraying as much abolitionist muck on Lincoln as possible. Arriving in Jacksonville on September 6, he attacked Lincoln as a "lying, wooly-headed abolitionist," and when he zigzagged over to Carlinville on the eighth, he denounced "the rottenness of the compact by which Lincoln and Trumbull, in 1854, agreed to disorganize their respective parties," until a violent rain shower cut

him off and "mollified . . . the effects of bad whiskey." He made a whistle stop across the Mississippi in St. Louis to work on Illinoisans who
were attending the St. Louis Agricultural & Mechanical Association
Fair, then worked his way down to Belleville and finally Chester on
September 13. That evening, Douglas, Adele, and the rest of his traveling staff boarded the St. Louis–Memphis riverboat *James H. Lucas* and
steamed down to Cairo, at the very southern tip of the state.[44]

At any other time, this would have been Douglas territory. In 1852,
the first state house district gave the Democrat Franklin Pierce 1,372
votes for the presidency against only 386 for the Whig candidate, Winfield Scott; an antislavery third-party candidate garnered exactly 1. In
1856, the turnout was almost comic: Buchanan won 2,157 votes for the
presidency while Frémont walked away with only 82; John Dougherty,
running for the district seat in the state legislature, handily beat off not
one but two challengers. But this was 1858. Southern Illinois (which
had been nicknamed "Egypt" from the presence of Cairo as its principal commercial center) had been a Democratic stronghold for longer
that Stephen A. Douglas had been in politics, and its underlying loyalties were to the national party. Dougherty had turned into one of the
prime movers of the Danites, and Douglas was being warned, through
Thomas Harris's contacts, that two of the state senators from districts
in "Egypt" had secretly "given in their allegiance to the Administration." Douglas could not afford "to let the opposition get a foothold in
Egypt," wrote Samuel S. Marshall, who had represented Egypt in
Congress in 1856. "If they do the State is gone beyond redemption." So
the Douglas loyalists were doing their best to paint the Republicans
"as occupying the strongest kind of abolishion grounds," and "they
also dig up the Skeletons of all those who died on the plains of Mexico and attempt to prove . . . that they all died at the hands of *Abe
Lincoln*."[45]

Despite the Danites and the damage Cairo sustained in the June
floods, "great preparations were made for a reception and ball" at the

Taylor House on the evening of September 14. Adele Douglas, "never weary of service in the cause of her noted husband," danced with all the local notables, and in a display of Democratic egalitarianism, even pitched in afterward with cleanup in the Taylor House kitchen. (Adele was a good trouper; privately, she loathed Illinois and wrote her mother that "you can never imagine until you come here how forlorn one feels after being accustomed to interesting & very refined people.") Usher F. Linder, whose help Douglas had begged on August 22 ("For God's sake, Linder . . ."), had finally appeared at St. Louis (after Douglas promised to pay his expenses), and at Cairo they joined forces with Samuel Marshall and the Democratic congressional district candidate, John Logan.

The next morning, a six-car excursion train, with Douglas's palace car and the little brass cannon on its flatbed attached behind, set off on the thirty-five-mile trek up the line to the all-temperance station stop of Anna. From there, with "Professor" Joseph Terpnitz's brass band at their head, they would march in triumph into Jonesboro.[46]

Jonesboro was the county seat of Union County, one of the oldest counties formed in Illinois. The town itself was incorporated in 1821, and in 1858 it had just finished a new brick courthouse. But Union County was among the poorest in the state, and its adult illiteracy rate was over 45 percent (compared with the statewide average of 16.5 percent). Its population numbered less than ten thousand, and the other two counties which formed the first state house district had scarcely half that between them. The planners of the Illinois Central stunted Jonesboro's growth even more by routing the ICRR's main line northward (from Cairo to Centralia) a mile and a half to the east, through the village of Anna. (Jonesboro would not get a rail connection until 1875, and its population in 1858 was under one thousand.) Taken as a whole, Egypt had the state's highest concentration of people born in slaveholding states (nearly 40 percent) and its most hostile attitudes toward blacks. Frémont had gotten only 4 percent of Union County's vote in 1856, and across the counties of Egypt, votes for Republicans rarely made it out of the low two figures.[47]

Lincoln came down the Illinois Central to Anna on the afternoon of September 14, staying with David L. Phillips, the Republican congressional candidate from the Ninth Congressional District (which embraced the eighteen southern counties of Illinois), while the *Tribune*'s team, Robert Hitt and Horace White, put up for the night at the Union Hotel. Phillips was an odd man out in Egypt: his parents had emigrated from Massachusetts, and he was a cousin of the abolitionist Wendell Phillips. As the rare abolitionist in Egypt, he had a wryly practical view of the political possibilities Lincoln faced in Jonesboro: "The Buchanan folks will give you a cordial welcome on the score of undying hostility to Douglas," but there was little more than that to be expected. Lincoln could hardly disagree. He had marked Union County as one of the places where there was "no use in trying," and only Douglas's designation of Jonesboro for one of the debates had drawn him this far south. There were no committees of well-wishers to deal with, so Lincoln drove to Jonesboro in the morning to look over the debate location and returned just in time for the Douglas train to pull into the Anna station with its little howitzer banging. The Little Giant "stepped forth, waved his hand," climbed into "a carriage prepared for hire," and set off for Jonesboro with the Terpnitz band and the brass howitzer in tow.[48]

This time, there was no great procession, neither for Douglas nor for Lincoln. A "speaking stand" was set up at the county fairgrounds a half mile north of the courthouse with the little howitzer unlimbered beside it, while "Professor" Terpnitz ("in a tall plug hat" and "rather long-tailed coat") and his band blared and thumped their way onto the grounds. Only about a hundred people had been on hand to greet Douglas at the Anna station, and in Jonesboro the townspeople looked on lethargically—not only were the Buchanan loyalists undisposed to show up for Douglas's benefit, but the Illinois State Fair had opened

the day before up the Illinois Central line in Centralia, and that pulled
still more of Union County's thin population away from the debate. A
Buchananite banner billowed in the breeze:

> MY SON, IF BOLTERS ENTICE THEE,
> CONSENT THOU NOT

At least there was none of the rowdiness which had punctuated the
Freeport debate: "There was no attempt made to interfere with either
of the speakers and all went orderly and well." But this was largely because there was none of the same turnout. The crowd which shuffled
out to the fairgrounds was probably no more than fifteen hundred
strong.[49]

This time, Douglas had the opening speech. But without a respon-
sive crowd to feed on, Chester Dewey thought Douglas was unin-
spired: "The delivery was very bad—a sort of school boy monotone."
The senator led off, as he had at Ottawa, with the "two great political
parties known as Whig and Democratic" as they were in the halcyon
days of 1854. Since then, however, "the Whig party has been transformed into a sectional party, under the name of the Republican party"
and "all men of Abolition . . . principles, no matter whether they were
old Abolitionists or had been Whigs or Democrats, rally under the sectional Republican banner."[50]

How had this happened? Because "certain restless, ambitious, and
disappointed politicians . . . took advantage of the temporary excitement created by the Nebraska bill to try and dissolve the old Whig
party and the old Democratic party, to abolitionize their members and
lead them, bound hand and foot, captives into the abolition camp." The
chief culprits in managing this transformation in Illinois were, of
course, Abraham Lincoln and Lyman Trumbull. They believed "that
hereafter no more slave States should be admitted into this Union,
even if the people of such State desired slavery; that the fugitive slave
law should be absolutely and unconditionally repealed; that slavery

should be abolished in the District of Columbia; that the slave trade should be abolished between the different States, and, in fact, every article in their creed related to this slavery question."

This bargain was supposed to have secured the Senate for Lincoln in 1855, but Trumbull had played "a yankee trick" on Lincoln and won the seat himself. In 1858, Trumbull and the "abolitionized Democrats"—and Douglas named a mixture of ex-Democrats and Danites, "John Wentworth, of Chicago, Gov. [John] Reynolds, of Belleville, Sidney Breese, of Carlisle," and most noteworthy of all, "John Dougherty, of Union"—were obliged to back Lincoln. This was, Douglas claimed, why the state Republican convention nominated Lincoln "as the 'first, last and only choice' of the Republicans for United States Senator," to "quiet Lincoln's suspicions; and assure him that he was not to be cheated by Lovejoy, and the trickery by which Trumbull outgeneralled him" in 1855.[51]

Douglas expended more than half an hour on the Trumbull-Lincoln conspiracy charge, and only then did he turn and "invite your attention to the chief points at issue between Mr. Lincoln and myself in this discussion." The first among those "chief points" was the House Divided speech and the assertion that slavery and freedom could not go on together in the Union, one half one way and the other half the other. As he had in Chicago and at Ottawa, Douglas simply asked, *Why not?* "Why can it not last if we will execute the government in the same spirit and upon the same principles upon which it is founded?" That was the way the Founders had constructed the Union in the beginning, and if it was good enough for them, and had been good enough the seventy years afterward, why not for the indefinite future? "It has stood thus divided into free and slave States from its organization up to this day," Douglas declared.

It was not slavery which was rending the Union but the agitation which the abolitionists had stirred up in Congress. The Supreme Court, "a tribunal established by the Constitution of the United States," had tried to settle the dispute in the *Dred Scott* decision, but

Lincoln "makes war on the decision." And he indulges this contempt
for the absurd reason that "it deprives the negro of the rights of citizenship." *The Negro? rights? citizenship?* This was ridiculous: "I hold
that this government was made on the white basis, by white men, for
the benefit of white men and their posterity forever, and should be administered by white men and none others." However, just because "a
negro is not your equal or mine," that does not mean "he must necessarily be a slave." That, Douglas asserted, "is a question which each
State of this Union must decide for itself." But if any "State of this
Union" did so decide, Douglas knew of no rights he shared with blacks
which would cause him to object. And if Lincoln and his kind would
only let the people of the territories, like the people of the states, make
up their own minds by popular sovereignty, the national harmony the
Founders had established would once more prevail.[52]

David Phillips stood up to introduce Lincoln, who came forward
with only a short three-point outline in his hand:

> *Brief answer to his opening.*
> *Put in the Democratic Resolutions.*
> *Examine his answers to my questions.*[53]

Just as he had at Ottawa, Lincoln began giving away the points he considered unnecessary to defend. "In so far as he has insisted that all the
States have the right to do exactly as they please about all their domestic relations, including that of slavery, I agree entirely with him." He
even agreed that slavery ought to be treated in "the way our fathers
originally left the slavery question." Where they parted ways was on
Douglas's fundamental premises, that the Founders had envisioned a
republic in which slavery and freedom cohabited forever, like two parallel lines stretching into infinity and that the territories had the same
self-determining autonomy as the states. "I say when this government
was first established it was the policy of its founders to prohibit the
spread of slavery into the new Territories of the United States, where

it had not existed," not to tolerate it. "Judge Douglas and his friends have broken up" the Founders' real expectations; and even worse, they have placed slavery on the path to becoming what the Founders had never dreamed of at all, "to become national and perpetual."[54]

Lincoln also had no difficulty joining with Douglas in saying that there should "be a variety in the different institutions of the States of the Union. . . . I agree to all that." The difficulty came when they had to examine what those "institutions" were. If it was only a question of growing sugar in Louisiana or making flour in Illinois, then Lincoln had no more objection to diversity than Douglas. These differences have never "produced any difficulty amongst us." But when we consider slavery, "have we not always had quarrels and difficulties over it?" And when would they cease? Only when slavery was put back into the box the Founders had created for it. It was not the agitation of antislavery fanatics which made an issue out of slavery, but the determination of slaveholding profiteers to trample on the original design of the Founders. And it was only when Douglas lent his hand to helping them through the Nebraska bill and popular sovereignty that slavery put North and South at each other's throats. "Whenever it has been limited to its present bounds and there has been no effort to spread it, there has been peace." Americans had, therefore, no right to "hope that the trouble will cease—that the agitation will come to an end—until it shall either be placed back where it originally stood and where the fathers originally placed it, or on the other hand until it shall entirely master all opposition." Douglas and his popular sovereignty doctrine, by turning a cheerful indifference to whether any future states went for slavery or freedom, was obviously not going to give people the latter.[55]

This was logical and fluent, but it was also bland and abstract. Lincoln did, however, have one new line of argument he wanted to try out: *Put in the Democratic Resolutions.* "At the suggestion of friends," Lincoln decided to read off "some resolutions and the like of abolition caste, passed by Douglas friends, some time ago, as a Set-off to his attempts of a like character against me." Two could play the game of embarrass-the-candidate-with-his-friends, and since Douglas thought there was political tar in the "production of those Springfield Resolutions at Ottawa," Lincoln wanted to know how well certain Democratic resolutions tarred his opponent. "Judge Douglas has . . . spoken of the platforms for which he seeks to hold me responsible." But the Illinois Democrats had not one but two platforms—one for the Douglasites, adopted in April, and the other for the Danites, adopted in June. It made as much sense to hold Douglas accountable for the Danites as it did for Douglas to look "up resolutions of five or six years ago, and [insist] that they were my platform, notwithstanding my protest that they are not, and never were my platform." In 1850, the Democratic candidate for Congress in Elihu Washburne's First District, Thompson Campbell, had responded to a series of "interrogatories" similar to Douglas's at Ottawa and gave exactly the answers Lincoln gave. What kind of a Democrat did that make Thompson Campbell—or Stephen A. Douglas? And there was another candidate in another district, plus a convention in the fifty-sixth state house district, and even a Democratic newspaper in DeKalb, announcing that "we have ever been rather in favor of the equality of the blacks"—all of them Democratic and all of them from 1850. So if Douglas wanted to play the resolutions game, he had better be prepared to answer for his own party. "I will say I do not think the Judge is responsible for this . . . but he is quite as responsible for it, as I would be if one of my friends had said it. I think that is fair enough."[56]

Finally, Lincoln had reminded himself to "examine his answers to my questions" at Freeport:

- *Would Douglas vote to admit Kansas to the Union if it came back with another proslavery, Lecompton-like constitution?* "He does not give any answer which is equivalent to yes or no—I will or I won't," and he finally makes "such statements as induce me to infer that he . . . will, in that supposed case, vote for the admission of Kansas." And Kansas will become a slave state.
- *Can the people of a territory, in any lawful way, exclude slavery before*

the formation of a state constitution? Douglas believed "that it can be done by the Territorial Legislature refusing to make any enactments for the protection of slavery in the Territory." But how was this to be squared with *Dred Scott*, which made it clear that such "enactments" mean depriving the slave owner "of that property without due process of law"? And, what was more, it occurred to Lincoln that "history" itself "shows that the institution of slavery was originally planted upon this continent without these 'police regulations' which the Judge now thinks necessary for the actual establishment of it."[57]

Lincoln now had only about fifteen minutes left, so he dropped the third and fourth Freeport questions and turned to a new question he wanted to add to the others: *If the slaveholding citizens of a United States Territory should need and demand Congressional legislation for the protection of their slave property in such territory, would you, as a member of Congress, vote for or against such legislation?* In other words, if slaveholders moved into a territory and found that their way was hampered by "unfriendly legislation," could they appeal to Congress to enact a *federal* slave code—and would Douglas vote for it? And if so, how would that sit alongside the Supreme Court's declaration that Congress had no business passing legislation binding the territories on the question of slavery? Either way, just as at Freeport, Douglas stood to lose: if he answered *no*, he further aggravated the South; if he answered *yes*, he alienated free-Soilers. (The idea for this question had come in a letter Lyman Trumbull sent to Lincoln the day before; Trumbull thought "this would effectually use him up with the South & set the whole proslavery Democracy against him.")[58]

Douglas now charged to the front, speaking rapid-fire and in no "monotone." He had not brought up the Aurora resolutions merely to embarrass Lincoln but to establish the direction in which the Republican party's compass was pointing and make Lincoln "avow whether or not he stood by the platform of his party." The exact details of who constructed it, where they constructed it, and when they constructed it were irrelevant. "Mr. Lincoln cannot and will not deny that the doctrines laid down in these resolutions were in substance . . . voted for by a majority of his party, some of them, if not all, receiving the support of every man of his party."

Take the first of the questions he had posed to Lincoln at Ottawa, "whether he would vote to admit any more slave States into the Union." This had been adopted by "a majority of all the counties of this State which give Abolition or Republican majorities," and Douglas merely wanted to know whether Lincoln stood by that. Lincoln said he was not *pledged* to that position. "The Abolitionists up North" interpreted "this answer" to mean that he was "not committing himself on any one territory now in existence," but in "Egypt," he was vague enough on this point that people were allowed to think he would always stand that way in the future. "Men running for Congress in the northern districts" take "that abolition platform for their guide," but "Mr. Lincoln does not want to be held to it down here in Egypt and in the centre of the State, and objects to it so as to get votes here."[59]

The same thing was true about Lincoln's denial of the "abolitionizing" conspiracy. Lincoln swore that no evidence of any such conspiracy existed. But it was "beyond denial" that Lincoln was once a Whig and "then undertook to Abolitionize the Whigs and bring them into the Abolition camp," just as "Trumbull up to that time had been a Democrat, and deserted, and undertook to Abolitionize the Democracy." And "they are both now active, leading, distinguished members of this Abolition Republican party, in full communion."

Lincoln was practicing the same trickery with those Democratic platforms he had thrown up. Thompson Campbell wrote his answers two days before the election and never made them public, or he would not have been elected; the fifty-sixth district convention was under the "tutelage" of Long John Wentworth, and Douglas had nothing in common with Wentworth. "These facts are well known, and Mr. Lincoln can only get up individual instances, dating back to 1849, '50, which are contradicted by the whole tenor of the democratic creed," Douglas asserted. But at this hour, Lovejoy and the other black Republicans were running around Illinois endorsing exactly the positions that Lincoln claimed he was not pledged to. And to uproarious laughter, Douglas added, "Let me tell Mr. Lincoln that his party in the northern part of the State hold to that abolition platform, and that if they do not in the south and in the centre they present the extraordinary spectacle of a house divided against itself, and hence cannot stand." [60]

Last, Douglas turned to Lincoln's belated fifth question, about a federal slave code. The answer, as always, was popular sovereignty. "It is a fundamental article in the Democratic creed that there should be non-interference and non-intervention by Congress with slavery in the States or territories." Turning the tables, Douglas asked how Lincoln would answer his own question: "I answer him direct, and yet he has not answered the question himself." In fact, "I have asked him three times, whether he would vote to admit Kansas whenever the people applied with a constitution of their own making . . . but I cannot get an answer from him." But there was no time left to rake Lincoln further over these coals. Douglas could only close with one last appeal to the peace-giving potential of popular sovereignty: "Maintain the rights of the States as they are guaranteed under the constitution, and then we will have peace and harmony between the different States and sections of this glorious Union." [61]

It had not been a glorious encounter for either debater. Douglas's opening was little more than a reprise of the Lincoln-Trumbull conspiracy charge, followed by a paean to popular sovereignty. Lincoln tried to question the connection of popular soveriengty with the intentions of the Founders, but his real excitement was in posing the slave-code question and exposing the same contradictions between Douglas and the Democrats that Douglas had set up between Lincoln and the abolition radicals in the Republican party. Neither proved very effective. Picking out the same flaw in Douglas was as much as admitting that Douglas had been right to deride it in Lincoln; and Douglas had just as effective, and much more rapid, a rejoinder. In fact, Douglas's frenzied final half hour was the most interesting and successful part of an otherwise lackluster encounter.

The "grid" for Jonesboro looks like this:

DOUGLAS	LINCOLN
Lincoln and Trumbull conspired to abolitionize the old parties [repeated in rejoinder]	Denied
Lincoln advocates racial equality	
House Divided speech means the dissolution of the Union	Denied
Lincoln attacks the Supreme Court [repeated in rejoinder]	Douglas's answer to the Freeport Question is a contradiction of the Supreme Court
Popular sovereignty is the key to national growth	Slavery is not an issue popular sovereignty can settle
	If Douglas wants to fasten the Aurora resolutions on Lincoln, Lincoln should be allowed to fasten other Democrats' answers to the Freeport Questions on Douglas
Lincoln refused to answer Douglas's questions at Ottawa and offered inadequate replies at Freeport	
"Unfriendly legislation" allows for legal exclusion of slavery from the territories	

There may have been more than relief in the minds of the crowd when Usher Linder was at once "lively called for" to climb up on the "stand" and make "a short Douglas speech," followed by John

Dougherty and "a stirring Buchanan speech."[62] On the other hand, Lincoln had little at stake in Egypt. His work would be in the Whig Belt. Both candidates bolted northward the next morning, Lincoln sticking straight to the Illinois Central, Douglas taking a quick (but still northward) detour to show the flag in the third, fifth, and eighth state house districts and running a day behind Lincoln in reaching Centralia. The next day, September 18, they would debate in Charleston, the Whig Belt's most important eastern outpost. For the first time, Lincoln and Douglas would be meeting on the ground that neither could claim for certain but both needed to win.

★ CHAPTER 5 ★

IN THE FACE OF THE NATION

F ROM TIME OUT of mind, comets were regarded as supernatural warnings of a great calamity. The comets themselves were thought to drag through the atmosphere trains of disease, famine, and a general drying up of human blood, which produced wars and insurrections. Unhappily for the people who made livings from interpreting portents, the scientific revolution of the seventeenth century cut the ground from under the metaphysics of comets. Edmund Halley's discovery that the comet of 1682 was in fact the same comet which had appeared at fixed intervals in 1531 and 1607 (and would again in 1758) reduced comets to harmless bits of material substance flashing mechanically and predictably through the sky. "Wars between princes spring from various reasons of state, or passions which change with a trifle," concluded Pierre Bayle, the notorious maker of the *Historical and Critical Dictionary* (1697). "There's no connection in nature between what passes here below after the appearance of comets."[1]

So when Giovanni Donati first detected the approach of a new comet on June 2, 1858, in the observatory in Florence where he worked as a staff astronomer, it generated no particular anxiety. It could not help but generate interest, though. Nathaniel Hawthorne, sketching out the first drafts of *The Marble Faun* in a rented villa out-side Florence, watched "the mighty and brilliant comet of Donati" as it "stretched itself across the valley in a great fiery arch, and remained in view till near morning." Orville Hickman Browning first noted the comet in his diary on August 23, "in the West, almost in the track of the Sun." And by the time of the Jonesboro debate, Donati's comet was nearing its perihelion and making a spectacular display across night skies in Illinois. "The comet blazes in the evening sky with a lustre which is nightly increasing," reported the *Illinois State Register*, and "is now the most brilliant and attractive object in the heavens. . . . Nightly there are thousands of eyes turned towards it." Stephen A. Douglas sat outside on the balcony of the Pennsylvania House in Mattoon through the "bright, clear and beautiful night . . . looking northward over the grand prairie, with Donati's comet lighting up the clear blue sky" while he argued the justice of "his course and opposition to the Admin-istration of Mr. Buchanan" with a youthful admirer, Theophilus van Deren. Horace White, traveling with Abraham Lincoln, thought "the splendid appearance of Donati's comet in the sky" was far more inter-esting than Jonesboro, and Lincoln, who "greatly admired this strange visitor," stayed outside "for an hour or more" in the evening, just "look-ing at it."[2]

Lincoln was the least of all men to attribute supernatural meanings to comets. Henry Villard, "accidentally" thrown together with Lincoln "at a flag railroad station," was asked by the candidate whether "most of the educated people in Germany were 'infidels.'" Maybe not openly, Villard said, but "most of them were not church-goers." Lincoln was not surprised: "My own inclination is that way," he said. It was not reli-gion but science which Lincoln saw as the key to understanding the operation of the universe. Joseph Gillespie remembered that Lincoln "wanted something solid to rest upon and hence his bias for mathemat-ics and the physical sciences." William Herndon thought "his tendency in philosophy was materialistic," and he watched Lincoln plow his way through a number of the most revolutionary scientific treatises of the nineteenth century, beginning with Robert Chambers's *Vestiges of the Natural History of Creation* and Sir Charles Lyell's epochal *Principles of Geology*, and reaching out to David Wells's Boston-based *Annual of Scientific Discovery* (1850–1871). Although John Todd Stuart recalled that Lincoln "made Geology . . . a special study," Gillespie thought Lincoln "was fond of astronomy," too, and his "conversation drifted into a discussion of the comet, a subject that was then agitating the scientific world, in which [Lincoln] took the deepest interest."[3]

But the interest was devoid of any hint that the icy messenger (with a tail estimated to be 6 million miles in length) had anything more to say to Lincoln than ice. This was the man who had looked out over the Niagara Falls—the falls which nineteenth-century Americans regarded as the most sublime natural feature on the planet and which inspired the greatest American painting of the century, Frederick Edwin Church's *Niagara* (1857)—and merely remarked, "Where in the world did all that water come from?" As Herndon despairingly explained, "He had no eye for the magnificence and grandeur of the scene, for the rapids, the mist, the angry waters, and the roar of the whirlpool, but his mind, working in its accustomed channel, heedless of beauty or awe, followed irresistibly back to the first cause. It was in this light he viewed every question."[4] There was no suggestion that the enormous comet might, as of old, be the premonition of cataclysm, war, and the death of kings.

The State Fair at Centralia was pulling in as many as eleven thousand people a day when Stephen Douglas's train wheezed into view, its brass howitzer banging out arrival notices, on September 17. The Buchananites hustled into Centralia the day before to head Douglas off, and R. B. Carpenter and old John Reynolds staged an evening rally on one side of the town square to argue that "Stephen A. Douglas had deserted the Democracy and gone over to Black Republicanism; he wintered with them in 1857–58, and *hasn't got back yet*." But the Douglasites were ready to give as good as they were given. Across the square, Usher F. Linder stood up in the rear flatbed of a carriage and "divertingly went to work at a counter fire." Linder and Reynolds ended up roaring like rival auctioneers, with Reynolds finally bawling out that "if St. Paul were running I wouldn't vote for him if he was a Douglas man." When Douglas arrived the next day, he pitched into working the crowd, "and enthusiastic Douglas men claim that he has shaken hands with the full number" in attendance at the fair. That evening, Douglas took over the town square and opened up vigorously on the Buchananites. But the cream of his spite was reserved for Lincoln, and he gleefully billboarded race hatred and the evils that abolition would scatter across Illinois. He "was particularly severe on the unfortunate odor of the black man [and] asked if his audience wished to eat with, ride with, go to church with, travel with, and in other ways bring Congo odor into their nostrils."[5]

If anything, Douglas was moving appeals to white racial fear further and further to the front of his campaign. Elect Lincoln to the Senate, Douglas warned, and he will move heaven and earth to abolish slavery in the South. When that happened, "he would then give" the freed slaves "citizenship, the right to vote, to hold office, to become legislators, jurors and judges, and finally to marry white women." When Frederick Douglass gave a speech in Poughkeepsie, New York, to celebrate the twenty-fifth anniversary of British West Indian emancipation, the "Black Douglas" pointed to "the contest going on just now in the state of Illinois" as "at bottom" a struggle between "Slavery and Anti-Slavery" and called for the defeat of the Little Giant—and thus allowed the Little Giant to shriek at Centralia that black abolitionists and "Black Republicans" had one and the same object, "nigger equality."[6]

Queasy-stomached old Whigs in Centralia had no particular love for Douglas, "with all his past objectionable conduct"; but he was "sound on niggers," whereas anyone who read Lincoln's speeches had to wonder whether Lincoln "of late years" had "gone off into the wildest stretches of Abolitionism." One nervous Whig-turned-

Republican from neighboring Bond County begged Lincoln to say "that the Republicans are not in favor of making the Blacks socially and politically equal with the Whites," because that was the conclusion Douglas, by sheer volume of repetition, was driving the Whig Belt toward. Thomas Marshall, who was running for the state senate as a Republican from Coles County (where the Charleston debate would be held), sent Lincoln a seamy list of talking points he hoped the candidate would use to convince people in his district that Lincoln had no intention of promoting slave emancipation or black equality:

> *That as for Negro equality in the sense in which the expression is used you neither believe in it nor desire it. You desire to offer no temptations to negroes to come among us or remain with us, and therefore you do not propose to confer upon them any further social or political rights than they are now entitled to— As a citizen of a free State or as a member of Congress you would have no right to interfere with Slavery in the States, & you have no such desire, and you consider the idea of changing the Constitution so as to give Congress control over the subject of slavery in the States as impracticable & absurd.*

"Negro Equality," added John M. Palmer in a letter of advice to Lincoln, "goes down hard" with any old Whigs or Fillmoreite Know-Nothings "that want an excuse for joining the Douglassites."[7]

And old Whigs and Fillmoreites were exactly what awaited Lincoln in Charleston. Under almost any other circumstances, Charleston (the county seat for Coles County) ought to have been home territory for Lincoln. It was the eastern anchor of the Whig Belt, and the *Chicago Journal* noticed that "most of the leading men here are . . . of the old Henry Clay Whig stamp." Until 1856, Coles County had given its majorities to Whig presidential candidates for as long as Lincoln had been in politics, and it gave a majority to Buchanan in 1856 only because the Whig vote was split by Frémont for the Republicans and Fillmore for the Know-Nothings.

Lincoln himself had practiced law in Charleston while it was part of the Eighth Judicial Circuit and tried fifty-one cases there over the years—an average of one each circuit term for as long as he had been a lawyer—so as both a politician and a lawyer, he had more personal visibility in Charleston than in any of the other debate sites. He also had a family stake in Coles County. When the Lincoln family had quit Indiana in 1830 and moved to Illinois, Lincoln's father and stepmother settled first in Macon County, then moved again in 1837 to a farm on Goosenest Prairie, twelve miles east of Charleston. There, Thomas Lincoln died in 1851, and the extended family which had trekked into Illinois with him mostly stayed put in Coles County. By 1858, Lincoln's stepmother, Sarah Bush Lincoln, was seventy-eight years old and living with her granddaughter, Harriet, and Harriet's husband, Augustus H. Chapman, in Charleston. Lincoln was not exactly a frequent visitor (he had last been down to see his stepmother "a little over a year" before). But early in the campaign, Chapman wrote to Lincoln, hoping that "if Douglass comes out & makes us a speech this season that you will do the same."[8] Chapman was now about to get his wish.

Both Lincoln and Douglas arrived in Mattoon, twelve miles west of Charleston on the Illinois Central line, late in the evening of September 17. The Democratic county committees from Coles and Moultrie (which together made up the twenty-fifth state house district) informed Douglas a week beforehand that he and Adele would be met in Mattoon and the next morning "conveyed by carriage to Charleston accompanied by citizens of the above mentioned counties." Lincoln, likewise, set out by carriage from Mattoon, "drawn by a splendid span of cream colored horses," and was met en route "by a large delegation from Charleston" led by Thomas Marshall and Judge Henry Bromwell. (Bromwell was Usher F. Linder's law partner, but this had not discouraged Bromwell from running, unsuccessfully, for Congress as a Republican in 1856.)

The weather had turned hot and cloudless again, and the roads converging on Charleston were clogged for "fifteen and twenty miles . . . marked here and there by clouds of dust." This crowd, eventually numbering between fifteen and twenty thousand, was more like Ottawa than Jonesboro, and it promised to be even more rambunctious than Freeport. The Douglas procession featured a parade of "thirty-two young ladies on horseback, representing the Federal Union, sixteen of whom carried the national colors waving from ash sticks"—the ash tree being the symbol of Henry Clay's Kentucky estate, Ashland—and "the other sixteen carrying the same colors on hickory sticks" for Andrew Jackson, as a none too subtle reminder that Douglas was the Union-loving embodiment of "the union between the Whigs and Democrats when our country was endangered by the agitation of sectional men in 1850." Lincoln's procession was headed by a brass band imported from Terre Haute (someone, with an eye on the Democratic blueprints, included a "mammoth" wagon with its own "thirty-two young ladies") and stretched backward for "a mile in length." Young Theophilus van Deren thought it was the "largest assemblage of people that I had ever before or have since then seen here."[9]

The Republican and Democratic clubs in Charleston had agreed beforehand to form a joint arrangements committee, and they directed the Douglas procession to arrive by the north road and the Lincoln procession by the south road "to avoid conflicts." But even before the parades had begun, political pranks were popping up. "Some Lincoln men" painted an eighty-foot long banner, with the motto OLD ABE THIRTY YEARS AGO and a full-length painting (by "a local painter of no ordinary ability") of the young Lincoln behind a plow and three oxen, and they climbed up into the cupola of the courthouse to begin stringing it across the street. A handful of Douglasites, who had their own banner, WELCOME DOUGLAS, "immediately scampered up to the Court House cupola" to get it strung up, only to have a gust of wind wrap it into a knot around the "flag rope." Once the marching columns arrived in Charleston, the restraints began to waver still more. Douglas's marchers stopped to deposit the Little Giant at the Union Hotel for lunch, but a welcoming speech there from Orlando Bell Ficklin, another ex-Whig turned Democrat, was drowned out by some noisy musical horseplay from the Terre Haute band. Meanwhile, the Lincoln wagon, with its thirty-two Republican "young ladies," sported a banner which proclaimed a subtly erotic interest in Lincoln as a fit successor to Henry Clay:

WESTWARD THE STAR OF EMPIRE TAKES ITS WAY
THE GIRLS LINK-ON TO LINCOLN, AS THEIR MOTHERS DID TO CLAY

A band of Douglasites hurriedly worked up a banner with its own erotic countermessage, "representing a white man standing with a negro woman, and followed by a negro boy, with the inscription of 'NEGRO EQUALITY,' over it."[10]

The Charleston joint committee reserved the county fairgrounds on the east side of town for the debate and built a sizable platform, eighteen by thirty feet, which could accommodate not only Lincoln, Douglas, and the reporters but as many as sixty other dignitaries—all three local Republican candidates (Richard Oglesby, who was running for Congress; Thomas Marshall for state senate; and William Craddock for the state house), and Usher F. Linder, who had been persuaded to run for the state senate from Coles County. (The Democratic nominees for Congress and the state house, James Robinson and Harvey Worley, decided it would be safer not to be seen on the same platform with Douglas.) And from across the state line, Indiana Republican John P. Usher (who would serve in Lincoln's cabinet during the Civil War) joined the platform party to give Lincoln a patina of out-of-state celebrity.[11]

As at Freeport, a small amount of rough plank seating had been sawn and nailed together. But most of the crowds were going to have to stand if they wanted to hear the debate, and with the speaking scheduled to start at two o'clock and the platform facing eastward, a good portion would have to stare into the afternoon sun as it sank toward its autumnal horizon. The atmosphere only got more edgy once lunch was over and the huge processions sluggishly started out for the fairgrounds. Douglas was irked by a banner strung across the road featuring Lincoln with "an uplifted war club felling the Little Giant to the ground," and when Douglas reached the fairgrounds, "some of the more ardent Republicans" rushed the platform and tried to plant a banner there showing Lincoln as a mastiff, sinking his teeth into Douglas's throat, over the legend LINCOLN WORRYING DOUGLAS AT FREEPORT. Lincoln tried to quiet the uproar by asking for the removal of the banner. But some equally ardent Douglasites instead tried to plant the NEGRO EQUALITY banner in its place, and two Republicans on the platform jumped down and tore the banner up. By the time Lincoln and Douglas had both pleaded for order and the introductions had been done, the start of the debate had been delayed by forty-five minutes, and the platform reminded Lew Wallace, a Douglasite state senator from Indiana who had come to Charleston to hear the debate, of "an island barely visible in a restless sea." [12]

Lincoln was due to take the opening speech at Charleston. And it is a measure of how deeply weighed down he felt by the pleas of Republican advice givers to shuck off the "Negro equality" accusation that he began with the words every Lincoln admirer since then wishes he had never uttered: "While I was at the hotel to-day an elderly gentleman called upon me to know whether I was really in favor of producing a perfect equality between the negroes and white people." This was the preface to a lengthy and improvised ("I had not proposed to myself on this occasion to say much on that subject") disclaimer of any interest in "bringing about in any way the social and political equality of the white and black races." Lincoln had struggled to keep the race issue at arm's length. Back in July, he had tried to dismiss "quibbling" about race as vicious and demeaning and promptly saw Douglas convert this into a damaging racist asset; and at Lewistown and Ottawa, he had labored to keep up his careful distinction between the *natural* racial equality which made black slavery a violation of natural law and the *civil* equality which communities were free to deal with as a separate issue. But careful distinctions were lost in the vile heat that arose from any discussion of race in Illinois, and Douglas did his best to make sure they were lost by speaking of *equality* as though it meant a black man in every white woman's bed.

In Ottawa, Douglas's racial smearing had had less force, since the audience had been hostile to almost everything he said anyway, and it meant less in Jonesboro, since nothing Lincoln said there about race was going to chip away at the rock-hard Democratic loyalties of Egypt. But in Charleston, Lincoln faced old Whig voters who loved to hate slavery but who could be poisoned by the slightest departure from white supremacy. So with the burden of the state committee's timidity around his neck, Lincoln plunged into a disgraceful catalog of all the civil rights he, fully as much as Douglas, believed blacks could be routinely deprived of:

> *I am not nor ever have been in favor of making voters or jurors of negroes, nor of qualifying them to hold office, nor to intermarry with white people; and I will say in addition to this that there is a physical difference between the white and black races which I believe will for ever forbid the two races living together on terms of social and political equality. And inasmuch as they cannot so live, while they do remain together there must be the position of superior and inferior, and I as much as any other man am in favor of having the superior position assigned to the white race. . . . I will add to this that I have never seen to my knowledge a man, woman or child who was in favor of producing a perfect equality, social and political, between negroes and white men. . . . I will also add to the remarks I have made, (for I am not going to enter at large upon this subject), that I have never had the least apprehension that I or my friends would marry negroes if there was no law to keep them from it [this drew "laughter" from the crowd] but as Judge Douglas and his friends seem to be in great apprehension that they might, if there were no law to keep them from it [this time "roars of laughter"], I give him the most solemn pledge that I will to the very last stand by the law of this State, which forbids the marrying of white people with negroes.*[18]

This was a callous way of driving civil equality as harmlessly far from natural equality as he could, and all the more callous as a concession to racial animosities he had otherwise never shown much respect for. Yet, for all its ugliness, it was a carefully calculated statement. What was the "physical difference"—color? intelligence? And was the "position of superior and inferior" merely an "assigned" one, not a natural one, to which Lincoln acquiesced out of simple political self-interest? But calculated or not, it was still an exercise in racial pandering, aimed at a constituency which expected pandering as the price of its votes, and it was twisted out of him by Douglas's racial demagoguery. And almost as if he was eager to wash his hands of a bad business, Lincoln abruptly declared that "I do not propose dwelling longer at this time on this subject," and went on to what he thought was the real beginning of the debate.

Lincoln's fundamental purpose, ever since 1854, had been to expose the Kansas-Nebraska bill and the popular sovereignty doctrine as shams designed to sweeten the extension of slavery into the territories. He was particularly eager to show that Douglas had known they were shams from the start. At Ottawa, Lincoln had cited the Chase amendment as proof that Douglas had no interest in any form of genuine popular sovereignty, and Lyman Trumbull had produced an even more damaging example of Douglas duplicity in the form of the Toombs amendment. Coming from a southern partisan like Robert Toombs, rather than an abolitionist like Chase, it was keenly embarrassing for Douglas to have his agreement to embargo the Toombs amendment shouted around Illinois—so embarrassing, in fact, that Lincoln had been advised repeatedly to slip "the Trumbull argument in to him as to striking out the submission clause," that Lincoln should *"make him eat . . . altering Toombs' bill"*—and Lincoln wrote to Trumbull to obtain "certain official documents" connected with the Toombs amendment for his own preparations.[14]

And so Lincoln began the Charleston debate by taking up the

Toombs amendment where Trumbull had left off. "When Judge Trumbull, our other Senator in Congress, returned to Illinois in the month of August," Lincoln began, he accused Douglas of being party to "a plot entered . . . to have a constitution formed for Kansas and put in force without giving the people an opportunity to vote upon it." Lincoln then made heavy weather of Douglas's various refutations of Trumbull—that territorial organization bills never included provisions for referendums, that Trumbull was using forged documents as proof that the Little Giant had suppressed the referendum provision, that Toombs's bill had never really contained a referendum provision—and all for the purpose of demonstrating that Douglas had never had any real interest in popular sovereignty but only in satisfying his Southern patrons. Lincoln challenged, "I ask him whether he took the original provision out, which Trumbull alleges was in the bill? If he admits that he did take it, I ask him what he did it for? It looks to us as if he had altered the bill. If it looks differently to him—if he has a different reason for his action from the one we assign him—he can tell it. I insist upon knowing why he made the bill silent upon that point when it was vocal before he put his hands upon it." [15]

Squeezing every drop from the Toombs bill took Lincoln so long that, when he stopped to ask the moderator, Dr. W. M. Chambers, how much time he had left, Chambers imperturbably replied that he had three minutes, only enough room to leave this question hanging in midair: if the Kansas-Nebraska bill was a perfect expression of popular sovereignty, why had Douglas spiked Robert Toombs's requirement that any Kansas state constitution "be submitted to a vote of the people"?

Douglas came forward, his face knotted in puzzlement. I thought, he began, that "the rule of such discussions is, that the opening speaker shall touch upon all the points he intends to discuss in order that his opponent, in reply, shall have the opportunity of answering them." But what "questions of public policy . . . has Mr. Lincoln discussed before you?" Lincoln had stolen Douglas's racial thunder at the outset "by saying, that he was not in favor of social and political equality between the white man and the negro," and Douglas could only say that he was pleased to have finally been able to drag such an admission out of Lincoln. "I am glad that I have at last succeeded in getting an answer out of him upon this question of negro citizenship and eligibility to office, for I have been trying to bring him to the point on it ever since this canvass commenced."

Otherwise, Lincoln seemed interested only in talking about Lyman Trumbull. And Trumbull, of course, was completely unreliable on any topic. "When Mr. Trumbull returned from the East," Douglas went on, "the first thing he did when he landed at Chicago was to make a speech wholly devoted to assaults upon my public character and public action . . . entirely without provocation and without excuse." As for the Toombs bill, it meant nothing at all. Trumbull "knew that Toombs denied that there ever was a clause in the bill he brought forward calling for and requiring a submission of the Kansas constitution to the people." Yes, Douglas admitted, he had refused to support the Toombs amendment—but that was only because the "question at issue was, whether we would admit Kansas with a population of 25,000, or, make her wait until she had the ratio entitling her to a representative in Congress, which was 93,420." The only reason Trumbull had for raking this up was to distract attention from "Lincoln's Abolitionism and negro equality doctrines," because "I was driving Lincoln to the wall, and white men would not support his rank Abolitionism." [16]

This provided the perfect transition to Douglas's inevitable message, that Lincoln and Trumbull had struck conspiratorial hands to abolitionize the Whigs and Democrats, and "to conceal from this vast audience the real questions which divide the two great parties." But something about the Toombs accusation was bothering Douglas, and so he turned back to Lincoln's challenge with redoubled fury. "I wish you to bear in mind that up to the time of the introduction of the Toombs bill, and after its introduction, there had never been an act of Congress for the admission of a new State which contained a clause requiring its constitution to be submitted to the people." And on it went, through a rehearsal of Douglas's chairmanship of the Senate Committee on Territories, through the niceties of Trumbull's speeches at Chicago and Alton a month before, through extracts from Douglas's speeches on the floor of the Senate, which had been pasted into the same "memorandum book" Douglas had used at Ottawa. (Lincoln, obviously, was not the only one who had been compiling "original documents" about the Toombs bill; what was curious was how unusually well prepared Douglas was to produce just the right clippings at just the right debate. Something like this had happened at Jonesboro, when Douglas had easily produced exact recollections of what certain Illinois Democrats had said at certain times about abolition, all of which raises the tantalizing question of whether there was a Douglas mole in the Republican state committee.)[17]

This went on for half an hour before Douglas finally worked his indignation out and returned to his barely started attack on the Lincoln-Trumbull conspiracy. "You know that prior to 1854 this country was divided into two great political parties, one the Whig, the other the Democratic." This was not the wisest thing to be reminding the voters in a onetime Whig stronghold, but Douglas was determined to brass it out: "I, as a Democrat for twenty years . . . fought you Whigs like a man on every question that separated the two parties." Douglas's opposition had always been aboveboard, he claimed, and was always conducted with "the highest respect for Henry Clay as a gallant party leader, as an eminent statesman, and as one of the bright ornaments of this country." At the time of the Compromise of 1850, "Clay . . . became the leader of all the Union men whether whigs or democrats . . . only animated by one common, patriotic sentiment to devise means and measures by which we could defeat the mad and revolutionary scheme of the northern abolitionists and southern disunionists." Those "means and measures" were, of course, "founded upon the great fundamental principle that the people of each State and each territory ought to be left free to form and regulate their own domestic institutions."

But now, "many of the leaders of the Whig party" had "led off and attempted to abolitionize the Whig party, and transfer all your old Whigs bound hand and foot into the abolition camp." And "who led that crusade against National principles in this State? I answer, Abraham Lincoln." He and Lyman Trumbull had "formed a scheme by which they would abolitionize the two great parties in this State," and thereby get both Lincoln and Trumbull elected to the Senate. "They have entered into a conspiracy to break me down by these assaults on my public character, in order to draw my attention from a fair exposure of the mode in which they attempted to abolitionize the old Whig and the old Democratic parties and lead them captive into the Abolition camp." The conspiracy was so etched with deceit that "Lincoln, Trumbull, Breese, Reynolds, and Dougherty" could not take the risk of advertising themselves in the Whig Belt to old-time Whigs as Republicans but instead, like Joseph Gillespee, ducked under names like the "Peoples Party" or "a convention of all men opposed to the Democratic party." What possible "object have these Black Republicans in changing their name in every county?" *To cheat people*, came the response from the crowd.[18]

Above all, they should not concede one ounce of credibility to Lincoln's disclaimers about "the social and political equality of the negro with the white man." Yes, Lincoln "has declared that he was not in favor of the social and political equality of the negro." But notice that Lincoln "would not say whether or not he was opposed to negroes voting and negro citizenship." He was an opponent of the *Dred Scott* decision, which found blacks incapable of citizenship; if he disagrees with *Dred Scott*, then "he must be in favor of conferring the right and privilege of citizenship upon the negro!" Lincoln has taken every opportunity to state that the Declaration of Independence makes everyone—including "the negro"—"equal to the white man, and that under Divine law." If that is what Lincoln thinks the Declaration says, then it would only be "rational for him to advocate negro citizenship." But with Douglas, no white man ever needed to bother with guessing or deducing: "I say to you in all frankness, gentlemen, that in my opinion a negro is not a citizen, cannot be, and ought not to be, under the constitution of the United States." All of this got Douglas "immense applause." But it also ran out the clock, and he had only half a minute to take a parting shot at the House Divided speech, and "stopped on the minute." [19]

Lincoln stood up to repeat, in the event Douglas had not seemed to notice it, "that I am not in favor of negro citizenship." But that was because Illinois as a state had made that determination on the basis of a sovereign, majoritarian decision of its citizens—"popular sovereignty," if Douglas would allow—and Lincoln, for his own reasons, acquiesced in it. He still believed, though, that "the different States have the power to make the negro a citizen, under the Constitution of the United States, if they choose." What made *Dred Scott* objectionable was the Supreme Court's claim that *it*, and not the states, should make that decision, because that pointed inevitably toward the fatal corollary that the Supreme Court could also decide about the legality of slavery in the states, too. Even if, in the spirit of appeasement, "I should be opposed to" black citizenship in Illinois, that was a decision Illinois should make, not Roger Taney.

Lincoln had no similar excuses to offer about the House Divided speech. "Have we ever had any peace on this slavery question?" he asked. "Judge Douglas and his friends" tell us that when we allow popular sovereignty or the Supreme Court to begin deciding *natural* rights there will be peace. But this slavery is not a question which will lie down and be peaceful, because the majoritarian decisions that govern civil law have no power to rewrite natural law, and the proof lay in how the nation has "been wrangling over this question for at least forty years." At every point between the Compromise of 1850 and the Lecompton constitution, people like Douglas had been promising that "we are just at the end of the slavery agitation." But we are not. "Now, at this day in the history of the world we can no more foretell where the end of this slavery agitation will be than we can see the end of the world itself." There are only two ways to get peace on the subject of slavery—"put it back upon the basis where our fathers placed it . . . re-strict it forever to the old States where it now exists," and put it "in the course of ultimate extinction," or else "cease speaking of it as in any way a wrong—regard slavery as one of the common matters of prop-erty, and speak of negroes as we do of our horses and cattle." If saying that cost Lincoln old Whig votes, so be it.[20]

That was not the point he wanted to spend time on, though. Lin-coln had to defuse Douglas's charge that he and Trumbull had entered into some unholy bond, and he challenged Douglas to bring forth the evidence that "Trumbull and myself" had "made a bargain to sell out the entire Whig and Democratic parties in 1854." It took more than a little turning of the cheek for Lincoln to add that never "in all the years that I have known Lyman Trumbull, have I known him to fail of his word or tell a falsehood, large or small." (A Douglasite heckler, James Brown, interrupted Lincoln with a loaded question: what did Gover-nor Thomas Ford's popular *History of Illinois,* which had been pub-lished four years before, say about Trumbull? Ford, who had clashed with Trumbull politically and then fired him as secretary of state in 1843, described Trumbull as "devoured by ambition for office . . . a man of strong prejudices, and not remarkable for liberal views"; but Lincoln provoked "roars of laughter and applause" by pointing out that Ford "talks a great deal worse of Judge Douglas)."[21]

If there was anyone in Illinois politics who was peddling false-hoods, Lincoln continued, it was Stephen A. Douglas, and the proof was in Douglas's "old charge against me, in reference to the Mexican War." This was the moment Lincoln had been waiting for ever since he spied Orlando Ficklin on the platform. Not only was Ficklin a onetime Whig, but he had sat with Lincoln in the same Congress which heard Lincoln deliver his demand for the "spot" on which American blood had been spilled. Lincoln turned on his heel, walked back to Ficklin's chair, grabbed the left-hand collar of Ficklin's frock coat "in no gentle manner," and walked him to the apron of the platform "to tell the whole truth about this Mexican business."

Ficklin had been an eyewitness, a decade before, that whenever the issue was "the origin and justice of the war, I . . . voted against it," Lincoln declared. But whenever the vote was about supplying and supporting American soldiers, Ficklin saw that "I never voted against the supplies for the army, and . . . whenever a dollar was asked . . . for the benefit of the soldiers, I gave all the votes that Ficklin or Douglas did, and perhaps more." And the hapless Ficklin grudgingly agreed to at least half of Lincoln's statement: on resolutions which "declared that the Mexican war was unnecessarily and unconstitutionally commenced by the President—my recollection is that Mr. Lincoln voted for that resolution." That was enough for Lincoln. "You know they have charged that I voted against the supplies, by which I starved the soldiers who were out fighting the battles of their country. I say that Ficklin knows it is false." And if this charge was false, what kind of credibility attached to Douglas's other charges about Lincoln and Trumbull? "Judge Douglas is playing cuttlefish," Lincoln said and grinned, "a small species of fish that has no mode of defending itself when pursued except by throwing out a black fluid"—like, for instance, Negro equality—"which makes the water so dark the enemy cannot see it and thus it escapes." *Roars of laughter*, scribbled Horace White for the *Tribune*.[22]

This brought Lincoln back to his—and Trumbull's—original question: if Douglas was so fervent a lover of popular sovereignty, and believed that it was the universal sedative to all questions concerning slavery in the territories, why had Douglas allowed a provision for a popular referendum in Kansas to be deleted from the Kansas-Nebraska bill? Unless, of course, Kansas-Nebraska was another "black fluid" to disguise Douglas's role in advancing the Slave Power. And until Douglas "gives a better or more plausible reason than he has offered" about why he failed to speak out for the Toombs amendment—and here, Lincoln was ready with a personal shot—"I suggest to him it will not avail him at all that he swells himself up, takes on dignity, and calls people liars." *Great applause and laughter,* jotted White. Douglas, cut to the bone, began erupting "to some of his friends" in bursts of profanity so boisterous that Robert Hitt had trouble hearing Lincoln; and with his eye on his watch, Douglas jerked up, began pacing "up and down the platform," and interrupted to complain that "Lincoln has overspoken his time two minutes now." [23]

Lincoln's time actually had run out, so he said, "Therefore I close." But he had done three things which made the Charleston debate memorable. First, he had slugged hard at Douglas's credibility and made expensive fun of Douglas's attempt to squirt "black fluid" across his inconsistencies about popular sovereignty. Second, Lincoln had conjured up, if only briefly, the argument for which Douglas had no real reply: for Douglas, slavery was simply an ordinary fact of American life, and the only question it posed was how it should be regulated. For Lincoln, slavery was a moral wrong which should be tolerated only because it was less disruptive to let it die than to kill it outright. Douglas might believe, and always had believed, that discussions of moral absolutes had no business intruding on discussions of policy; Lincoln was not a moral absolutist, but he could not believe that public policy could afford to ignore all absolutes. The Constitution might not include any invocation of natural law, or give standing to any particular morality. But no democratic polity was likely to survive for long if it pretended that these were purely private hypotheses, with no more significance for public affairs than a taste for Madeira or a game of rounders.

But at that moment, the most important accomplishment of the Charleston debate was to make people notice, and frequently for the first time, that the most famous debater in the United States Senate had still not managed to knock down this minor Republican lawyer from Springfield. A straw poll taken "among the passengers on the railroad" (the only way pollsters of the 1850s had of getting a reliable cross section of voters in one place and keeping them there to poll) showed "63 for Lincoln and 51 for Douglas" on the line from Vandalia and Ramsay; another taken between Sandoval and Centralia gave Lincoln 286 votes and Douglas 198. Lincoln was not only on his feet but jabbing back enthusiastically at Douglas, and it began to occur to a host of onlookers that this was a surprise of major proportions. "No one" who had heard the Charleston debate "could ever after doubt Lincoln's ample ability to meet Douglas," recalled Isaac Arnold. "Mr. Lincoln is winning golden opinions in the present canvass," observed Galena's *Weekly North-Western Gazette* (which persistently misspelled his name as Abram) on September 28. "The consummate ability which he has evinced has surprised many of his friends."

Among those friends, Governor William Bissell wrote Elihu Washburne five days after the Charleston debate that the "Republican cause is unquestionably gaining. . . . *Lincoln is doing well.*" Wherever Lincoln has been, enthused the *Illinois State Journal,* "the skies are bright and the prospects good." And David Davis wrote Lincoln to say, "Your concluding speech on Douglass at Charleston was admirable." Even more revealing, Davis wrote to his son, a student at Beloit College, that

> *the joint debates between Mr. Douglass & Mr. Lincoln you must read.*
>
> *The one at Jonesboro and the one at Charleston have already taken place. You can purchase the Chicago Tribune & keep the papers that have the debates in them. Mr. Lincoln's friends think he has sustained himself admirably in the debates & that his prospects for election are very fair. . . . Whether Mr. Lincoln or Judge Douglass shall go to the Senate, absorbs the people.*[24]

It absorbed them even after the debate ended. The crowd broke up for dinner, Stephen and Adele Douglas (who had listened to the debate in the comfort of the Ficklin family carriage) heading back to town with Orlando Ficklin. Lincoln took his dinner with his stepmother at Augustus Chapman's house on Jackson Street, then paid a courtesy call at Thomas Marshall's home. But once fed, the crowds turned out into the streets for more speeches, the Democrats cheering on Usher F.

Linder on the steps of the courthouse, and Richard Oglesby giving the Republican faithful two hours' worth of oratory "on the southwest corner of the public square." And then, at ten o'clock, there was "an informal reception and conference" for Lincoln and the local candidates at Marshall's home. "The enthusiastic supporters of Mr. Lincoln did not disperse until after midnight."[25]

The grid for Charleston looks like this:

LINCOLN	DOUGLAS
Denies that Republicans favor racial equality	
Rebuts Douglas's attack on Trumbull and the Toombs amendment	
Denied in rejoinder	Lincoln is evading the issues of the campaign
	Toombs amendment is irrelevant
	Lincoln falsely accuses two presidents and the Supreme Court of conspiracy
Denied in rejoinder	Lincoln and Trumbull conspired to abolitionize the old parties
Denied in rejoinder	Republicans favor racial equality
	Lincoln speaks one way in northern Illinois and another in southern Illinois
Slavery must be returned to containment	
Denies voting against troop supplies in Mexican War	
Douglas's failure to accept Toombs amendment to Kansas–Nebraska bill shows ulterior motive	

The debate at Charleston marked the end of the third phase of the Lincoln-Douglas campaigns, as well as the end of the only swing either candidate would bother to make into southern Illinois. With just a little over six weeks left before election day in November, Lincoln and Douglas would turn their energies entirely toward crisscrossing the broad western angle of the Whig Belt. The three remaining debates— at Galesburg, Quincy, and Alton—all lay within this western angle and would form "the real battleground" on which the last two phases of the campaigns would be fought.[26]

Charleston, however, did not mark anything close to the end of the edginess the two campaigns were showing. Sheahan's *Chicago Times* whooped with delight when a religious newspaper in Chicago, the *Congregational Herald*, chastised Lincoln for trying to discount the race card at Charleston. The *Congregational Herald* was the house organ of New England's midwestern diaspora in the 1840s and '50s, and it irritably condemned Lincoln's decision at Charleston to make "color and race the ground of political proscription. He forsook *principle*, and planted himself on *low prejudice*." Henry Villard smirked in his dispatches to the *New-Yorker Staats-Zeitung* over Lincoln's volte-face: "The entire Republican press of Chicago took up this declaration, and the Negro had no stauncher advocate . . . than Lincoln. . . . Now, the same Lincoln declared, that the Negro, 'created as a race inferior to White by the Lord Almighty,' must remain in his condition."[27]

The Republican press was less worried about the fevered brows of émigré abolitionists and more about the rumors which were circulating about Douglas's cozy relationship with the Illinois Central Railroad. "It is a well-known fact that Mr. Douglas claims to be the father of the Illinois Central Railroad" and "that he is a pet of the Company," complained a Republican newspaper. The contrast between Douglas's palace car and the flatcar with its cannon, and Lincoln catching rides in ordinary passenger cars and, sometimes, cabooses, shortened Republican tempers and lengthened the reach of Republican suspicions. "During the present canvass the company have given [Douglas] a special car to himself," raged the same newspaper. "In this car he carries his provisions, liquors, &c., and if we are not misinformed, the company furnishes him with servants." Henry Clay Whitney, however, could not persuade an Illinois Central conductor even to unlock an empty car "hitched on to the rear of the train" as they were headed to Charleston, so that Lincoln could get some peace and quiet. "The conductor refused," and from that moment, Whitney concluded that "every interest of that Road and every employee was against Lincoln and for Douglas." Lincoln himself was growing irked enough with the Illinois Central's behavior that, at a rally at Pekin on October 5, he accused the ICRR of providing Douglas "with special trains free of expense for the accommodation of himself and his famous cannon" and "an immense tract of land of the railroad company for so small a sum that a poor man would be enriched by the operation." Railroad officials hotly denied this, and the vice president of the Illinois Central (whom Lincoln would meet again under very different circumstances only three years hence) finally wrote an open letter to the *Chicago Tribune,* insisting that

> *this company has taken, and will take no part in politics; and that neither Senator Douglas, nor any other gentleman engaged in politics, ever has had, or can have, the slightest influence as to the removal or appointment of any officer or employee of this Road.*
>
> Geo. B. McClellan[28]

But the rumors persisted—and not without cause. The Illinois Central owed a tremendous debt to Douglas for sponsoring the federal legislation in 1850 which funded the construction of the long-delayed railroad through the sales of publicly held lands. Not content with a free pass to fund its creation, the Illinois Central continued over the next eight years to whine for tax immunity from Illinois counties and for the cancellation of a 7 percent gross earnings tax owed to the state, and stories were flying across Illinois that Douglas would shake all the right hands on the railroad's behalf. "There is an effort now being made by the Company to be released from the contract to pay these earnings to the State," and the "effort" was rumored by central Illinois newspapers to have Stephen A. Douglas as its promoter as soon as he was reelected. This was the reason, Whitney suspected, that "McClellan was in person taking Douglas around in a special car and Special Train," and McClellan himself had privately volunteered to fund a proposal to have a Douglas campaign worker, Richard Merrick, tag along to the debates to deliver follow-up speeches after Lincoln (which Merrick did at Charleston).[29]

In all likelihood, any threat posed by Merrick and McClellan would probably have small consequences. What was more troubling to underdog Republicans was what the Illinois Central might do with the large numbers of immigrant—usually Irish—laborers it employed up and down the lines of the railroad, from Galena and Chicago to Cairo. Voting rights in the 1850s were a state prerogative—one of those civil rights Lincoln painfully distinguished from natural rights—and in Illinois, the statutes were notoriously vague. Even if "a year's residence in the State is required as a qualification of the voter," the actual *"length or time of residence"* in "the county and township in which his ballot is offered . . . *is not defined."* And since it was the state legislature which did the voting for U.S. senators, the election would be decided not by the state at large, "but upon the ballots cast for members of the Legislature, in the districts." That meant that all the Douglasites had to do was infiltrate "one or two hundred votes" into a few "decisive" districts to "give Mr. Douglas the legislature."[30]

This being 1858, the slowness of travel and the greatness of distance across districts made it unlikely that anyone, even Douglas, could recruit "two thousand men" who could be dropped simultaneously into ten or so of the Whig Belt districts—except, of course, if they happened to be workers on the Illinois Central Railroad. As early as the beginning of September, the Republican state committee began sending up little balloons of complaint about the legislative elections being "overborne by illegal and fraudulent votes" cast by laborers in the pay of the Illinois Central. One campaign worker warned the Republican campaign treasurer, John C. Bagby, that "from all I can learn the principles of the Road are in favor of Douglas" and are "flooding the Road . . . in every County in this district that a Road passes through."[31]

In almost every case, the "fraudulent voters" carried with them the added stigma of being "Irish." In 1850, Irish-born immigrants to America numbered over 900,000, almost twice the size of the next largest immigrant group, the Germans. The great railroad construction boom begun by the Illinois Central made Illinois the fourth largest magnet for Irish immigrants in America, and the largest in the Midwest. The ICRR alone required between eight and ten thousand workers to grade the lines, lay the track, build the bridges and trestles, crew the work trains, and construct shanties and temporary quarters along the lines. The railroad's chief engineer finally resorted to contracting with brokers and immigrant aid societies in New York, Brooklyn, and Philadelphia to recruit German, Swedish, and Irish laborers, fresh off the immigrant boats. The demand for railroad labor was so great that other Illinois railroads entered into bidding wars for laborers, and by the mid-1850s, the ICRR's competition was offering up to $1.50 an hour, forcing the railroad to promise "two fifty for track layers" and forcing Illinois farmers, who also required short-term labor at harvest, to pay as much as "$2 per day and board to work at harvest."[32]

The Irish were, by Illinois standards, overpaid, dangerously and overwhelming male (with all the potential unattached gangs of young males had for mayhem), and growing in numbers with every steamer's offload of immigrant laborers onto Chicago's docks. In 1843, the Irish population accounted for about 10 percent of the whole city of Chicago; seven years later, the national census showed that the percentage of Irish-born Chicagoans had doubled. It mattered little that the Irish suffered miserable work conditions, disease-riddled camps, and larcenous employers and brokers, or that the labor demand which brought the Irish to Illinois in the first place had peaked in 1854. In the eyes of Illinois storekeepers whose windows were broken during railroad workers' drunk sprees, or Illinois farmers forced to pay top dollar for Irish labor, or Illinois Protestants who loathed the Irishman's Catholicism, or Illinois Whigs who looked upon them as an ignorant rabble waiting to sell their votes to the next demagogue, the Irish *b'hoy* reared up in the imagination as a malevolent genie. "Of the different nationalities," the *Chicago Tribune* had no doubt that "the Germans and the French, the English, and the Scotch, and the Scandinavians" would always "be counted on the side of free institutions." The Irish, however, "have signally failed to comprehend the spirit of freedom," partly because they were beastly and ignorant by "their instincts," but even more because they were Roman Catholic. "Popery and Slavery have been the hard masters of the American people," complained the *Illinois State Journal,* because both depend on blind submission to authority and reverence for hierarchy. Little surprise, then, that Irish Catholics would gravitate toward the Democratic party. Democrats were less imbued with a prying Protestant moralism than Whigs and Republicans, and more likely to be sympathetic to the plight of unskilled immigrants in an unfamiliar American world. And it was not lost on the immigrants themselves that the Whigs nursed a soft spot for nativism, and that many of the Republicanized Whigs had turned Republican only after a detour in the mid-1850s through the Know-Nothings. For both friend and foe, "Irish Democracy and Irish Catholicism are one and the same thing. . . . There is not to-day more than an infinitesimal fraction of Roman Catholic voters who do not profess the Democratic faith, and who do not bow to the usages and support of the candidates of the Democratic party." [33]

It took only a very small push to make Republicans imagine that the Illinois Central Railroad was cementing its corrupt cooperation with Stephen A. Douglas by sending road gangs of Irish Catholics down the line, dropping them off in strategic districts days or weeks before the election to perform grading and repairs, and to turn up on Election Day to vote as though they were permanent residents. It is the intention "of the Douglas Democracy to overrun the interior counties of this State with fraudulent votes," declared Ray and Medill in the *Tribune*. "Irishmen are daily pouring into Illinois by the hundred from the North" and "are seen and marked on all the interior railroads, particularly on the Illinois Central." In Bloomington, "one hundred Irishmen . . . were dumped by the road side" and "scattered out among the Douglas men," where they would not be seen again "until election day."[34]

The alarm over this "Celtic invasion at Bloomington, Lexington, Chenon, Towanda, etc." was, in part, just another rancid expression of nineteenth-century nativism. But another part of it was pure calculation by the state committee. For one thing, fear of a fraudulent vote would "arouse the whole country," and excited Republicans would turn out "en masse to the polls," and propel the party "clear of this point of danger." Similarly, dangling the Irish bogeyman was one way to draw uncommitted old Whigs and Fillmoreite Know-Nothings in the Whig Belt over to Lincoln, by portraying him as the target of an immigrant conspiracy. "If the Americans & republicans can unite on the same ticket," wrote one of Lyman Trumbull's political advisers, "we can surely carry the state vs. the pro-slavery, nullification Democratic party." In the Whig Belt, "the Nativists form a 'balance-of-power' whereas the two other parties have to entice voters from the Know-Nothings to gain a majority."

Singling out the Irish as the culprits also allowed the Republican state committee to drive a wedge between the Irish and the Germans, so that the Irish could be used to frighten the old Whigs into voting for Lincoln candidates while leaving the Germans unsullied and open to Republican appeals. In places like St. Clair County, at the southern curve of the Whig Belt, that might mean the difference between winning or losing the twelfth state house district's two representatives.

There, the Irish vote was insignificant, but the Germans outnumbered "Anglo-Americans" by three to one and German had almost "replaced English as the major language in business and public life." As much as the Germans resented Yankee moralists peering severely into their beer gardens, "the Dred Scott decision is the great bugbear of the German republican leaders and speakers" and is driving "two-thirds of the Germans in Illinois" into the arms of the Republicans.[35]

Lincoln was one Whig who had never put any faith in nativism. "I am not a Know-Nothing. That is certain," he wrote in 1855. "How can anyone who abhors the oppression of negroes, be in favor of degrading classes of white people?" Lincoln's sublime confidence in the universality of natural law led to him to see in "Hans and Baptiste and Patrick, and all other men from all the World" the same natural rights and yearnings for life, liberty, and the pursuit of happiness that any native-born American had. But he had also seen Winfield Scott's Whig presidential campaign self-destruct in 1852, when Scott tried to ingratiate himself with "the gallant men of Erin" who had served under him in the Mexican War. And Lincoln had his own suspicions about the willingness of Douglas and the Illinois Central to use its track workers as special squads of illegal voters in key districts. He told Norman Judd that he had "met about fifteen Celtic gentlemen, with black carpet-sacks in their hands" in Rushville and learned that "they had crossed over from the Railroad in Brown county, but where they were going no one could tell."

Lincoln guessed that Douglas and the ICRR "will introduce into the doubtful districts numbers of men who are legal voters in all respects except residence and who will swear to residence and thus put it beyond our power to exclude them." Lincoln, accordingly, would put his chips on appealing to the German vote and let the state committee use the threat of "the Irish" to rally the nativists. "Large numbers of Lincoln's speeches (published in German)" were sluiced into the mails, and prominent German Republicans—Carl Schurz from Wisconsin, Anton Hesing from Chicago, and Gustave Koerner—were recruited to

take the stump among the German towns. Lincoln himself tried his
hand at a direct appeal to the Germans. When Joseph Gillespie
arranged for a rally at Highland, Lincoln was "delighted with the idea
of visiting Highland, as he said he understood that place was a little
Germany." Of course, Gillespie warned him, Lincoln was going to
have to be prepared for a little convivial beer swilling. "Lincoln said
then, we will not go to Highland," because Lincoln was as much a tee-
totaler as any come-outer revivalist, and "I can't drink." Gillespie
pleaded with him to no avail until Gillespie hit on the expedient of
telling the Highland Germans that Lincoln "had an infirmity which
precluded him from indulging," and so "they would excuse him." So
they "went to Highland & had a good time." [56]

But this act of robbing Irish Peter to pay German Paul required a
delicacy of operation which the Douglasites knew how to shatter into
pieces. For every vote Republicans gained by their cries for anti-Irish
vigilance, they lost tribes of them by playing directly into the hands of
Douglasites who knew how to paint the Republicans as the enemies of
all immigrants and all Catholics, not just the Irish ones on the railroad.
In 1856, Douglas had managed the presidential campaign in Illinois by
adroitly splitting the Frémont-Republican vote and the Fillmore-
Know-Nothing vote. Two years later, Douglas wanted it the other way
round: by nailing the flag of Negro equality to the Republican mast, he
could attract the votes of both immigrants (who wanted no economic
or social competition from free blacks) *and* the Know-Nothings, who
simply wanted no blacks in any form. He recruited Buckner Morris,
the Fillmoreite candidate for governor in 1856, to take the stump
against Lincoln, and filled Lanphier's *State Register* and Sheahan's
Chicago Times with appeals "to every foreigner, read the actions of the
Black Republican party . . . and then vote according to your better
judgement. . . . They would grant the negro rights that foreign born
white citizens would be deprived of." When William Herndon ("Lincoln's man Friday") took the stump at a Danite rally in Springfield, "a
drunken man was somewhat noisy," and the *State Register* was de-

lighted to report that Herndon picked the drunk up "and brutally hauled him down stairs, yelling 'God damn the Irish, I want it distinctly understood that *we* . . . are willing to have war with them.'" The *State Register* cheerfully followed this up with the reminder that "the coming election will probably furnish republicanism with another class upon which to war—the Germans" and "any and every class who refuse to recognize the negro as the white man's equal." To make sure every immigrant understood which party was the white man's party, the *State Register* fastened its sights on a freelance campaigner, a twenty-six-year-old black Chicagoan named Hezekiah Ford Douglass, the owner of the *Provincial Freeman*, who was touring northern Illinois as an antislavery lecturer, and began touting him as a Lincoln Republican. Douglass had been on the antislavery lecture circuit since 1856; he was on the circuit again in the summer and fall of 1858, and Charles Lanphier was happy to announce that his "abolition speeches . . . extolled the political virtues of Mr. Lincoln," who was willing "to swallow every greasy nigger that comes along." (It would have come as no pleasant surprise for Lanphier to discover that H. Ford Douglass had written to the Little Giant in January to ask for the addition of his name to Douglas's regular mailing list of printed congressional speeches: "I am opposed to you in Politics," wrote Douglass, "but like you for your consistency in the advocacy of the 'Kansas-Nebraska Bill.'")[37]

But Douglas continued to be dogged by griefs of his own. The Danites still harassed him on the campaign trail, and they were confident that, although he "fights in his rough vulgar way like a tiger," the long campaign had "used him . . . nearly up." Other Danites begged Sidney Breese, as the Danite Senate candidate, to "give us a lift" by actively stumping the state against Douglas. If Breese would strike out vigorously, they would not leave even so much as "a greasy spot" to remind people where Douglas had stood. Meanwhile, the heads of Douglas patronage appointees, which had rolled so frequently in July, now underwent another round with the Buchanan guillotine, and "one by one the heads of adherents of Mr. Douglas come off. . . . We are assured that every post Master—great and small—and every other Federal office-holder who fails to do the work of the Administration is to be removed."

Douglas was having difficulty even among his own loyalists. "I have had some trouble," wailed Samuel Marshall to Charles Lanphier on October 9, "in guarding against the danger of local questions and personal rivalries that have to some extent endangered the success of our cause." In Madison County, arguments over railroad litigation might drive just enough Democrats away from the polls or into the arms of the Danites; there were also "railroad questions" in Wayne and Edwards counties; in the tenth state house district, the Douglasite candidate, Robert Forth, was too ill and "cannot take the stump at all." He was opposed by A. R. Kinear, "a Smooth, intelligent, pleasant gentleman" who "is personally popular with the people—Especially the old Whigs." [38]

Douglas did his cause no favor by drinking ever more heavily. At Charleston, there were rumblings that his antagonistic behavior during Lincoln's rejoinder could only have been fueled by booze, and Lincoln smirked that at least *he* did not have "to have his wife along to keep him sober." A week after Charleston, Charles Wilson's *Chicago Journal* passed along a report from a campaign stop in Oquawka that Douglas's speech "was observed to be very difficult, as though his tongue was much swollen. The peculiar manner in which he spoke of Misha Linka was highly suggestive."

And then the weather turned. At the beginning of the campaigns, Illinois had been soaked by torrential rains, but the weeks that followed in July and August had been baking dry and hot, interrupted by only a brief low-pressure front during the week of the Freeport debate. Now, the autumnal rains and damp swept in with a vengeance: Orville Hickman Browning recorded September 24 as a "cloudy, chilly, misty looking fall day," and the week following provided rain "quite heavily in the night" and "gusty" winds, and finally "heavy white frost this morning." Worn down with the strain, Douglas caught a cold, which swiftly developed into bronchitis—and which he treated with still more liquor. No wonder the *Chicago Tribune* thought that Douglas's voice "is growing hollow and husky, his temper is bad, and his whole appearance jaded and worn." Herndon told Theodore Parker that the Little Giant looked as "bloated as I ever saw him; he drinks very hard indeed; his look is awful to me, when I compare him as he now looks with what he was in February, 1858."[39]

Unfortunately, Douglas was now going to need every ounce of his depleted energies to turn back ever more rambunctious and confident Republican crowds. "The Republican Party . . . has been resorting to regular ruffianism in attempting to break up meetings Mr. D. was addressing," complained one Democratic newspaper, and in fact incidents of heckling and fistfights were on the rise as the campaigns swung into their fourth phase. At a Republican rally for Lyman Trumbull at Rock Island, the banners were literally nauseating: one showed Douglas "with a pair of shears, cutting the clause from the Toombs bill," while another showed him swallowing a large pig marked DRED SCOTT at Chicago, then vomiting up the pig at Freeport. Two days after Charleston, Lincoln and Douglas were both in Sullivan, the county seat of Moultrie County (which shared the twenty-fifth state house district with Charleston in Coles County), and there, a Douglas meeting on the town square stood in the path of a Republican parade to a "grove" in "the north part of town." While the "Black Republican marshal" argued with the Douglasites to make way, "a band of music, which had been employed by the friends of Mr. Lincoln . . . commenced blowing and drumming with all their might to drown the voice of Senator Douglas." Finally, the "band wagon," led by "a few persons with badges, inscribed 'A Lincoln,'" tried to force its way through the Douglas crowd, and predictably, a street brawl broke out.

On the other hand, the Douglasites still had plenty of "dirty tricks" left in their own bags, too. Within three weeks of the Charleston debate, Lincoln was informed that "A pamphlet containing what is purported to be the speeches delivered by Judge Douglass & yourself in the debate at Charleston" was circulating to the tune of ten thousand copies. "Your speech," warned one of Lincoln's correspondents, was so embarassingly rewritten that "it is well calculated to work a great injury to yourself & our party's cause." It carried no printer's frank, but "the pamphlet has doubtless issued from the Times office Chicago."[40]

A little less than three weeks separated the Charleston debate from the next debate on the schedule, at Galesburg, the county seat of Knox County. Neither candidate showed much disposition to rest or repair. In the week following Charleston, Douglas slugged onward through Danville on September 21, west to Urbana on the twenty-third, then north to Kankakee on the twenty-fifth. If anything, he was reaching for increasingly dramatic shows. He was now traveling with "four extra cars and platform car for his cannon," and at Urbana, he was met by the Urbana Saxhorn and Military Band, a long parade of "ladies and gentlemen on horseback" and a "string of wheeled vehicles." From there, he turned up the Illinois River, touching by steamboat at Metamora, Washington, Peoria, and Pekin. With five days left before the debate, Douglas struck due west from Pekin to Oquawka on the Mississippi River and then sprang back through Monmouth in order to arrive at Galesburg on October 7.[41]

Lincoln gave himself no more rest than Douglas. Even after the "collision" at Sullivan, Lincoln paced after Douglas, following him to Danville and Urbana until September 25, when he broke off to return to Springfield, where the local Republican Club greeted him at the station and a local band played outside his house until "Mr. Lincoln appeared on the portico" to acknowledge them. He was then on the road again, with thirteen "densely-packed" cars of supporters for a rally in the heart of the Whig Belt at Jacksonville. Lincoln was finally receiving reinforcements from the larger Republican world—although in this case it was only from nearby St. Louis, in the form of Frank P. Blair, who had just lost a hard-fought campaign in Missouri, and from

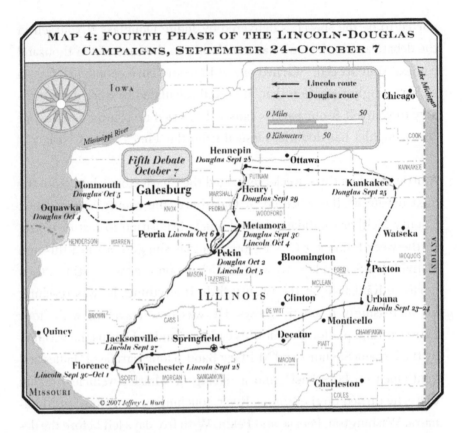

MAP 4: FOURTH PHASE OF THE LINCOLN-DOUGLAS CAMPAIGNS, SEPTEMBER 24–OCTOBER 7

Springfield lawyer James Cook Conkling. (He would not, however, get help from Indiana's Caleb B. Smith, or Ohio's Thomas Corwin, Samuel Galloway, or Benjamin Wade, despite Joseph Medill's pleas. Like so many of Douglas's fair-weather Democratic friends, prominent Republicans would sit this one out until they could be certain not only of the winner but whether, if the winner was Douglas, he might turn Republican, and an unforgiving one at that). In Jacksonville a parade led by the Beardstown Independent Guards, a local rifle company, an artillery company, and the Rescue Fire Company tramped noisily from the Great Western Railroad station to the Morgan County courthouse square, bearing banners that read,

MORGAN, SANGAMON

UNITED IN THE STATE SENATE FOR LINCOLN

(Morgan and Sangamon counties composed a single state senate district, the fifteenth, where a Republican, Cyrus Vanderen, was a "holdover" and not up for reelection in 1858.) At the courthouse, a "stand" had been put up for all three Republicans to speak from. But "as the crowd continued to increase," another "stand" had to be erected for Conkling so that the overflow of the fifteen thousand people who eventually packed the courthouse yard could also have someone to listen to. From Jacksonville, Lincoln spoke at Winchester, Florence, and Pittsfield, then followed Douglas's path up the Illinois river to arrive on October 6 at Peoria, within striking distance (on the Peoria & Oquawka Railroad) of the debate at Galesburg.[42]

Galesburg was a colony and became a town only because the colony couldn't help it. It was the brainchild of the Reverend George Washington Gale, but its ultimate reason for existence was the great wave of evangelical revivals which swept out of New England and across upstate New York between 1815 and 1831. The revivals took their pattern from the Great Awakening of the 1740s, which had pitched George Whitefield and Jonathan Edwards to the peak of American attention. But this second Great Awakening was simultaneously more mobile and more ambitious. New Englanders converted in the first onset of the Awakening carried its fires with them as they migrated westward into New York in search of land, and their converts, in turn, carried it still farther, in a wide band that covered the Western Reserve of Ohio, lapped along the Great Lakes, and planted its westernmost outposts in southern Michigan and northern Illinois. Behind it, the Awakening scattered neat replicas of New England towns (with replica names like Amherst, Litchfield, Norwalk, Deerfield, Stockbridge) designed by earnest spirits who were determined to create miniature evangelical commonwealths. The most famous of these "colonies" was Oberlin, in northern Ohio, where the first settlers had actually signed a "covenant" to eat, dress, and drink in puritanical simplicity: "first religion, second work; and third study."[43] The opportunity for study was supplied by Oberlin's most famous asset, the

Oberlin Collegiate Institute, which had lured the most successful of the Awakening's preachers, Charles Grandison Finney, to become its president. And Finney's mentor was George Washington Gale.

Galesburg was not, at first inspection, unlike several other self-contained "colonies" which had been created in Illinois. New Englanders with the same purposes as Gale's in mind established "Yankee colonies" at Hoyleton and Rosemond in the 1850s; Norwegians were lured to the Augustana Lutheran Synod's settlement at Paxton; Eric Janson and Swedish pietists founded Bishop Hill in 1846; a collection of British gentleman freethinkers led by Morris Birkbeck organized a settlement at English Prairie as early as 1816; and between 1839 and 1846, Nauvoo became the capital of Mormon settlement in Illinois. But Galesburg's primary kinship was to Oberlin: George Washington Gale had infused "a deep and ardent religious sentiment" into the colony, and in 1837, Gale established a college on the Oberlin model, named for the morning star of Scottish Presbyterianism, John Knox. And as evangelical benevolence increasingly went hand in hand with abolitionism, Galesburg became an enclave in Illinois "well known among the negroes" as a place where "a runaway slave was considered as free from capture when within its limits as if in Canada." Gale himself had been indicted for harboring fugitive slaves, and the college's first president, Hiram H. Kellogg, was a delegate at the World's Anti-Slavery Convention in 1843. The first black member of the U.S. Senate after the Civil War had been a student at Knox College; so had Varveel Florville, the son of Springfield's (and Lincoln's) black barber.[44]

Still, by the 1850s, the intrusion of commerce had begun to displace the zeal for religion. Galesburg sat squarely on the old Military Road that once linked Chicago with Fort Madison on the Mississippi, and it made an ideal link for the Chicago, Burlington & Quincy Railroad (as it reached west to Burlington, Iowa) and the newly finished Peoria & Oquawka, and a branch of the Northern Cross Railroad. But none of these compromises with the larger world had entirely quenched the embers of the town's abolition enthusiasm. Galesburg had gone consistently for Republicans at every level in 1856: the fifty-eighth state house district (which embraced Galesburg and all of its surrounding Knox County) had gone Republican by 64 percent; and as part of the ninth state senate district, Galesburg and Knox County gave 66 percent of its vote to the Republican Thomas Henderson. Yet the Douglasites were determined to make a fight of it. James Davidson, the Douglasite federal marshal for northern Illinois, whose head had been one of the first to fall into President Buchanan's basket, was put up to face William Pitt Kellogg for the Fourth Congressional District, and at the Douglasite county convention in early September, "one and a half hours was consumed in making arrangements for the reception of Douglas at Galesburg." As one of Lincoln's correspondents wrote, "The Democrats are calculating largely on the effect of their reception" to overawe Galesburg's Republicans.[45]

And they did not do badly. Douglas (along with "eleven carloads" of spectators) arrived in Galesburg at ten o'clock on the morning of the debate on the Chicago, Burlington & Quincy Railroad; the local Democratic worthies—John T. Barrett, Josiah Tilden, and George Elwell—met him and offered "a well-prepared but somewhat fulsome address." The students of Lombard University, the town's nonabolition college, made up a white silk banner with a hand-embroidered laurel wreath, "emblematic of Mr. Douglas' course," and the motto PRESENTED TO STEPHEN A. DOUGLAS, BY THE STUDENTS OF LOMBARD UNIVERSITY. A little more risqué was the inscription embroidered "on the dresses of a number of young ladies," which played Douglas's race card at its most blunt level: WHITE MEN OR NONE.[46]

But Galesburg was Republican territory, and the local Republican arrangements committee had determined to "turn out 10 republicans to one democrat." Rather than merely get off the train in Galesburg, Lincoln was to stop the afternoon before the debate in Knoxville, a station two miles east of Galesburg on the Burlington line. He would be met there by William Kellogg, and the following morning, "a cavalcade of at least 12 to 1500 persons" would escort Lincoln by carriage into Galesburg at the same hour as Douglas's train was due to pull in. They "marched through the principal street of the city, from the east to the public square, thence south two squares, thence east and north two squares, crossing its own track." The local Republican committee, headed by Judge Henry Sanderson, gave the official greeting to Lincoln from the steps of Sanderson's house north of the town square, and "the Republican ladies of Galesburg" had an embroidered banner of their own to present to Lincoln, with an "American Shield" on one side and a "scroll" (meant to portray the Declaration of Independence) painted on the other.

Between then and one o'clock (when the debate was to begin), the fields around Galesburg sprouted tents and camps, the wooden sidewalks filled up with people, and the streets became jammed with "carriages and wagons ... driving about ... in search of hitching places." The banners they had made to carry in the parade to the debate were evidence of the increasingly virulent tone of the campaigns: one portrayed Douglas and Toombs, and showed Douglas slashing a Kansas constitution with his pen; another carried a crude picture of a headless James Davidson; yet another showed Douglas "coming from Egypt," and roaring with pain under the blows of a cane wielded by Lincoln. "The Douglas-Lincoln war rages fiercely on the Western prairie," reported one Pennsylvania newspaper. "The combatants begin to lose temper, and hurl epithets which are neither polite nor savory."[47]

The estimates on the size of the crowd packing into Galesburg varied wildly, from 10,000 to 25,000; what was not in dispute, however, was that this crowd would probably be the most actively hostile audience Douglas had faced since Freeport. Just as hostile would be the weather. From Indian summer conditions only a few days before, the temperatures suddenly dropped off the edge the evening before the debate as a powerful cold front brought a "semi-deluge or rain" over Galesburg, followed by a killing "Artic frost ... and a sour northwest wind" on the morning of the debate. "Notwithstanding the sun shone bright and clear," the "elements seemed to have conspired to dampen and congeal all political ardor."

The arrangements committees had originally planned to use the town square for the debate, and a platform had been constructed there for the usual collection of reporters, dignitaries, and the two principals. But the open platform, in an open square, offered no shelter and no acoustic compromise with the whipping wind, and at noon the platform was dragged bodily over to the Knox College campus, where it was set up under the lee of the east side of the three-story classroom building, Old Main. This delayed the start of the debate till two o'clock, and the relocation made access awkward—the platform rose flush to the sills of the tall windows on the side of Old Main, and the window sashes had to be removed so that Lincoln and Douglas could use them as makeshift doorways onto the platform. But the enormous crowd dutifully followed the platform to the college, and students at the college ranged themselves on the roof of the one-story dormitory facing the east side of Old Main "as the best vantage ground for seeing and hearing." [48]

It was plain from the start that Douglas, who would have the lead-off position in this debate, was in trouble. The Little Giant's struggle with his deepening bronchitis quickly rendered his voice hoarse, and despite the "small round box" of lozenges "in his hand," he began sounding "so rough and harsh" that his words "carried only a comparatively short distance in the great crowd." One Knox student found Douglas "very hard to listen to," and up on the dormitory roof, another student doubted "if he was heard, so as to be understood, by a third or the audience." He also tired rapidly: "His style of speaking . . . was disjointed as if he could not be heard if he spoke two words without pause between."

And at first, Douglas's argument seemed as lacking in energy as his style. All of his policies, including Kansas-Nebraska, were based on "the great fundamental principle" of popular sovereignty, "that the people of each State and each territory of this Union . . . ought to be permitted to exercise the right of regulating their own domestic concerns in their own way, subject to no other limitation or restriction than that which the Constitution of the United States imposes upon them." When he discovered that the Lecompton constitution would violate this "great fundamental principle," he "carried the banner of Popular Sovereignty aloft, and never allowed it to trail in the dust, or lowered my flag until victory perched upon our arms." He had not done this with any thought about slavery: "My opposition to the Lecompton constitution did not rest upon the peculiar position taken by Kansas on the subject of slavery." Slavery was something he did not meddle in, and did not want Congress meddling in, and he believed the people of Kansas were the only ones fitted to decide it. "I held then, and hold now, that if the people of Kansas want a slave State, it is their right to make one and be received into the Union under it; if, on the contrary, they want a free State, it is their right to have it, and no man should ever oppose their admission because they ask it under the one or the other." Slavery was not the issue at stake; popular self-government was.[49]

His real enemy in this struggle was the Buchanan administration, which wanted "to break me down" in retaliation for his opposition to Lecompton. But the Republicans were hoping to use this to their partisan political advantage "and put another man in the U.S. Senate in my place." These Republicans had opposed Lecompton as much as Douglas had, but they "now form an alliance with federal office holders, professed Lecompton men, to defeat me, because I did right." What shall we make of "a political organization that will try to make an unholy and unnatural combination with its professed foes to beat a man merely because he has done right?"

Nor was that the only thing wrong with the Republicans. Political parties in this country had once been "national in their character" with principles that applied "alike in the Slave and the Free States." The Republicans are something more sinister—"a sectional organization . . . which appeals to northern passion, northern pride, northern ambition, and northern prejudices, against southern people, the southern States and southern institutions"—and are willing even to entertain the idea of disunion and civil war in pursuit of their program. Not that they do so openly. Instead, they whip up abolition frenzy among the abolitionists; but then, because the abolitionist vote could never get them elected, they peddle a phony moderation among Union-loving moderates to garner their support. Take Lincoln, for example: "In the extreme northern part of Illinois he can proclaim as bold and radical abolitionism as ever . . . Lovejoy, or Garrison enunciated, but when he gets down a little further South he claims that he is an old line Whig." Lincoln denies this, but just contrast what Lincoln said in Chicago—and here Douglas trotted out Lincoln's deadly words against "quibbling" over "this race and that race, and the other race being inferior"—with what he said in Charleston about never favoring "the social and political equality of the white and black races." Douglas, however, would never turn his coat: "I will never conceal my opinions, or modify or change them a hair's breadth in order to get votes." And so he had no fear in telling a Republican audience "that this Chicago doctrine of Lincoln's—declaring that the negro and the white man are made equal by the Declaration of Independence and by Divine Providence—is a monstrous heresy." [50]

Douglas's one, true and constant principle would always be "that each State has the right to do as it pleases on all these questions, and no other State, or power on earth has the right to interfere with us, or complain of us merely because our system differs from theirs." Of course, there was the problem of *Dred Scott*. If no territory had the constitutional power to bar slavery, the same logic seemed to imply that no state should, either. But Douglas disposed of that with the unfriendly-legislation strategy. "Chief Justice Taney has said in his opinion in the Dred Scott case, that a negro slave being property, stands on an equal footing with other property, and that the owner may carry them into United States territory the same as he does other property." But what do you do with various kinds of property? A merchant who sells liquor does not try to transport liquor into a "dry" state like Maine, because he knows that "the Maine liquor law . . . prohibits the sale or use of his property." Just so with slave property: "The slaveholder when he gets his slaves there finds that there is no local law to protect him in holding them, no slave code, no police regulation maintaining and supporting him in his right, and he discovers at once that the absence of such friendly legislation excludes his property from the territory, just as irresistibly as if there was a positive constitutional prohibition excluding it." Hence, the will of the people triumphs. If Kansas votes itself free, every antislavery man can congratulate himself on the success of antislavery; if Kansas votes itself slave, no antislavery man can oppose that vote without opposing the root principle of democracy itself. The "one path of peace in this republic" is not to make the house all one thing or all the other but "to administer this government as our fathers made it, divided into free and slave States, allowing each State to decide for itself whether it wants slavery or not."[51]

This was as slow and listless a performance as Douglas had given during the debates (his rate of speaking had dropped to just under a hundred words a minute), and at the close he wrapped himself in an overcoat and a white, wide-brimmed hat, and sat down glumly to smoke a cigar. His comments were enlivened only by the smarminess of his remarks about Lincoln, who had now descended in Douglas's description from being a political sharpie trying to abolitionize the Whigs to being a routine hypocrite with no better goal than gaining office. Lincoln rose, doffing "a long light colored duster" which he wore over his black suit, and as he passed Douglas, the Little Giant muttered (from Psalm 13), "How long, O Lord, how long?" Lincoln, never to be outdone in the volume of Scripture he had memorized as a boy, instantly shot back, "The days and years of the wicked are short" (Proverbs 10:27). And to the "surprise and delight" of the students festooning the roof of the Knox dormitory, Lincoln's "high tenor . . . voice rang out over the great assembly clear as a bell" and "with extraordinary carrying power."

He would not try to respond to everything Douglas had said, Lincoln explained, because "a very large portion of the speech which Judge Douglas has addressed to you" was simply the same thing he had been saying since July. But there were some points he wanted to speak to, and based "upon some notes which I have taken," he would reply in reverse order, beginning with Douglas's dismissal of the Declaration of Independence as "heresy." [52]

"I believe the entire records of the world, from the date of the Declaration of Independence up to within three years ago, may be searched in vain for one single affirmation, from one single man, that the negro was not included in the Declaration of Independence." If it was true that the Declaration of Independence was never intended to include blacks, then the burden of proof was on Douglas, and it was proof which he would never be able to find, since no such proof existed. Thomas Jefferson, even while he was "the owner of slaves," admitted that he "trembled" over the injustice of slavery, and precisely because his own words about all men being created equal actually meant *all*. Douglas, by contrast, seemed never to have trembled at all at the injustice of slavery, and Lincoln was ready to offer "the highest premium in my power to Judge Douglas if he will show that he, in all his life, ever uttered a sentiment at all akin to that of Jefferson." (This stung: it was followed by *great applause* and cries of *"Hit him again."*)

Douglas also seemed to have trouble understanding any distinction, any explanation, or any logic higher than the level of a slogan. "The Judge will have it that if we do not confess that there is a sort of inequality between the white and black races, which justifies us in making them slaves, we must, then, insist that there is a degree of equality that requires us to make them our wives." This is absurd. Natural "equality between the white and black races" had nothing to do with "perfect social and political equality," and Douglas was only raising this as a distraction from the real question, which was slavery. "There is no misunderstanding this, except by men interested to misunderstand it." What was slavery? An outrage on "moral and abstract right." Why? Because it violated the natural rights every black man, woman, and child had as an equal member of the human race to life, liberty, and the pursuit of happiness.

Lincoln's concern was with the containment and extinction of this outrage, not making it a matter of popular vote, as though majority rule in a democracy had the same authority over gravity that it had over turnpikes. "We are now far advanced in this Canvass," Lincoln continued, pressing home his sharpest rhetorical weapon. "Judge Douglas and I have made perhaps forty speeches apiece, and we have now for the fifth time met face to face in debate, and up to this day I have not found either Judge Douglas or any friend of his" able to point to anything in the Republican opposition to slavery "that is wrong." Douglas calls his opponents *Black Republicans, Nigger-lovers, sectional*—what he has not been able to do is "demonstrate them to be wrong." (In fact, if anybody was turning sectional, it was Douglas: "All the Democrats of the Free States are agreeing with him, while he omits to tell us that the Democrats of any Slave State agree with him.")

The problem with Kansas-Nebraska, and ultimately with Douglas himself, is that he fiddles industriously over the question of whether a majority of the people in a territory have the right to choose something and ignores the fire he sets when he licenses any majority to do what is *wrong.* "I suppose that the real difference between Judge Douglas and his friends, and the Republicans on the contrary, is that the Judge is not in favor of making any difference between Slavery and Liberty—that he is in favor of eradicating, of pressing out of view, the questions of preference in this country for Free over Slave institutions; and consequently every sentiment he utters discards the idea that there is any wrong in Slavery."

If there was no hint of *wrong* in slavery—if there was no natural law of equality, or if power and self-interest were the only guiding stars of a democracy, so that democracy had nothing more transcendent at its heart than dumb self-satisfaction—then Douglas would be a hero and popular sovereignty would be the only question at stake. "If you will

take the Judge's speeches, and select the short and pointed sentences expressed by him—as his declaration that he 'don't care whether Slavery
is voted up or down'—you will see at once that this is perfectly logical, if
you do not admit that Slavery is wrong." But if it is wrong . . . then you
"cannot logically say that anybody has a right to do wrong." Slavery
was a question of morals and whether democracy rested on a moral
basis, not a discussion about the mechanisms of process.[53]

Perhaps, Lincoln added, Douglas has some difficulty discerning the
morality of democracy because he has a basic trouble understanding
that politicians have a responsibility to distinguish right from wrong.
"I want to call to the Judge's attention an attack he made upon me in
the first one of these debates, at Ottawa, on the 21st of August," imput-
ing the Aurora resolutions to the entire Illinois Republican party. As
soon as Lincoln had shown Douglas the error in this charge, "that the
resolutions which he read had not been passed at Springfield at all, nor
by a State Convention," Douglas had promptly blamed Charles Lanphier and Thomas Harris for misleading him, "and he promised in that
speech that when he went to Springfield he would investigate the matter." But "a month has passed . . . and so far as I know, he has made no
report of the result of his investigation." Nor did Lincoln expect him
to, because the whole business was a "fraud." But why should Illinoisans put any faith now in Douglas when he accuses Lincoln of
hypocrisy? Douglas, Lincoln drolly said, was like "the fisherman's wife,
whose drowned husband was brought home with his body full of eels."
When she was asked, "What was to be done with him?" her reply was
"Take the eels out and set him again." Likewise, "Harris and Douglas
have shown a disposition to take the eels out of that stale fraud . . . and
set the fraud again."[54]

The crowd was whooping now—*Great cheering. . . . Hit him
again. . . . Give it to him*—but Lincoln still had one more bomb to
throw. Douglas had innocently alluded to "Chief Justice Taney" and
how the unfriendly legislation strategy would permit popular sovereignty to operate freely despite the ruling in *Dred Scott*. Lincoln had

pressed Douglas at Freeport to explain, in response to Lincoln's third question there, why a decision which struck down laws against slavery in the territories couldn't logically be used as a precedent for one day striking down the laws against slavery in the free states. Lincoln quoted Taney directly: *Now, as we have already said in an earlier part of this opinion, upon a different point, the right of property in a slave is distinctly and expressly affirmed in the Constitution.* From that, Lincoln constructed this syllogism:

> *Nothing in the Constitution or laws of any State can destroy a right distinctly and expressly affirmed in the Constitution of the United States.*
>
> *The right of property in a slave is distinctly and expressly affirmed in the Constitution of the United States;*
>
> *Therefore, nothing in the Constitution or laws of any State can destroy the right of property in a slave.*

So far, Douglas has offered no contradiction of this logic other than a "sneer" that the Supreme Court would never do something like that. Sneers, however, do not offer much protection from logic, or from another *Dred Scott*–like decision. The only real insurance would be the election of Republicans to Congress—and especially the Senate. "My own opinion is," Lincoln went on, "that the new *Dred Scott* decision, deciding against the right of the people of the States to exclude slavery, will never be made, if that party is sustained by the elections." Douglas only tells us that he has a strategy which accommodates *Dred Scott* and still promises freedom. Well, elect Douglas, and we will go on accommodating *Dred Scott* until the second *Dred Scott* decision is handed down, and by that point, Douglas will have talked everyone into believing that they don't need to care whether slavery is voted up or voted down, that "whoever wants Slavery has a right to have it," and that "there is no inconsistency between free and slave institutions." Is this a strategy for ensuring freedom, or the preparation of the way for making "the institution of Slavery national!"[55]

Lincoln began at this moment to launch into "a consideration of the question of territorial acquisition in its relation to slavery." But "just here" came another parade, numbering eighteen hundred people, onto the college campus "with music." (It was a massive Lincoln delegation from Peoria, whose twenty-two car train on the Peoria & Oquawka line had broken down from the sheer weight of the passengers in two coaches and an assortment of boxcars and flatcars. Two locomotives had been dispatched to the rescue, but even then the passengers had been forced to get out of the cars and push to get the train up some steep grades. Only now, at nearly five o'clock, had they pulled into Galesburg.) In the noise and hurrahing, Lincoln lost all track of his time, along with the attention of the crowd, and he stopped in mid-stride to "give way to Judge Douglas." (Lincoln had actually come up slightly short, which was why the moderator, the former Republican congressman James Knox, had not yet called time.)

Douglas had been stewing unhappily over Lincoln's fire, and he now barreled to the front of the platform "under great mental excite-ment." Did Lincoln believe that he had nothing new to say? That was only because, unlike Lincoln, he did not have one message for northern Illinois and an entirely different one for the south. "The first criticism that Mr. Lincoln makes on my speech was that it was in substance what I have said everywhere else in the State where I have addressed the people. I wish I could say the same of his speech." Lincoln tells you in Charleston that he doesn't believe in "negro equality," while today, in Republican territory, "I understand him to reaffirm the doctrine of negro equality, and to assert that by the Declaration of Independence the negro is declared equal to the white man." *We believe it,* a voice bel-lowed up from the crowd, to be followed by so many "cat calls, groans, cheers, and other noises" that Douglas stopped speaking and Lincoln had to stand up and ask for quiet.

Douglas tried to continue, accusing Lincoln of making slavery a question of morality in Galesburg and only "a question of degree" in

Charleston. But again the crowd erupted with cries of *He's right* and *Both*, and this time an infuriated Douglas began arguing back with his tormentors: "He is right then, sir, in your estimation, not because he is consistent, but because he can trim his principles any way in any section, so as to secure votes." Lincoln has "used hard names; has dared to talk about fraud, about forgery, and has insinuated that there was a conspiracy between Mr. Lanphier, Mr. Harris, and myself to perpetrate a forgery." But Douglas was interrupted again, this time by laughter.[56]

Douglas's temper, frayed by weariness and the severity of Lincoln's attack, now gave way completely. "His grand manner was gone," recalled one observer. "He shook his fist in wrath as he walked the platform. A white foam gathered upon his lips, giving him a look of ferocity." Lincoln might not have signed off on those abolitionist resolutions in 1854, Douglas doggedly insisted, but he agrees with them all the same. And as an added shot, the Little Giant snarled that Lincoln "takes to himself great merit because he thinks they were not adopted on the right spot for me to use them against him, just as he was very severe in Congress upon the government of his country when he thought that he had discovered that the Mexican war was not begun in the right *spot*." Douglas demanded to know if "there was an honest man in the State of Illinois who doubted that I had been led into the error, if it was such, innocently, in the way I detailed." Except, of course, Lincoln. "Does Mr. Lincoln wish to push these things to the point of personal difficulties here?" Douglas demanded, backing around and shaking "his clinched fist within a few inches of Lincoln's face." Lincoln says that the logic of *Dred Scott* "would carry slavery into the free States . . . and goes into a long argument to make you believe that I am in favor of . . . the doctrine that would allow slaves to be brought here." Rubbish: "Mr. Lincoln knows that there is not a member of the Supreme Court who holds that Doctrine." What Lincoln really wants to do is "to bring the Supreme Court into disrepute among the people" and change "the government from one of laws into that of a mob."[57]

This was the worst performance Douglas had given during the debates, and the best Lincoln had given. The grid for Galesburg looks like this:

DOUGLAS	LINCOLN
Popular sovereignty is the great principle Douglas has stood for in opposing Lecompton	
Republican party is a sectional party	
Lincoln speaks one way in northern Illinois and another in southern Illinois [repeated in rejoinder]	Denied
Republicans favor racial equality [repeated in rejoinder]	Denied
Unfriendly legislation allows for legal exclusion of slavery from the territories	
	Douglas repudiates the Declaration of Independence
	Natural equality is not the same as civil equality
Denied	Douglas denies that slavery is a moral wrong
	Douglas has not retracted the Aurora resolutions accusation— corollary: Douglas is deceitful
	Douglas's answer to the Freeport Question is a contradiction of the Supreme Court
Denied	Douglas is conspiring to nationalize slavery
Lincoln is descending into name-calling	

Douglas sat down to a smattering of applause, but unlike Charleston, there would be no elaborate postdebate festivities. The cold and the coming-on of evening, together with Douglas's exhaustion, precluded anything larger than a reception afterward for the Little Giant at the Bonney House. Nor were the pressures on Douglas going to get any easier: he had unwisely packed the final two debates of the series, at Quincy and Alton, into the week following Galesburg, and he was now less equal to the strain than when he began his campaign. It was the worst possible sign of the way the Little Giant's tide was ebbing that Charles Wilson's *Chicago Journal* could casually remark, the day after Galesburg, that "we wish these joint debates before the people . . . could be more frequent," perhaps even "two or three times a week" and "in all the principal towns of each Congressional district." If they were, the people "would be so strongly and sweepingly in favor of Lincoln before election day that Douglas would have to abandon himself utterly to despair."

Nor, thanks to Hitt's and Binmore's "phonography," were the stakes limited to Illinois. By the time of the Charleston debate, Lincoln had become conscious that "the readers of this debate" were forming a second audience, and his passing comment, during the Galesburg debate, that the transcribed texts of the debates had been "put in print and all the reading and intelligent men in the community would see them and know all about my opinions," was an offhand testimony to the work the papers had performed in bringing each debate under the scrutiny of every newspaper reader in Illinois, and beyond. Lincoln had suspected, "when it was first agreed that Judge Douglas and I were to have these seven joint discussions," that they would begin to take the shape of "successive acts of a drama"; what he had not expected was that the drama, like Donati's comet, would "be enacted not merely in the face of audiences" in seven Illinois towns "but in the face of the nation, and to some extent . . . in the face of the world."

But so they had. "Illinois is now justly regarded as the central battleground, or turning-point," not just for Lincoln and Douglas, but for "the powers of Slavery and the hosts of Freedom," and "the pending contest in this State" will likely "settle the next Presidency." And the debates had become "the greatest assizes that were ever assembled at any time . . . for the life of the nation, for the liberty of a race, for the triumph of eternal principles."[58]

★ CHAPTER 6 ★

THE SAME TYRANNICAL PRINCIPLE

> *Would I might rouse the Lincoln in you all,*
> *That which is gendered in the wilderness*
> *From lonely prairies and God's tenderness.*
> *Imperial soul, star of a weedy stream,*
> *Born where the ghosts of buffaloes still dream,*
> *Whose spirit hoof-beats storm above his grave,*
> *Above that breast of earth and prairie-fire—*
> *Fire that freed the slave.*
>
> VACHEL LINDSAY, *GENERAL WILLIAM BOOTH ENTERS INTO*
> *HEAVEN AND OTHER POEMS*, 1913

NOTHING TESTIFIED MORE widely to how the debates were turning into a kind of national "assize" than the wave of imitators they spawned. In early September, a Douglasite and a Republican in the seventeenth state house district took the opportunity provided by the meeting of the circuit court in Mount Carmel to stage a debate, and on September 17, the rival candidates for the Fourth Congressional District, Jackson Grimshaw and Isaac Morris, squared off at Nauvoo for what turned out to be something more energetic even than a debate. "Morris called [Grimshaw] a liar, whereupon Grimshaw struck Morris and knocked him headlong off the stand." On September 25, two Republicans—Shelby Cullom and William Jayne (Lyman Trumbull's brother-in-law)—"joined issue" with two Democrats in a "joint debate" at Chatham. Three weeks later, Cullom and Jayne crossed words in another debate at Pleasant Plains. As far away as upstate New York, a novice Republican candidate for Congress, Roscoe Conkling, threw the glove down to his Democratic opponent, challenging him to debate on the same terms being popularized by Lincoln and Douglas. "The practice of making direct avowals of political views, and submitting to open interrogation and scrutiny, has commended itself of late to candidates for nearly every elective office in the country," Conkling wrote on September 28. "Every eye," agreed the *Philadelphia Press*, "is now turned to Illinois."[1]

The eyes of Lincoln and Douglas, however, would be turned to the Whig Belt. Little more than three weeks now remained before the Illinois elections, and in this last phase of their campaigns, both candidates would concentrate entirely on the Belt's seventeen house districts—and the twenty-four representatives those districts would send to the state house—and the Belt's two state senate districts where the seats were up for grabs in 1858. Concentrated in these districts were the votes which would swing the election, and they were votes which would be cast by politically homeless Whigs who had either gone for Fillmore in 1856 or given a combined majority to Fillmore and Frémont. They were, in other words, Lincoln's to lose. And as the Little Giant weakened and slowed, Illinois Republicans jubilantly scented a catastrophic upset in the wind. Pennsylvania's early-bird legislative elections in October gave Republicans a thumping 61 percent of the vote, followed by deadly Republican sweeps in Ohio and Indiana. "Keep up the cry, boys," urged the *Chicago Journal*, and not only "in the U.S. Senate of 1859" but in "the Presidential contest of 1860, we shall again have occasion to repeat with redoubled enthusiasm, 'Hurrah for Lincoln!'"[2]

Lincoln's greatest opportunity to seal the old Whig vote would come in the remaining two debates, since both—in Quincy on October 13 and in Alton on October 15—would take place in the vote-rich districts of the western Whig Belt, along the Mississippi. Lincoln wasted no time in picking up the Peoria & Oquawka railroad at Toulon (where he also spoke in the town square) and bolting westward to begin pumping the Mississippi river towns. He spoke at Oquawka on the afternoon of October 9 and crossed the river to Burlington, Iowa, to speak at the state fair. He stayed with Iowa governor James W. Grimes, and Grimes, who "had read his debates with Mr. Douglass up to that time," sat down over the next day (a Sunday) and "frankly discussed & criticized the points made by each of the disputants."

The next day, Lincoln was back on Illinois soil, speaking at Monmouth. The weather was as chill and gloomy as it had been at Galesburg, and the rain was so constant that the Monmouth Republicans were ready to cancel their outdoor rally and "go to a hall" where Lincoln could address a smaller audience. But shortly after noon, the rain stopped, and "at one o'clock we concluded to go to the stand," where the Monmouth Republican Glee Club "gave us one of their original songs." Lincoln was conscious that this was Whig territory, and he aimed his comments at any former Whig who had caught the strains of the siren song of Douglas the friend of Clay. "Judge Douglas," Lincoln complained, is trying to act as administrator of the political will of Henry Clay. Normally, the requirement for an administrator is "to be a creditor or of kin to the deceased." But Clay "did not owe anything politically to his old enemy, Douglas," and that made Douglas "a pretty man to undertake to wrap the mantle of Clay around him, and strut about trying to palm himself off as his political administrator." Douglas was also up and doing. He, too, made a beeline from Galesburg westward to the river towns, speaking in Macomb on October 8, Ply-

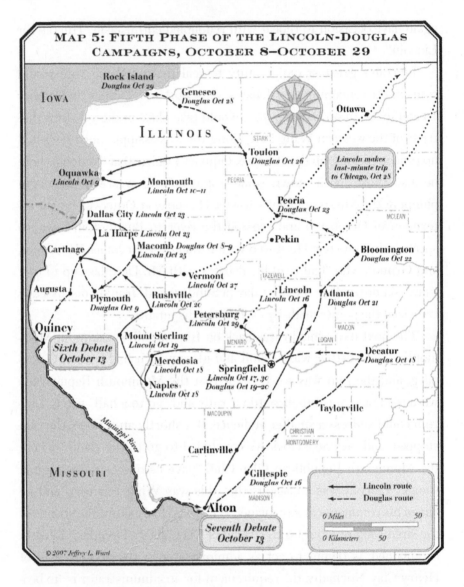

MAP 5: FIFTH PHASE OF THE LINCOLN-DOUGLAS CAMPAIGNS, OCTOBER 8–OCTOBER 29

mouth on October 9, and Carthage on October 11, where Orville Hickman Browning heard him speak to "about 2500 or 3000 people." The bleak turn in the weather was giving Douglas no respite: it was a "cloudy, muddy day," wrote Browning, and it brought forth "a very dull speech."[3]

But if Douglas seemed to be wobbling as he headed toward Quincy, it would have been folly to assume that the Little Giant was about to collapse. By mid-October, Democratic loyalists who had been cheering President Buchanan's massacre of the Douglasites as the punishment due a party rebel were beginning to have uneasy second thoughts about the wisdom of running an interference campaign against the Little Giant. With Democrats meeting "crushing defeat" in Pennsylvania, Ohio, and Indiana, deposing the most prominent Democrat in the Senate over an intraparty fracas began to look less and less like wisdom. "The course of Judge Douglass in the last Congress . . . meets our unqualified disapprobation," wrote the *Dallas Weekly Herald,* "but as between him and Lincoln our sympathies are all with Douglas." The *Houston Telegraph* decided that "between Mr. Douglas and Mr. Lincoln, few southerners can be long in making a choice. The one is democrat, though an erring one . . . while the other is a rank, rampant, poisonmouthed, tearing, raving and raging Abolitionist." And for the half-hearts who steered only in the direction that the political winds were blowing, the Pennsylvania elections were held up "pretty much as the handwriting upon the wall" for Buchanan's political standing. Prudence, or at least a grubby regard for one's own future political employment, dictated a switch to endorsing Douglas. James L. Orr, the Speaker of the House of Representatives, announced that, much as he deplored "the course of . . . Judge Douglas, on the issue of Kansas," nevertheless "all my sympathies . . . are with him in his contest with Lincoln." On the same day as the Quincy debate, Virginia governor Henry Wise wrote a six-page public letter, endorsing Douglas and denouncing the "Tyrannical Proscription which would, alike foolishly & wickedly, lop off one of the most vigorous limbs of National Democracy—the limb of glorious Illinois!" And one of the Democratic survivors in Ohio, Congressman Clement Laird Vallandigham, wrote in a similar letter on the nineteenth that "my sympathies are wholly with Douglas & against Lincoln; & I express . . . almost the unanimous voice, I believe, of the Democracy of Ohio."[*]

Nor was Quincy, sitting on its high bluff above the Mississippi, exactly a dead zone for Douglas. Although it sat at the westernmost point of the Whig Belt, Quincy had briefly been Douglas's home base once he moved into political prominence, and it had sent him to Congress in the 1840s. Even more surprising, Quincy was the heart of a state house district—the twenty-ninth—which went for Buchanan in 1856 and sent two Democrats to the state house. And for a decade it had consistently elected Douglas's chief lieutenant, William A. Richardson, to Douglas's old seat in the House of Representatives. But Democratic victories were not always guaranteed; Quincy had elected a Whig mayor in 1856 by a wafer-thin majority of forty-four votes. The task facing Lincoln was to win over voters who had gone for Whigs when they felt free enough but who defected to the Democrats whenever they sniffed abolition. Orville Hickman Browning, whose home and law practice were in Quincy, was an ominous case in point. Although Browning was an old friend of Lincoln's, and had joined Lincoln in moving to the Republicans in 1856, his name appeared nowhere on the Quincy arrangements committee for Lincoln when it met on October 5. Although he agreed to lend his home in Quincy as a temporary headquarters for Lincoln during the debate, Browning somehow contrived to be out of town, "attending court," on the day of the event.[5]

The Republican arrangements committee was itself a testimony to the shakiness of Lincoln's prospects in Quincy. Of the twenty-three members, only one—Illinois's Republican lieutenant governor John Wood—was a statewide political figure. Five others had some local prominence, but only modestly so. George Bond was a two-term city alderman who had moved to Quincy from Boston in 1835 and set up a successful meatpacking firm; James Arthur was an immigrant from northern Ireland (and therefore passed as Protestant, in contrast to the Catholic Irish who generated the *Chicago Tribune*'s dread of "colonization" on Election Day) with a modest butcher's business worth about $3,000, who rarely pushed himself onto the political stage and had "refused frequent solicitation to accept official positions." John

Wheeler, another city alderman and a miller who owned $27,000 worth of property, was a longtime Whig who had voted for William Henry Harrison in 1840 and was now "a sturdy Republican"; Joel Rice, a Kentuckian by birth, was like George Bond in meatpacking; and Alonzo Swarthout, yet another alderman, was a riverboat captain. Once past these few, the social standing of the committee fell off considerably. Quincy had a substantial German-speaking immigrant population (six of the town's twenty churches held German-language services; there was even a German Jewish synagogue), so the committee included Ferdinand Flack, a twenty-five-year-old druggist from Germany, and Otto Bertschanger, a twenty-four-year-old Swiss-born clerk. And rounding out the humbler pursuits, it also numbered Timothy Rogers and John Bernard, "wagon-makers," and Joseph van Doom, a twenty-two-year-old "confectioner."[6] This did not make Quincy's embrace of Republicanism look all that firm.

Even the weather smiled for Douglas in Quincy, as the lowering clouds and "cold, dismal storms" of the preceding week broke to reveal a "bright day, mild & windy" for the debate. The Little Giant arrived on the Great Western Railroad from Augusta the evening before ("and was received at the depot by a small sized Irish mob," grumbled the *Tribune*). Lincoln came in at nine o'clock the next morning, riding on the same train with Carl Schurz, who had his first chance to meet the Republican candidate personally. "Although measuring a little over six feet myself," Schurz remembered, "I had, standing quite near to him, to throw my head backward in order to look into his face." But Lincoln's "benignant, melancholy eyes," and his freedom from "any semblance of pretension or superiority" as he talked "about the points he and Douglas made in the debates at different places," soon made Schurz feel "as if I had known him all my life."

The Republican train was met at the Quincy station by a "Republican procession" led by Steig's Brass Band, the Adams County Republican clubs, and a long string of "carriages and wagons." The Republican and Democratic arrangements committees had planned their parading with almost military precision: the Republicans, guided by marshals wearing blue scarves and Lincoln badges, would march through the streets, wheeling at Jersey Street, Eighth Street, Hampshire Street, Fourth Street, Maine Street, and Fifth Street, with each turn moving closer and closer to the county courthouse on Washington Square, where Lincoln would "be received and welcomed by the Committee of Reception." At the head of the Republican procession was a "model ship on wheels, drawn by four horses, labeled 'CONSTITUTION'" and featuring a live raccoon—the emblem of Henry Clay—at the helm. Douglas's parade was to assemble at the courthouse at nine thirty, marching up Broadway and meeting the Little Giant at his hotel, the Quincy House, where he "saluted it" from his second-story room window. Farther up Broadway, at Twelfth Street, the parade tacked on the "delegations from the northern part of the county" (who were drawn up in readiness at Twelfth Street), followed by "the delegations from the east and southern part of the county" (at Maine Street), and finally "the river delegations" (who had come downriver by steamboat) at the Virginia House, ending up at the courthouse for Douglas to make "a few remarks" just after the Lincoln procession had dismissed. Lincoln, meanwhile, was driven from the courthouse to Orville Hickman Browning's home, where John Tillson (the Republican candidate for the state senate, who was running against the deposed Douglasite postmaster Austin Brooks) made another welcoming speech and a local choir sang "Columbia, the Gem of the Ocean."[7]

The debate was scheduled to begin at one thirty in Washington Square, just three blocks up from the wharves along the Mississippi. The platform faced southwest, "toward the old Quincy house," and with approximately twelve thousand people piling into the square, the "whole street was full of teams and people entirely around the park." But the construction work (by "Mr. N. Pinkham") had been slipshod, and "shortly before the arrival of the speakers," a part "of the railing around the platform" came apart and dumped "twelve or fifteen persons . . . backward on the ground" along with a "heavy wooden bench."

Three people (including the wife of Democratic state house candidate Moses Bane) ended up "badly bruised, though not dangerously injured," but it was two thirty before the injuries had been attended to and emergency repairs made to the platform, and only then was the "chief marshal," I. T. Wilson, ready to begin his introduction of Lincoln.[8]

For the first time, Lincoln came forward, slashing and cutting at Douglas. The Judge, Lincoln opened as though he was shaking out a whip, is a man who likes to find people guilty of crimes they did not commit. The Republican party had adopted a national platform in 1856, and the Illinois Republicans had adopted two state platforms, in 1856 and most recently in June. But so far in these debates, Douglas had not spoken to any issue in those platforms. Instead, beginning at Ottawa, he "attempted to hold me responsible for a set of resolutions" which "had not been passed by any State Convention anywhere—had not been passed at Springfield, where he supposed they had, or assumed that they had, and that they had been passed in no Convention in which I had taken part." The error of this "forgery"—and Lincoln turned back to Douglas, repeating, "Yes, Judge, I did dare to say forgery"—had repeatedly been explained, but Douglas just as regularly had ignored this, so Lincoln decided at Jonesboro "that if he thought I was responsible for every man or every set of men everywhere, who happen to be my friends, the rule ought to work both ways ... and gave him a pretty long string of resolutions, passed by men who are now his friends, and announcing doctrines for which he does not desire to be held responsible."

In the same spirit, Douglas "undertakes to establish that I ... make speeches of a certain sort in the North, among the Abolitionists, which I would not make in the South, and that I make speeches of a certain sort in the South which I would not make in the North." But Lincoln had said the same things in Ottawa that he had said in Jonesboro, and he asked people "to notice how very nearly they are the same as Judge Douglas says were delivered by me down in Egypt." Finally, Douglas had concocted the fantastic story that Lincoln and Trumbull "had entered into a bargain, one of the terms of which was that Trumbull was to abolitionize the old Democratic party, and I was to abolitionize the old Whig party—I pretending to be as good an Old Line Whig as ever." Douglas, not to put too fine a point upon it, was a liar.[9]

Not only a liar but a dodger. On three occasions, Lincoln had asked why, by the logic of the *Dred Scott* decision, it would not be possible for the Supreme Court to legalize slavery "in all the States as well as in the Territories." Douglas, who promised that he could reconcile *Dred Scott* with popular sovereignty by using unfriendly legislation to keep slavery out, "had not directly answered that question, but had merely contented himself with sneering at it." But Douglas needed more than a sneer to deal with the threat of *Dred Scott*. Lincoln went on, "I have examined that decision with a good deal of care, as a lawyer examines a decision, and so far as I have been able to do so, the Court has no where in its opinions said that the States have the power to exclude slavery," whether by unfriendly legislation or any other means, any more than it was allowing the territories to exclude it.

Douglas needed to do more in reply to this question than invent fairy tales about Lincoln and Trumbull and platforms and "negro equality," and stop whining about how Lincoln "was pushing this matter to a personal difficulty, to avoid the responsibility for the enormity of my principles." It was principles and the direction of public policy that Lincoln wanted to talk about, and Douglas didn't. "I say to the Judge and to this audience now, that I will again state our principles as well as I hastily can," and if "the Judge hereafter chooses to confine himself to a war upon these principles," instead of cock-and-bull stories about conspiracies and his love for Henry Clay, "he will probably not find me departing from the same course."

Principle number one, then, was this: "We have in this nation this element of domestic slavery," and it has proven to be "a disturbing" and a "dangerous element." Why is there such a disturbance? Because there is a fundamental and irreconcilable "difference of opinion" about slavery which has set one American at another's throat, and that is "the difference between the men who think slavery a wrong and those who do not think it wrong." Lincoln believed it "is a moral, a social and a political wrong," wrong in itself and wrong in its "tendency" to extend its sway to "the whole nation." The Republican cure for this "dangerous element" was simply to "prevent its growing any larger, and so deal with it that in the run of time there may be some promise of an end to it." Lincoln claimed "no right at all to disturb it in the States where it exists," and even where the Constitution permitted "us to disturb it, in the District of Columbia," he only proposed "making the emancipation gradual and compensating the unwilling owners." Even in the face of the provocation offered by *Dred Scott*, he did not propose to call for "a mob" to attack the Court or to free Scott.

Opposed to this is a genuinely lawless "sentiment in the country . . . which holds that slavery is not wrong, and therefore it goes for policy that does not propose dealing with it as a wrong." That sentiment "is the . . . central idea of the Democratic party" and of Stephen A. Douglas, who has "the high distinction . . . of never having said slavery is either right or wrong." Understanding that this, and not race or property or choice, is the fundamental issue would "get the question distinctly stated." It would also get it stated in precisely the way the Whigs had always wanted to state it, so that "all these men who believe that slavery is in some of these respects wrong" can "stand and act with us in treating it as a wrong." By painting slavery as a threat to virtue, the Union, and natural law, rather than as an option to be decided by democratic majorities, Lincoln was playing flawlessly with the political language of the Whigs and sponging away old Whig suspicions of abolitionism. He was not preaching outright emancipation; he was simply promising "an end of this slavery agitation." And what disciple of Henry Clay and Daniel Webster could object to that?[10]

That was exactly what Douglas thought Lincoln had always been too clever by half about, and when Lincoln finished, his opponent unsteadily stood up in his own defense. He was not in good form, and the reporter for the *Missouri Democrat* (who had come over from St. Louis to hear Douglas) thought that "even in his manner of address a great difference is perceptible between Douglas four months ago and Douglas now." Carl Schurz was impressed by how "natty and well-groomed" Douglas looked in his "excellently fitting broadcloth and shining linen"; but the impression was ruined by Douglas's "puffy" face and loose demeanor, which implied "that he had been drinking hard with some boon companion either on his journey or since his arrival." And the *Democrat*'s reporter noticed uneasily that Douglas spoke "very slowly," as though "bad whiskey and the wear and tear of conscience have had their effect." (He was, as Horace White told Jesse Weik many years later, "at that very time drinking himself to death.")

And so Douglas would do little more than sluggishly ward off Lincoln's blows. He waved away the suggestion that, because Lincoln thought slavery was a moral wrong, *he* must somehow be guilty of believing it right. Douglas, after all, had never thought of slavery the way proslavery apologists in the 1850s did, that it was a "positive good." Douglas clearly thought of slavery as personally regrettable, and perhaps an undeserved misfortune for black people, and the practical proof lay in the diceyness he had displayed over his first wife's plantation legacy. But if blacks were people, they were not the same kind of people as whites, and their misfortunes not so remarkably regrettable that they were worth disrupting the fabric of the American democracy. Douglas saw the real issue of 1858 as the sinister designs of lunatic-pious abolitionists, who wanted to disturb the racial status quo, thwart the will of the people, and plunge the whole country into pointless conflict. For Douglas, the agitation was the problem, and slavery merely the occasion; for Lincoln, slavery was the problem, and containment the best solution.

And so the Little Giant ignored Lincoln's challenge to debate "principles" and went to work, rooting up everything in his opponent's opening speech that he had taken as a personal insult. "I regret that Mr. Lincoln should have deemed it proper for him to again indulge in gross personalities and base insinuations in regard to the Springfield resolutions," Douglas announced, and then he indulged in a few "gross personalities" of his own. The obnoxious Aurora resolutions *were* Republican party resolutions and were adopted, if not exactly in Springfield, then by "nearly all the Republican county conventions in northern Illinois where his party is in a majority." Merely because Douglas had erred about the "spot"—a nudge to the ribs; the Mexican War accusation again—Lincoln had no right to "quibble about the place rather than meet and discuss the merits of the resolutions themselves." [11]

And on it went. Lincoln used the House Divided speech to slander Chief Justice Taney as a partner in "a conspiracy . . . by which the Dred Scott decision was to be made by the Supreme Court, in order to carry slavery everywhere under the constitution." Douglas "called upon him to retract his false charge," but "instead of coming out like an honest man and doing so, he reiterated the charge." Lincoln slandered "President Buchanan with having been a party to the conspiracy." Again, "although I have called upon him over and over again . . . to take back his false charge," when Lincoln's slanders are exposed, he "either remains silent, or, resorts to other tricks to try and palm his slander off on the country." At Ottawa, "I read the resolutions, and put the questions to him, and he then refused to answer them." At Freeport, he asked whether Lincoln would "vote to admit Kansas into the Union, with just such a constitution as her people want, with slavery or without as they shall determine." The result? "He will not answer." And the reason? "He wished to make the old line Whigs believe that he would stand by the compromise measures of 1850." In northern Illinois, Lincoln preaches "the abolition creed . . . while down south, in Adams county, in Coles, and in Sangamon, he and his friends are afraid to advance that doctrine." In Chicago, "he declared that all distinctions of race must be discarded and blotted out, because the negro stood on an equal footing with the white man. . . . Did Lovejoy, or Lloyd Garrison, or Wendell Phillips, or Fred. Douglass, ever take higher abolition grounds than that?" But, Douglas snarled in mock apology, "I forgot—

he would not be a Republican if his principles would apply alike to every part of the country." [12]

This took Douglas almost forty minutes into his reply, and he now began to meander alcoholically from pillar to post. Lincoln was not just plotting to abolitionize the old Whigs: he was plotting genocide. "Mr. Lincoln thinks that it is his duty to preach a crusade in the free States, against slavery, because it is a crime, as he believes, and ought to be extinguished." Well, "how is he going to abolish it?" If Lincoln was telling the truth about not wanting to "interfere with slavery in the States, but intends to interfere and prohibit it in the territories," then the result could only be that the "natural increase" of the slave population would create more slave mouths than the South could feed, and "his policy would drive them to starvation." This, Douglas said with a smirk, "is the humane and Christian remedy that he proposes for the great crime of slavery." Or if not genocide, then perhaps Lincoln was plotting treason. "The Dred Scott decision was pronounced by the highest tribunal on earth" and "from that decision there is no appeal this side of Heaven." Lincoln, however, "says he is going to reverse that decision." How? "Will he stir up strife and rebellion in the land and overthrow the court by violence?" Maybe Lincoln had never preached rebellion quite that starkly, but it was still true that "he who attempts to stir up odium and rebellion in the country against the constituted authorities, is stimulating the passions of men to resort to violence and to mobs instead of to the law." [13]

Lincoln's real problem with *Dred Scott* was that he had never understood how it offered the ideal way to keep slavery out of the territories. "Chief Justice Taney, in his opinion in the Dred Scott case, said that slaves being property, the owner of them has a right to take them into a territory the same as he would any other property." But property is always subject to local regulation. "Any man has a right to go to Kansas and take his property with him, but when he gets there he must rely upon the local law to protect his property, whatever it may be." The owner of slaves who goes to Kansas and finds "no law to protect him when he arrives there" discovers that he also "has no remedy if his slaves run away to another country: there is no slave code or police regulations, and the absence of them excludes his slaves from the territory just as effectually and as positively as a constitutional prohibition could."

So, if Free-Soilers want slavery banned from Kansas or any other territory, let them take the responsibility upon themselves, rally the votes they need in Kansas, get Kansas to adopt laws which give no protection to slavery, and the thing will be done without any further wrangling or paralysis in Congress. "I would not vote in Congress for any code of laws either for or against slavery in any territory. I will leave the people perfectly free to decide that question for themselves," Douglas declared. And this, he added with a rolling eye on the Whig Belt's voters, was the same position taken by "Clay's compromise measures" in 1850. If standing by these principles cost Douglas the support of the "little corrupt gang" who were now running the Democratic party in Washington—"and wish to elect Lincoln in preference to me"—then he would "stand by that great principle, no matter who may desert it." Popular sovereignty had, in effect, made Douglas into a sort of honorary Whig.[14]

No one in Quincy should be fooled by Lincoln's attempt to make slavery itself the issue, Douglas went on. Lincoln "tells you that I will not argue the question whether slavery is right or wrong," and Lincoln is perfectly correct: "I hold that under the Constitution of the United States, each State of this Union has a right to do as it pleases on the subject of slavery." Decisions about the rightness or wrongness of slavery are matters for private conscience, and if the people of one state accumulate enough private conscience about slavery to ban it, they have the "sovereign right" to do so, just as Illinois has done. But that decision has no bearing on Missouri. Illinois's decision about slavery is an opinion of the people of Illinois, not a statement of eternal right and wrong, and under the Constitution, "Missouri is a sovereign State of this Union, and has the same right to decide the slavery question for herself that Illinois has to decide it for herself." It is not the business of

"Mr. Lincoln, or anybody else, to tell the people of Kentucky that they have no consciences, that they are living in a state of iniquity, and that they are cherishing an institution to their bosoms in violation of the law of God." Enactments of conscience are not what democracies concern themselves with; enactments of the will of the people are. "Hence," Douglas wound up, "I do not choose to occupy the time allotted to me in discussing a question that we have no right to act upon."[15]

The time had actually fled faster than Douglas thought. "I am told that my time is within two minutes of expiring," he noted, and with a sonorous flourish, he thanked his listeners for what seemed—after Freeport, Charleston, and Galesburg—like an extraordinary "kindness" and "courtesy." The crowd had, in fact, been surprisingly receptive to Douglas, repeatedly interrupting him with cheers and giving him "nine cheers" at the close. But by spending half of his time on personal attack, and the other half insisting that the morality of slavery was a question entirely separate from the political process *about* slavery, the unsteady Little Giant had given Lincoln a generous opening for his rejoinder.

The problem with Douglas's argument, Lincoln began curtly, was that slavery *was* the problem, and Douglas's concentration on process was a cynical attempt to avoid what everyone knew to be the real issue. The Founders understood this, which was why they "cut off the source of slavery by the abolition of the slave trade, and adopted a system of restricting it from the new Territories where it had not existed." And this restriction would have eventually, and peacefully, brought an end to slavery, had it not been for "the invention of the cotton gin" and the profits to be made from cheaply produced cotton. It was greed, and not popular sovereignty, which "made the perpetuation of the institution of slavery a necessity in this country." So the effect has been that "Judge Douglas" has taken slavery from the position under which the Founders placed it and "put it upon the cotton gin basis." Douglas was not an apostle of democracy; he was an agent of the Slave Power. (A fifteen-year-old named Seneca Selby slipped around to the rear of

the platform and watched Lincoln begin speaking from eye level, noticing how vigorously Lincoln moved to the attack and "stood up once in
awhile and raised up on his tiptoes.")[16]

If Douglas was so worried about the pristine constitutionality of
Dred Scott, then how did he reconcile that with his notion of "do nothing
Sovereignty"? Lincoln picked out a "gentleman" in the crowd at random
and proceeded to hold a mock cross-examination. "We will say you are a
member of the Territorial Legislature, and like Judge Douglas, you believe that the right to take and hold slaves there is a constitutional
right." If slaveholding is a right guaranteed by the Constitution to all
Americans, then how can "the Territorial Legislature . . . by withhold-
ing necessary laws, or by passing unfriendly laws, nullify that constitutional right?" It was a principle in law, Lincoln insisted, that "what you
cannot do directly, you cannot do indirectly." There was no middle
ground in the territories for popular sovereignty to operate: either no
one could legislate against slavery (and that was the drift of *Dred Scott*)
or everyone (including Congress) could. "The Dred Scott decision cov-
ers the whole ground, and while it occupies it, there is no room even for
the shadow of a starved pigeon to occupy the same ground."[17]

But from here, Lincoln's enthusiasm for an argument from "principle" began to peter out; he, too, needed to play to the old Whigs in the
crowd. In the first place, Lincoln hoped no one would put much stock in
Douglas's attempt to make old Whigs believe that those noxious Buchanan Democrats were whooping for Lincoln's election. (The Danite
candidate for Quincy's state senate district, William H. Carlin, was sitting on the platform, and Lincoln turned wryly to ask Carlin whether he
"will vote for me"; Carlin shook his head *no*). Lincoln had so little interest
in becoming the darling of any Democratic faction that he was perfectly
happy telling Douglas, *Give it to them* and telling "Carlin, and Jake Davis"
[the Danite candidate for the Fifth Congressional District] and "this
man Wagley [William C. Wagley, the Danite state senate candidate in
the neighboring district] up here in Hancock, *Give it to Douglas.*"

Nor should they take seriously Douglas's bizarre suggestion that

Lincoln was going to incite some kind of national rebellion against *Dred Scott.* There were more ways than rebellion to overturn Supreme Court decisions, as Douglas himself could well remember—just as every old Whig could remember how Andrew Jackson had wrecked the Whigs' largest pet project, the Second Bank of the United States. "Did not he and his political friends find a way to reverse the decision of that same Court in favor of the constitutionality of the National Bank? Didn't they find a way to do it so effectually that they have reversed it as completely as any decision ever was reversed—so far as its practical operation is concerned?" In fact, back in 1838, hadn't Douglas found a way "to reverse the decision of [the Illinois] Supreme Court" when that court upheld the Whig secretary of state, Alexander Field, against dismissal by William Carlin's father, old Governor Thomas Carlin, and get himself appointed to that office instead? And wasn't it "General Jackson" who "once said each man was bound to support the Constitution 'as he understood it.'" Douglas "understood" the Constitution by endorsing *Dred Scott* and signing on to every one of its implications; Lincoln understood "it another way," he explained, "and therefore I am bound to support it in the way in which I understand it." If this was treason, it was taken right from Andrew Jackson's mouth.[18]

As for Douglas's charges that he had been tailoring his platform to his audiences, depending on whether he was in northern or southern Illinois, Lincoln was ready to pull out one of his notebooks and "show you . . . the substance of the Chicago speech I delivered two years ago . . . down at Springfield," except for "lack of time." Nor had what he said in Chicago about the Declaration of Independence been a mess of abolitionist claptrap, the way Douglas had claimed; it was no more than "the sentiments that Henry Clay used to hold," and those "sentiments" were what he did read from. Nor had Douglas dealt honestly with the Aurora resolutions. The Judge would never have conceded his error at all if "the newspapers of our Side" had not "discovered and published it, and put it beyond his power to deny it." And yet he was still trying to pin them to Lincoln.[19]

Lincoln was prepared to go on with this point-by-point rebuttal, but his time finally ran out. It was not his most dramatic performance—that prize still remained with Freeport—but it was certainly his best organized, and it was clearly his most concentrated effort to win the support of swing Whig voters. Douglas had done little more than scatter nasty innuendos. The Quincy debate's grid looks like this:

LINCOLN	DOUGLAS
Denies that the Aurora resolutions are Republican platform— corollary: Douglas is deceitful [repeated in rejoinder]	Lincoln endorses the *spirit* of the Aurora resolutions even if not endorsing the letter
Denies that he speaks one way in northern Illinois and another in southern Illinois—corollary: Douglas is deceitful	
Popular sovereignty contradicts *Dred Scott* [repeated in rejoinder]	Unfriendly legislation allows for legal exclusion of slavery from the territories
Denies that Lincoln and Trumbull conspired to abolitionize the old parties	
Slavery is morally wrong [repeated in rejoinder]	Slavery agitation was the result of abolitionist agitation, not moral wrong
	Questions of moral right and wrong are not germane
	Republicans favor racial equality
Denied	Lincoln advocates defiance of the Supreme Court
The Founders intended the extinction of slavery	
Denies that Douglas has any real conflict with Buchanan	

The crowd had been unusually restrained, almost sedate, thanks to the heavy lock the arrangements committees had put on rowdiness. That evening, the courthouse was "literally jammed with people" to hear still more Republican speeches, by Carl Schurz (in "the German language"), by Jackson Grimshaw (the Republican candidate for the Fifth Congressional District), and by Benjamin M. Prentiss.[20] In less than two and a half years, all three would be in uniform, and Prentiss would be the hero of a battle far away beside the Tennessee River, named for a nearby church called Shiloh.

As with the Jonesboro and Charleston debates, Douglas's original debate proposal bracketed the last two debates at Quincy and Alton into a single week—in this case, within two days. Both were river towns, and both had long-standing Whig loyalties. But Alton, which only lay 120 miles to the south along the Mississippi, was almost twice the size of Quincy and served as the western terminal for two of Illinois's major east-west rail lines, the St. Louis, Alton & Chicago (which connected with the Illinois Central north at Bloomington) and the Alton & Terre Haute (which bisected the main line of the Illinois Central at Pana and the ICRR's Chicago line at Mattoon, and from there ran eastward to Indiana), and in 1858 it stood a reasonable chance of challenging St. Louis for dominance of the northern Mississippi. It was the only debate site Douglas had chosen which was not a county seat, but the county it sat in, Madison county, had good reason for thinking of itself as the commercial jewel of the Whig Belt. Madison county constituted the fourteenth state house district and was one of only seven counties in the state to have gone straight for Fillmore in 1856; control of the surrounding Sixth Congressional District had seesawed between Richard Yates as a Whig in 1850 and 1852, and Douglas's other principal lieutenant, Thomas L. Harris, in 1854 and 1856.

The town also had the bleak notoriety of having been, twenty years before, the site of the murder of Elijah Lovejoy, the brother of Owen Lovejoy. The elder Lovejoy had originally planted himself in St. Louis in 1833 as the editor of the *St. Louis Observer,* a church newspaper which quickly became an abolitionist sounding board, and which soon enough got his press office smashed by a mob. Lovejoy hoped that Alton, twenty miles upriver, would offer a happier pulpit from which to preach abolition, but it did not. Mobs broke into his office twice and threw his printing press into the Mississippi; the third time, in November 1837, Lovejoy and his friends barricaded themselves in the office and fought back, and Lovejoy was killed in the shoot-out. Elijah Lovejoy became abolitionism's first martyr and the inspiration of his younger brother Owen (not to mention Wendell Phillips and John Brown). Illinois Whigs deplored the murder—in one of Lincoln's earliest public addresses, in January 1838, he had attacked the "mobocratic spirit" which would "throw printing presses into rivers, shoot editors, and hang and burn obnoxious persons at pleasure"—but they also did nothing about it.[21]

Twenty years later, abolition was still unmentionable in Alton. The Democratic county convention was addressed by an "old-line Whig," a forty-five-year-old Alton lawyer named Henry W. Billings, who had come over to Douglas's side because "he could have no sympathy with the Republican party," whose "action tended to an equality of the races." Billings, who had been born in Massachusetts, was exactly the solid, middle-class Whig type that Lincoln could not afford to alienate. And Lincoln's supporters had been forced in September to strike a deal with the Fillmoreites in Madison County, nominating a slate of candidates at a convention of Fillmoreites in the morning, and then having it ratified that afternoon by a "People's Convention" (rather than a Republican one). And the nominees would run not as Republicans but as "anti-Douglas men."

Like the arrangements committees in Quincy, the burghers of Alton were determined to repress any untoward demonstrations. A joint planning committee had been formed, and all had agreed to build the debate platform on the long south side of the new city hall (a three-story affair with an enormous cupola), looking down toward the Mississippi. Henry Billings, the Whig lawyer turned Democrat, would preside on the platform and be joined by three local Republicans and three local Democrats, plus the usual corps of Chicago reporters and stenographers, and other local political worthies—including, for the first time in the campaigns, Lyman Trumbull. All banners "and campaign devices" were banned from the platform (although this did nothing to prevent Altonites from stringing across the streets banners of their own—OLD MADISON FOR LINCOLN;—OLD ABE AND FREE LABOR; STATE SOVEREIGNTY—NATIONAL UNION). And there would be no uproarious party meetings after the debate, either. The Republicans, the Douglasites, and the Danites would have to hold their own party rallies the evening *before*.[22]

Like the Quincy arrangements committee, the Alton joint committee was proof of how much clout the Little Giant could call upon, even in a traditional citadel of Illinois Whig politics. Of the twelve members of the committee who can be identified, six were Republican, five were Douglas Democrats, and one was a die-hard Danite. The Republicans (or, as they were careful to call themselves, "the People's Party Club") represented only a modest share of Madison County's prosperity—a real estate developer, Henry Guest McPike (whose abolitionist father had edited the local Whig newspaper and who would build Alton's most famous mansion in 1869), a banker, a druggist, and two lawyers. The wealthiest of the Republicans, Vermont-born lawyer Friend S. Rutherford, was listed in the 1860 census with twelve thousand dollars' worth of real and personal property (about on a par with Lincoln himself); the poorest, a thirty-year-old lawyer named Tribble, had no property assessment listed at all. It was the Democrats who held the economic upper hand, starting with Zephaniah Job, a real estate speculator who had first moved to Madison County in 1836, left to become a Forty-Niner in the California Gold Rush, and struck it big enough to come back to Madison County in 1851 and break into major real estate investments. The census put Job down at $99,800, making him one of the richest men in Illinois, and that wealth was currently underwriting Job's campaign to win one of the state house district's two seats. The state senate seat was being contested by Virginia-born Samuel Buckmaster, who sat on a fairly substantial swath of property worth $59,000 and who had lost a bid for the state house in 1856 by only seventy-eight votes. The poorest of the committee's Democrats was also the Democrats' outcast: Dr. Thomas M. Hope, a Virginia-born physician and the lone Danite. Weighing racist fear and Democratic money together gave Douglas more than an even chance at carrying off Madison County's two fourteenth state house district seats and the state senate district it shared with Montgomery County and tiny Bond County.[23]

The joint committee let out the contract to build the platform (with "seats to accommodate ladies") and stipulated that "the reception of Messrs. Douglas and Lincoln shall be a quiet one." Indeed it was. Both candidates booked passage on the river steamer *City of Louisville* on the day after the Quincy debate and arrived without much ado downriver in Alton at five o'clock in the morning of October 15, to be promptly whisked off to their respective hotels. The debate had been optimistically scheduled by the joint committee for half past one o'clock. But with trains full of spectators (plus a troop of militia cadets, Merritt's Cornet Band, and for the first time in the debates, Mary Lincoln and the fifteen-year-old Robert Todd Lincoln) coming in from Springfield and points east on the Alton & Terre Haute and the Chicago & Alton lines, and the steamers *White Cloud* and *Baltimore* bringing "up a full load from St. Louis," the debating did not actually get started until two.

Despite the enforced tranquility which the Alton joint committee hoped to impose, there was a general sense that "this closing debate" would form "a sort of climax following the preceding arguments, which had been widely discussed throughout the Nation." Milling through the town, the "great American People" had taken possession of Alton as though it were a stage flat for a Mark Twain story (and Twain, of course, was a twenty-two-year-old cub pilot, somewhere out on the Mississippi, when the Alton debate took place):

> It went up and down the streets—it hurrahed for Lincoln and hurrahed for Douglas—it crowded to the auction rooms—it thronged the stores of our merchants—it gathered on the street corners and discussed politics—it shook its fists and talked loudly—it mounted boxes and cried the virtues of Pain Killer—it mustered to the eating saloons, and did not forget the drinking saloons—it was here and there and everywhere, asserting its privileges and maintaining its rights.[24]

Or if not Mark Twain, then perhaps the O.K. Corral. Just before two o'clock, Douglas emerged from the Alton House and walked up to the city hall, arm in arm with Henry Billings, while Lincoln stepped off from the Franklin House flanked by Friend Rutherford, Henry McPike, and sixty-five-year-old Cyrus Edwards, a distant relation by marriage and onetime Whig candidate for governor. (Sixteen years before, Lincoln nearly *had* fought a duel here—or rather, on a mudflat in midriver that he could almost see from the platform—when he challenged James Shields *mano a mano* with "cavalry broadswords of the largest size"; it was an idiotic piece of political exuberance which Lincoln discouraged anyone now from recalling.)

The Alton debate was Douglas's last chance at leading off—and it was promptly spoiled by the neglected Danite, Dr. Hope. Douglas had hardly sucked in his first breath when Hope popped up in front of the platform to demand the opportunity to interrogate the candidate: "Judge, before you commence speaking, allow me to ask you a question." Nonplussed, Douglas patiently agreed, "if you will not occupy too much of my time." Satisfied, Hope read out his question: "Do you believe that the Territorial legislatures ought to pass laws to protect slavery in the territories?" It is hard to understand what Hope thought he was gaining by this question, since Douglas's whole campaign had been built around opposition to the idea that territorial legislatures *ought* to protect slavery (or *ought* to outlaw it, in the sense of being compelled by some exterior authority), and Douglas brushed him aside with the backhand comment that Hope would "get an answer in the course of my remarks." The audience happily applauded—Hope had the reputation of being something of a crank—but Hope's interruption was a signal that Douglas was in for some rough steerage. And not only because of Hope. Gustave Koerner was "really shocked at the condition he was in. His face . . . was bloated, and his looks were haggard, and his voice almost extinct." The harder he tried, the more "his words came like barks," and he "frothed at the mouth when he became excited."[25]

But the barks still had bite to go with them. Almost as though he was delivering a summation to a jury, Douglas reached back to June and the House Divided speech to pull up two "principles" Lincoln had staked his entire campaign upon:

- "that this government could not endure permanently divided into free and slave States"
- that "the Supreme Court was guilty of a monstrous crime in the Dred Scott decision"—not because of what *Dred Scott* did in forbidding Congress to deal with slavery in the territories but because "it deprived the negroes of . . . all the rights, privileges, and immunities of the citizens of the several States." And Lincoln had trumped this in Chicago in July by uttering even stronger "sentiments in regard to the negro being on an equality with the white man."[26]

If Lincoln wanted to talk about *principles*, here they were—race and civil war.

Douglas recalled that he had taken Lincoln's "positions" out into the debates, "analyzed them, and pointed out what I believed to be the radical errors contained in them." To say that the government "was in violation of the law of God which says, that a house divided against itself cannot stand" was a "slander upon the immortal framers of our constitution." There was no reason not to suppose that "this government can endure forever, divided into free and slave States as our fathers made it," if only the abolition agitators would permit "each State . . . to prohibit, abolish or sustain slavery just as it pleases." It was under the steady operation of this principle that the free states had abolished slavery and "the South lost her power as the majority section in this Union." What purpose would be served by abandoning this peaceful procedure to declare "war against the Southern States and their institutions until you force them to abolish slavery everywhere"?

The clever Lincoln, however, had evaded Douglas's refutations of these "principles," beginning at Ottawa (where Lincoln "began to crawfish a little") and running through every debate since. At Ottawa, Douglas had "propounded certain questions to him"; Lincoln would not answer. "I have asked him whether he would vote to admit Nebraska if her people asked to come in as a State with a constitution recognizing slavery, and he refused to answer." Douglas had gone through each of the territories, one by one, and put "the same question to him with reference to each, and he has not said, and will not say, whether, if elected to Congress, he will vote to admit any territory now in existence with such a constitution as her people may adopt." Douglas, of course, had never had any difficulty answering questions like these, because the answer was popular sovereignty. "I have said everywhere, and now repeat it to you, that if the people of Kansas want a slave State they have a right, under the constitution of the United States, to form such a State, and I will let them come into the Union with slavery or without, as they determine. . . . It is their business not mine." [27]

And Douglas did not mind adding, for the benefit of any uncertain Illinois Whigs, that he had suffered for this principle at the hands of his own party. He had broken with James Buchanan and his bullies over Lecompton because "I hold that it is a violation of the fundamental principles of this government to throw the weight of federal power into the scale, either in favor of the free or the slave States," and the result was that "in this State, every postmaster, every route agent, every collector of the ports, and every federal office holder, forfeits his head the moment he expresses a preference for the Democratic candidates against Lincoln and his abolition associates." In fact, Douglas had bled for the same principles which motivated Henry Clay and the Whigs in their struggle against Andrew Jackson. "I hold that an attempt to control the Senate on the part of the Executive is subversive of the principles of our constitution." This may have surprised anyone who remembered a younger Douglas's reverence for Old Hickory in 1837. But these were different times, when it was "important for the Democratic party, for all national men, to rally and stand together." Just as it had been in 1850, when "Clay left the quiet and peace of his home, and again entered upon public life to quell agitation and restore peace to a distracted Union" without respect to party, so it should be in 1858, with "all united as a band of brothers" for the cause of "the peace, harmony, or integrity of the Union."[28]

The real enemies of this unity were not Whigs, or even reasonable Southern Democrats (and here Douglas read off snippets of speeches made by James Orr and Jefferson Davis within the past few weeks that seemed to endorse popular sovereignty) but "the Abolition party." They were possessed by the notion that "under the Declaration of Independence the negro is equal to the white man," and this had driven them "to agitate this country, to array the North against the South, and convert us into enemies instead of friends." And Douglas had just begun to crank around to describing how "a few ambitious men" were planning to exploit that agitation in order to "ride into power on a sectional hobby," when his hour ran out and time was called. "I am told that my hour is out," he grumbled and added suspiciously, "It was very short."[29]

All through Douglas's opening, Lincoln had sat at the rear of the platform, tilting backward in his chair "against the wall of the City Hall" and gazing fixedly down, "nor did he make notes of any remark that Douglas was making."[30] He had heard this same thread of argument at place after place—Lincoln wanted civil war, Lincoln wanted "negro equality," Stephen A. Douglas was a martyr to democracy, the Whigs should be moved to pity and vote for him, and so on. And even though Douglas seemed to have given up trying to pin the Aurora resolutions and the Trumbull conspiracy to his coat, he had also set the fundamental issue out as plainly as Lincoln could desire. Did popular government exist merely to ratify the decisions of its majorities, no matter what those decisions were, or was democracy wedded to a set of fundamental propositions that those majorities were accountable to? And where did those propositions come from?

Lincoln rose to confess that he had actually enjoyed hearing Douglas speak so agonizingly of his sufferings at the hands of the Buchananites. In fact, his opponent had been getting more agonized the more time he spent in Whig territory. "At Quincy, day before yesterday, he was a little more severe upon the Administration than I had heard him upon any former occasion," and this afternoon "I take it he has now vastly improved upon the attack he made then upon the Administration." All Lincoln could say about the spectacle of two Democrats, Douglas and Buchanan, at each other's throats was the same thing the battered wife had said when she saw her husband attacked by a bear: *Go it, husband!—Go it, bear!* (He had them laughing now, even "uproariously.") Maybe it was "inconsistent" of Buchanan to behave that way. But Douglas was by far the best judge of inconsistency. Since 1856, "the Judge" has been "very valiantly fighting for the Nebraska bill and the repeal of the Missouri Compromise." But only a few years before that, "he was the valiant advocate of the Missouri Compromise." James Buchanan certainly has "as much right to be inconsistent as Douglas"; or does the Little Giant have "the exclusive right, in this country, of being on all sides of all questions? . . . Is he to have an entire monopoly on that subject?" *Great laughter.* Gustave Koerner marveled at Lincoln's ease and banter, saying he seemed "as fresh as if he had just entered the campaign, and as cool and collected as ever."[31]

The serious business had to begin, however, and it would begin with *Dred Scott.* Douglas had missed entirely the point of Lincoln's criticism of that decision. The menace of the *Dred Scott* decision was not that "it held that a negro could not be a citizen"—that was a simplification aimed at stirring up the basest of racial prejudices. On the other hand, criticizing *Dred Scott* was nothing compared with the way Douglas freely criticized the Declaration of Independence. "Three years ago there never had lived a man who had ventured to assail it in the sneaking way of pretending to believe it and then asserting it did not include the negro," and if there was something worth criticizing in *Dred Scott*, it was the way Chief Justice Taney, "and . . . next to him . . . our friend Stephen A. Douglas," concluded that the black man had no rights which a white man was obliged to recognize.

Since Lincoln was "surrounded to some extent to-day, by the old friends of Mr. Clay," it would be useful to contrast Taney and *Dred Scott* with what Henry Clay had to say about the Declaration—and here Lincoln brought out the creased notebook again. Clay "says it is true as an abstract principle that all men are created equal." Neither Clay nor Lincoln ever meant we could "practically apply it in all cases." No one in 1858 was suggesting that "females, minors and insane persons" be given equal *civil* rights. But it *is* certainly true "as an abstract principle in the organization of society as well as in organized society, and it should be kept in view as a fundamental principle," and not blotted out in order to rationalize the stripping away of *natural* rights to life, liberty, and the pursuit of happiness.

> *I desire no concealment of my opinions in regard to the institution of slavery* [Lincoln read from one of Clay's speeches]. *I look upon it as a great evil; and deeply lament that we have derived it from the parental government; and from our ancestors. But here they are and the question is, how can they be best dealt with? If a state of nature existed and we were about to lay the foundations of society, no man would be more strongly opposed than I should be, to incorporating the institution of slavery among its elements.*

To the extent that the western territories represented this "state of nature," (by Clay's prescription) slavery ought to be banned there. "What have I done, that I have not the license of Henry Clay's illustrious example here in doing?" Lincoln asked his listeners.[32]

Then there was the business of the House Divided speech. "The sentiments expressed in it, have been extremely offensive to Judge Douglas," Lincoln wisecracked. "He has warred upon them as Satan does upon the Bible." (Given that the house divided image really was a biblical one, what did that make Douglas?) And with approximately the same expectation, too. All that Lincoln had said in the House Divided speech was that "the agitation" over slavery "would not cease until a crisis should have been reached and passed." One way of getting to that point and beyond it was by "arresting the further spread of it and placing it where the fathers originally placed it," on the road to "ultimate extinction." (What else could the Founders have had in view but its extinction when they banned its spread into the Northwest in 1787, restricted the amount of congressional representation slaveholders could demand on the basis of the numbers of their slaves, dodged the very mention of *slavery* in the Constitution, and banned the transatlantic slave trade in 1808?) It is a "falsehood" for Douglas to claim that "our fathers . . . made this government part slave and part free" and expected it to stay that way perpetually. "The exact truth is, that they found the institution existing among us," but in "making the government they left this institution with many clear marks of disapprobation upon it."[33]

Lincoln had no objection to popular sovereignty. What he objected to was the notion that popular sovereignty provided the same authority to enslave other human beings as it provided to pass cranberry laws. "Judge Douglas has intimated . . . that all this difficulty in regard to the institution of slavery is the mere agitation of office seekers and ambitious Northern politicians." But since when had the ambitions of politicians divided the national parties, broken up the great religious denominations, and raised the furies "in politics, in religion, in literature, in morals, in all the manifold relations of life"? And how could a question which had torn the fabric of the country from top to bottom be settled by a ballot initiative?

Or look at popular sovereignty from a practical angle: if the territories were to be left perfectly open and undecided, and "if you go to the Territory opposed to slavery and another man comes upon the same ground with his slave," doesn't the advantage subtly shift to the slaveholder, and "you have no part of it your way"? How many in this audience, Lincoln stopped to ask (in the same way he had reached out into the crowd in Quincy), had moved from the slave states to Illinois to get away from slavery, and away from competition with plantation-style labor? Voices chorused out, *a thousand*. Would you have moved here if you had known that slaveholders were also free to move here and that a final decision about slavery in Illinois would be made only at a later date? Did anyone doubt what the result would be at that later date? Would anyone have moved? Well, then: when the next generation gets the itch (or the economic squeeze) to move for itself, if they, too, "wish to be rid of the institution, where will they find the place to go to?" [34]

The applause was now "loud and long continued," and Lincoln was finally ready to bring the debate down to what he had insisted at Quincy was its bedrock—the inherent immorality of slavery itself. "The real issue in this controversy—the one pressing upon every mind—is the sentiment on the part of one class that looks upon the institution of slavery as a wrong, and of another class that does not look upon it as a wrong." Understanding that is what enables everyone to understand why the issue of slavery has divided the house, and must come to a crisis. Lincoln was not asking people to be "so impatient of it as a wrong as to disregard its actual presence among us and the difficulty of getting rid of it suddenly in a satisfactory way, and to disregard the constitutional obligations thrown about it." But understanding that slavery *is* a moral wrong is what determines people to oppose its further spread and desire its "ultimate extinction." Not ambition, not sectional hatred—just the "the sentiment that contemplates the institution of slavery in this country as a wrong." Did anyone really wish to be on the other side of that proposition, and insist that slavery was morally *right?* Probably not. But by pretending that slav-

glory of a democratic society is that "there is no permanent class of hired laborers amongst us"—no permanent class, in fact, of any-thing—so that "the hired laborer of yesterday, labors on his own ac-count today; and will hire others to labor for him tomorrow." This, Lincoln insisted, "is the order of things in a society of equals." But not if slavery were treated as though it had no more moral content than freedom. "Those who deny freedom to others, deserve it not for them-selves," he would warn in another year, "and, under a just God, can not long retain it." We must "repulse them," Lincoln wrote, "or they will subjugate us."[37]

This was the rhetorical high point of the debates, and years after-ward, one spectator declared that "the melting pathos with which Mr. Lincoln said this and its effect on his audience cannot be described." If Lincoln, who knew good theater when he saw it, could have ended at this climax, he would have. But he had been working along at so un-usually rapid a clip that when he turned to Henry Billings to check on the time, Billings told him he had ten minutes yet to go. There was no point to sitting down with the clock still running, so Lincoln launched into an addendum on the incompatibility of *Dred Scott* and popular sov-ereignty, no matter what Douglas was promising with his unfriendly legislation solution. How can anyone "withhold the legislation which his neighbor needs for the enjoyment of a right which is fixed in his favor in the Constitution of the United States which he has sworn to support?" The tautness thus went out of his argument. But his denun-ciation of the "tyrannical principle" of slavery had provided the most powerful flail Lincoln had yet swung against Douglas, and it was going to take an extraordinary effort from his opponent to turn back Lincoln's surge.[38]

And he could not do it. The weariness of the campaigns, the phlegmy weights in his head and chest, the mental fogginess from too much liquor over too many days, and the temperamental incapacity of a Jacksonian Democrat to discuss morality as a matter of policy all combined to lower Douglas's rejoinder to a collection of irritated snaps. Yes, Lincoln certainly hopes that Buchanan's bear will tear him up, because "his hopes of success, and the hopes of his party depend solely upon it." And it was about time Lincoln was "in favor of prosecuting one war vigorously," because back during the Mexican War, he had "voted that the war was wrong, that our country was in the wrong, and consequently that the Mexicans were in the right." That was Lincoln's notion of right and wrong—betray your country. Lincoln was doing the same thing now, talking "about his being an old line Clay Whig" here in Alton. "We did not hear much about the old Clay Whig party up in the Abolition districts," Douglas said with a leer. Yes, it was true that the Founders "did not establish slavery in any of the States." But they didn't abolish it, either, and in order to "form a government uniting them together," they agreed to "guarantee forever to each State the right to do as it pleased on the slavery question." Worst of all, Douglas resented Lincoln's appeal "to the moral sense of justice, and to the Christian feeling of the community to sustain him." On that basis, "Mr. Lincoln proposes to govern the territories without giving the people a representation, and calls on Congress to pass laws controlling their property and domestic concerns without their consent and against their will." *Now* who was governing by divine right?[39]

And yet, watching the clock squeeze him down to his last minutes, Douglas dropped the savage mask and pleaded with as much sincerity as his weariness and his political logic could muster: "My friends, if, as I have said before, we will only live up to this great fundamental principle there will be peace between the North and the South." Let the North make holy war upon slavery or "any other peculiar institution of the opposite section," and the result will be bloodshed of the unholiest kind. "The only remedy and safety is that we shall stand by the constitution as our fathers made it, obey the laws as they are passed, while they stand the proper test and sustain the decisions of the Supreme Court and the constituted authorities." It was the last word Douglas and Lincoln would ever exchange in debate.[40] And the grid looks like this:

DOUGLAS	LINCOLN
Lincoln misconstrues the intentions of the Founders about slavery	
Lincoln refuses to answer the questions Douglas has put to him	
Douglas has joined Clay in promoting the saving of the Union over party politics	
Trouble over slavery has been fed by abolitionist agitation	
	Douglas's break with Buchanan is simply an example of inconsistency, not courage
	Douglas repudiates the Declaration of Independence
	Lincoln takes the same position as Henry Clay
	Douglas misconstrues the House Divided speech
The Founders adopted popular sovereignty as the means of dealing with slavery [in rejoinder]	Popular sovereignty does not have the authority to settle the slavery issue
Popular sovereignty is the only guarantee of peace [in rejoinder]	Popular sovereignty grants slaveholders an advantage in settling the territories
	Slavery is morally wrong
	Popular sovereignty contradicts *Dred Scott*
Lincoln betrayed his country in the Mexican War	
Lincoln speaks one way in northern Illinois and another way in southern Illinois	

At dinner that evening at the Franklin House, Lincoln asked Lyman Trumbull "whether any impression had been made upon the people" in the debate. Trumbull, who up to this point had still managed to avoid mentioning Lincoln in his stump speeches and concentrated entirely on damning Douglas, replied diffidently that, in general, "public meetings in Madison County were usually undemonstrative." But in this case, Trumbull allowed that "a favorable impression had been made."

Other Illinois Republicans were ecstatic. William Herndon's cousin Rowan wrote to Lincoln after the Alton debate that in Quincy "the duglasites are stedfast" and "the Lincolnites is the same way," but among the "floting vote," he had heard "that iff they sent Dug to Congress, he had No Party to goe with that . . . and would Be of N[o] use." They "would vote for Lincon." A friend of Republican campaign treasurer John Bagby wrote excitedly, "John, if we elect Lincoln I believe I will get drunk. I do not know what more foolish & desperate thing I could do to express my joy for I have not tasted a drop of raw liquor for more than seven years. Hurrah for Lincoln." The state committee was still worried about the "intentions of the Douglas Democracy to overrun the interior counties of this State with fraudulent votes," and in Peoria, suspicious Republicans kept track of "the agents of the [Illinois] Central company" who were bringing "hundreds of Irish voters over into Illinois, free of expense." Even Lincoln was beginning to get edgy about the rumors of "fraudulent votes." It was worth the state committee's while, Lincoln advised Norman Judd, to hire an undercover detective to mingle with them and "control their votes." Otherwise, Lincoln had "a high degree of confidence that we shall succeed," and "carry the day." In Carthage, he spoke to over six thousand people at a rally where "the shaking of hands and rejoicing of the Republicans reminded" one onlooker "of a great revival among the Methodists, all bound for heaven together." After Alton, "all our folks are in the best of spirits and are working as if the devil were after them," reported one of John Bagby's correspondents. "Nothing but the 'Colonization Society' can beat us here."[41]

But Alton was only the last of the debates, not the end of the campaign, and there were still two weeks to run before Election Day. Two weeks, as Harold Wilson once said, is a long time in politics, and in the final run, the campaigns skidded to new levels of nastiness. After Alton, Lincoln made a brief stop back in Springfield, then set out for one last tour through the western Whig districts. But in Rushville on October 20, the local Douglasites greeted him by nailing a black flag to the cupola of the county courthouse, and when Lincoln spoke from a platform beside the courthouse, a claque of hecklers hooted at him from the upstairs windows and dangled a black doll adorned with the banner HURRAH FOR LINCOLN! Three days later, in Dallas City, Lincoln found himself facing a banner "stretched across the street" with "a large Negro" painted on it and "over the head . . . a circle" marked 'Equality.'" But he had been in politics long enough to know how to give as well as he was given. In Dallas City, he thanked the local Democrats for honoring him "with their favourite banner," and when a local loudmouth repeatedly interrupted Lincoln and "called him a liar," Lincoln asked him to stand up, and "Great God, how Lincoln scored him. You could have heard the boys shout a mile."

By the time Lincoln made his final turn through Macomb and Petersburg, Democratic hecklers were concentrating almost entirely on the race card. One veteran Sangamon County Whig, James N. Brown, was so unnerved by the race-baiting that he tremblingly wrote to Lincoln to beg for assurances that the candidate "disclaimed all intention to produce social and political equality between the whites and blacks." Lincoln actually sent one of his notebooks to Brown to carry around with him as proof that "I believe the negro is included in the word 'men' used in the Declaration of Independence," and that "all men are created equal," and therefore "that negro slavery is violative of that principle; but that, by our frame of government, that principle has not been made one of legal obligation." This pacified old Brown, but it did nothing to dampen the racist ardor of the Douglasites. "Vote the WHITE MAN's ticket," screamed the headlines of the *Montgomery County*

Herald on October 29, "and don't forget that Lincoln is an Abolitionist up North but opposed to negroes down in Egypt."[42]

At the same time, the Little Giant was meeting a rising tide of heckling and disruption at his own meetings. Douglas struck north from Alton to Gillespie on October 16, but his speech there was interrupted by the editor of the *Carlinville Free Democrat*, who ("wishing to break the force of the speaker's remarks") called on Douglas to explain his opposition to the Toombs amendment. "What's that, sir?" Douglas snapped. "Didn't you strike out the submission clause in the Toombs bill?" "That's a lie," Douglas roared back, and "hundreds of men" rushed the wagon in which the Carlinville editor was standing and "attempted to drag him backwards." But not even Douglas's allies could deny that "his voice is broken so that tis hardly possible to understand him." Horace White almost felt sorry for him. Douglas "looked jaded, used up and badly under the weather. . . . It was almost pitiful to listen to his husky, half-uttered sentences, many of his words being clipped and entirely inaudible." One Democrat even wondered whether "he should quit speaking," or else let Adele campaign for him, since "she is beautiful."

But Stephen A. Douglas had never seen a risk—even a risk to his health—that he would not take, and the Little Giant stuck doggedly to his campaign schedule up to the last day, October 29, in Rock Island. Parading through the town, the Rock Island Democrats flourished banners that summed up every tactic, every argument, every point Douglas had scored against Lincoln:

POPULAR SOVEREIGNTY NOW AND FOREVER

THIS COUNTRY WAS MADE FOR WHITE MEN

DOWN WITH NEGRO EQUALITY

OLD ABE HAS GOT ON THE WRONG SPOT

FROM THE IRISH SCUM AND HALF CIVILIZED GERMANS
HAVE DESCENDED AMERICA'S BRAVEST SONS

DOUGLAS FOR PRESIDENT IN 1860[43]

Every point, that is, except one last lethal arrow that Douglas had kept in his quiver since July, against the day when he would need to launch an October surprise.

Theophilus Lyle Dickey was the typical central Illinois Whig who found the Republicans too intermixed with abolition for his taste, and he had created a minor sensation on August 9, when he issued a public endorsement of Douglas. But Dickey was not exactly a host in himself. What he had, however, were contacts with Whigs who once commanded such hosts, and chief among them was John J. Crittenden.

Hardly anyone, after Clay and Webster, owned better Whig credentials than John Crittenden. A Kentuckian like Clay, Crittenden had first been elected to the Senate as long ago as 1817 and served as attorney general in the short-lived Whig administrations of William Henry Harrison and Millard Fillmore. He filled Clay's seat in the Senate, stood as best man at Lincoln's father-in-law's second marriage, and for all practical purposes, inherited the mantle of what was left of the Whig leadership. Lincoln first met Crittenden in 1847, during his lone term in the House of Representatives, and he stood with Crittenden in opposing the Mexican War and in backing Zachary Taylor for the Whig presidential nomination. He was "flattered" in 1849 "to learn that Mr. Crittenden" remembered him, and even though it was not more than a "slight general recollection," Crittenden had allowed that Lincoln was "a rising man."[44]

But Crittenden was not happy to see his "rising" done as a Republican. Crittenden had no sympathy with the new Republican party, or with Lincoln joining it. "You have I suppose seen . . . the speech of Mr. Lincoln made to the Republican Convention in Springfield," wrote one of Crittenden's Illinois correspondents on July 17. "I do not believe there is any Western State that can upon a fair canvass be brought to endorse the sentiments of that Springfield speech. It is abolition and disunion so absolutely expressed that it should be made to burn Mr. Lincoln as long as he lives." On the other hand, Crittenden was pleasantly startled by Stephen A. Douglas's defiance of Buchanan and the Lecompton constitution. Crittenden advised Lyman Trumbull "to have no controversy with Douglas" and sit out the 1858 campaign, since Douglas had ranged himself on the side of angels by "opposing the Administration," and he had privately told Douglas's lieutenant, Thomas Harris, that, "he would do anything we desired—he would write to any body—& give his views & wishes in your favor." Lincoln could sustain the defection of Lyle Dickey, but he could not shrug off the impact of Crittenden announcing his support for Douglas's reelection. "He will control 20,000 American [Know-Nothing] or old line Whig votes in the center & south" of the state, and Lincoln's margin of victory was going to be thin enough without Crittenden putting that many votes into jeopardy.

The prospect of a Crittenden endorsement of Douglas weighed so heavily on Lincoln's mind that he wrote to Crittenden on July 7, before the campaigns had begun, delicately feeling out the old Kentuckian's "inclination" and hoping to persuade him to do nothing. "I am prompted ... by a story being whispered about here that you are anxious for the re-election of Mr. Douglas to the United States Senate, and also of Harris, of our district, to the House of Representatives, and that you are pledged to write letters to that effect to your friends here in Illinois, if requested. I do not believe the story, but still it gives me some uneasiness." Crittenden waited almost an entire month to reply, and the answer could not have provided Lincoln with much reassurance: "Mr. Douglas & myself have always belonged to different parties, opposed, in politics, to each other." But Douglas's opposition to Lecompton "was highly gratifying to me," and while he had actually made no endorsement of Douglas, and had not "a single particle of personal unkindness or opposition to you," Crittenden couldn't help at least hoping that a Douglas victory in Illinois would embarrass the Buchananites.[45]

At best, Lincoln could hope that Crittenden would remain a benevolent neutral. But the best was not what ensued. On July 19, even before announcing his own defection to Douglas, Lyle Dickey wrote to Crittenden, appealing to him to allow Dickey to release "the substance of a conversation between us in relation to Judge Douglas." Crittenden did him one better—he retailed the details of the conversation himself, dwelling on how "the people of Illinois little knew how much they really owed" Douglas, that Douglas "had had the courage and patriotism to take an elevated, just and independent position on the Lecompton question," and that, best of all, "there was a heroism" in Douglas's "course calling not only for approbation but applause."

Maddeningly, Crittenden immediately assured Dickey that he did not want to be seen "as an officious intermeddler in your elections," and Dickey seems to have read that as a request that the letter not be used except as a last resort. But Douglas was now down to his last resort, and on October 19, Dickey took the opportunity of a Douglas rally in Decatur to read Crittenden's letter aloud. It was promptly published in Sheahan's *Chicago Times* and Lanphier's *State Register,* and within a week it was being reprinted in the East Coast newspapers. Douglas now leapt forward to attack Lincoln for having "betrayed Henry Clay," adding with a snarl, "Isn't he a pretty man to be claiming Old Line Whig support?"[46]

The collective clatter of the Republican state committee's jaws bouncing on the floor could have been heard as far downstate as Cairo. Norman Judd and Charles Ray wanted to send off a member of the state committee to pin Crittenden down personally, and maybe extract a recantation. William Herndon wrote to Crittenden, begging him to explain why he had ever consented to write his letter for Dickey, and in an effort to stanch the flow of Whig voters away from Lincoln, the state committee sent Lincoln's and Crittenden's July letters to the *Missouri Daily Republican.* Some Republicans tried to pretend the Dickey letter was a forgery: "We are assured by the personal and political friends of Mr. Crittenden that his sympathies are with Lincoln, and that his letter is only to be regarded as an admission of a conversation." Others tried to huff and puff their way past the letter. "Talk of honorable, conservative old Whigs like Crittenden supporting Douglas in his present absurd political position!" exclaimed Charles Wilson in the *Chicago Journal*. "Could anything more preposterous be imagined?" Or else they tried to sniff out evil motivations in waiting until the eve of the election to publish it: "Where has it been all this time?" the *Illinois State Journal* demanded querulously. "Why has it been held back for THREE MONTHS AND NEVER TILL NOW ALLOWED TO SEE THE LIGHT?"

Despite all the Republican counterflooding, the impact was devastating. Lincoln would afterward rebuke Crittenden for having "contributed largely" to Douglas's last-minute recovery. But far from regretting it, Crittenden instead turned on Lincoln and upbraided *him* for allowing "the St. Louis Republican (I think that is the paper)" to quote from "our private correspondence." The best that Lincoln and the state committee could do was to turn Lincoln's last speeches into testimonies to "the wisdom and conservatism of the Republican platform" and his own "consistency with the action and views . . . of Henry Clay," while the *Illinois State Journal* ran two parallel columns on its front page, dovetailing the speeches of Clay and Lincoln.[47]

There was one last rally for Lincoln, at home, in Springfield, on Saturday, October 30. The gloom and the rain came sweeping back over Illinois in this final week of campaigning, but on the day of the rally, a thirty-two-coach excursion train, bearing on its first car the banner A. LINCOLN THE PRIDE OF ILLINOIS and posters of Clay and Lincoln, chugged doggedly into Springfield, followed by another nine-coach train from Jacksonville. The rain stopped long enough for a platform to be set up on the east side of the city square, along the iron railing that surrounded the statehouse, where Lincoln had delivered the House Divided speech four and a half months before.

"To-day closes the discussions of this canvass," Lincoln told his well-wishers, with a touch of weariness. "The planting and the culture are over; and there remains but the preparation, and the harvest." He had come into this "painful" campaign not out of "ambition" (as Douglas had accused him) but because of the "tendency" of legalized slavery "to subvert the first principle of free government itself." He had been "bespattered with every immaginable odious epithet," and even "some who were friends"—was John J. Crittenden a *friend?*—had "made themselves most active in this." In a moment of frank self-revelation, Lincoln told this crowd of neighbors and friends from every point on the old Eighth Circuit that he would not try to make them believe he was a plaster saint, devoid of "insensibility to political honors." But if he could put the whole political clock back to the Missouri Compromise, and put slavery "on the old ground of 'toleration' by necessity" and "unyielding hostility to the spread of it," then he would gladly put Douglas in the Senate and himself back in his law office, "so long as we both or either, live." And so they all went to dinner.[48]

The "preparation" Lincoln referred to was the organization of systems of polling places all over the state, and the printing of tickets by the parties and in the newspapers for Illinois voters to use in voting. In 1858, there was no system of party membership rolls, or even voter registration lists, in Illinois. Instead, "all over the state census takers are at work preparing lists of voters," and the census rolls provided the single qualification any white male Illinoisan needed, which was residence. Polling places might be set up almost anywhere, from county courthouses to rural post offices and storefronts; the one requisite was a sufficiently large room to set up a ballot box and a "voting window." It was to this window that voters, armed with tickets, would present themselves. The tickets were usually printed in the local party newspapers or as long slips of paper, with only that party's nominees. On November 2, this would include candidates for U.S. Congress, Illinois state treasurer, the state superintendent of public instruction, and the candidates for the state house and state senate (if that senate district seat was open). Because "our U.S. Senators are not elected by the direct vote of the people," explained the *Freeport Weekly Journal,* "but by our legislature," the names of Lincoln and Douglas would appear nowhere on any ticket; in Freeport, and everywhere else, "to vote for Lincoln" was to "vote for John H. Addams for [state] Senator, and John A. Davis for Representative—both good men and true."[49]

Tickets could be cut out of the newspapers or collected from party workers and would then be brought to the polling place. Voters would approach the polling place, shoulder their way through party workers waving printed ballots they were eager to thrust into the voters' hands, and hand in their tickets through the ticket window. On the other side of the window, judges of elections would receive the tickets, and if there was no challenge to the eligibility of the voters, the tickets went into the ballot box. Both poll watchers and judges had the authority to challenge a vote, but if there were no reliable census lists, a voter could (under Illinois law) take an oath, swearing to legitimate age and residency, and proceed with voting.

This process opened up generous opportunities for fraud, as Norman Judd had feared. At polling places, "whiskey already flows as freely as water, & presents of coats, hats, boots, shoes, etc." were handed out to entice the unscrupulous, and "clubs, pistols, and stones" could be used on the faint of heart. Almost anyone, especially in towns and cities, could swear "their votes through, and how many of this number were guilty of perjury, nobody will ever know." Lincoln pored over the Illinois voting statutes in mid-October to determine if there was some way a fraudulent voter who nevertheless took the oath could still be disqualified. Both he and Judd recommended "cross-examining the prop[os]ed voter," asking not just "Do you reside in this precinct?" but asking "a question as their wives and children, where they are, and so forth," so that poll watchers could "obtain enough information so that the Judges can determine the right of the voter." Judd wished that "a tried and firm magistrate and constable" could be recruited to watch every "place of voting." But at least, as Henry Whitney suggested, the state committee could distribute "circulars" to the Republican faithful, "teaching them their whole duty" and how to confront frauds.[50]

Above all, the people had to be gotten out to vote. Under weather as frowning as early November promised to be—and on Monday, November 1, the rain "continued all day without the least intermission accompanied by cold East wind"—the party newspapers rang every bell they could and made each vote sound like the hinge of fate. "If Lincoln is elected," promised the *Illinois State Journal*, "the nominee of the [next] Democratic [national] convention will certainly be defeated in 1860. The contest in Illinois has assumed a national importance. The eyes of the country are on us. Let us do our duty." [51]

★ EPILOGUE ★

ONE SUPREME ISSUE

Oh, Judge, the time of artful men will come at length! How were
you to foresee a certain day under the White Dome of the Capi-
tol? Had your sight been long, you would have paused before
your answer. Had your sight been long, you would have seen this
ugly Lincoln bareheaded before the Nation, and you are holding
his hat. Judge Douglas, this act alone redeemed your faults. It
has given you a nobility of which we did not suspect you. At the
end God gave you strength to be humble, and so you left the name
of a patriot.

WINSTON CHURCHILL, *THE CRISIS* (1901)

T HE FAVORABLE BREAK in the weather that cleared the skies over
Quincy and Alton disappeared by the last week before the election.
Right up to the eve of Election Day, the weather turned "dark" and
"cloudy," with increasing rain. It would continue pouring bleakly
through the day of the election, November 2, and for the week following, when the season's first snow fell. Despite all the apprehensions,
the polls were orderly, and "everything passed off quietly." In Chicago,

"at an early hour, the city was alive" and "an unusual excitement pre-vailed," and in Bloomington, hardy poll workers bravely strung up a banner in the soaking rain, TODAY FREEDOM AND SLAVERY JOIN BATTLE ON THE PRAIRIES OF ILLINOIS.[1]

By the evening, Lincoln knew that he had lost. "I had been reading the returns," he recalled on another Election Day, six years later (which was just as "dark, rainy & gloomy"), "and had ascertained that we had lost the Legislature." It is not clear exactly how Lincoln fig-ured this out so early. The *Chicago Tribune* was hoping against hope as late as Thursday that the results were "Still in Doubt" and that nine of the state house races, and three of the state senate races, were still "un-decided." Not until Friday, November 5, did the Douglas newspapers finally feel sure enough to print an enormous rooster at the head of their columns, gleefully underlined with DOUGLAS SUSTAINED! LIN-COLN'S COMB IS CUT! And not until Friday did the *Tribune* and other Lincoln papers finally concede. Even then, certified returns in Morgan and Scott counties were not published until November 12, and seven other counties still had not filed final reports.[2]

However, all Lincoln needed to know that night was the result in the Whig Belt, and there, the news was almost all bad. The onetime Whig stronghold of the fourteenth district, where two Democratic candidates for the state house lost by a 3.2 percent margin in 1856, now went Democratic in 1858 by almost exactly the same margin (gar-nering 51.6 percent of the vote), so sending two Democratic state rep-resentatives and a Democratic state senator to Springfield to vote for Douglas when the new legislature convened. In the twenty-eighth dis-trict (Pike and Brown counties, on the Illinois River), Democrats ex-panded the narrow 1.6 percent victory margin they had won in 1856 (by dividing Republicans and Whigs) by three percentage points in 1858; in the twenty-seventh district (Morgan and Scott counties, across the Illinois River from the twenty-eighth district), the two De-mocratic representatives, Cyrus Epler and Elisha Hitt, went from squeaking margins of 129 and 35 votes (respectively) in 1856 to reelection margins of 640 and 611 votes in 1858 (the votes for the two Republican candidates for the legislature actually went *down* in the twenty-seventh district by 10 and 11). Overall, in the Whig Belt, the nineteen state house districts that had given either a majority to Fillmore or a majority to a combination of Frémont and Fillmore in the 1856 presidential election, now went fourteen to five for Douglas candidates, including all but one of the two-representative districts:[5]

VOTING IN THE "WHIG BELT" DISTRICTS—STATE HOUSE

District	Representatives sent to state house	Democratic— Douglas	Republican— Lincoln
6th	1	1,063	985
11th	1	1,283	463
13th	1	1,617	1,045
14th	2	4,411	4,021
21st	1	2,021	1,545
22nd	1	1,539	777
24th	1	1,400	1,453
25th	1	2,223	2,291
26th	2	6,102	5,476
27th	2	6,101	4,850
28th	2	6,642	5,179
31st	1	2,389	2,032
32nd	1	1,957	1,765
33rd	2	6,479	5,942
35th	1	2,208	2,130
36th	1	3,285	3,861
39th	1	1,955	1,783
41st	2	6,466	7,014
42nd	1	2,512	2,608

* Gray indicates the majority.

The same pattern held true in the state senate races. In 1856, the voters in the eighth, eleventh, and most of the fourteenth, eighteenth, and twenty-first state senate districts had gone for Fillmore, or for a combination of Frémont and Fillmore. Now, however, they elected Douglasites by a margin of three to two.

VOTING IN THE "WHIG BELT" DISTRICTS—STATE HOUSE

State Senate District	Democratic—Douglas	Republican—Lincoln
8th	5,093	5,213
11th	4,578	4,112
14th	4,623	3,011
18th	4,834	5,457
21st	4,135	3,593

* Gray indicates the majority.

At the end of the day, Republican state house candidates won thirty-five seats, while Douglasites won forty; Republicans held eleven state senate seats and Democrats fourteen. On a party-line vote, the new legislature would reelect Douglas over Lincoln by 54 to 46.

And yet, it was by no means a rout. If only *three* more of the Whig Belt districts had gone to Republicans—or even *two* more, provided one of them was a two-representative district, like the fourteenth—Republicans would have controlled the state house; and if they could have added the eleventh state senate district (which contained two counties, one which went for Frémont and one which went for Fillmore, in 1856), Republicans would have almost controlled the senate, too, and handed the ensuing senatorial election to Lincoln. And none of these outcomes were wishful thinking. Some of the Whig Belt districts fell to Douglas men by maddeningly narrow margins. In the thirty-fifth district, the Douglasite victory was razor-close (78 votes, or 50.8 percent); in the thirty-third, the change of 150 votes would have given the district's two representatives to the Republicans, while in the thirty-ninth (Tazewell County) the change of 90 votes would have elected a Republican.

In fact, Lincoln gained much more ground than it looked. In every version of the 1858 campaigns (from Isaac Arnold's 1866 biography of Lincoln onward), the yardstick used to measure Republican vote getting has been the two statewide offices up for election, state treasurer and state superintendent of public instruction. The tally of these elections was published nationally, and it was easy to conclude from them what the voting must have been for the legislative candidates as well. Horace Greeley's *Tribune Almanac* gives 125,430 votes for the Republican candidate for state treasurer, James Miller, and 121,609 for his Democratic opponent, William B. Fondey; in almost the same proportions, the Republican candidate for superintendent of public instruction, Newton Bateman, beat his Democratic rival, Augustus C. French, by 124, 993 to 122,413. Averaged between the two races, Republicans could be said to have outscored Democrats by 125,212 to 121,810. So, if it is assumed that the same voters who elected Miller and Bateman cast their ballots in the same way for Lincoln and Douglas, then it can be said that Lincoln (or at least Lincoln candidates) won a popular, but very narrow, majority of 3,402 votes (or 50.6 percent).

But because of the voting in districts which elected multiple representatives (and because not everyone who might vote for Lincoln would also vote for Bateman or Miller), the actual number of votes cast in the legislative elections on November 2 was substantially higher than votes cast for just these two state offices. There were actually 366,983 votes cast in the state house districts of which 166,374 were for Democratic candidates and 190,468 for Republican, with a smattering of 9,951 for the Buchananites, and a scattering of write-ins. If Illinois voters were consciously voting for legislative candidates who would, in turn, vote for Lincoln or Douglas, then we have to say that

Lincoln "won" the votes cast for the house races by over 24,000—or a much more decisive 51.9 percent of the votes cast, whereas Douglas "won" only 45.3 percent. The same story holds true in the state senate races. Of the 99,842 votes cast in the twelve open state senate races, 44,750 went to Democrats, but 53,784 went to Republicans (the Buchananite candidates garnered only 1,308).[4] So, Lincoln also "won" the state senate votes with a hefty 53.86 percent of the votes cast.

What saved Douglas was that, even though in both senate and house races Lincoln candidates won substantial victories, they won them unevenly. Representation in the legislature, based on the state's 1854 reapportionment plan, rewarded votes cast in "safe" Democratic districts with greater representation than those cast in the Republican districts in the north. "If the State had been apportioned according to population," complained Joseph Medill, "the districts carried by the Republicans would have returned forty-one Lincoln representatives, and fourteen Lincoln Senators, which of course would have elected him. . . . On a fair appointment, Douglas would have been beaten seven in the House and three in the Senate." Combined with the failure to win over enough of the Whig districts, the apportionment doomed Lincoln's chances of election. "The State apportionment . . . has given Mr. Douglas an apparent victory," wailed the *Chicago Journal.* "Madison [County] with 4,000 votes, and Fulton [County] with 5,500 votes elect two members each, while the Will [County] district with 10,000 votes, elects *three,* and Cook [County] with 19,000 elects *four!*"[5]

Lincoln had expected to do better than he did; but he still did almost well enough to snatch the Senate seat away from Douglas and send the Little Giant to the political junk heap. Oddly, it was the candidate whose gospel was popular sovereignty who would be reelected to the Senate on the basis of a popular vote he had, technically, lost. Even more oddly, when Lincoln and Douglas faced each other two years later for the 1860 presidential contest, it would be Lincoln who would garner only 40 percent of the popular vote but win the presidency on the strength of Northern control of the Electoral College.

So, despite an overall Republican majority among votes cast, Douglasite Democrats narrowly retained control of the legislature after all, and made Douglas's reelection a foregone conclusion. When the legislature cast its electing vote on January 5, "the announcement of the result called forth much applause from the crowded galleries and lobbies, and the House adjourned in great confusion, while the victors exercised their lungs vigorously, and the noise of a cannon recalled to our mind the famous little one that Mr. D. used to trudge around with him during the canvass." Charles Lanphier wired Douglas in Philadelphia, "Glory to God and the Sucker Democracy. Douglas 54, Lincoln 46. Announcement followed by shouts of immense crowd present." Douglas wired back, without a trace of irony, "Let the voice of the people rule."[6]

It was not irony but rage which governed the attitudes of Republicans, who were convinced that Lincoln had been, once more, unfairly robbed of the victory he deserved. "The defeat of Mr. Lincoln grieves me beyond measure," David Davis wrote to his son on November 7, and, writing the same day to Lincoln, he added, "The result in Illinois has both astonished and mortified me beyond measure." George Rives, in Edgar County, moaned to Ozias Hatch, "O my God, it is too bad." Lincoln had "done his duty nobly" and was "too good a man to be thus treated by these D——Sons of bitches." The most obvious weapon in this robbery was the apportionment. "Had the people voted directly for you instead of for Members of the Legislature," wrote Judge Anson Miller to Lincoln, "you would be our U.S. Senator to-day by a handsome majority." But even under the unfair terms of the apportionment, argued David Davis, Lincoln would still have won had it not been for "the Irish colonization." William Grimshaw, writing to Lincoln on November 11, agreed with Davis: "We had a hard fight in Pike [County]" and lost because "the Rail Road & other Irish overwhelmed us." So did

William Herndon, who blamed the loss on "thousands of wild, roving, robbing, bloated, pock-marked Irish."

But by far the most frequent objects of blame were the old-line Whigs, especially Lyle Dickey and John J. Crittenden. As one Democratic newspaper chortled, the Whigs were suckers for the race card. "Negro equality is 'no go'" among the "old Line Clay Whigs" and so they "chose to vote with the Democrats." Leonard Swett was convinced that Lincoln had done a great deal to lose the Whig vote himself, by the "first ten lines" of the House Divided speech. But even Swett conceded that it was the Crittenden letter which decisively tipped the Whigs toward Douglas. David Davis thought "it was perfectly outrageous in Mr. Crittenden to have written any thing," but it was even worse for Lyle Dickey "to have kept that letter from 1st August & then published it a week before the election." Joseph Medill thought "the letter from Mr. Crittenden . . . damaged the Republican party more than any other" factor, and Herndon agreed in seeing the Crittenden letter as the reason why "thousands of Whigs dropped us on the eve of the election."

Both Herndon and Medill also blamed the inaction of East Coast Republicans. "The East was for Douglas by silence," Herndon complained, and the editor of the *Carlinville Free Democrat* (who had been set upon by Douglas's heavies when he heckled Douglas at the campaign stop in Gillespie) bitterly blamed Lincoln's loss on Republican faint-hearts "following the instructions of Greeley, Seward, Wilson & Co., and voting for the friends of Douglas, believing him to be the most reliable anti-slavery man." Elihu Washburne, who at least had the satisfaction of holding on to his congressional seat, was still stewing at the end of November over Greeley's betrayal of Lincoln early in the campaign: "Don't Illinois Republicans feel grateful to [the] N.Y. Tribune and others who were so earnest to . . . adopt Douglas?"[7]

There were also plenty of fingers being pointed at targets within Illinois's Republican leadership. One ex-Whig Republican told Ozias

Hatch that "we have deferred too much to the Democratic elements in our party," and that could mean only one person in particular, namely Norman Judd. "You know as well as I do," Hatch's correspondent irritably remarked, "that the back bone of the Republican Party is the Whig portion of it," and handing the reins of party leadership to the likes of Judd was only asking old Whigs to look elsewhere. David Davis, along with Charles Wilson of the *Chicago Journal* and Samuel Baker of the state committee, fingered Judd as the principal reason the campaign had been ineptly managed. And they were joined by Judd's bitter personal enemy, the ever-opportunistic "Long John" Wentworth, in sending up a chorus of mourning over Judd's "political inexperience." Wentworth even accused Judd of using the state committee chairmanship to promote his own ambitions "to be Governor . . . I look upon the whole management as making Lincoln incidental to the project of certain men for the future." A few of the blame assessors even turned to the weather for an explanation of the Republicans' loss. "Our Republicans are too many of them of the dry weather sort," wrote one. "I don't often swear but I say Damn a man that will talk big before elections and then excuses [himself] on the day, because of the weather."[8]

There is a faint possibility that "colonization" may have played a role in Lincoln's defeat, even allowing for the steep discount one has to impose on nativist paranoia about "Irish cattle." One of Ozias Hatch's correspondents told him on November 8 that "illegal votes were Cast in this county to the number of at least 100," and in the Whig Belt districts, even a number that small would have been enough to nudge Douglas past Lincoln. But although another of Hatch's correspondents declared that "we have some now under arrest for Perjury" at the polls, there is no record, in the months after the election, of any widespread pattern of voter-fraud convictions, nor did Lincoln lay any weight on "colonization" as an explanation for his defeat. The same is true for the weather, which, presumably, neither Douglas nor Lincoln could blame on the other.

	COUNTY		STATE HOUSE DISTRICT		U.S. CONGRESSIONAL DISTRICT	
	Dem.	Rep.	Dem.	Rep.	Dem.	Rep.
Ottawa	6,795	8,228	9,795	12,242	14,988	22,313
Freeport	1,500	2,131	1,500	2,131	6,457	15,811
Jonesboro	566	620	1,442	757	15,878	2,796
Charleston	1,641	1,777	2,223	2,291	13,588	11,760
Galesburg*	1,900	2,930	1,900	2,930	16,860	19,487
Quincy*	6,789	5,971	6,789	5,971	13,529	11,648
Alton*	4,411	4,021	4,411	4,021	11,490	8,410

* County and district boundaries coterminous.

Going by the county numbers, we would have to conclude that Lincoln "won" the first five debates—which is, in fact, counterintuitive, since Ottawa was hardly a moment of oratorical sparkle for him, and Jonesboro was even less so. Going by the state house district numbers, however, the pattern remains pretty much the same, the only change being in Jonesboro's first state house district, which was the farthest reach of Democratic "Egypt." (Oddly, the same pattern holds true of the votes in the debate towns themselves: in Freeport, Republicans outpolled Democrats 503 to 370; in Galesburg, Republicans won again, 789 to 225; but in Quincy, Democrats eked out a 1,061-to-1,006 majority, as they did in Alton, 583 to 487 and Charleston, 333 to 303).[10] Only when attention shifts to the U.S. congressional districts do things seem to change. But they change erratically—if we rely on those numbers, Lincoln won Ottawa but lost Charleston, won Galesburg but lost Quincy and Alton.

But more striking than any assessment of who "won" is the remarkable difference of arguments deployed by Lincoln and Douglas. Douglas staked out his basic points in his campaign opener in Chicago and then in the Ottawa debate, and kept hitting away at them in place after place; Lincoln also kept the threads of his most significant arguments going throughout the debates, but only as threads. He also composed new arguments for each debate. In fact, it has often puzzled commentators that once Lincoln struck certain blows against Douglas, particularly the Freeport Question, he seemed to lose interest in them and failed to repeat them before other debate audiences. But rather than indicating the unimportance of the Freeport Question, the fact that Lincoln asked it only once underscores the key role he came to see in the transcription and reprinting of the debate texts in the newspapers. Douglas made more or less the same arguments in every debate town because he was trying only to persuade the audience hearing him at that moment; he saw the debates as rhetorical events, where all that was required for victory was a triumph in front of the voters who happened to be on hand. Everything he said in one debate could, and should, be repeated in front of a different audience who had heard nothing of the preceding debate. Lincoln, however, saw the debates, at least from Freeport onward, as a newspaper serial. He had no need to repeat himself in each debate town, because he counted on audiences in one place having read the texts of the debates in the others. This induced Lincoln to treat the debates as cumulative and move on in developing new arguments as the debates themselves developed. For Douglas, the debates were principally oratory; for Lincoln, they became texts, something which was more apparent after the close of the campaigns, when Lincoln began assembling the debate transcriptions from the *Chicago Tribune* to issue them in book form.

The numbers, in the end, really tell us nothing about whether voters listened dispassionately as Lincoln and Douglas scored points or allowed the point spread to persuade them and then voted accordingly. There are no large ethnoreligious patterns, and nothing which looks like politics-as-usual, managed from the top downward. What there is, however, is the surprise national politicos felt at noticing the Illinois lawyer whom Douglas could not seem to knock down and whose words, even in cold type, crackled with authority. "Mr. Lincoln is a man of very great ability; few men in the nation would willingly encounter him in debate," wrote the *National Era* two weeks after the election. "We have heard many men in all parts of the Union, and think, for clear statement, the simplifying of difficult points, taking into consideration his rectitude and singleness of purpose, he is our choice." [11]

No one had more reason to rejoice over the results than Stephen A. Douglas. He had made fifty-nine full-dress speeches (of the two to three-hour variety) and seventeen shorter ones, plus thirty-seven brief responses to welcoming committees, and covered 5,227 miles in the course of the campaign. Despite the wearing down of his voice and his health, Douglas had missed not a single event on his published schedule. And he had won a double victory, over Lincoln and the Republicans, and over James Buchanan's administration. "The eloquent popular addresses made by Lincoln, and the eloquent unpopular appeals made by the administration equally fell short of their design," wrote one Douglasite. Standing on the same Tremont House balcony where he had begun his campaign, Douglas told a "grand Demonstration" of his loyalists on November 17, "You have a right to be proud of this glorious triumph. . . . It is the triumph of the glorious principles of the Union over fanaticism and sectionalism" as well as "the triumph over the principle of self-government over Congressional interference and Executive usurpation." And he happily told Charles Ray that the election looked like a complete endorsement of his course: "He will be the first to denounce any legislation which is designed for the restriction of slavery in the territories," but "he will not give up his notion that the organizers may refuse to legislate for it if it is there." Harriet Martineau, writing on American affairs for the London *Spectator* on November 27, thought Douglas was "the least like a Northern Republican and free-soiler that can be accepted," but that would probably be enough to induce "the entire South" to "join a portion of the North to carry Douglas" into the White House in 1860 "over the head of any genuine anti-slavery candidate."[12]

The biggest losers were the Danites and, behind them, James Buchanan. The losses the Buchanan administration suffered over Lecompton in October were only the overture to the farce of November. In New England, Maine, Vermont, and Massachusetts all went Republican; New Jersey split its five-man congressional group three to two in favor of the Republicans; in New York, Republicans and Douglas Democrats won twenty-nine of the thirty-three congressional seats, took 99 out of 128 seats in the state assembly, and elected Republican Edwin D. Morgan as governor; in Michigan, three out of the four congressional seats went to Republicans. In all, the Democrats remained in control of the Senate, thirty-eight to twenty-five, but they were upended in the House of Representatives, where Republicans captured 113 seats, Buchanan Democrats were left with 93 (almost exactly reversing their numbers for the previous session), and Douglas Democrats won 8.

But the worst beating was in Illinois. Despite the patronage decapitations, despite John Slidell's cynical attempt to use the Mississippi plantation issue to embarrass Douglas, and despite Isaac Cook's effort to erect a Danite political tower to challenge Douglas, the Buchananites failed miserably to undermine the Douglas machine in Illinois. Fewer than 10,000 votes went to Danite candidates for the state house—less than 3 percent of the total—and only 1,308 for Danite state senate candidates (little more than 1 percent). In fact, the Danites managed to field candidates in only thirty-five of the fifty-eight state house districts and failed to recruit challengers for three of the twelve state senate races. Only in the fifth, forty-first, and forty-second state house districts would the Danite vote have made any difference, and then only if every Danite vote had been thrown behind *Republicans*; only in the eighth state senate district (along the Illinois River) did the Danite vote pull enough Democrats away from Douglas to ensure a

Republican candidate's victory. "Will you not take one Danite with you," taunted the *Mongomery County Herald*, as the Republicans made "arrangements for a long sojourn at the head of Salt river" ("Salt river" meaning the freshet of tears the Republicans had to shed over the results). "He has not enough to paddle his own canoe, and he helped you all he could, you ought to give him a seat in your boat." [13]

Oddly, it was precisely the Danites' decision to declare themselves in open revolt against Douglas so early in the campaign which doomed them to irrelevance. By forcing a showdown with Douglas's Illinois supporters at the April state Democratic convention, Isaac Cook (and behind him, James Buchanan) forced administration sympathizers to declare themselves openly—and be openly proscribed by John Moore's state Democratic committee. Had the Danites held their fire until after November, and allowed Danite sympathizers to be elected as Democrats in good standing, with the full support of the state Democratic committee, the Buchananites might have won a secret beachhead of their own in the state legislature. After the November election, patronage threats (and patronage deals) would have had more impact on unprepared Illinois Democratic legislators, and deals could have been cut with opposition Republicans from a position of strength. And once the voting for U.S. senator began in the new legislature in January, a "compromise" candidate—Sidney Breese, John Wentworth, even Lyle Dickey—could have been trotted out and Douglas buried politically.

Lincoln had been in this position himself in 1855, and there was nothing which guaranteed that it might not happen again, this time to Douglas. Some of the Danites actually believed this was still possible between November and January. "Whether Stephen A. Douglas will be elected to the United States Senate is still a matter of doubt, notwithstanding the apparent majority in both Houses of the Legislature," puffed one Danite newspaper in Egypt, and Isaac Cook assured Buchanan that there were enough Democrats "not unfriendly to the Administration" in the legislature that no one could achieve a majority and thus "prevent the election of a U.S. Senator during the coming session." James Sheahan even overheard "one federal officer" offering a "blank commission to important federal offices" for any Democrats in the state senate who "would refuse to vote for Douglas." This, of course, was pipe dreaming. Douglas was elected by the legislature on a strict party-line vote on January 5, without dissenters, horse swapping, or multiple ballots.[14]

But there were other ways in which Douglas could still be wounded. For three weeks after the November elections, the haggard Little Giant stayed in Chicago to monitor the final count of the votes and ensure the practical loyalty of the new legislature. But then he and Adele took off cross-state to Alton, and thence by steamboat down the Mississippi to New Orleans, and from there to Havana, for a much-needed vacation. What he found, however, was the first inkling of how angrily Southern Democrats were going to hold his answer to Lincoln's Freeport Question against him. Speaking to an audience at Odd-Fellows Hall in New Orleans on December 6, he struggled (as Lincoln predicted he would) to convince slaveholders that popular sovereignty was never intended to allow a territory to forbid the *entry* of slaves, or that unfriendly legislation could run as far as to prevent slaveholders from recovering runaway slaves. In the weeks following, Douglas began writing a formal article on popular sovereignty, "The Dividing Line Between Federal and Local Authority," which he published in the September 1859 issue of *Harper's Monthly* (and as a separate pamphlet). In his eagerness to win back Southern support, he declared that "Slave property . . . is entitled to the same rights and immunities" as any other property, "even though it was always dependent upon the local authorities and laws for protection." The problem for Douglas had always been in deciding how far those "local authorities and laws" could infringe on the "rights and immunities" of slaveholders who happened to move next door. Within those "rights and immunities," Douglas conceded, was the power of the slaveholder "to reclaim his slave property"; but surely anyone who exercised his "rights and immunities" by recapturing his runaway slave could not be

constitutionally restrained by some local "police power." In fact, anyone who could recapture runaways by the strength of his constitutional "rights and immunities" had nothing he needed from any local
"authorities and laws." If the Constitution guaranteed a sovereign
right to reclaim fugitives, then all the local unfriendly legislation a territory could adopt was legally pointless.[15]

This did nothing to placate Southerners, however. Speaking at
Vicksburg as Douglas was happily cruising past on the Mississippi
River, Mississippi senator Jefferson Davis warned against allowing the
Little Giant's reassurances "to lull his constituents into false security."
Even the slightest unfriendliness to slavery in territorial legislation
was no longer acceptable, and in the next Congress, Davis began pushing for a federal slave code which would prevent interference by a territorial legislature "whether by direct legislation or legislation of an
indirect and unfriendly nature . . . with the constitutional right of any
citizen of the United States to take his slave property into the common
Territories." When Douglas finally arrived in Washington for the
opening of the lame-duck session of the Thirty-fifth Congress, Edmund Ruffin, who had hoped that Douglas's "immeasurable and unscrupulous ambition" against Buchanan would destroy his "hopes for
the presidency," greeted him as "a great political scoundrel."

Douglas had hardly occupied his seat before "a killing frost" descended on him. On December 9, the Senate Democratic caucus, the
last reserve of the Buchananites' political strength, relieved him of the
chairmanship of the Committee on Territories, which Douglas had
held for thirteen years. Mississippi's junior senator, Albert Gallatin
Brown, led a vicious attack on Douglas on the floor of the Senate, declaring that *Dred Scott* made it "the whole duty of this Government towards slave property . . . to protect it," and by *protect*, Brown could
understand only "*adequate* protection, *sufficient* protection," and not
unfriendly legislation.[16]

And when Douglas tried to fight back, it was invariably Freeport
which was waved under his nose. Up till Freeport, Douglas had been

able to speak from both sides of his mouth about popular sovereignty, promising Northerners that it would stop slavery and promising Southerners that it wouldn't, and all in the mighty hope that no one would pay too-careful attention. Freeport ended that. Douglas "held out to us here, when we advocated and supported the Kansas-Nebraska bill . . . that the Democratic party should be a unit on the question," complained Louisiana senator Judah P. Benjamin, "but when he goes home, and is pressed in a local contest, and he sees the glittering prize of a seat in this Chamber slipping from his grasp . . . he tells his people, as he says he has told them a hundred times before" that "he has, in the Kansas-Nebraska act, obtained . . . a perfect right to make a free Territory of every Territory in the Union, notwithstanding the decision of the court." Douglas's "anti-Lecomptonism was bad," commented the *Louisville Courier,* but "his Freeport speech was worse."

Even after the far sharper threat to slavery posed by John Brown's raid on Harpers Ferry in October 1859, and the rapid descent of James Buchanan into political paralysis, Douglas could still not sponge away the onus of Freeport. When the Democratic national convention met in Charleston in the spring of 1860, no other serious national Democratic figure stood in Douglas's way for the even-more glittering prize of the party's presidential nomination. That made no difference to the Southern Democrats. "The Mississippians have the Freeport speech of Douglas with them," wrote Cincinnati journalist Murat Halstead, and they "intend to bombard him in the convention with ammunition drawn from it."[17]

The Slave Democrats walked out of the Charleston convention rather than nominate Douglas; a second convention, in Baltimore, managed to nominate him, but only after another wave of Southern walkouts. Rather than contaminate themselves with Douglas, the Slave Democrats organized a nominating convention of their own and ran John C. Breckinridge—Buchanan's vice president, who had refused Douglas's plea to campaign with him in Illinois in 1858. If Douglas wanted the presidency, he would have to get it without the help of the

Southern half of his party. Nor could he turn to the old Whigs, as he had in 1858. In a vain effort to call up the ghost of the Whig party, the veteran survivors of Whiggery in the border states organized themselves as a "Constitutional Union" party and nominated John Bell to run for them. Douglas would be able to muster only the votes of Northern Democrats. And those votes would not be anywhere near enough to hold off the rising tide of the Republicans across the North, and the candidate they nominated for president, who—to the general surprise of all concerned—turned out to be Abraham Lincoln.

Lincoln's first reaction to the last-minute tail dive of his campaign for the Senate was depression. Henry C. Whitney found Lincoln the night of the election, in his Springfield law office, "gloomy as midnight . . . brooding over his ill-fortune." It seemed to him that people "are always putting me in the place where somebody has to be beaten and sacrificed for the welfare of the party or the common good," and he had now been beaten enough times that he expected everyone to desert him except his law partner, William Herndon.

He and Herndon faced a backlog of work which made Lincoln more than usually testy, especially when clients demanded opaquely to know why judgments had not been executed or collections made. "You perhaps need not to be reminded how I have been personally engaged the last three or four months," Lincoln wrote to one particular pest who wanted to know why "the lands of those against whom we obtained judgments last winter for you, have not been sold." He was also more weary from the incessant traveling and speaking than he seemed. He had made sixty major speeches and covered more than 4,300 miles of Illinois territory. Writing to Norman Judd two weeks after the election, he said that "I am convalescent and hoping these lines may find you in the same improving state of health," so even for Lincoln the campaign had taken its toll. But one of the characteristic marks of Lincoln's temperament was resiliency. Henry Rankin marveled at "how well he held up in his mental ability" to the end of the campaign, "as any one who read those speeches will observe." That resiliency now came to his aid in the cave of defeat. Returning home the night of the election, "the path" he walked on his way back to the clapboard house at Eighth and Jackson streets "had been worn hog-backed & was slippering. My foot slipped from under me, knocking the other one out of the way, but I recovered myself & lit square: and I said to myself, '*It's a slip and not a fall.*'"[18]

A slip and not a fall. By any other standards for measuring political shelf life, Lincoln's would, by this point, have been close to expiration. He had spent one term in the House of Representatives, mostly fruitless; he had failed in one bid for the Senate in 1855, switched parties, and now had been defeated again for the Senate when it had looked as though he had every expectation of winning. Judd and the Republican state committee had run the campaign "upon the most economical plan" possible, but they still ended up $65,000 in the hole, with the *Chicago Tribune* mortgaged to the chin to generate the loans and another $2,500 in borrowing made by the committee directly. Judd had no choice but to write out $300 assessments for each of the state committee members, and for Lincoln.

This did not make Lincoln happy. He complained to Judd, "I have been on expences so long without earning any thing that I am absolutely without money now for even household purposes . . . all which being added to my loss of time and business, bears pretty heavily upon one no better off in this world's goods than I." Still, he recognized that "as I had the post of honor, it is not for me to be over-nice," and he agreed to "put in two hundred and fifty dollars . . . towards discharging the debt of the Committee," which, alongside "an outstanding note" he had already written for Judd, would take him over the mark of "five hundred dollars." And, a little reluctantly, he agreed to help Judd collect assessments from the other state Republican candidates. To anyone else than Judd, though, he admitted how glad he was to have gotten off with as little pain as "a few hundred dollars," and even turned down a loan from the Bloomington lawyer William H. Hanna,

who had "supposed Lincoln poor" from his spartan demeanor. "I am
not so poor as you suppose," Lincoln wrote back, amused, "though
much obliged to you." [19]

Nor did Lincoln stay "convalescent" for long. "A few weeks at home
after [the debates] had ended," recalled Henry Rankin, and "he was
entirely restored by his regular home life." Three weeks after the election, Lincoln was back in legal harness, scheduling cases and "making
sales." Soon, he began dismissing the sympathy letters and writing
notes to buck up the letter writers' spirits. "You are feeling badly," he
wrote to Norman Judd; but remember, "this too shall pass away." He
heard, through Ozias Hatch, that Charles H. Ray was "feeling like
h———ll yet." With determined cheer, Lincoln exhorted him to "quit
that. You will soon feel better. Another 'blow-up' is coming; and we
shall have fun again." It also gave Lincoln some uplift to see his defeat
as no more than one battle in a much larger war on behalf of liberty, a
battle that "must go on. The cause of civil liberty must not be surrendered at the end of one, or even, one hundred defeats." And "go on" it
certainly would, so long as Stephen A. Douglas "had the ingenuity to
be supported in the late contest both as the best means to break down,
and to uphold the Slave interest. No ingenuity can keep those antagonistic elements in harmony long. Another explosion will soon come."
When Archibald Williams, another unsuccessful Republican candidate, walked into Lincoln's law office on the day of Douglas's confirma-
tion by the Illinois legislature and complained that "the Democrats are
making a great noise over their victory," Lincoln looked up and commented patiently, "Yes, Archie, Douglas has taken this trick, but the
game is not played out yet." [20]

He did not try to pretend that the loss hadn't wounded him. When
Douglas's election was confirmed by the Illinois legislature in January,
Lincoln admitted to Charles Zane, a fellow lawyer in Springfield, that
"it hurts too much to laugh and I am too big to cry." Nor did Lincoln
try to hide his irritation that, just as in 1855, he had been let down by
his old party, the Whigs: "Nearly all the old exclusive silk-stocking

whiggery is against us." He rushed to qualify that by saying, "I do not mean nearly all the old whig party," which contained so many self-improvers like himself, "but nearly all of the nice exclusive sort," who were perfectly content to lose elections and sink back down into their leather chairs without any real feeling of loss. But that had never been his notion of the Whig party anyway, and "the fight" would do very well without them. He was also irked at the subtle role played in his defeat by the legislative apportionment, and he hoped Judd and the Republican state committee would "draft an apportionment law" which would be "strictly & obviously just in all particulars."

But the one black dog which Lincoln could not dismiss from his mind was the question of what his future role in "the fight" was likely to be. Lincoln told his physician, Anson G. Henry, that he was "glad I made the late race" because "it gave me a hearing on the great and durable question of the age, which I could have had in no other way." He had made "some marks which will tell for the cause of civil liberty long after I am gone." But *gone*, at least politically, was what he expected to be. "I now sink out of view, and shall be forgotten," he predicted. And to Norman Judd, he confided that in any future political fight over Douglas, slavery, and popular sovereignty, "I shall fight in the ranks" and "shall be in no ones way for any of the places."[21]

This sort of self-pity—and self-pity it was, since no politician ever declares that he is renouncing ambition for political office without the hope that someone will feel sorry enough to call him conveniently back—sits oddly beside what turned out to be the real feeling among Illinois Republicans, that Lincoln had lost only by a technicality and, even more, that he had performed far above anyone's expectations against the Little Giant and needed to be given a fresh platform on which to try again. "Your Defeat is only due to unfortunate circumstances by which [Douglas] has had an unfair advantage," explained Henry Bromwell. Lincoln needed to look up, wrote Chester Dewey, who had covered the debates for the *New York Evening Post*, and see that he had "made hosts of warm friends at the East." Through the debates, Lincoln had "made a national reputation that I would much rather have this day, than that of S. A. Douglas," wrote William Hanna on the day the *Chicago Tribune* conceded the election. "I give you my hand on the next great fight and when it comes [I] shall not fail to be with you." One campaign worker told Ozias Hatch that, in spite of the defeat, "I would rather vote for him than for any man living."

And not only in Illinois. Jesse Fell told Lincoln, "Seriously, Lincoln, Judge Douglas being so widely known, you are getting a national reputation. . . . Your discussion with Judge Douglas had demonstrated your ability and your devotion to freedom; you have no embarrassing record; you have sprung from the humble walks of life, sharing in its toils and trials; and if only we can get these facts sufficiently before the people, depend on it, there is some chance for you." But chance for what? When Thomas Harris, one of Douglas's great confidants, suddenly spiraled downward after his election to the Sixth U.S. congressional seat and died on November 24, Lincoln was at once bombarded with requests that he throw his hat into a special election for the seat in December. But even more dramatically, people now began attaching the words *vice president* or even *president* to Lincoln's name. Benjamin Lundy, the son of a famous abolitionist editor and himself the editor of the *Hennepin Tribune*, sent Lincoln a clipping from his paper which "hoisted the names of *Seward* and *Lincoln* as our choice for Presidential & Vice Presidential candidates in '60." (Lundy left it up to Lincoln whether he wanted to "again bare the Republican Standard" for "President, Vice-President, or Governor of the State.") George Rives, fresh from "the sad news of Lincoln's defeat," immediately told Ozias Hatch that "now I am for Lincoln for the nomination for president in 1860!" By December, even the *Chicago Tribune* was beginning to hint at endorsing Lincoln for the presidential race in 1860. "Let me assure you," wrote the *Tribune*'s Horace White. "Your popular majority in the state will give us the privilege of naming our man on the national ticket in 1860."[22]

Lincoln was not entirely sure what to make of this. "Just think of such a sucker as me as president!" he laughed to Henry Villard. And, more seriously, he told Thomas J. Pickett, the editor of the *Rock Island Weekly Register,* who had been booming the idea of a Lincoln presidential nomination, "I must, in candor, say I do not think myself fit for the Presidency" and thought it "best for our cause that no concerted effort, such as you suggest, should be made." The notion of *the cause* had played such a salving role in coping with his defeat that Lincoln kept pushing on the idea that he was no more than a foot soldier in a larger army in the service of freedom. But it was often hard to disentangle his self-denying pledge of service to *the cause* from his continuing private fury at the free skate through life enjoyed by Stephen A. Douglas. The stature Lincoln had gained in the debates now earned him invitations from Republican candidates in other states, and in September 1859 he stumped Ohio, Indiana, and Wisconsin. But he spent his best efforts in Ohio, on behalf of Salmon Chase, who was in the running for the U.S. Senate—because Chase was the one major Republican figure who had come to Lincoln's aid in Illinois, and also because Douglas was stumping Ohio, too, on behalf of Chase's competitor.

The result became something like an extension of the 1858 debates, with Lincoln spending more time on Douglas than on Chase. Lincoln had learned the hard way about the magic of the words *popular sovereignty,* so he put his shoulder to the task of making "a broad distinction between real popular Sovereignty and Douglas popular sovereignty." Real sovereignty means "that a state, or any minor political community, shall control what exclusively concerns it." This was a simple statement of political independence, and this, "no republican opposes." But Douglas's popular sovereignty was a glorification of raw power over the rule of natural law: "If any organized political community, however new and small, would enslave men . . . neither any nor all may interfere." As he had promised Charles Ray, Lincoln was once again having "fun." [23]

It was also hard for Lincoln to reconcile the humble posture of a footman to *the cause* with the turbulent froth of his "little engine" of ambition, something which surfaced only weeks after the close of the 1858 Illinois campaign in the form of an idea for a book version of the debate texts. He wrote Charles H. Ray only two weeks after the campaign ended to ask if Ray could supply him with a double set of all the issues of the *Chicago Tribune* which contained the debate texts, "in order to lay one away in the raw, and to put the other in a Scrap-book." After waiting ten days and getting no answer, Lincoln wrote to Henry Clay Whitney in Chicago and asked Whitney to "procure them and forward them to me by Express." Ray claimed never to have received Lincoln's letter and, worse, had on hand only the *Tribune's* morgue copies, so Whitney volunteered to send Lincoln his own set.

By then, Lincoln was already receiving inquiries from Republican editors across the North for copies of the debate texts, and he had to say that, at least so far, "the joint discussions between Judge Douglas and myself have been published in no shape except in the first newspaper reports." But by March 1859, Lincoln was talking with at least one publisher about collecting not just the debate texts from the *Tribune* but matching pairs of texts (his speeches from the *Tribune*, Douglas's from Sheahan's *Chicago Times*—"this would represent each of us, as reported by his own friends, and thus be mutual, and fair") plus a number of the incidental campaign speeches and "the correspondence between Judge Douglas and myself which led to the joint discussions," in book form as *The Illinois Political Canvass of 1858.*[24]

Nothing came of Lincoln's feelers about publication that spring, and so the first and most practical use for the "Scrap-book" was similar to the use he developed for his notebooks during the 1858 campaign, as a resource for the speeches he would give in Ohio in 1859. The Ohio state Republican committee was so grateful for Lincoln's help that in December 1859 the committee chairman, George Parsons, offered to underwrite the publication of the "Scrap-book" and put Lincoln in touch with Ohio's principal political publisher, Follett & Foster of

Columbus. (Oran Follett was also the editor of the *Ohio State Journal* and "one of the founding fathers of the Republican party in the state.") By March 20, 1860, Follett & Foster were ready to offer copies of what they had entitled, with a cooler marketing eye than Lincoln's, *Political Debates Between Hon. Abraham Lincoln and Hon. Stephen A. Douglas in the Celebrated Campaign of 1858, in Illinois.* Although this version of the title was more lugubrious, the book sold surprisingly well—four printings were off the press by May 21, with the fourth selling sixteen thousand copies.[25]

But by May, of course, Abraham Lincoln was the Republican presidential nominee.

The publication of the debates annoyed Stephen A. Douglas, who wrote to Follet & Foster on June 9, "to protest the unfairness of this publication, and especially against the alterations and mutilations in the Reports of my speeches." This seemed hard to credit, since Lincoln had taken the trouble to use the transcriptions made by Douglas's shorthand reporters, Binmore and Sheridan, and printed in Sheahan's *Chicago Times.* But Douglas's complaint centered on the difficulty of using any transcriptions of "speeches . . . delivered in the open air to immense crowds of people, and in some cases in stormy and boisterous weather, when it was impossible for the Reporters to hear distinctly and report literally." And he suspected very loudly that Lincoln (or Follett & Foster) had gone to work prettifying Lincoln's speeches and "mutilated" his. He was particularly incensed that the publisher had barged ahead with the project without ever bothering to consult him, or allowing him to make corrections, and he demanded that Follet & Foster insert his protest letter "as a Preface to all future editions of these Debates." The publisher indignantly denied that they had performed any editorial surgery on either debater. (Ironically, Lincoln had indeed made a number of editorial changes in the margins of the cuttings he made from the *Chicago Tribune* for his "Scrap-book," but there are only thirty-three of them, and twenty-three of those appear to have been taken from Sheahan's *Chicago Times*.) Follett & Foster did agree to include Douglas's letter in a subsequent printing of the book and add two of the Little Giant's 1859 Ohio campaign speeches.[26]

By June 1860, though, Douglas had far more pressing matters on hand. The Democratic party was splintering under his feet, and behind that could be heard the cracking-up of the Union itself. The split of the Democrats into Douglas and Breckinridge parties, and the additional distraction of the Constitutional Union party, doomed Douglas's chances for the final prize he had for so long sought. In November 1860, the nation trooped to what looked like the last presidential election it would ever hold, and the unhappy Douglas came out of it 490,000 votes short of Lincoln and won only 12 electoral votes (against Lincoln's 180). In Illinois, Lincoln once again carried the popular vote (by almost 12,000 votes) and by exactly the same percentage he had won in 1858 (51.9 percent). But he still lost in the Whig Belt— Peoria by 199 votes, Menard County by 73 votes, Macoupin by 496 votes, Hancock by 392 votes, Adams (where the Quincy debate took place) by 454 votes.

Lincoln's election was the signal which set off waves of secession by the slaveholding states, and those secessions finally came to violence over the status of Fort Sumter. Douglas used the Senate seat he had won in 1858 to attack secession as "wrong, unlawful, unconstitutional, criminal." But all he had to offer as a formula to "banish the slavery question from the Halls of Congress and the arena of Federal politics" was popular sovereignty, and by January 1861, no one was listening. When the artillery of the newly organized Confederate States began battering the walls of Fort Sumter, Douglas wearily agreed that "the shortest way now to peace is the most stupendous and unanimous preparation for war." At Lincoln's inauguration, Douglas stood on the platform on the east side of the capitol, and when Lincoln rose to take the oath and discovered he had no place to rest his top hat, Douglas obligingly stepped forward and held it for him. The Senate adjourned at the end of March 1861, but Douglas was still in Washington when the news of the fall of Sumter arrived, and he hurried to the White House to pledge "the President his most earnest and active co-operation toward putting down the rebellion." He spoke at rallies on the train route back to Illinois, telling a crowd in Columbus that "the Union must be preserved and the insurrection must be crushed," addressing both houses of the Illinois legislature on April 25 at the same rostrum from which Lincoln had delivered the House Divided speech. The next day, Douglas told Orville Hickman Browning that he was "unqualifiedly for the government against all attempts to over-throw it, and said very emphatically that we ought to meet the traitors beyond the line, and fight the battles on their own soil." And in Chicago on May 1, Douglas announced emphatically, "There can be no neutrals in this war; *only patriots and traitors.*"[27]

The strain literally killed him. Stephen A. Douglas had never been a paragon of health, and he never entirely recovered from the battering he took in the 1858 campaign. But he had taken the risk in 1858 be-cause, in the end, risks were the ultimate witchery for Douglas, and in the spring of 1861, he took them again for what he saw as the final threat to the Union he thought he had been christened to save. Even at the end, Douglas could not resist the lure of the party game. Much as "there was but one path of duty left to patriotic men" in the current cri-sis, he wanted people to understand that "I am neither the supporter of the partisan policy nor the apologist for the errors of the Administra-tion," and he hoped eventually "to regain and perpetuate the ascen-dancy of our party."

But this was one risk he would not live to play out. On the evening of his last speech, Douglas began to feel unwell, and by May 10, his ill-ness had developed into "a severe attack of rheumatism," which may have been either a minor stroke or a heart attack. He took to his bed, but his condition did not improve, and on the morning of June 3, with Adele and his two sons beside him, the Little Giant died.[28]

·   ·   ·

The Civil War washed over the memory of Stephen A. Douglas, leaving him with little for a legacy except the fact that he had once crossed words with Abraham Lincoln. It was Douglas now who had become dependent on Lincoln for what remained of a reputation, rather than, as in 1858, the other way round. When commemorations of the 1858 campaigns began in 1896, it was Robert Todd Lincoln who was induced to make one of his rare public speeches at a celebration of the Galesburg debate, not either of the sons of Douglas. Freeport followed with a celebration in 1903, when a Republican president, Theodore Roosevelt, was the guest of honor and was introduced by Robert Hitt, the onetime shorthand reporter who was now a Republican congressman. Five years later, Quincy staged a fifty-year celebration, as did Alton (where the aged Henry McPike resumed his place on the platform, joined by Horace White) and Freeport, which produced a full-dress reenactment of its debate on the same site as the original. In 1929, Freeport unveiled a commemorative statue—of "Lincoln the Debater," by Leonard Crunelle, as though Douglas had never even been there. In Charleston, the home of the only museum devoted to the debates, the monument on the courthouse grounds depicts Lincoln delivering the House Divided speech, and the local hospital is named for Lincoln's stepmother.

Not until 1936—at the beginning of a new Democratic ascendancy in national politics—did Douglas begin to appear in celebrations of the debates. At Quincy, Lorado Taft executed a monument of Lincoln and Douglas together (although Lincoln is standing and speaking, while Douglas is seated), and Douglas's great-grandson Robert D. Douglas was the featured speaker. For the centennial of the debates, Freeport's Lincoln-Douglas Society commissioned a play by Norman Corwin, *The Rivals*, in which Martin Gabel played Stephen A. Douglas against Raymond Massey as Lincoln, and sponsored another reenactment of the debates. (And almost on cue for the exhumation of Douglas's reputation as a heroic nationalist, a member of Freeport High School's graduating class of 1958 delivered a commencement speech lauding Douglas's championship of "the growth and progress of the nation through opening up new territory, leaving the people to decide whether it should be slave or free territory.")

In 1975, Chicago mayor Richard J. Daley, long an admirer of the Little Giant, founded a Stephen A. Douglas Association, and in 1994, Harold Holzer, a onetime Democratic staffer for Bella Abzug and Mario Cuomo, published an edition of the debates, reversing the order Lincoln had adopted in the Follett & Foster edition and printing Lincoln's speeches as published by the *Chicago Times* and Douglas's as published by the *Chicago Tribune*. That same year, C-Span televised a series of reenactments of the debates, stimulated by Holzer's new book but now tamely vetted of Lincoln's moralism and made over into "a celebration of the right to disagree."[29]

But none of this minor rehabilitation of Douglas's reputation has ever amounted to an eclipse of Lincoln's role in the debates, nor should it. From a starting point well in the shade of Lyman Trumbull and the schemes of James Buchanan, Lincoln emerged over the course of his campaign as an opponent of formidable intellectual stature on the slavery question. "He entered upon the canvass with a reputation confined to his own state," wrote Joseph Medill. "He closes it with his name a household word wherever the principles he holds are honored and with the respect of his opponents in all sections of the country." Lincoln had forced Douglas into admitting that the Little Giant stood immovably by popular sovereignty in the territories, which ended forever any hope that Douglas could be embraced by the Republican national leadership and reduced to vanishing the possibility that he could be reconciled to the administration and the Southern Democrats. Douglas "was dreaming of a seat in the White House, and to please or conciliate the negro-breeders . . . clasped to his embrace the black imp Dred Scott," wrote a disgusted Horace Greeley. "He staked his soul against the Presidency, in a game with the Demon of Slavery, and he has lost!"[30]

In a state and a region where Democratic majorities were usually taken easily for granted, and against the most prominent Northern Democratic politician, Lincoln had carved his way to within a few districts of toppling Douglas and winning the Senate seat he craved so earnestly. That, fully as much as the debates, gave Lincoln a national profile he had never enjoyed, or thought to enjoy. "Until June," recalled Shelby Cullom, "Mr. Lincoln was unknown outside of Illinois and Indiana," but by September, "Lincoln's character was understood and his ability was recognized in all the non-slaveholding States of the Union." Years later, in the White House, Lincoln would offer to Charles Morehead of Kentucky his own interpretation of the outcome of the debates when he said that he "was accidentally elected president of the United States" and would never have been at all "but from the fact of his having made a race for the Senate of the United States with Judge Douglas in the state of Illinois." As a result of "running that race in a local election, his speeches had been published," and from that "his name became prominent," and on that basis "he was accidentally selected" as a Republican dark horse candidate "and elected afterwards as president of the United States."[31]

But at the deepest level, what Lincoln defended in the debates was the possibility that there could be a moral core to a democracy. The fundamental premise of Douglas's popular sovereignty was that democratic decision-making, in order to be free, has to be unencumbered by the weight of factors which are nonpolitical in nature, such as kinship, ethnic identity, or moral and religious obligations. The purpose of politics is not to lead "the good life" or to pursue what is good and true but to ensure fair play, toleration, and personal autonomy. As Theodore Parker wrote to Herndon after the election, Douglas did "not deal with *principles* which a man may spread abroad from the pulpit or by the press, but only with *measures* that require political place to carry out." In this way, no one particular path to virtue is laid out, no one morality is held against others as a standard, and the civil conflicts that emerge over differing standards of virtue and morality are held to a minimum. It creates a world, as T. S. Eliot once remarked, "of systems so perfect that no one will need to be good," where no one recognizes the right of anyone else in himself, where desire is the only reality and the only ends those we have chosen for ourselves. Solidarity becomes sentimentality; morality, a socially useless prejudice. Paul Berman, writing in *Terror and Liberalism*, speaks despairingly of the ways in which liberal democracy, at the moment of its greatest triumph with the fall of the Soviet empire, still managed "in its pure version . . . to seem mediocre, corrupt, tired, and aimless, a middling compromise, pale and unappealing—something to settle for, in spirit of resignation." He might as well have been talking about Douglas.

This was also the spirit Francis Fukuyama described in *The Last Man and the End of History* in 1992—with the fall of Soviet Communism, liberal democracy had triumphed, had at last freed humanity, and had removed any need to search further for a better politics. "There is no struggle or conflict over 'large' issues, and consequently no need for generals or statesmen," Fukuyama wrote in 1989, "what remains is primarily economic activity." But to what end? To sit at the end of the historical tracks, *free*, but free only to indulge one's personal preferences? Fukuyama's, and Berman's, nightmare was that the "last man" would turn out to be the "comfortable burgher, blinking stupidly and wondering about dinner . . . cowardly, greedy and self-absorbed," a society "with no ability or inclination to defend itself or anyone else." The assault on liberal democracy mounted by Islamic terrorism in the 1990s and culminating in 9/11, represented a judgment by Islamism that the West in general (and the United States in particular) was too fat, dumb, and happy to mount any effective response to its Islamized versions of fascism—just as Hitler and Stalin had judged the Western democracies in the 1930s and '40s as too morally vacuous to offer serious resistance to their aggressive and militarized ideologies.[32] Little in the response of those democracies after 9/11 suggests that the Islamists had been wrong.

The great exception to democratic stagnation, argues Berman, has been the United States, which in the 1850s "took the notion of a liberal society and, with a few earnest twists of the screwdriver, rendered the whole concept a little sturdier." Sturdier, in the sense that the United States turned the principles of self-government into a natural morality and then wedded those principles to a universalism, part Christian and part Enlightenment, which made them universally right—not merely convenient or useful but transcendently right. And among the possible candidates for chief turner of the screwdriver, Berman had only one worth talking about: "It was Lincoln who did this." [33]

We have been so content to take the Lincoln-Douglas debates as a purely historical event that we miss how much the great debates really are a defining moment in the development of a liberal democracy, and how much Lincoln is our greatest preceptor and Douglas our most tempting but disastrous alternative—for these are not the lessons modern liberal democracy wishes to hear. The "procedural republic" described by Michael Sandel at the beginning of this book treats its citizens strictly as independent individuals who have *rights*, which must always trump any appeal to morality, to responsibility, or to the general welfare of everyone else. In 1858, in the midst of the deepening crisis over slavery in America, a commitment to the procedural republic pointed Stephen A. Douglas in the direction of arguing that slavery was a constitutionally guaranteed and morally neutral right, that it was no business of anyone in the free states to interfere with the free exercise of that right, and that the only way of dealing with slavery in the West was to leave to the people actually settling in the West the privilege of determining whether they wanted to legalize slavery or not.

Lincoln represented an entirely different perspective. For him, politics was not about helping people exercise rights apart from doing what was right; and slavery was so clearly a violation of the rights of black slaves that it was tantamount to a moral wrong. In the face of Douglas's belief that liberal democracy existed only to provide a procedural framework for exercising rights, Lincoln insisted that liberal democracy had a higher purpose, which was the realization of a morally right political order. No one managed to state this more clearly than Robert Todd Lincoln, speaking at the Galesburg celebration in 1896:

> *Now, as then, there can be but one supreme issue, that between right and wrong. In our country there are no ruling classes. The right to direct public affairs according to his might and influence and conscience belongs to the humblest as well as to the greatest. . . . But it is times of danger, critical moments, which bring into action the high moral quality of the citizenship of America. The people are always true. They are always right, and I have an abiding faith they will remain so.*[34]

And so Lincoln and Douglas pose anew a dilemma which has haunted Americans from the time of Plymouth Rock—what was the American experiment about? Finding space to be free, or finding an opportunity to do right? The Puritan Commonwealth or the Weimar Republic? A city on the hill or Sodom-by-the-Sea? Enlightened self-interest or beloved community? And was there a way to hold on to one without entirely losing a grip on the other? Although the Civil War eventually settled this question as it applied to slavery, it has continued to be a fundamental dilemma for American democracy and for liberal democracy everywhere else, even now, in the Age of Terror. The great debates in Illinois in 1858 turned out to be a more important victory than Lincoln could have imagined, for they pointed him to his national political debut in New York City in 1860, the Republican national convention, and finally his election as the sixteenth—and greatest—American president. And beyond even that, a beacon to us all.

NOTES

INTRODUCTION

1. "Failures for 1857," *Illinois State Register*, January 18, 1858; *The Reminiscences of Carl Schurz* (New York: Doubleday, Page & Co., 1907), volume 2, p. 75; William Lyman Fawcett, *Gold and Debt; an American Hand-book of Finance* (Chicago: S. C. Griggs, 1877), p. 160; Horace Greeley, *An Overland Journey, from New York to San Francisco in the summer of 1859* (New York: C. M. Saxton, Barker, 1859), pp. 9–10; "Great Religious Awakening!" *Peoria Daily Transcript*, March 9, 1858, and "Religious Revivals," *Illinois State Register*, March 26, 1858; Charles H. Coleman, "The Lincoln-Douglas Debate at Charleston, Illinois, September 18, 1858," *Eastern Illinois University Bulletin* 220 (October 1, 1957), p. 21; "The Ohio River Still Rising," *Philadelphia Evening Bulletin*, June 13 and 15, 1858.

2. *Dallas Weekly Herald*, August 14, 1858; "Speaker Orr," *Missouri Daily Republican*, August 28, 1858; "The Douglas Campaign in Illinois," *Missouri Daily Republican*, September 15, 1858; *Memoirs of Henry Villard, Journalist and Financier, 1835–1900* (Boston: Houghton Mifflin, 1904), volume one, p. 91; Anson Miller to Abraham Lincoln, November 15, 1858, Abraham Lincoln Papers, Library of Congress (hereafter LOC); "The Illinois Fight" and "Douglas," *Philadelphia Evening Bulletin*, August 23, 1858; "The Vermont Convention—Greeley and the Tribune—Douglas and Lincoln in Illinois," *The Liberator*, July 30, 1858, p. 124; "Douglas-Lincoln," *Montgomery County Herald* [Hillsboro, IL], September 17, 1858; Alexander Davidson, *A Complete History of Illinois from 1673 to 1873* (Springfield: Illinois Journal, 1874), pp. 709–10; Richard Allan Heckman, *Lincoln vs. Douglas* (Washington: Public Affairs Press, 1967), p. 78; Robert W. Johannsen, *Stephen A. Douglas* (Urbana: University of Illinois Press, 1973), p. 645.

3. Isaac Arnold, *The History of Abraham Lincoln and the Overthrow of Slavery*, (Chicago: Clarke & Co., 1866) p. 134; Joseph Barrett, *Life, Speeches and Public Services of Abraham Lincoln*, (Washington, D.C.: Moore, Wolstach & Baldwin,

1865) p. 189; Ida M. Tarbell, *The Life of Abraham Lincoln* (New York: McClure, Phillips & Co., 1904), volume one, p. 322.

4. Daniel Fish, *Legal Phases of the Lincoln and Douglas Debates: Annual Address before the State Bar Association of Minnesota at Minneapolis, July 14, 1909* (Minneapolis, 1909), p. 11; Allan Nevins and Willard L. King, "The Constitution and Declaration of Independence as Issues in the Lincoln-Douglas Debates," *Journal of the Illinois State Historical Society* 52 (Spring 1959), p. 12.

5. Neil Postman, *Amusing Ourselves to Death: Public Discourse in the Age of Show Business* (New York: Penguin Books, 1985), pp. 44–49.

6. Ibid., pp. 48, 60, 80.

7. Albert Beveridge, *Abraham Lincoln, 1809–1858*, volume two, p. 635; William O. Lynch, "The Character and Leadership of Stephen A. Douglas," *Proceedings of the Mississippi Valley Historical Association*, volume ten, 1920–21 (Cedar Rapids, IA: Torch Press, 1923), p. 461; James Garfield Randall, *Lincoln the President: Springfield to Gettysburg* (New York: Dodd Mead, 1945), volume one, p. 128; Kirk Jeffrey, "Stephen Arnold Douglas in American Historical Writing," *Journal of the Illinois State Historical Society* 61 (Autumn 1968), pp. 255–58.

8. George Beatty reminiscence, Ida Tarbell Papers, Special Collections, Pelletier Library Allegheny College, Meadville, Pa.

9. I. M. Short, *Abraham Lincoln: Early Days in Illinois* (Kansas City, MO: Simpson Pubs., 1927), p. 97; Heckman, *Lincoln vs. Douglas*, pp. 1–2; Michael P. Kramer, *Imagining Language in America: From the Revolution to the Civil War* (Princeton: Princeton University Press, 1992), p. 138.

10. Lee Benson, *The Concept of Jacksonian Democracy: New York as a Test Case* (Princeton: Princeton University Press, 1961), p. 269; Joel H. Silbey, "The Surge of Republican Power: Partisan Antipathy, American Social Conflict, and the Coming of the Civil War," in *Essays on American Antebellum Politics, 1840–1860*, ed. Stephen Maizlish and John J. Kushma (College Station: Texas A&M University Press, 1982), pp. 201–2; Glenn C. Altschuler and Stuart M. Blumin, "The Limits of Political Engagement in Antebellum America: A New Look at the Golden Age of Participatory Democracy," *Journal of American History* 84 (December 1997), pp. 865, 870–71, 877; John L. Brooke, " 'To Be Read By the Whole People': Press, Party, and Public Sphere in the United States, 1789–1840," *Proceedings of the American Antiquarian Society* 110 (part 1, 2002), p. 52; Michael D. Pierson, " 'Prairies on Fire': The Organization of the 1856 Mass Republican Rally in Beloit, Wisconsin," *Civil War History* 48 (June 2002), pp. 104–5.

11. Mark E. Neely, *The Boundaries of American Political Culture in the Civil War Era* (Chapel Hill: University of North Carolina Press, 2005), 31; Louis Menand, "Fractured Franchise," *The New Yorker* (July 9/16, 2007), pp. 88–91.

12. David Potter, *The Impending Crisis, 1848–1861* (New York: Harper & Row, 1976), pp. 334–35, 338; David Zarefsky, *Lincoln, Douglas and Slavery: In the Crucible of Public Debate* (Chicago: University of Chicago Press, 1990), p. x. Indeed, the *American Almanac* for 1859 does not mention the debates; but this is because the *Almanac*'s listing of "General Events for 1858" stopped at August 25,

1858—just after the first of the debates at Ottawa, and nine weeks before the general legislative election in Illinois—in order to make the *Almanac*'s December press deadline. See *The American Almanac and Repository of Useful Knowledge for the Year 1859* (Boston: Crosby, Nichols, and Co., 1859), p. 371.

13. Allan Nevins, *The Emergence of Lincoln: Douglas, Buchanan, and Party Chaos, 1857–1859* (New York: Charles Scribner's Sons, 1950), pp. 377, 399; Don E. Fehrenbacher, *Prelude to Greatness: Lincoln in the 1850's* (Stanford: Stanford University Press, 1962), p. 104; Harry V. Jaffa, *Crisis of the House Divided: An Interpretation of the Issues in the Lincoln-Douglas Debates* (Garden City, N: Doubleday, 1959), p. 229; John Channing Briggs, *Lincoln's Speeches Reconsidered* (Baltimore: Johns Hopkins University Press, 2005), p. 52; Damon Wells, *Stephen Douglas: The Last Years, 1857–1861* (Austin: University of Texas Press, 1990), p. 126.

14. Michael Sandel, *Democracy's Discontent: America in Search of a Public Philosophy* (Cambridge, MA: Harvard University Press, 1996), pp. 21–24; Paul Berman, *Terror and Liberalism* (New York: W. W. Norton, 2003), pp. 170–71.

15. G. S. Hillard, *Life and Campaigns of George B. McClellan, Major-General U.S. Army* (Philadelphia: J. B. Lippincott, 1864), p. 126.

16. Lincoln, "Speech at Peoria, Illinois" (October 16, 1854) and "Speech at Springfield, Illinois" (June 26, 1857), in *Collected Works of Abraham Lincoln* (hereafter *C.W.*), ed. Roy P. Basler et al. (New Brunswick, NJ: Rutgers University Press, 1953), volume two, pp. 256, 405.

17. Lincoln, "Fragment on Sectionalism" (c. July 23, 1856), in *C.W.*, volume two, p. 352; James L. Huston, "Democracy by Scripture Versus Democracy by Process: A Reflection on Stephen A. Douglas and Popular Sovereignty," *Civil War History* 43 (September 1997), pp. 192–93.

1: THE LEAST MAN I EVER SAW

1. "The Territory of Nebraska" (January 4, 1854), *Congressional Globe*, 33rd Congress, 1st session, p. 115; Robert W. Johannsen, *Stephen A. Douglas* (Urbana: University of Illinois Press, 1973), p. 403.

2. Frank E. Stevens, "Life of Stephen Arnold Douglas," *Journal of the Illinois State Historical Society* 16 (April–July 1923), pp. 255–57; SAD, "Autobiographical Sketch, September 1, 1838," in *The Letters of Stephen A. Douglas*, ed. Robert W. Johannsen (Urbana: University of Illinois Press, 1961), pp. 57–58; Joseph Howard, "Reminiscences of Stephen A. Douglas," *Atlantic Monthly* 8 (August 1861), p. 206. The family spelled its name *Douglass*, but by the 1840s, Stephen Arnold Douglas had dropped the second *s*.

3. Stevens, "Life of Stephen Arnold Douglas," pp. 267–68.

4. Howard, "Reminiscences of Stephen A. Douglas," p. 207; Stevens, "Life of Stephen Arnold Douglas," pp. 273, 275–76, 279; Johannsen, *Stephen A. Douglas*, pp. 20–21; William Gardner, *Life of Stephen A. Douglas* (Boston: Roxborough Press, 1905), pp. 12–13; Clark E. Carr, *Stephen A. Douglas: His Life, Public Services, Speeches, and Patriotism* (Chicago: A. C. McClurg, 1909), p. 7.

5. Daniel Feller, *The Jacksonian Promise: America, 1815–1840* (Baltimore: Johns

Hopkins University Press, 1995), pp. 55–56; Sean Wilentz, *The Rise of American Democracy: Jefferson to Lincoln* (New York: W. W. Norton, 2005), pp. 47–48; Eric Foner, "Free Labor and Nineteenth-century Political Ideology," in Melvyn Stokes and Stephen Conway, eds., *The Market Revolution in America: Social, Political, and Religious Expressions, 1800–1880* (Charlottesville: University Press of Virginia, 1996), pp. 101–2.

6. SAD, "Autobiographical Sketch," pp. 62, 68; Howard, "Reminiscences of Stephen A. Douglas," p. 210; Gardner, *Life of Stephen A. Douglas*, pp. 14, 15–17, 19–20, 25, 29, 48; Johannsen, *Stephen A. Douglas*, pp. 30–31, 56, 68, 87, 97.

7. Carr, *Stephen A. Douglas*, pp. 4, 7; John Forney, *Anecdotes of Public Men* (New York: Harper & Bros., 1873–1881), p. 21; Gardner, *Life of Stephen A. Douglas*, 89; Stevens, "Life of Stephen Arnold Douglas," pp. 367–69; James W. Sheahan, *The Life of Stephen A. Douglas* (New York: Harper & Bros., 1860), pp. 71–72, 184; Matthew Warshauer, *Andrew Jackson and the Politics of Martial Law* (Knoxville: University of Tennessee Press, 2006), pp. 129–31; Carlton Jackson, "A History of the Whig Party in Alabama, 1828–1860" (unpublished Ph.D. dissertation, University of Georgia, 1961), p. 28; SAD, "To the Democratic Republicans of Illinois" (November 1837), "To Francis B. Cutting *et al*" (May 3, 1851), and "To Twenty-five Chicago Clergymen" (April 6, 1854), in *Letters of Stephen A. Douglas*, pp. 42–43, 49, 216, 313; Saul Sigelschiffer, *The American Conscience: The Drama of the Lincoln-Douglas Debates* (New York: Horizon Press, 1973), pp. 75–77.

8. Johannsen, *Stephen A. Douglas*, p. 313; Carr, *Stephen A. Douglas*, pp. 23, 25, 27; Sheahan, *Life of Stephen A. Douglas*, p. 354; Gardner, *Life of Stephen A. Douglas*, pp. 89, 105–6, 111.

9. George Murray McConnell, "Recollections of Stephen A. Douglas," *Transactions of the Illinois State Historical Society for the Year 1900*, p. 41; Johannsen, *Stephen A. Douglas*, pp. 90–92, 211, 334, 335; Stevens, "Life of Stephen Arnold Douglas," p. 636; Carr, *Stephen A. Douglas*, pp. 49, 50; Anita Clinton, "Stephen Arnold Douglas—His Mississippi Experience," *Journal of Mississippi History* 50 (Spring 1988), pp. 58–59; Allan Nevins, *The Ordeal of the Union: A House Dividing, 1852–1857* (New York: Charles Scribner's Sons, 1947), pp. 148–49; Gardner, *Life of Stephen A. Douglas*, pp. 29, 48, 63; Elizabeth Fries Ellet, *The Court Circles of the Republic; or, The beauties and celebrities of the nation; illustrating life and society under eighteen presidents: describing the social features of the successive administrations from Washington to Grant* (New York: J. D. Denison, 1869), pp. 469, 475, 487.

10. Johannsen, *Stephen A. Douglas*, pp. 304–6; SAD, "To Asa Whitney" (October 12, 1845), in *Letters of Stephen A. Douglas*, p. 127; SAD, "Speech in the Senate on the Pacific Railway" (April 17, 1858), in Carr, *Stephen A. Douglas*, pp. 247, 248, 250; Stevens, "Life of Stephen A. Douglas," p. 422; "Eighteen Fifty-Two and the Presidency," *Democratic Review* 163 (January 1852), p. 12.

11. Robert Taft, "The Appearance and Personality of Stephen A. Douglas," *Kansas Historical Quarterly* 21 (Spring 1954), pp. 10–1, 16–7; Horace White, *The*

Lincoln-Douglas Debates: An Address before the Chicago Historical Society, February 17, 1914 (Chicago: University of Chicago Press, 1914), pp. 7–8; Robert Bruce Warden, *A Voter's Version of the Life and Character of Stephen Arnold Douglas* (Cincinnati: Follett & Foster, 1860), p. 111; Sigelschiffer, *The American Conscience*, pp. 148–49, 151; Carr, *Stephen A. Douglas*, pp. 42–43, 44; Forney, *Anecdotes of Public Men*, pp. 146–47; Wead, "Illinois & Her Politicians: The Observations of Hezekiah Morse Wead, Delegate to the 1847 Illinois Constitutional Convention," ed. Thomas F. Schwartz, *Journal of Illinois History* (Spring 2000), p. 47; Stevens, "Life of Stephen Arnold Douglas," pp. 297–98; Shelby Cullom, *Fifty Years of Public Service: Personal Recollections of Shelby M. Cullom* (Chicago: A. C. McClurg, 1911), p. 62; Stephen L. Hansen, *The Making of the Third Party System: Voters and Parties in Illinois, 1850–1876* (Ann Arbor: UMI Research Press, 1978), p. 21.

12. Gardner, *Life of Stephen A. Douglas*, p. 56; James Pinckney Hambleton, *A Biographical Sketch of Henry A. Wise, with A History of the Political Campaign in Virginia in 1855* (Richmond: J. W. Randolph, 1856), p. 183.

13. "Illinois," in M. W. McCluskey, ed., *The Political Text-book, or Encyclopedia Containing everything necessary for the reference of the politicians and statesmen of the United States* (Philadelphia: J. B. Smith, 1859), p. 249.

14. Sheahan, *Life of Stephen A. Douglas*, pp. 9–11; Stevens, "Life of Stephen Arnold Douglas," p. 365; SAD, "Speech in the Senate on Territorial Expansion and Foreign Aggression" (March 10, 1853), in Carr, *Stephen A. Douglas*, p. 183; Graham A. Peck, "Was Stephen A. Douglas Antislavery?" *Journal of the Abraham Lincoln Association* 26 (Summer 2005), pp. 2–3, 8, 15, 19.

15. Michael F. Holt, *The Rise and Fall of the American Whig Party: Jacksonian Politics and the Onset of the Civil War* (New York: Oxford University Press, 1999), pp. 476–82; Robert Remini, *Henry Clay: Statesman for the Union* (New York: W. W. Norton, 1991), pp. 758–59.

16. Douglas, "Slavery in the Territories" (February 12, 1850), *Congressional Globe*, 31st Congress, 1st session p. 343; Robert W. Johannsen, "Stephen A. Douglas, Popular Sovereignty and the Territories," *The Historian* 22 (August 1960), pp. 384–85; David Zarefsky, *Lincoln, Douglas and Slavery: In the Crucible of Public Debate* (Chicago: University of Chicago Press, 1990), p. 119; Johannsen, *Stephen A. Douglas*, pp. 275–76, 294; David F. Ericson, *The Shaping of American Liberalism: The Debates over Ratification, Nullification, and Slavery* (Chicago: University of Chicago Press, 1993), pp. 117–18.

17. James C. Malin, "The Motives of Stephen A. Douglas in the Organization of Nebraska Territory: A Letter Dated December 17, 1853," *Kansas Historical Quarterly* 19 (November 1951), p. 336; Robert W. Johannsen, "Stephen A. Douglas and the Territories in the Senate," in *The Frontier, the Union, and Stephen A. Douglas* (Urbana: University of Illinois Press, 1989), p. 106.

18. SAD to Asa Whitney (October 15, 1845) and SAD to J. H. Crane, D. M. Johnson, and L. J. Eastin (December 17, 1853), *Letters of Stephen A. Douglas*, pp. 127, 271; "Kansas and Nebraska Act of 1854," *The Whig Almanac and United States*

Register for 1855 (New York: Greeley & McElrath, 1855), p. 18; Gardner, *Life of Stephen A. Douglas*, pp. 64–65.

19. George E. Baker, *The Life of William H. Seward with Selections from His Works* (New York: Redfield, 1855), pp. 165–66.

20. J. W. Schuckers, *The Life and Public Services of Salmon Portland Chase* (New York: D. Appleton, 1874), p. 141; David Donald, *Charles Sumner and the Coming of the Civil War* (New York: Alfred A. Knopf, 1960), p. 252; Holt, *Rise and Fall of the American Whig Party*, p. 815; Bingham, *The Rise and Fall of the Democratic Party—Speech . . . Delivered in the United States Senate, May 24, 1860* (n.p.: Republican Congressional Committee, 1860), p. 13; Botts, *The Great Rebellion: Its Secret History, Rise, Progress and Disastrous Failure* (New York: Harper & Bros., 1866), pp. 125–26; Foote, *Casket of Reminiscences* (Washington: Chronicle Publishing, 1874), pp. 92–93; E. W. Hazard to Lyman Trumbull, May 23, 1856, Lyman Trumbull Papers, Library of Congress.

21. Carroll, *A Review of Pierce's Administration; Showing Its Only Popular Measures to have Originated with the Executive of Millard Fillmore* (1856), pp. 40–41.

22. Wead, "Illinois & Her Politicians," p. 45; *Speech of the Hon. Thomas Ewing, at Chillicothe, Ohio, before a Republican Mass Meeting, September 29th, 1860* (Cincinnati: Rickey, Mallory & Co., 1860), p. 4; Stevens, "Life of Stephen Arnold Douglas," pp. 438, 440, 442, 490; SAD, "To Samuel Wolcott" (April 26, 1854), in *Letters of Stephen A. Douglas*, p. 324; SAD, in Nevins, *Ordeal of the Union: A House Dividing*, p. 96; Johannsen, *Stephen A. Douglas*, p. 412; F. I. Harriott, "Senator Stephen A. Douglas and the Germans in 1854," *Transactions of the Illinois State Historical Society* (1912), pp. 144–45.

23. SAD to Howell Cobb (April 2, 1854), in *Letters of Stephen A. Douglas*, p. 300; SAD, "Speech in the Senate on the Kansas-Nebraska Bill" (March 3, 1854), in Carr, *Stephen A. Douglas*, pp. 190, 191, 192–93, 214.

24. Johannsen, *Stephen A. Douglas*, pp. 428–31; Baker, *Life of William H. Seward*, pp. 163–64, 168; Yonatan Eyal, "With His Eyes Open: Stephen A. Douglas and the Kansas-Nebraska Disaster of 1854," *Journal of the Illinois State Historical Society* 91 (Winter 1998), pp. 212–13; SAD, "Clerical Protest" (March 14, 1854), *Congressional Globe*, 33rd Congress, 1st session, p. 621; Nevins, *Ordeal of the Union*, pp. 144–45, 154–57; Thomas E. Schott, *Alexander H. Stephens of Georgia: A Biography* (Baton Rouge: Louisiana State University Press, 1988), pp. 172–73; William W. Freehling, *The Road to Disunion: Secessionists at Bay, 1776–1854* (New York: Oxford University Press, 1990), pp. 558–59.

25. Fehrenbacher, *Prelude to Greatness*, pp. 38–39; Gardner, *Life of Stephen A. Douglas*, pp. 85, 87; Zarefsky, *Lincoln, Douglas and Slavery*, pp. 4–6; Stevens, "Life of Stephen Arnold Douglas," pp. 480–81; Cullom, *Fifty Years of Public Service*, p. 42; Alexander Davidson, *A Complete History of Illinois from 1673 to 1873* (Springfield: Illinois Journal, 1874), p. 691.

26. SAD, "Kansas Affairs" (June 9, 1856), *Congressional Globe*, 34th Congress, 1st session, p. 1369; Damon Wells, *Stephen Douglas: The Last Years, 1857–1861* (Austin: University of Texas Press, 1971), p. 67.

27. "The Case of Dred Scott," *Tribune Almanac and Political Register for 1857* (New

York: Tribune Association, 1858), pp. 37–44; Mark A. Graber, *Dred Scott and the Problem of Constitutional Evil* (New York: Cambridge University Press, 2006), pp. 18–20.

28. Archibald Cox, *The Court and the Constitution* (Boston: Houghton Mifflin, 1987), pp. 106–9; Benjamin Chew Howard, *Report of the Decision of the Supreme Court of the United States, and the Opinions of the Judges thereof, in the Case of Dred Scott versus John F. A. Sanford* (Washington, DC: Cornelius Wendell, 1857), pp. 45, 48.

29. Johannsen, *Stephen A. Douglas*, p. 569; Don E. Fehrenbacher, *The Dred Scott Case: Its Significance in American Law and Politics* (New York: Oxford University Press, 1978), p. 379.

30. George W. Jones to Sidney Breese, September 28, 1858, Sidney Breese Papers, Abraham Lincoln Presidential Library & Museum (hereafter ALPLM), Springfield, IL. SAD, "To Samuel Treat" (February 5, 1857), in *Letters of Stephen A. Douglas*, p. 372; Johannsen, *Stephen A. Douglas*, pp. 550–51.

31. Johannsen, *Stephen A. Douglas*, p. 586; Gardner, *Life of Stephen A. Douglas*, pp. 128–31; SAD, "The President's Message" (December 9, 1857), *Congressional Globe*, 35th Congress, 1st session, p. 18; SAD, "To John A. McClernand" (November 23, 1857), in *Letters of Stephen A. Douglas*, p. 403.

32. SAD, "Kansas-Lecompton Constitution" (March 22, 1858), *Congressional Globe*, 35th Congress, 1st session (appendix), pp. 195, 200.

33. Wells, *Stephen Douglas: The Last Years*, p. 27; David E. Meerse, "Origins of the Douglas-Buchanan Feud Reconsidered," *Journal of the Illinois State Historical Society* 67 (April 1974), p. 160; O. M. Dickerson, "Stephen A. Douglas and the Split in the Democratic Party," *Proceedings of the Mississippi Valley Historical Association for the Year 1913–1914* (Cedar Rapids, IA: Torch Press, 1914), pp. 197–98; Carr, *Stephen A. Douglas*, p. 65.

34. Schott, *Alexander H. Stephens*, pp. 249–51; Wells, *Stephen Douglas: The Last Years*, pp. 36–37.

35. Paul M. Angle, ed., "The Recollections of William Pitt Kellogg," *Abraham Lincoln Quarterly* 3 (September 1945), p. 320.

36. Jackson, "History of the Whig Party in Alabama," p. 15.

37. Dennis Hanks interview with William Henry Herndon (June 13, 1865) and letter to Herndon (January 26, 1866), A. H. Chapman written statement (September 8, 1865), in *Herndon's Informants: Letters, Interviews and Statements about Abraham Lincoln*, ed. Douglas L. Wilson and Rodney O. Davis (Urbana: University of Illinois Press, 1998), pp. 41, 99, 176; AL, "Autobiography Written for John L. Scripps" (June 1860), in *The Collected Works of Abraham Lincoln*, ed. Roy P. Basler et al. (New Brunswick: Rutgers University Press, 1953), volume four, pp. 61–62.

38. Harry L. Watson, *Liberty and Power: The Politics of Jacksonian America* (New York: Farrar, Straus & Giroux, 1990), pp. 243–47; Thomas Brown, *Politics and Statesmanship: Essays on the American Whig Party* (New York: Columbia University Press, 1985), pp. 44–46; Henry H. Simms, *The Rise of the Whigs in Virginia, 1824–1840* (Richmond: William Byrd Press, 1929), pp. 42, 86; Arthur Charles Cole, *The Whig Party in the South* (Washington, D.C.: American Historical Asso-

ciation, 1913), pp. 30–31; Herbert Ershkowitz, *The Origin of the Whig and Demo-
cratic Parties: New Jersey Politics, 1820–1837* (Washington: University Press of
America, 1982), pp. 95, 102, 207–8; Holt, *Rise and Fall of the American Whig
Party*, p. 574.

39. AL, "Handbill Replying to Charges of Infidelity" (July 31, 1846), in *C.W.*, volume one, p. 382; Clay, "The American System" (1832), in Daniel Walker Howe,
ed., *The American Whigs: An Anthology* (New York: Wiley & Sons, 1973), p. 40;
Robert C. Winthrop, "Protection to Domestic Industry" (1837), in *Addresses and
Speeches on Various Occasions* (Boston: Little, Brown, 1852), p. 206.

40. Nathaniel Grigsby, Silas Richardson, Nancy Richardson, and John Romine
interviews (September 14, 1865) and Orlando B. Ficklin to W. H. Herndon
(June 25, 1865), in *Herndon's Informants*, pp. 58, 118, 181; "Conversation with
Hon. S. T. Logan at Springfield, July 6, 1875," in *An Oral History of Abraham Lin-
coln: John G. Nicolay's Interviews and Essays*, ed. Michael Burlingame (Carbon-
dale: Southern Illinois University Press, 1996), p. 36; John Minor Botts and
John E. Roll, in *Recollected Words of Abraham Lincoln*, ed. Don and Virginia
Fehrenbacher (Stanford: Stanford University Press, 1996), pp. 37, 383; Paul
Simon, *Lincoln's Preparation for Greatness: The Illinois Legislative Years* (Norman:
University of Oklahoma Press, 1968), p. 28; Stevens, "Life of Stephen Arnold
Douglas," pp. 290–91.

41. Douglas L. Wilson, *Honor's Voice: The Transformation of Abraham Lincoln* (New
York: Alfred A. Knopf, 1998), pp. 223, 239; Johannsen, *Stephen A. Douglas*,
pp. 65, 66, 76, 77, 78–79; Kenneth J. Winkle, *The Young Eagle: The Rise of Abraham Lincoln* (Dallas: Taylor, 2001), pp. 170, 194–95; Henry B. Rankin, *Intimate
Character Sketches of Abraham Lincoln* (Philadelphia: J. B. Lippincott, 1924),
p. 159; Elizabeth Todd Edwards and Harriet A. Chapman interviews, in *Herndon's Informants*, p. 444; Michael Burlingame, *The Inner World of Abraham Lincoln*
(Urbana: University of Illinois Press, 1994), pp. 309, 623, 646.

42. *Utica Herald* (June 21, 1860), in *Recollected Words*, p. 5; Burlingame, *Inner World*,
p. 262; AL, "Fragment on Stephen A. Douglas" (December 1856) and "Speech at
Tremont, Illinois" (August 30, 1858), in *C.W.*, volume two, p. 382, and volume
three, p. 77; Ward Hill Lamon, *The Life of Abraham Lincoln: From His Birth to His
Inauguration as President* (Boston: J. R. Osgood, 1872), pp. 195–96, 341.

43. Cullom, *Fifty Years of Public Service*, p. 23.

44. John Todd Stuart interview (June 1865), in *Herndon's Informants*, p. 64; Herndon, in Emmanuel Hertz, ed., *The Hidden Lincoln, From the Letters and Papers of
William H. Herndon* (New York: Viking, 1938), pp. 68, 77, 88, 96; Paul Findley,
A. Lincoln: The Crucible of Congress (Jacksonville, IL: Findley Books, 1979),
pp. 151–52.

45. AL, "To Edward Wallace" (October 11, 1859) and "Autobiography Written for
John Locke Scripps" (June 1860), in *C.W.*, volume three, p. 487, and volume four,
p. 67.

46. AL, "To Albert G. Hodges" (April 4, 1864), "Speech at Kalamazoo, Michigan"
(August 27, 1856), "Fragment on Free Labor" (September 17, 1859), "Notes
for Speeches" (August 21, 1858), and "Reply to New York Workingman's

Democratic Republican Association" (March 21, 1864), in *C.W.*, volume two, p. 364, volume three, pp. 315, 462, and volume seven, p. 259; Burlingame, *Inner World*, p. 34; Charles S. Zane, "Lincoln as I Knew Him," *Journal of the Illinois State Historical Society* 14 (1921–22), p. 79; James A. Stevenson, "Lincoln vs. Douglas over the Republican Ideal," *American Studies* 35 (Spring 1994), p. 66.

47. AL, "The Perpetuation of Our Political Institutions" (January 27, 1838), in *C.W.*, volume one, p. 115.

48. "A Word to Southern Democrats," *American Whig Review* 10 (August 1849), p. 196; AL, "Speech at Bloomington, Illinois" (September 12, 1854) and "To Henry L. Pierce and Others" (April 6, 1859), in *C.W.*, volume two, p. 232, and volume three, p. 376; Joseph Gillespie interview (January 31, 1866), in *Herndon's Informants*, p. 183; Julian Kune and Robert Browne, in *Recollected Words*, pp. 61, 280; Kinley J. Brauer, *Cotton Versus Conscience: Massachusetts Whig Politics and Southwestern Expansion, 1843–1848* (Lexington: University of Kentucky Press, 1967), pp. 23–24.

49. AL, "Speech at Worcester, Massachusetts" (September 12, 1848), "Speech at Bloomington, Illinois" (September 26, 1854), "To Joshua F. Speed" (August 24, 1855), and "Speech at Princeton, Illinois" (July 4, 1856), in *C.W.*, volume two, pp. 239, 321–22, 347; Albert J. Beveridge, *Abraham Lincoln, 1809–1858* (Boston: Houghton Mifflin, 1928), volume two, p. 241.

50. AL, "Speech at Springfield, Illinois" (October 4, 1854), "Speech at Peoria, Illinois" (October 16, 1854), and "Autobiography Written for John Locke Scripps" (June 1860), in *C.W.*, volume two, pp. 242–43, 282, and volume four, p. 67; Joseph Gillespie interview (January 31, 1866), in *Herndon's Informants*, p. 183.

51. W. H. Herndon to Jesse Weik (October 28, 1885), in *The Hidden Lincoln*, p. 96.

52. I. M. Short, *Abraham Lincoln: Early Days in Illinois* (Kansas City: Simpson Publishing, 1927), p. 87; Benjamin F. Irwin to W. H. Herndon (February 8, 1866) and Samuel C. Parks to W. H. Herndon (March 25, 1866), in *Herndon's Informants*, pp. 198, 239; Stevens, "Life of Stephen Arnold Douglas," pp. 480–81, 485; AL, "Speech at Springfield, Illinois" (October 4, 1854) and "Speech at Peoria, Illinois" (October 16, 1854), in *C.W.*, volume two, pp. 245, 266–67; John Channing Briggs, *Lincoln's Speeches Reconsidered* (Baltimore: Johns Hopkins University Press, 2005), p. 138; Johannsen, *Stephen A. Douglas*, pp. 457–58; Fehrenbacher, *Prelude to Greatness*, pp. 34–35.

53. Stevens, "Life of Stephen Arnold Douglas," p. 480; William E. Gienapp, *The Origins of the Republican Party, 1852–1856* (New York: Oxford University Press, 1987), pp. 116–24, 127; Charles A. Church, *History of the Republican Party in Illinois, 1854–1912* (Rockford, IL: Wilson Bros., 1912), pp. 20–21, 23; Victor B. Howard, "The Illinois Republican Party," *Journal of the Illinois State Historical Society* 64 (Summer–Autumn 1973), pp. 125–26.

54. AL, "To Thomas J. Henderson" (November 27, 1854), "To Joseph Gillespie" (December 1, 1854), and "List of Members of the Illinois State Legislature in 1855," in *C.W.*, volume two, pp. 288, 290, 296–98; John G. Nicolay memorandum (October 25, 1860), in *With Lincoln in the White House: Letters, Memoranda, and Other Writings of John G. Nicolay, 1860–1865*, ed. Michael Burlingame (Carbon-

dale: Southern Illinois University Press, 2000), p. 7; Burlingame, *Inner World*, pp. 243–44.

55. AL, "To Elihu B. Washburne" (December 14, 1854) and "To William H. Henderson" (February 21, 1855), in *C.W.*, volume two, pp. 293, 305, 307; SAD, "To Charles H. Lanphier" (December 18, 1854), in *Letters of Stephen A. Douglas*, pp. 331–32; Trumbull to J. M. Palmer (February 24, 1855), in G. T. Palmer, "A Collection of Letters from Lyman Trumbull to John M. Palmer, 1854–1858," *Journal of the Illinois State Historical Society* 16 (April–July 1923), pp. 24–25; John W. Bunn interview (August 21, 1879), in *An Oral History of Abraham Lincoln*, p. 3; Fehrenbacher, *Prelude to Greatness*, pp. 38–39; Mark Krug, "Lyman Trumbull and the Real Issues in the Lincoln-Douglas Debates," *Journal of the Illinois State Historical Society* 14 (1921–22), p. 382.

56. Hansen, *Making of the Third Party System*, pp. 69–70; Holt, *Rise and Fall of the American Whig Party*, pp. 838, 867; Linder, in John S. Wright, *Lincoln and the Politics of Slavery* (Reno: University of Nevada Press, 1970), p. 71; AL, "To Joshua F. Speed" (August 24, 1855) and "Speech at Bloomington, Illinois" (May 29, 1856), in *C.W.*, volume two, pp. 323, 341; Don E. Fehrenbacher, *Chicago Giant: A Biography of "Long John" Wentworth* (Madison, WI: American History Research Center, 1957), p. 137; Johannsen, *Stephen A. Douglas*, pp. 455–56, 534.

57. Paul Selby, "Genesis of the Republican Party in Illinois," *Transactions of the Illinois State Historical Society* 11 (1906), p. 271; Wright, *Lincoln and the Politics of Slavery*, pp. 71–72; Victor B. Howard, "The Illinois Republican Party," pp. 150–51, 304–5; Palmer, in Elwell Crissey, *Lincoln's Lost Speech: The Pivot of His Career* (New York: Hawthorn Books, 1967), p. 240; Winkle, *The Young Eagle*, pp. 295–96.

2: TAKE CARE OF YOUR OLD WHIGS

1. Robert W. Johannsen, "Spectators of Disunion: The Pacific Northwest and the Civil War," in *The Frontier, the Union, and Stephen A. Douglas*, p. 61; George H. Mayer, *The Republican Party, 1854–1964* (New York: Oxford University Press 1964), p. 26; Gienapp, *Origins of the Republican Party*, pp. 416–17; Eric Foner, *Free Soil, Free Labor, Free Men: The Ideology of the Republican Party before the Civil War* (New York: Oxford University Press 1970), p. 165; Michael F. Holt, "Making and Mobilizing the Republican Party, 1854–1860" in *The Birth of the Grand Old Party: The Republicans—First Generation*, ed. R. F. Engs and R. M. Miller (Philadelphia: University of Pennsylvania Press 2002), p. 47; David Davis to AL, June 14, 1858, and John H. Bryant and Stephen G. Paddock to AL, June 4, 1858, Abraham Lincoln Papers.

2. Crissey, *Lincoln's Lost Speech*, pp. 118–19, 132–38; Fehrenbacher, *Chicago Giant*, pp. 134–40; E. T. Bridges to AL, May 18, 1858, Abraham Lincoln Papers; AL, "Fragment on Sectionalism" (July 23, 1856), in *C.W.*, volume two, p. 352; "How to Succeed," *National Era*, October 21, 1858.

3. Davidson, *Complete History of Illinois*, p. 690; G. F. Ross to Lyman Trumbull April 25, 1858, in Lyman Trumbull Papers (volume 13), Loc; Ray, in Lloyd

Wendt, *Chicago Tribune: The Rise of a Great American Newspaper* (New York: Rand McNally, 1979), p. 86.

4. Potter, *Impending Crisis*, pp. 264–65; Paul M. Angle, *"Here I Have Lived": A History of Lincoln's Springfield, 1821–1865* (Chicago: Abraham Lincoln Bookshop, 1935), p. 223; "Illinois Politics," *Chicago Press & Tribune*, July 12, 1858.

5. John Moses, *Illinois Historical and Statistical Comprising the Essential Facts of its Planting and Growth as a Province, Territory, and State* (Chicago: Fergus Printing, 1892), pp. 1137–39; "The Apportionment," *Chicago Press & Tribune*, November 6, 1858.

6. AL, "To Lyman Trumbull" (June 7, 1856), "Editorial on the Right of Foreigners to Vote" (July 23, 1856), "To John Bennett" (August 4, 1856), "To Lyman Trumbull" (August 11, 1856), and "Speech at Petersburg, Illinois" (August 30, 1856), in *C.W.*, volume two, pp. 342, 355–56, 358, 359–60, 373; Thompson, *The Illinois Whigs Before 1846*, p. 130; Beveridge, *Abraham Lincoln*, volume two, p. 390; *The Tribune Almanac and Political Register for 1857* (New York, 1858), pp. 44–63; Jediah Alexander to AL, May 1, 1858, Abraham Lincoln Papers.

7. AL, "Fragment on the Dred Scott Case" (January 1857), "Speech at Springfield, Illinois" (June 26, 1857), "To Lyman Trumbull" (November 30, 1857), in *C.W.*, volume two, pp. 388, 401, 427; Don E. Fehrenbacher, "The Galena Speech: A Problem in Historical Method," in *Lincoln in Text and Context: Collected Essays* (Stanford: Stanford University Press, 1987), pp. 21–23; Graber, *Dred Scott*, pp. 182–83.

8. Trumbull to AL, January 3, 1858, in Abraham Lincoln Papers; James Parton, *The Life of Horace Greeley* (Boston: James Osgood, 1872), p. 252; William Harlan Hale, *Horace Greeley: The Voice of the People* (New York: Harper & Bros., 1950), pp. 174, 204; Robert C. Williams, *Horace Greeley: Champion of Freedom* (New York: New York University Press, 2006), pp. 195–201; Wells, *Stephen Douglas: The Last Years*, pp. 50–51; Wendt, *Chicago Tribune*, pp. 84–85; Beveridge, *Abraham Lincoln*, volume two, p. 555; "The True Sovereignty," *Philadelphia North American and Gazette*, July 16, 1858; "From Washington," *Springfield (MA) Republican*, February 9, 1858; "The Religious Revival," "Our Late Fellow-Laborer," *New York Tribune*, April 3 and May 4, 1858. On Washburne, see AL, "To Elihu Washburne" (April 26, 1858, and May 10, 1858), in *C.W.*, volume two, pp. 443–44, 445–46, offering "to now forget it entirely" if Washburne would come out and endorse him at the state Republican convention.

9. Carl F. Wieck, *Lincoln's Quest for Equality: The Road to Gettysburg* (DeKalb: Northern Illinois University Press, 2002), p. 67; Clifton H. Moore (Jesse W. Weik interview), in *Herndon's Informants*, p. 731; Johannsen, *Stephen A. Douglas*, pp. 593–94, 603, 634, 637–38; Douglass, "Freedom in the West Indies: An Address Delivered in Poughkeepsie, New York, August 2, 1858," in John Blassingame, ed., *The Frederick Douglass Papers, Series One, Speeches, Debates and Interviews, Volume 3, 1855–1863* (New Haven: Yale University Press, 1985), p. 234; Wendt, *Chicago Tribune*, p. 105; Eliza Grimshaw to O. M. Hatch January 4, 1858, and A. M. Knappe to O. M. Hatch, March 31, 1858, Ozias Mather Hatch Papers, Abraham Lincoln Presidential Library & Museum (ALPLM), Spring-

field, IL.; William Kellogg to Jesse K. Dubois, April 25, 1858, in Jesse K. Dubois Correspondence (SC 427), Abraham Lincoln Presidential Library & Museum (hereafter ALPLM), Springfield, IL.; Mildred C. Stoler, "The Democratic Element in the New Republican Party in Illinois, 1856–1860," *Papers in Illinois History and Transactions for the Year 1940* (1944), pp. 54–55.

10. Ebenezer Peck to Lyman Trumbull, April 15, 1858, Lyman Trumbull Papers (volume 13), LOC; Herndon, in David Donald, *Lincoln's Herndon: A Biography* (New York: Alfred A. Knopf, 1948), pp. 114–15; Johannsen, *Stephen A. Douglas*, pp. 555–56, 637–38; George W. Jones to Sidney Breese, September 17, 1858, Sidney Breese Papers, Abraham Lincoln Presidential Library & Museum (ALPLM), Springfield, IL.; Richard Allen Heckman, "Out-of-State Influences and the Lincoln-Douglas Campaign of 1858," *Journal of the Illinois State Historical Society* 59 (Spring 1966), pp. 34–35, 39.

11. Donald, *Lincoln's Herndon*, p. 116; C. H. Ray to Trumbull, March 8, 1858, and Jesse K. Dubois to Trumbull, April 8, 1858, Lyman Trumbull Papers (volume 13), LOC; "Douglas—His Position and Prospects," *Peoria Daily Transcript*, February 1, 1858; "Arts of John Wentworth," *Illinois State Register*, January 4, 1858; "Illinois Senator," *New Hampshire Patriot & Gazette*, June 23, 1858; AL, "To Lyman Trumbull" (December 28, 1857), in *C.W.*, volume two, p. 430.

12. AL, "To Jediah F. Alexander" (May 15, 1858) and "To Charles L. Wilson" (June 1, 1858), in *C.W.*, volume two, pp. 446, 457.

13. AL, "To Ward Hill Lamon" (June 11, 1858), in *C.W.*, volume two, p. 459.

14. SAD, "To William S. Prentice" (August 30, 1841), in *Letters of Stephen A. Douglas*, pp. 99–100; Watson, *Liberty and Power*, pp. 174–75, 234; Holt, *Rise and Fall of the American Whig Party*, pp. 31–32, 100; Howard, "The Illinois Republican Party," pp. 135–36, 137; "Baltimore Convention—The Future," *Democratic Review* 30 (May 1852), p. 472.

15. W. H. Herndon to Lyman Trumbull, April 12, 1858, Lyman Trumbull Papers (volume 13), LOC; "Democratic State Convention," *Jacksonville Sentinel*, April 23, 1858; Fehrenbacher, *Prelude to Greatness*, pp. 48–49.

16. "Douglas's Probable Successor," *Cincinnati Weekly Gazette*, April 28, 1858; "Republican State Convention," *Peoria Daily Transcript*, April 28, 1858; Wendt, *Chicago Tribune*, p. 89; "Republican State Convention," *Quincy Daily Whig & Republican*, April 30, 1858; "The Republicans of Schuyler," *Quincy Daily Whig & Republican*, June 12, 1858; "Illinois Senator," *New Hampshire Patriot & State Gazette*, June 23, 1858; Grimshaw to AL, April 3, 1858, Jackson Grimshaw Correspondence (SC 606), Abraham Lincoln Presidential Library & Museum (hereafter ALPLM), Springfield, IL.; C. D. Way to Lyman Trumbull, May 29, 1858, Lyman Trumbull Papers (volume 14), LOC; Harry E. Pratt, "Abraham Lincoln in Bloomington, Illinois," *Journal of the Illinois State Historical Society* 29 (April 1936), p. 56.

17. William E. Baringer, "Campaign Technique in Illinois—1860," *Transactions of the Illinois State Historical Society for the Year 1932*, p. 204; Wilson to AL (May 31, 1858), in David C. Mearns, ed., *The Lincoln Papers* (Garden City, NY: Doubleday

& Co., 1948), volume one, p. 208; "What Long John Says," *Illinois State Register*, April 28, 1858; AL, "To Lyman Trumbull" (June 23, 1858), in *C.W.*, volume two, p. 472; Fehrenbacher, *Chicago Giant*, p. 148; Don E. Fehrenbacher, "The Nomination of Lincoln in 1858," *Abraham Lincoln Quarterly*; Jeffrey N. Lash, *A Politician Turned General: The Civil War Career of Stephen Augustus Hurlbut* (Kent, OH: Kent State University Press, 2003), p. 48.

18. AL, "To Elihu Washburne" (May 15, 1858), in *C.W.*, volume two, p. 447; *The American Almanac and Repository of Useful Knowledge for the Year 1859* (Boston: Crosby, Nichols, and Co., 1859), p. 369; "Tornado in Illinois," *New York Sun*, June 2, 1858; "Another Tornado in Illinois," *Cincinnati Weekly Gazette*, June 10, 1858; "The River Still Rising—Condition of the Levee," *Quincy Daily Whig & Republican*, June 14, 1858; "The Floods at the West," *New York Times*, June 19, 1858.

19. "Republican State Convention," *Peoria Daily Transcript*, April 28, 1858; "Illinois," *National Era*, July 22, 1858; "The Flood," *Illinois State Register*, June 17, 1858; Robert W. Johanssen, "The Lincoln-Douglas Campaign of 1858—Background and Perspective," *Journal of the Illinois State Historical Society* 73 (Winter 1980), p. 242; Jack Nortrup, "Lincoln and Yates: The Climb to Power," *Lincoln Herald* 73 (Winter 1971), p. 251.

20. "Republican State Convention," *Jacksonville Sentinel*, June 25, 1858; Ida M. Tarbell, *The Life of Abraham Lincoln* (New York: McClure, Phillips, 1904), volume one p. 305; Davidson, *Complete History of Illinois*, pp. 696–97; Horace White, *The Lincoln-Douglas Debates: An Address before the Chicago Historical Society, February 17, 1914* (Chicago: University of Chicago Press, 1914), p. 17.

21. Cullom, *Fifty Years of Public Service*, p. 29; "The Recollections of William Pitt Kellogg," Paul Angle, ed., *Abraham Lincoln Quarterly* 3 (September 1945), p. 325; Paul Selby, *Anecdotal Lincoln: Speeches, Stories and Yarns of the "Immortal Abe"* (Chicago: Thompson & Thomas, 1900), p. 35; AL, " 'A House Divided': Speech at Springfield, Illinois" (June 16, 1858), in *C.W.*, volume two, p. 461.

22. AL, "Campaign Circular from Whig Committee" (March 4, 1843), "To George Robertson" (August 15, 1855), and "Fragment of a Speech" (c. May 18, 1858), in *C.W.*, volume one, p. 315, and volume two, pp. 318, 452; Zarefsky, *Lincoln, Douglas and Slavery*, pp. 42–43; "Speech of Mr. Webster, of Massachusetts" (January 26–28, 1830), in Herman Belz, ed., *The Webster-Hayne Debate on the Nature of the Union: Selected Documents* (Indianapolis: Liberty Fund, 2000), p. 81.

23. AL, " 'A House Divided': Speech at Springfield, Illinois" (June 16, 1858), in *C.W.*, volume two, p. 461; Donald, *Lincoln's Herndon*, pp. 118–9; White, *The Lincoln-Douglas Debates*, p. 16; John Armstrong (W. H. Herndon interview, February 1870), in *Herndon's Informants*, p. 575; Herndon, in *Recollected Words*, pp. 250–51.

24. AL, " 'A House Divided': Speech at Springfield, Illinois" (June 16, 1858), in *C.W.*, volume two, pp. 463, 465–66.

25. Ibid., p. 465.

26. Ibid., pp. 467–68; "Republican State Convention," *Jacksonville Sentinel*, June 25, 1858; "The Republican Convention," *Quincy Daily Whig & Herald*, June 21,

1858. The House Divided speech was also printed in full in the *New York Tribune*, June 24, 1858.

27. Greeley to Joseph Medill, July 24, 1858, in Abraham Lincoln Papers, Wendt, *Chicago Tribune*, p. 91; Jeter Allen Iseley, *Horace Greeley and the Republican Party, 1853–1861: A Study of the New York Tribune* (Princeton: Princeton University Press, 1947), p. 245; "Senator Douglas—Speaker Douglas" and "The Douglas Contest in Illinois," *Springfield Republican*, June 10 and 18, 1858; Greeley, *Recollections of a Busy Life* (New York: J. B. Ford & Co., 1868), p. 357; Carl Wieck, *Lincoln's Quest for Equality: The Road to Gettysburg* (DeKalb: Northern Illinois University Press, 2002), pp. 109–10; R. M. Burton to SAD, June 26, 1858, Stephen A. Douglas Papers, Special Collections, Regenstein Library, University of Chicago; "Mr. Lincoln Showing His Spots," *Illinois State Register*, June 26, 1858.

28. Fehrenbacher, *Prelude to Greatness*, pp. 82–83; Winkle, *The Young Eagle*, p. 301; John Armstrong interview with W. H. Herndon (February 1870) and Swett to W. H. Herndon (January 17, 1866), in *Herndon's Informants*, pp. 162–63, 576; Scripps to AL, June 22, 1858, Abraham Lincoln Papers.

29. AL, "To John L. Scripps" (June 23, 1858), in *C.W.*, volume two, p. 471; "President Buchanan's Administration," *United States Democratic Review* (September 1858), p. 190; "Where Do They Stand?" *Illinois State Register*, September 20, 1858; "Lincoln In A Snarl—Abolitionism Holds Him to His Work," *Illinois State Register*, October 8, 1858; "A Bitter Dose," *Jacksonville Sentinel*, June 23, 1858.

30. James A. Farrell to Alexander H. Stephens, April 7, 1858, Alexander H. Stephens Papers (volume 5), LOC; "New Postmaster at Clinton," *Central Transcript*, June 26, 1858; William L. Harris to Charles H. Lanphier, January 21, 1858, Charles H. Lanphier Papers, Abraham Lincoln Presidential Library & Museum (ALPLM), Springfield, IL; Fehrenbacher, "Political Uses of the Post-Office," in *Lincoln in Text and Context*, pp. 27–28.

31. "Removal of the Post-Master of Chicago," *Illinois State Register*, February 22, 1858; A. T. Andreas, *History of Chicago from the Earliest Period to the Present Time* (Chicago: A. T. Andreas, 1884), volume two, p. 385; "The Guillotine," *Quincy Daily Whig & Republican*, March 22, 1858; Auchampaugh, "The Buchanan-Douglas Feud," *Journal of the Illinois State Historical Society* 25 (April–June 1932), pp. 10–16; David E. Meerse, "Origins of the Douglas-Buchanan Feud Reconsidered," *Journal of the Illinois State Historical Society* 67 (April 1974), pp. 157, 165; Hansen, *Making of the Third Party System*, pp. 21, 24; Sheahan, *Life of Stephen A. Douglas*, pp. 395, 397; John Pearson to SAD, June 21, 1858, Stephen A. Douglas Papers; Robert B. Carpenter to James Buchanan, June 23, 1858, in R. B. Carpenter Correspondence (SC 254), Abraham Lincoln Presidential Library & Museum (ALPLM), Springfield, IL.

32. *Register of Officers and Agents, Civil, Military, and Naval in the Service of the United States* (Washington: A. O. P. Nicholson, 1857), pp. 73, 168, 172–73, 326–49, 411–30; *Register of Officers and Agents, Civil, Military, and Naval in the Service of the United States* (Washington: William A. Harris, 1859), pp. 52–76, 171, 174–76, 432–52; Daniel McCook to Charles H. Lanphier, September 15, 1858,

Charles H. Lanphier Papers, Abraham Lincoln Presidential Library & Museum (ALPLM), Springfield, IL; Henry Villard, "Illinois Politics" and "Development of the Campaign," *New-Yorker Staats-Zeitung,* August 3 and September 16, 1858; "Illinois," *National Era,* July 22, 1858; "Confirmed," *Quincy Daily Whig & Republican,* March 3, 1858; Stevens, "Life of Stephen Arnold Douglas," p. 543; Foote, *Casket of Reminiscences,* p. 135; "Removed for His Democracy," *Jacksonville Sentinel,* July 2, 1858; "A Political Picture," *Philadelphia Press,* March 13, 1858; SAD, "To Samuel Treat" (February 28, 1858), in *Letters of Stephen A. Douglas,* p. 418.

33. Stevens, "Life of Stephen Arnold Douglas," p. 542; "Illinois Democracy," *Cairo Weekly Times & Delta,* March 17, 1858; Lew Wallace, *An Autobiography* (New York: Harper & Bros., 1906), volume 1, p. 248; Sheahan, *Life of Stephen A. Douglas,* pp. 388–89, 391; Davidson, *Complete History of Illinois,* pp. 694–95; "Personal and Political," *Springfield* (MA) *Republican,* January 22, 1858; "The Democracy in Council in Springfield," *Quincy Daily Whig & Republican,* April 24, 1858; "Illinois," *National Era,* July 22, 1858; O. Z. Skinner to Sidney Breese, August 24, 1858, Sidney Breese Papers, Abraham Lincoln Presidential Library & Museum (ALPLM), Springfield, IL; Beveridge, *Abraham Lincoln,* volume two, pp. 550–51, 553; "Illinois State Democratic Convention," *Cairo Weekly Times & Delta,* April 28, 1858.

34. "Democratic State Convention," *Jacksonville Sentinel,* April 23, 1858; "The State Convention—The Expression of the Democratic Party," *Illinois State Register,* April 22, 1858; "Illinois State Buchanan Convention," *Quincy Daily Whig & Republican,* June 12, 1858; "Illinois State Buchanan Convention," *Montgomery County Herald,* June 12, 1858; Sheahan, *Life of Stephen A. Douglas,* pp. 395, 397; Johannsen, *Stephen A. Douglas,* pp. 622, 624, 627; Ray to Lyman Trumbull, March 9, 1858, Lyman Trumbull Papers (volume 13), LOC; Heckman, *Lincoln vs. Douglas,* p. 50; Beveridge, *Abraham Lincoln,* volume two, pp. 553–55.

35. SAD, "British Aggressions" (June 15, 1858), *Congressional Globe,* 35th Congress, 1st session, pp. 3056, 3058; Hansen, *Making of the Third Party System,* p. 118; SAD, "To Samuel Treat" (February 28, 1858), in *Letters of Stephen A. Douglas,* p. 418; James May to SAD, June 21, 1858, Stephen A. Douglas Papers; Lyman Trumbull to John M. Palmer (May 20, 1858) in "Letters from Lyman Trumbull to John M. Palmer, 1854–1858," pp. 36–37.

36. Delahay to Lyman Trumbull, May 22, 1858, W. H. Herndon to Trumbull, April 24, 1858, and July 8, 1858, and E. L. Baker to Trumbull, May 1, 1858, Lyman Trumbull Papers (volume 14), LOC; Kellogg to Jesse K. Dubois, April 25, 1858, in Jesse K. Dubois Correspondence (SC 327), Abraham Lincoln Presidential Library & Museum (ALPLM), Springfield, IL; Rodney O. Davis, "Dr. Charles Leib: Lincoln's Mole?" *Journal of the Abraham Lincoln Association* 24 (Summer 2003), pp. 24–25.

37. *The American Almanac and Repository of Useful Knowledge for the Year 1858* (Boston: Crosby, Nichols, and Co., 1857), p. 325; Norman Judd to Elihu Washburne, September 20, 1858, Elihu Washburne Papers (volume 4), LOC; AL, "1858 Campaign Strategy" (July 1858) and "Response to a Serenade at Spring-

field, Illinois" (September 25, 1858), in *C.W.*, volume two, pp. 476–81, and volume three, p. 203; "Popular Vote of the State of Illinois," in Moses, *Illinois Historical and Statistical*, pp. 1156–57, 1208; *The Tribune Almanac for 1857, Comprehending the Politician's Register and The Whig Almanac* (New York: New York Tribune, 1857), pp. 60–61; AL to Trumbull (June 23, 1858), in *C.W.*, volume two, p. 472.

38. Gardner, *Life of Stephen A. Douglas*, pp. 150, 158; Gustave Koerner to AL, July 17, 1858, Henry C. Whitney to AL, August 26, 1858, and Lyman Trumbull to AL, June 12, 1858, Abraham Lincoln Papers; SAD, "To John A. McClernand" (December 23, 1856), in *Letters of Stephen A. Douglas*, p. 371; C. L. Higher to SAD, June 24, 1858, Stephen A. Douglas Papers; Norman Judd to Lyman Trumbull, April 19, 1858, Lyman Trumbull Papers (volume thirteen), LOC; Forest L. Whan, "Stephen A. Douglas," in Lionel Crocker, *An Analysis of Lincoln and Douglas as Public Speakers and Debaters* (Springfield, IL: C. C. Thomas, 1968), p. 117.

39. AL, "To Henry C. Whitney" (July 9, 1856) and "To Owen Lovejoy" (March 8, 1858), in *C.W.*, volume two, pp. 347, 435; David Davis to Ward Hill Lamon, May 25, David Davis Papers, Abraham Lincoln Presidential Library & Museum (ALPLM), Springfield, IL; Pratt, "Abraham Lincoln in Bloomington, Illinois," p. 59; David Davis to W. H. L. Wallace (June 7, 1858), in Isabel Wallace, *Life and Letters of General W. H. L. Wallace* (Chicago: R. R. Donnelly, 1909), p. 84; AL to C. H. Ray, June 27, 1858, Abraham Lincoln Papers Project, Springfield, IL; Hansen, *Making of the Third Party System*, pp. 95–97; Willard L. King, *Lincoln's Manager: David Davis* (Cambridge, MA: Harvard University Press, 1960), pp. 117–18.

40. Browning interview with John Nicolay (June 17, 1875) and letter to Edgar Cowan (September 6, 1864), in Michael Burlingame, ed., *An Oral History of Abraham Lincoln: John G. Nicolay's Interviews and Essays* (Carbondale: Southern Illinois University Press, 1996), pp. 6, 127; "Hon. O. H. Browning," *Quincy Whig*, June 14, 1858; Richardson to SAD, July 27, 1858, Stephen A. Douglas Papers; William J. Ramsay to John C. Bagby, August 18, 1858, John C. Bagby Papers, Abraham Lincoln Presidential Library & Museum (ALPLM), Springfield, IL; Diary entry for September 14, 1858, in *The Diary of Orville Hickman Browning*, ed. Theodore Calvin Pease and James G. Randall (Springfield: Illinois State Historical Library, 1925), volume one, p. 336; David Donald, *We Are Lincoln Men: Abraham Lincoln and His Friends* (New York: Simon & Schuster, 2003), p. 107; AL, "To Stephen A. Hurlbut" (June 1, 1858), in *C.W.*, volume two, p. 456.

41. AL, "To Jediah F. Alexander" (May 15, 1858), "To William Fithian" (September 3, 1858), and "To James W. Grimes" (August 17, 1857), in *C.W.*, volume two, pp. 413, 446, and volume three, p. 84; E. S. Miers, ed., *Lincoln Day-by-Day: A Chronology* (Dayton, OH: Morningside, 1991), pp. 218–19; Herndon to J. W. Weik (October 21, 1885), in *The Hidden Lincoln*, p. 95.

42. Gardner, *Life of Stephen A. Douglas*, pp. 161, 169; Gustave Koerner to AL, July 17, 1858, W. J. Usrey to AL, July 19, 1858, Norman Judd to AL, November 15, 1858, and Schuyler Colfax to AL, May 18, 1860, Abraham Lincoln Papers;

Baringer, "Campaign Technique in Illinois in 1860," pp. 204–5; Bessie Louise Pierce, *A History of Chicago: Volume 2, From Town to City, 1848–1871* (New York: Alfred A. Knopf, 1940), pp. 228–29; "Foreign Intervention in the Politics of Illinois," *Chicago Press & Tribune*, September 10, 1858; King, *Lincoln's Manager*, p. 125; Cornelius Bushnell to SAD, June 30, 1858, Stephen A. Douglas Papers; "Poor Little Dug!" *Chicago Press & Tribune*, September 28, 1858; Jonathan Birch, in *Herndon's Informants*, p. 728; "Speech of Senator Douglas at Clifton Springs, New York," *New York Times*, July 10, 1858; "Reception of Senator Douglas at Toledo," *Washington Union*, July 10, 1858; "Mr. Douglas at Toledo," *New York Times*, July 9, 1858; Thomas Wakefield Goodspeed, "Lincoln and Douglas: With Some Personal Reminiscences," *Journal of the Illinois State Historical Society* 26 (October 1933), p. 185; Beveridge, *Abraham Lincoln*, volume two, pp. 592–93; Andreas, *History of Chicago*, volume one, p. 635; George Fort Milton, *The Eve of Conflict: Stephen A. Douglas and the Needless War* (Boston: Houghton Mifflin, 1934), p. 310.

43. Villard, "Douglas's Reception," *New-Yorker Staats-Zeitung*, July 14, 1858; "The Douglas Demonstration," *Chicago Tribune*, July 10, 1858; "The Reception of Senator Douglas," *Chicago Daily Journal*, July 10, 1858; SAD, "The Political Campaign in Illinois—Speech of Mr. Douglas at Chicago," *Washington Union*, July 15, 1858; SAD, "The Lecompton Fraud—Speech of Senator Douglas," *New York Times*, July 13, 1858; SAD, "The Contest in Illinois—Senator Douglas on Popular Sovereignty—Extracts from His Speech, Delivered on the Occasion of His Reception at Chicago, July 9, 1858," *United States Democratic Review* 42 (August 1858), pp. 133–37; "Reception of Senator Douglas in Chicago," *New York Times*, July 12, 1858; "Mr. Douglas's Reception at Home," *Boston Daily Advertiser*, July 12, 1858; "Senator Douglas at Chicago," *Harrisburg Daily Telegraph*, July 13, 1858; Johannsen, *Stephen A. Douglas*, pp. 641–44.

44. SAD, "The Political Campaign in Illinois"; Carr, *Stephen A. Douglas*, p. 79.

45. SAD, "The Political Campaign in Illinois"; SAD, "The Contest in Illinois," pp. 138, 142–43.

46. SAD, "The Political Campaign in Illinois"; "The Political Campaign in Illinois," *New York Tribune*, July 13, 1858.

47. "Lincoln To-Night," *Chicago Tribune*, July 10, 1858; "Mr. Douglas at Chicago—He Is a Douglas Man," *Washington Union*, July 13, 1858; "Illinois Politics," *New York Times*, July 13, 1858; "Reply to Senator Douglas," *Boston Daily Advertiser*, July 13, 1858.

48. "Speech of Mr. Lincoln," *New-York Tribune*, July 15, 1858.

49. Joshua Whitmore to W. H. L. Wallace (June 5, 1858), in *Life and Letters of General W. H. L. Wallace*, pp. 83–84; "Speech of Senator Trumbull at Chicago," *Quincy Daily Whig & Republican*, August 25, 1858; "What Would Be The Effect of Negro Equality?" *Illinois State Register*, October 9, 1858; Kenneth Winkle, "Paradox Though It May Seem: Lincoln on Antislavery, Race and Union, 1837–1860," in Brian Dirck, ed. *Lincoln Emancipated: The President and the Politics of Race* (DeKalb: Northern Illinois University Press, 2007), pp. 15, 19.

50. AL, "Speech at Carlinville, Illinois" (August 31, 1858), in *C.W.*, volume three,

p. 79; William Lee Miller, *Lincoln's Virtues: An Ethical Biography* (New York: Alfred A. Knopf, 2002), pp. 277–78; Joseph R. Fornieri, *Abraham Lincoln's Political Faith* (DeKalb: Northern Illinois University Press, 2003), pp. 89–90; Stewart Winger, *Lincoln, Religion, and Romantic Cultural Politics* (DeKalb: Northern Illinois University Press, 2003), pp. 108–9.

51. AL, "Speech at Peoria, Illinois" (October 16, 1854), in *C.W.*, volume two, p. 256; Michael Lind, *What Lincoln Believed: The Values and Convictions of America's Greatest President* (New York: Doubleday, 2004), p. 133.

52. "Mr. Lincoln on the Declaration," *Illinois State Register*, July 28, 1858; "The Mask Off in Illinois," *Pittsfield Sun*, July 29, 1858; "What Does He Believe?" *Freeport Weekly Bulletin*, August 5, 1858; on Douglas's opaqueness on the subject of rights, see Harry V. Jaffa, *A New Birth of Freedom: Abraham Lincoln and the Coming of the Civil War* (Lanham, MD: Rowman & Littlefield, 2000), p. 476.

53. Davidson, *Complete History of Illinois*, pp. 709–10; "Douglas at Bloomington," *Bloomington Pantagraph*, July 19, 1858; "Douglas at Bloomington and Springfield" and "Douglas and Lincoln in Springfield," *Chicago Press & Tribune*, July 19 and 20, 1858; "At Springfield" and "Mr. Lincoln on the 'Declaration,'" *Illinois State Register*, July 19 and 28, 1858; Milton, *Eve of Conflict*, p. 321.

54. Gardner, *Life of Stephen A. Douglas*, pp. 150, 158; Milton, *Eve of Conflict*, p. 322.

55. John Mathers to AL, July 19, 1858, Abraham Lincoln Papers; "Senator Douglas" and "Mr. Lincoln's Last Speech," *Illinois State Register*, July 20 and 22, 1858; "Abraham R. Lincoln," *New York Sun*, June 26, 1858; Wendt, *Chicago Tribune*, p. 94.

56. Miers, ed., *Lincoln Day-by-Day*, p. 222.

3: A DAVID GREATER THAN GOLIATH

1. Villard, "Development of the Campaign," *New-Yorker Staats-Zeitung*, September 16, 1858; Beveridge, *Abraham Lincoln*, p. 628; Sigelschiffer, *The American Conscience*, p. 204; Davidson, *Complete History of Illinois*, pp. 696–97; "Senator Douglas at Chicago," *New York Tribune*, July 12, 1858; Wendt, *Chicago Tribune*, p. 95; Fehrenbacher, *Prelude to Greatness*, p. 99; AL to Alban Jaspar Conant, in *Recollected Words*, p. 117; W. J. Usrey to AL, July 19, 1858, Abraham Lincoln Papers, AL, "To Joseph Gillespie" (July 25, 1858) and "To Stephen A. Douglas" (July 24, 1858), in *C.W.*, volume two, pp. 522–23.

2. Fehrenbacher, *Prelude to Greatness*, pp. 100–101; Sigelschiffer, *The American Conscience*, pp. 203–4; Stevens, "Life of Stephen Arnold Douglas," p. 553; Norman Judd (J. G. Nicolay interview), in *An Oral History of Abraham Lincoln*, p. 44; SAD, "To Abraham Lincoln" (July 24, 1858), in *Letters of Stephen A. Douglas*, pp. 423–24; Milton, *Eve of Conflict*, p. 329; SAD, "Second Debate with Stephen A. Douglas at Freeport, Illinois" (August 27, 1858), in *C.W.*, volume three, p. 63.

3. "Will Mr. Douglas Accept?" *Chicago Press & Tribune*, July 26, 1858; "Lincoln's Challenge to Douglas," *Chicago Daily Journal*, July 27, 1858; SAD, "To Abraham Lincoln" (July 24, 1858), in *Letters of Stephen A. Douglas*, p. 424.

4. Norman Judd to AL, July 27, 1858, Abraham Lincoln Papers, AL, "To Stephen

A. Douglas" (July 29 and July 31, 1858), in *C.W.*, volume two, pp. 528–30, 531; SAD, "To Abraham Lincoln" (July 30, 1858), in *Letters of Stephen A. Douglas*, pp. 424–25; Edwin Earle Sparks, ed., *Collections of the Illinois State Historical Library, Volume III: The Lincoln-Douglas Debates of 1858* (Springfield: Illinois State Historical Library, 1908), pp. 72–73. Henry Villard heard Lincoln make an announcement of the debates at a campaign rally at Monticello on July 29 and was under the impression that Lincoln was responding to a challenge from Douglas, instead of the other way round. See Villard's "Illinois Politics," *New-Yorker Staats-Zeitung*, August 3, 1858.

5. "How Jesse Fell Started the Debates," in Walter B. Stevens, *A Reporter's Lincoln*, ed. Michael Burlingame (Lincoln: University of Nebraska Press, 1998), p. 62; Johannsen, *Stephen A. Douglas*, pp. 76–77, 78–79; Lamon, *Life of Abraham Lincoln*, p. 236; Stevens, "Life of Stephen Arnold Douglas," pp. 323–24, 325, 327–28; Wilson, *Honor's Voice*, 199–200; Pratt, "Abraham Lincoln in Bloomington," p. 53.

6. Jeffrey L. Pasley, *The Tyranny of Printers: Newspaper Politics in the Early American Republic* (Charlottesville: University of Virginia Press, 2001), p. 5; James N. McElligott, *The American Debater: Being a Plain Exposition of the Principles and Practice of Public Debate* (New York: Ivison & Phinney, 1855), pp. 39, 128–31; Joseph Bartlett Burleigh, *The Legislative Guide, containing All the Rules for Conducting Business in Congress* (Philadelphia: J. B. Lippincott, 1856), pp. 156–59; Increase Cooke, *The American Orator; or, Elegant Extracts in Prose and Poetry* (New Haven: John Babcock, 1819), p. 13; Caleb Bingham, *The Columbian Orator: containing a variety of original and selected pieces* (Boston: J. H. A. Frost, 1832), p. 30; "Will Mr. Douglas Accept?" *Chicago Press & Tribune*, July 26, 1858; "Stump Speaking in Illinois," *Richmond Daily Dispatch*, September 2, 1858.

7. John L. Brooke, "To be 'Read by the Whole People': Press, Party, and Public Sphere in the United States, 1789–1840," *Proceedings of the American Antiquarian Society*, 110, Part 1 (2000) pp. 78, 80–81, 83–84; Pasley, *The Tyranny of Printers*, pp. 6, 9, 12–14, 15, 397; David M. Henkin, *City Reading: Written Words and Public Spaces in Antebellum New York* (New York: Columbia University Press, 1998), pp. 23, 104–5, 114–15; James L. Crouthamel, *Bennett's New York Herald and the Rise of the Popular Press* (Syracuse: Syracuse University Press, 1998), p. 43; Kimberly K. Smith, *The Dominion of Voice: Riot, Reason, and Romance in Antebellum Politics* (Lawrence: University Press of Kansas, 1999), pp. 124–25.

8. George Beatty reminiscence, Ida M. Tarbell Papers, Special Collections, Pelletier Library, Allegheny College.

9. Isabelle Lehuu, *Carnival on the Page: Popular Print Media in Antebellum America* (Chapel Hill: University of North Carolina Press, 2000), pp. 15–16, 37; Thomas C. Leonard, *News for All: America's Coming-of-Age with the Press* (New York: Oxford University Press, 1995), pp. 7, 13, 67; Dan Schiller, *Objectivity and the News: The Public and the Rise of Commercial Journalism* (Philadelphia: University of Pennsylvania Press, 1981), pp. 12, 13, 73; William E. Gienapp, " 'Politics Seem to Enter into Everything': Political Culture in the North, 1840–1869," in Stephen E. Maizlish and John J. Kushma, eds., *Essays on American Antebellum*

Politics, 1840–1860 (College Station: Texas A&M University Press, 1982), pp. 41–42; "Business at the Chicago Post Office," *Chicago Daily Journal*, August 16, 1858.

10. Crouthamel, *Bennett's New York Herald*, pp. 45, 46–47, 48–49; George Prescott, *History, Theory and Practice of the Electric Telegraph* (Boston: Ticknor & Fields, 1860), pp. 7, 9, 111–12, 124–25, 214.

11. Hansen, *The Making of the Third Party System*, pp. 28–29; "The Democratic Press of Illinois," *Illinois State Register*, June 22, 1858; John Moses, *Illinois, Historical and Statistical, comprising the essential facts of its Planting and Growth as a Province, County, Territory and State* (Chicago: Fergus, 1892), volume two, pp. 944–45; Fred Gerhard, *Illinois As It Is* (Chicago: Keen & Lee, 1853), pp. 439–43; Harry E. Pratt, *The Great Debates* (Springfield: Illinois State Historical Library, 1956), pp. 4–5; Smith, *The Dominion of Voice*, pp. 124–25; Heckman, *Lincoln vs. Douglas*, pp. 40–41; Wright, *Lincoln and the Politics of Slavery*, p. 154; Wendt, *Chicago Tribune*, pp. 39, 49–55, 57; Heckman, "Out-of-State Influences," pp. 44–45; "Salutatory," *Weekly Madison Press*, August 11, 1858.

12. James Aune, "Lincoln and the American Sublime," *Communication Reports* 1 (Winter 1988), pp. 15–16; James Perrin Warren, *Culture of Eloquence: Oratory and Reform in Antebellum America* (University Park: Pennsylvania State University Press, 1999), pp. 11, 18–19; Smith, *The Dominion of Voice*, pp. 92–93; Michael P. Kramer, *Imagining Language in America: From the Revolution to the Civil War* (Princeton: Princeton University Press, 1992), pp. 81–82.

13. William L. Gross, *Concerning Mr. Lincoln: In Which Abraham Lincoln Is Pictured as he Appeared to Letter Writers of his Time*, ed. Harry E. Pratt (Springfield, IL: Abraham Lincoln Association, 1944), p. 20.

14. Beatty reminiscence, Ida M. Tarbell Papers.

15. William D. Pierce, "Reminiscence of Lincoln," April 25, 1915, William D. Pierce Papers, LOC; Mildred Freburg Berry, "Abraham Lincoln: His Development in the Skills of the Platform," in William Norwood Brigance, ed., *A History and Criticism of American Public Address* (New York: McGraw-Hill, 1943), volume two, p. 844; Villard, "Douglas' Reception—Lincoln's Reply to the German Republicans," *New-Yorker Staats-Zeitung*, July 14, 1858; Seymour D. Thompson, "Lincoln and Douglas: The Great Freeport Debate," *American Law Review* (March–April 1905), pp. 162, 164; *Memoirs of Henry Villard, Journalist and Financier, 1835–1900* (Boston: Houghton Mifflin, 1904), volume one, pp. 93–94; Joseph Gillespie to W. H. Herndon (January 31, 1866), in *Herndon's Informants*, p. 184; "The Recollections of William Pitt Kellogg," p. 323; Herndon to Truman Bartlett (July 19, 1887), in *The Hidden Lincoln*, pp. 191–92; Jeese W. Weik, *The Real Lincoln: A Portrait* (New York: Houghton Mifflin, 1922), p. 313.

16. Beatty reminiscence, Ida M. Tarbell Papers.

17. Edmond Beall, "Recollections of the Lincoln-Douglas Debate Held in Alton, Illinois, October 15, 1858," *Journal of the Illinois State Historical Society* 5 (January 1913), p. 487; Stowe, in "The Appearance and Personality of Stephen A. Douglas," p. 12; Carr, *Stephen A. Douglas*, p. 15; William Cullen reminiscence, Ida M. Tarbell Papers, Allegheny College; Gustave Koerner, *Memoirs*, volume

two, p. 63; "Congressional Eloquence," *North American Review* 52 (January 1841), pp. 109–10; Schurz, *Reminiscences*, volume two, p. 95; William H. Pierce, "Reminiscence of Lincoln," William H. Pierce Papers, LOC; Michael Burlingame, "How Shorthand Reporters Covered the Lincoln-Douglas Debates of 1858," *Lincoln Herald* 96 (Spring 1994), p. 23; William Dickson, in *Recollected Words*, p. 141; "Lincoln and Douglas," *National Era*, November 11, 1858.

18. Berry, "Abraham Lincoln," in *American Public Address*, volume two, pp. 856–58; "The Lincoln Scrapbooks," in Stevens, *A Reporter's Lincoln*, p. 72; Lois J. Einhorn, *Abraham Lincoln the Orator: Penetrating the Lincoln Legend* (Westport, CT: Greenwood Press, 1992), p. 36; Burlingame, "How Shorthand Reporters Covered the Lincoln-Douglas Debates," p. 21; Charles S. Zane, "Lincoln As I Knew Him," *Journal of the Illinois State Historical Society* 14 (1921–22), pp. 76–77, 78–79, 81; Mary Cunningham Logan, *Reminiscences of a Soldier's Wife* (New York: Charles Scribner's Sons, 1913), pp. 61–62; Pratt, "Abraham Lincoln in Bloomington," p. 45; John Channing Briggs, *Lincoln's Speeches Reconsidered* (Baltimore: Johns Hopkins University Press, 2005), p. 6; William Butler interview (June 13, 1875) and Milton Hay interview (July 4, 1875), in *An Oral History of Abraham Lincoln*, pp. 20, 26–27.

19. Bingham, *Columbian Orator*, pp. 23, 25; Cooke, *American Orator*, pp. 58, 66; Epes Sargent, *The Standard Speaker, Containing Exercises in Prose and Poetry for Declamation* (Philadelphia: Charles DeSilver, 1852), p. 33; John Frost, *The American Speaker, Containing Numerous Rules, Observations, and Exercises* (Philadelphia: Thomas, Cowperthwait, 1845), p. 20; J. H. Blake, *An Abridgment of Lectures on Rhetorick by Hugh Blair* (Concord: Hill & Moore, 1822), pp. 196, 200–201; Berry, "Abraham Lincoln," in *American Public Address*, volume two, p. 836.

20. Smith, *The Dominion of Voice*, pp. 93, 107–9; Robert G. Gunderson, "The Southern Whigs," in *Oratory in the Old South, 1828–1860*, ed. Waldo W. Braden et al. (Baton Rouge: Louisiana State University Press, 1970), pp. 127–28; Kramer, *Imagining Language in America*, p. 114; "Congressional Eloquence," p. 112. If we were to employ Laban Movement Analysis, both Lincoln and Douglas would receive high marks for "versatility" by effectively coordinating phrasing, vocabulary, and message to their use of effort, shape, and space, with Lincoln effectively communicating crisis and urgency, and Douglas communicating reassurance and trust. See J. A. Levy and M. P. Duke, "The Use of Laban Movement Analysis in the Study of Personality, Emotional State, and Movement Style: An Exploratory Investigation of the Veridicality of 'Body Language,'" *Individual Difference Research* 1 (April 2003), pp. 39–63.

21. "Cost of the Performance," *Chicago Press & Tribune*, July 10, 1858; "The Ovation to Senator Douglas," *Chicago Daily Journal*, July 9, 1858; List of Distribution, C. B. Buckner to SAD, July 30, 1858, Stephen A. Douglas Papers; Johannsen, *Stephen A. Douglas*, pp. 317, 656–57; "Douglas at Hillsboro," *Illinois State Journal*, August 10, 1858; "I. N. Higgins bill for Campaign in 1858," Chauncey L. Higbee Papers, Abraham Lincoln Presidential Library & Museum (hereafter ALPLM), Springfield, IL; Neely, *Boundaries of American Political Culture in the Civil War Era*, pp. 65–66; White, *The Lincoln-Douglas Debates*, p. 17; H. Villard to

SAD, August 24, 1858, Stephen A. Douglas Papers; "Illinois Central Railroad Corruption Scheme," *Peoria Daily Transcript*, October 25, 1858; "Douglas and the Illinois Central Railroad," [Clinton] *Central Transcript*, September 3, 1858; Johannsen, *Stephen A. Douglas*, p. 659; Stevens, "Life of Stephen A. Douglas," pp. 549–50; Beveridge, *Abraham Lincoln*, volume two, p. 610; Willard L. King, *Melville Weston Fuller: Chief Justice of the United States, 1888–1910* (New York: Macmillan, 1950), p. 45; Logan, *Reminiscences*, pp. 62–63; George Fort Milton, *The Eve of Conflict: Stephen A. Douglas and the Needless War* (Boston: Houghton Mifflin, 1934), p. 320; Charles C. Patton, ed., *Glory to God and the Sucker Democracy: A Manuscript Collection of the Letters of Charles H. Lanphier* (privately printed, 1973), volume one, p. 102; Davidson, *Complete History of Illinois*, pp. 709–10.

22. "Douglas in Clinton," *Clinton Central Transcript*, July 30, 1858; "Senator Douglas at Clinton," *Illinois State Register*, July 30, 1858; Logan, *Reminiscences*, p. 64.

23. "Meeting on Monday," *Montgomery County Herald* (Hillsboro, IL), August 6, 1858; "Douglas at Hillsboro," *Illinois State Journal*, August 6, 1858; William H. Bissell to Joseph Gillespie, July 9, 1858, Joseph Gillespie Papers, Abraham Lincoln Presidential Library & Museum (ALPLM), Springfield, IL.

24. "Senator Douglas," *Weekly Madison Press*, August 11, 1858; "Douglas in Pike County," *Illinois State Journal*, August 13, 1858; "Douglas at Beardstown," *Chicago Press & Tribune*, August 16, 1858; "Douglas at His Old Home in Winchester," *Jacksonville Sentinel*, August 18, 1858.

25. King, *Lincoln's Manager: David Davis*, pp. 112–4, 120–1; Wright, *Lincoln and the Politics of Slavery*, pp. 105–6; "Conversation with Hon. T. Lyle Dickey" (October 20, 1876), in *Oral Biography of Abraham Lincoln*, p. 48; Leonard Swett to Herndon (January 17, 1866) and Dickey to Herndon (December 8, 1866), in *Herndon's Informants*, pp. 163, 504; Henry C. Whitney to AL, July 31, 1858, Abraham Lincoln Papers; "Judge T. L. Dickey for Douglas," *Illinois State Register*, August 9, 1858; "The Old Line Whigs for Douglas," *Jacksonville Sentinel*, August 18, 1858.

26. "Lincoln in the Field," *Illinois State Journal*, August 16, 1858; "Lincoln at Beardstown," *Quincy Daily Whig & Republican*, August 20, 1858; "Mr. Lincoln at Beardstown," *Weekly North-Western Gazette*, August 31, 1858.

27. Wilson to Lyman Trumbull, May 12, 1858, Lyman Trumbull Papers (volume 14), LOC; Jediah Alexander to AL, August 5, 1858, Abraham Lincoln Papers; AL, "Speech at Beardstown, Illinois" (August 12, 1858) and "Speech at Havana, Illinois" (August 14, 1858), in *C.W.*, volume two, pp. 536–40, 543; "Lincoln in the Field," *Chicago Daily Journal*, August 18, 1858; "Abe Lincoln and Judge Kellogg at Havana," *Chicago Press & Tribune*, August 20, 1858; William H. Herndon and Jesse W. Weik, *Herndon's Lincoln*, ed. Douglas L. Wilson and Rodney O. Davis (Urbana: University of Illinois Press, 2006), pp. 393–94.

28. Charles J. Stewart, "The People and the Lincoln-Douglas Campaign of 1858," *Register of the Kentucky Historical Society* 65 (1967), p. 288; AL, "Speech at Lewiston, Illinois" (August 17, 1858), in *C.W.*, volume two, p. 546.

29. Sheahan, *Life of Stephen A. Douglas*, p. 300; "Judge Douglas and the Germans,"

National Era, August 26, 1858; *Illinois State Register*, August 7, 1858; "The Lincoln Scrapbooks," in Walter B. Stevens, *A Reporter's Lincoln*, ed. Michael Burlingame (Lincoln: University of Nebraska Press, 1998), pp. 75, 85.

30. Elmer Baldwin, *History of Lasalle County Illinois* (Chicago: Rand McNally, 1877), pp. 209, 221, 226; Moses, *Illinois, Historical and Statistical*, pp. 1208–9; *Tribune Almanac, 1858*, p. 60; Richard Swainson Fisher, *A New and Complete Statistical Gazeteer of the United States of America* (New York: J. H. Colton, 1853), p. 305; "The Great Debate at Ottawa," *Chicago Press & Tribune*, August 18, 1858; *History of Lasalle County, Illinois* (Chicago: Inter-State Publishing, 1886), volume one, pp. 270–71; C. W. Waite to AL, August 4, 1858, Abraham Lincoln Papers; George Anastaplo, *Abraham Lincoln: A Constitutional Biography* (New York: Rowman & Littlefield, 1999), pp. 157–58; *Lasalle County, 1860 Federal Census* (Ottawa, IL: Lasalle County Genealogy Guild, 1993); *The 1850 Federal Census of Lasalle County, Illinois* (Yakima, WA: Yakima Genealogical Society, 1978), last column.

31. Sigelschiffer, *The American Conscience*, pp. 220–21; W. H. L. Wallace to AL, August 19, 1858, Abraham Lincoln Papers; "An Army with Banners," *Illinois State Journal*, August 21, 1858.

32. Beatty reminiscence, Ida M. Tarbell Papers.

33. White, *The Lincoln-Douglas Debates*, p. 18; Michael Cyprian O'Byrne, *History of Lasalle County, Illinois* (Chicago: Lewis Pubs., 1924), pp. 188–89; Frederick Trevor Hill, "The Battle of the Giants," in *Abraham Lincoln* (New York: Republican Club of the City of New York, 1907), pp. 6–7, 10; Logan, *Reminiscences*, pp. 67–68.

34. White, in Frank E. Stevens, "Life of Stephen Arnold Douglas," pp. 589–90.

35. Franklin W. Hart to Louis A. Warren, September 7, 1933, Lincoln Museum, Fort Wayne, IN; "The Illinois Campaign," *Daily Missouri Republican*, August 20, 1858; "Incidents at Ottawa," *Illinois State Journal*, August 25, 1858; Cullom, *Fifty Years of Public Service*, pp. 7, 8, 11; Michael Burlingame, "How Shorthand Reporters Covered the Lincoln-Douglas Debates of 1858," *Lincoln Herald* 96 (Spring 1994), pp. 18–19, 21; Wilson and Davis, eds. *Herndon's Lincoln*, pp. 387, 396–97; Harold Holzer, ed., *The Lincoln-Douglas Debates: The First, Complete Unexpurgated Text* (New York: HarperCollins, 1993), p. 9; Wendt, *Chicago Tribune*, p. 98; "The Lincoln Scrapbook," in *A Reporter's Lincoln*, pp. 73, 76, 77; Hitt, in *The Lincoln-Douglas Debates of 1858*, ed. Sparks, p. 79.

36. "Mr. Douglas' Speech," in *Lincoln-Douglas Debates*, ed. Sparks, pp. 86–90; "Mr. Douglas' Opening Speech," in *Lincoln-Douglas Debates*, ed. Holzer, pp. 45–49; "First Debate with Stephen A. Douglas at Ottawa, Illinois," in *C.W.*, volume three, pp. 1, 3, 5.

37. On August 19, the *Freeport Weekly Bulletin*, a Douglasite newspaper in northern Illinois edited by W. T. Giles, published a list of ten propositions (copied from the *Cincinnati Enquirer*), which cover almost exactly the same ground as Douglas's seven questions, posing the interesting possibility that Douglas based his questions on the *Weekly Bulletin*'s list. "Mr. Douglas' Speech," in *Lincoln-Douglas Debates*, ed. Sparks, pp. 92–94, 98; "Mr. Douglas' Opening

Speech," in *Lincoln-Douglas Debates*, ed Holzer, pp. 52–53, 58; "First Debate with Stephen A. Douglas at Ottawa, Illinois," in *C.W.*, volume three, pp. 5–6, 12.

38. "Mr. Douglas' Speech," in *Lincoln-Douglas Debates*, ed. Sparks, pp. 94–96; "Mr. Douglas' Opening Speech," in *Lincoln-Douglas Debates*, ed. Holzer, pp. 52–54; "First Debate with Stephen A. Douglas at Ottawa, Illinois," in *C.W.*, volume three, pp. 9–10.

39. "Mr. Douglas' Speech," in *Lincoln-Douglas Debates*, ed. Sparks, pp. 95, 97; "Mr. Douglas' Opening Speech," in *Lincoln-Douglas Debates*, ed. Holzer, pp. 56–57; "First Debate with Stephen A. Douglas at Ottawa, Illinois," in *C.W.*, volume three, pp. 10–12.

40. "Mr. Lincoln's Reply," in *Lincoln-Douglas Debates*, ed. Sparks, pp. 99, 102; "Mr. Lincoln's Reply," in *Lincoln-Douglas Debates*, ed. Holzer, pp. 59, 63; "First Debate with Stephen A. Douglas at Ottawa, Illinois," in *C.W.*, volume three, pp. 13, 16; John M. Rozett, "Racism and Republican Emergence in Illinois, 1848–1860: A Re-evaluation of Republican Negrophobia," *Civil War History* 22 (June 1976), p. 105.

41. "Mr. Lincoln's Reply," in *Lincoln-Douglas Debates*, ed. Sparks, pp. 102–4; "Mr. Lincoln's Reply," in *Lincoln-Douglas Debates*, ed. Holzer, pp. 63–65; "First Debate with Stephen A. Douglas at Ottawa, Illinois," in *C.W.*, volume three, pp. 17–19; Charles Hubert Coleman, "The 'Grocery-Keeper' and His Customer," *Journal of the Ilinois State Historical Society* (Winter 1959), p. 550.

42. "Mr. Lincoln's Reply," in *Lincoln-Douglas Debates*, ed. Sparks, pp. 108, 110, 114; "Mr. Lincoln's Reply," in *Lincoln-Douglas Debates*, ed. Holzer, pp. 66, 73–76; "First Debate with Stephen A. Douglas at Ottawa, Illinois," in *C.W.*, volume three, pp. 21–22, 23–24, 27–28. Both Sheahan's *Chicago Times* and Lanphier's *Illinois State Register* insisted that Lincoln ended thirteen (or fifteen, according to Lanphier) minutes short of his allotted ninety minutes, by which they intended to show how ill-prepared and tongue-tied he was (see David Zarefsky in *Lincoln, Douglas and Slavery*, p. 55). But Lincoln's reply runs to approximately 8,900 words, and given Horace White's recollection that he "began to speak in a slow and awkward way," and usually did not speak "in a rushing, unbroken stream" or faster than 100 words a minute, it seems likely that Lincoln did *not* stop short but used his full budget of time.

43. "An Army With Banners," *Illinois State Journal*, August 21, 1858; "Mr. Douglas's Rejoinder," in *Lincoln-Douglas Debates*, ed. Sparks, pp. 117–178, 120; "Mr. Douglas' Rejoinder," in *Lincoln-Douglas Debates*, ed. Holzer, pp. 78–79; "First Debate with Stephen A. Douglas at Ottawa, Illinois," in *C.W.*, volume three, pp. 30–31.

44. "Mr. Lincoln's Reply," in *Lincoln-Douglas Debates*, ed. Holzer, p. 80; "First Debate with Stephen A. Douglas at Ottawa, Illinois," in *C.W.*, volume three, p. 40.

45. "Mr. Douglas's Rejoinder," in *Lincoln-Douglas Debates*, ed. Sparks, pp. 122, 124; "Mr. Douglas' Rejoinder," in *Lincoln-Douglas Debates*, ed. Holzer, pp. 82, 84, 85; "First Debate with Stephen A. Douglas at Ottawa, Illinois," in *C.W.*, volume three, pp. 34–35, 37.

46. "The Great Debate at Ottawa," *Peoria Daily Transcript*, August 24, 1858; "The

Result of the First Lincoln-Douglas Debate," *Chicago Daily Journal*, August 23, 1858; "Conclusion of the Whole Matter," *Chicago Press & Tribune*, August 23, 1858.

47. David Davis to Lincoln, August 25, 1858, Henry Clay Whitney to Lincoln, August 26, 1858, and Lyman Trumbull to Lincoln, August 24, 1858, Abraham Lincoln Papers; King, *Lincoln's Manager*, p. 122; Thomas J. Pickett, in *Recollected Words*, p. 357; Tarbell, *Life of Abraham Lincoln* volume one, p. 308; "Discussion at Ottawa," *Freeport Weekly Bulletin*, August 26, 1858; "Douglas' Reply to Lincoln at Ottawa," *Jacksonville Sentinel*, September 3, 1858; Henry Villard, "Douglas and Lincoln," *New-Yorker Staats-Zeitung*, August 27, 1858; "The Campaign in Illinois—Great Discussion between Douglas and Lincoln," *Philadelphia Press*, August 26, 1858; "The Great Debate between Lincoln and Douglas at Ottawa," *Illinois State Journal*, August 23, 1858; "The Great Debate at Ottawa," *Chicago Press & Tribune*, August 26, 1858; "Douglas and Lincoln at Ottawa," *Jacksonville Sentinel*, August 27, 1858; *Chicago Times* (August 22, 1858), in *Lincoln-Douglas Debates*, ed. Sparks, p. 143.

48. David Zarefsky, "The Lincoln-Douglas Debates Revisited: The Evolution of Public Argument," *Quarterly Journal of Speech* 72 (May 1986), p. 165; David Zarefsky, *Argumentative Strategy in the Lincoln-Douglas Debates* (Waco, TX: Baylor University Press, 1982), pp. 8, 11–12; Forest L. Whan, "Stephen A. Douglas," in William Norwood Brigance, ed. *A History and Criticism of American Public Address* (New York: McGraw-Hill, 1943), volume two, pp. 806–8, 816–17; Marvin G. Bauer, "Persuasive Methods in the Lincoln-Douglas Debates," in Lionel Crocker, ed., *An Analysis of Lincoln and Douglas as Public Speakers and Debaters* (Springfield, IL: C. C. Thomas, 1968), pp. 64–65, 69, 70, 73; Zarefsky, *Lincoln, Douglas and Slavery*, pp. 109–10.

49. Tarbell, *Life of Abraham Lincoln*, volume one, pp. 320–21; AL to Joseph O. Cunningham (August 22, 1858), in *C.W.*, volume three, p. 36; Robert R. Hitt to Horace White, December 10, 1892, in Horace White Papers, ALPLM.

4: FOR GOD'S SAKE, LINDER, COME UP

1. Stevens, "The Lincoln Scrapbook," in *A Reporter's Lincoln*, pp. 80–81; Victor B. Howard, "The Illinois Republican Party," *Journal of the Illinois Historical Society* 64 (Summer–Autumn 1973), p. 140; Paul Selby, "Genesis of the Republican Party in Illinois," *Transactions of the Illinois State Historical Society* 11 (1906), p. 274.

2. SAD to Lanphier (August 15, 1858), in *Letters of Stephen A. Douglas*, pp. 426–27; "Senator Douglas at Galena," *Chicago Daily Journal*, August 27, 1858; Heckman, *Lincoln vs. Douglas*, p. 87; Harris, "Politics of the Country," (August 9, 1856) *Congressional Globe*, 34th Congress, 1st session (appendix), p. 1274; "Lincoln and Douglas at Ottawa," *Chicago Daily Journal*, August 23, 1858; "The Ottawa Fraud," *Chicago Press & Tribune*, August 24, 1858; Wendt, *Chicago Tribune*, pp. 99–100.

3. "More of the Ottawa Forgery," *Illinois State Journal*, August 30, 1858; "The Re-

publicans Catching at Straws," *Jacksonville Sentinel,* August 27, 1858; B. Lewis to AL, August 25, 1858, Abraham Lincoln Papers.

4. "Trying to Screen Lincoln's Defeat," *Jacksonville Sentinel,* August 27, 1858; "Introduction," in *The Lincoln-Douglas Debates,* ed. Holzer, pp. 12–13; Michael Burlingame, "The Accuracy of Newspaper Accounts of the 1858 Lincoln-Douglas Debates," and Stevens, "The Lincoln Scrapbook," in *A Reporter's Lincoln,* pp. 70–72, 230–31; "At Its Dirty Work Again," *Chicago Daily Journal,* August 30, 1858; "Douglas Puffers and Valets," *Illinois State Journal,* September 27, 1858; "Garbling Lincoln's Speeches," *Chicago Press & Tribune,* October 11, 1858.

5. Jesse K. Dubois to AL, September 7, 1858, Sydney Spring to AL, September 8, 1858, and Thomas C. Sharp to Ozias M. Hatch, August 11, 1858, Abraham Lincoln Papers; Fehrenbacher, *Prelude to Greatness,* pp. 113–14; Sheahan, *Life of Stephen A. Douglas,* p. 416; Donald, *We Are Lincoln Men,* pp. 82–83; Johannsen, *Stephen A. Douglas,* pp. 648–49; "The National Democracy of Illinois in Counsel," *Chicago Press & Tribune,* September 9, 1858; Thomas M. Ward to SAD, June 28, 1858, Stephen A. Douglas Papers.

6. "Douglas Electioneering," *Carlinville Free Democrat,* July 1, 1858; Clifton H. Moore to AL, August 10, 1858, Abraham Lincoln Papers; "Col. Carpenter at Clinton," *Quincy Daily Whig & Republican,* August 17, 1858; Henry Villard, "Illinois Politics," *New-Yorker Staats-Zeitung,* August 3, 1858; A. L. Dicket, "John Slidell and the Chicago Incident in 1858," *Louisiana History* (Fall 1964), p. 372; Heckman, "Out-of-State Influences and the Lincoln-Douglas Campaign of 1858," pp. 32–33; "The Contest in Illinois," *Philadelphia Press,* August 24, 1858; James Jackson to Sidney Breese, August 30, 1858, Sidney Breese Papers, ALPLM; Wright, *Lincoln and the Politics of Slavery,* pp. 62–63; Hansen, *The Making of the Third Party System,* pp. 22–23, 117–18.

7. William Harris to Lanphier, September 21, 1858, Charles H. Lanphier Papers, ALPLM; R. C. Coler to SAD, August 30, 1858, Stephen A. Douglas Papers; King, *Melville Weston Fuller,* pp. 45–46; J. M. Stratton to Lanphier, September 23, 1858, and John C. Breckinridge to Lanphier, October 4, 1858, Charles H. Lanphier Papers, ALPLM; SAD to Brown (August 29, 1858), and to Linder (August 22, 1858), in *Letters of Stephen A. Douglas,* pp. 427–28. Douglas's telegram to Linder fell into Republican hands and was plastered across the state so hilariously that Linder was tagged thereafter as "For-God's-Sake" Linder.

8. Beveridge, *Abraham Lincoln,* p. 545; Richardson to SAD, July 27, 1858, Stephen A. Douglas Papers; Mildred C. Stoler, "The Democratic Element in the New Republican Party in Illinois, 1856–1860," *Papers in Illinois History and Transactions for the Year 1940* (1944), pp. 50–51; Fehrenbacher, *Chicago Giant,* pp. 102, 148, 152–54, 156, 159; Hansen, *The Making of the Third Party System,* pp. 32, 97–98; Fehrenbacher, *Lincoln in Text and Context: Collected Essays* (Stanford: Stanford University Press, 1987), p. 40; Beveridge, *Abraham Lincoln,* pp. 522, 565; White, *The Lincoln-Douglas Debates,* p. 17; E. T. Bridges to AL, May 18, 1858, Abraham Lincoln Papers.

9. "From Illinois," *National Era,* November 18, 1858, p. 183; Medill to Elihu Wash-

burne, October 21, 1858, Elihu Washburne Papers, LOC; "Appointments for the Campaign," *Chicago Daily Journal*, October 22, 1858; "Interesting Reminiscences," *Peoria Daily Telegraph*, March 16, 1858; *Reminiscences of Carl Schurz*, volume two, p. 87; Wendt, *Chicago Tribune*, p. 91.

10. Ralph J. Roske, *His Own Counsel: The Life and Times of Lyman Trumbull* (Reno: University of Nevada Press, 1979), pp. 1, 4–5, 50–51; Trumbull to Palmer (June 19, 1858), in G. T. Palmer, "A Collection of Letters from Lyman Trumbull to John M. Palmer, 1854–1858," *Journal of the Illinois State Historical Society* 16 (April–July 1923), pp. 38–40; Horace White, *The Life of Lyman Trumbull* (New York: Houghton Mifflin, 1913), pp. 428–30.

11. Lyman Trumbull to John Trumbull, June 20, 1858, and to Julia Trumbull, October 10, 1858, in Lyman Trumbull Family Papers, ALPLM; Judd to Trumbull, July 11, 1858, Lyman Trumbull Papers, LOC; G. F. Ross to Lyman Trumbull, April 25, 1858, Lyman Trumbull Papers, LOC; Shelby M. Cullom, *Fifty Years of Public Service: Personal Recollections of Shelby M. Cullom* (Chicago: A. C. McClurg, 1911), p. 42; Mark Krug, "Lyman Trumbull and the Real Issues in the Lincoln-Douglas Debates," *Journal of the Illinois State Historical Society* 57 (1964), pp. 386, 389.

12. Sheahan, *Life of Stephen A. Douglas*, pp. 430–31; "Senator Trumbull's Speech on Saturday Night," *Chicago Daily Journal*, August 9, 1858; "Judge Trumbull's Great Speech," *Chicago Press & Tribune*, September 6, 1858; Medill to Elihu Washburne, August 24, 1858, Elihu Washburne Papers, LOC; "Another Intrigue of Trumbull—Cheating Round the Board," *Illinois State Register*, September 22, 1858; "Senator Trumbull's Alton Speech," *Illinois State Journal*, October 2, 1858; Lash, *A Politician Turned General*, p. 47; Beveridge, *Abraham Lincoln*, volume two, p. 628; Bruce Collins, "The Lincoln-Douglas Contest of 1858 and Illinois' Electorate," *Journal of American Studies* 20 (1986), p. 396; "The Alliance—Breese, Lincoln and Trumbull," *Montgomery County Herald* (Hillsboro, IL), October 8, 1858.

13. Horace White, in *Herndon's Lincoln*, p. 411; "Kansas Affairs" (June 23, 1858), *Congressional Globe*, 34th Congress, 1st session, p. 1439; "Senator Trumbull's Charges," *Illinois State Journal*, August 14, 1858; Nevins, *Ordeal of the Union: A House Dividing, 1852–1857*, pp. 470–71; Johannsen, *Stephen A. Douglas*, pp. 525–27, 674–75; Milton, *Eve of Conflict*, p. 334.

14. Bigler, "The President's Message," (December 9, 1857) and "Kansas Affairs" (December 21, 1857), *Congressional Globe*, 35th Congress, 1st session, pp. 21, 113–15; "Trumbull, Jonas, Prentiss and Grimshaw," *Quincy Daily Whig & Republican*, September 30, 1858; "Douglas in a Rage," *Chicago Daily Journal*, August 16, 1858; Johannsen, *Stephen A. Douglas*, pp. 674–75; Stewart, "The People and the Lincoln-Douglas Campaign in 1858," pp. 292–93.

15. Davis to Hatch (August 18, 1858), in *For the People: A Newsletter of the Abraham Lincoln Association* 4 (Autumn 2002), p. 6; Lincoln to Ebenezer Peck (August 23, 1858), in *C.W.*, volume nine, pp. 32–33; "Lincoln at Augusta and Macomb," *Chicago Press & Tribune*, August 26, 1858; "The Republican Convention—Lincoln at Augusta," *Quincy Whig & Republican*, August 27, 1858.

16. "Lincoln Refuses to Answer," *Chicago Daily Journal,* August 24, 1858; "Conversation with Hon. N. B. Judd, Washington, Feb 28 '76," in *An Oral Biography of Abraham Lincoln,* p. 45; Medill to AL [August 26, 1858] and Ray to AL [August 25, 1858], Abraham Lincoln Papers.

17. Fisher, *New and Complete Statistical Gazeteer,* p. 306; Gerhard, *Illinois As It Is,* p. 222; Horace Greeley and John F. Cleveland, *A Political Text-Book for 1860: Comprising a Brief View of the Presidential Nominations and Elections* (New York: Tribune Association, 1860), p. 221; William H. Johnston, *Sketches of the History of Stephenson County, Ill., and incidents connected with the early settlement of the North-West* (Freeport: J. O. P. Burnside, 1854), pp. 307–14; Mary X. Barrett, *History of Stephenson County* (Freeport: County of Stephenson, 1970), pp. 40–41; Robert Mize Sutton, *The Illinois Central Railroad in Peace and War, 1858–1868* (New York: Arno Press, 1981), p. 35; *The Freeport Debate and Its Centennial Commemoration* (Freeport: Lincoln-Douglas Society, 1959), pp. 190, 209.

18. "The Lincoln and Douglas Debate at Freeport," *Alton Weekly Courier,* September 2, 1858; "Great Debate between Lincoln and Douglas at Freeport," *Illinois State Journal,* September 1, 1858; "The Debate at Freeport," *Galesburg Semi-Weekly Democrat,* September 1, 1858; "Discussion at Freeport," *Freeport Weekly Bulletin,* August 19, 1858; "The Meeting at Freeport last Friday," *Weekly Northwestern Gazette,* August 31, 1858; "The Great Gathering at Freeport," *Rockford Republican,* September 2, 1858; Smith D. Atkins, "The Freeport Debate," in Nathan William MacChesney, ed., *Abraham Lincoln: The Tribute of a Century, 1809–1909* (Chicago: A. C. McClurg, 1910), p. 140; Elihu Washburne, in *Reminiscences of Abraham Lincoln,* p. 26; Louis Altenbern, in W. T. Rawleigh, *Freeport's Lincoln: Exercises Attendant Upon the Unveiling of a Statue of Abraham Lincoln; Freeport, Illinois, August 27, 1929* (Freeport: W. T. Rawleigh, 1930), pp. 198–99; "Lincoln-Douglas—E. B. Spaulding's Reminiscences of the Great Debate at Freeport," newspaper clipping, 1901, in the files of the Lincoln Museum, Fort Wayne, IN; *The Freeport Debate and Its Centennial Commemoration,* pp. 209–12; *The History of Stephenson County, Illinois* (Chicago: Western Historical Co., 1880), p. 383.

19. "E. B. Spaulding's Reminiscences"; "Discussion at Freeport," *Freeport Weekly Bulletin,* August 19, 1858; "The Wagon," *Freeport Weekly Bulletin,* September 2, 1858; William Clingman, in Rawleigh, *Freeport's Lincoln,* pp. 193–94; Dewey, "The Senatorial Contest in Illinois," in *Lincoln-Douglas Debates,* ed. Sparks, p. 193; Charles Coleman, "The Lincoln-Douglas Debate at Charleston, Illinois, September 18, 1858," *Eastern Illinois University Bulletin* 220 (October 1, 1957), p. 30; Stewart, "The People and the Lincoln-Douglas Campaign," pp. 288–89; Seymour D. Thompson, "Lincoln and Douglas: The Great Freeport Debate," *American Law Review* 39 (March–April 1905), pp. 168, 170–71.

20. "E. B. Spaulding's Reminiscences"; "Lincoln and Douglas at Freeport," *Quincy Daily Whig & Republican,* September 1, 1858; "Mr. Lincoln's Speech," in *Lincoln-Douglas Debates,* ed. Sparks, pp. 148–51; "Mr. Lincoln's Opening Speech," in *Lincoln-Douglas Debates,* ed. Holzer, pp. 92–93.

21. AL, "Second Debate with Stephen A. Douglas at Freeport, Illinois" (August 27,

1858), in *C.W.,* volume three, p. 40; Henry C. Whitney to Herndon (August 29, 1887), in *Herndon's Informants,* p. 636; Villard, "Douglas and Lincoln—The Second Debate at Freeport, Ill.," *New-Yorker Staats-Zeitung,* September 4, 1858.

22. "Mr. Lincoln's Opening Speech," in *Lincoln-Douglas Debates,* ed. Holzer, pp. 95–96; "Mr. Lincoln's Speech," in *Lincoln-Douglas Debates,* ed. Sparks, p. 152.

23. Thompson, "Lincoln and Douglas: The Great Freeport Debate," pp. 171–72; "Dr. Ward Woodbridge Writes His Recollections," *Cedar Rapids Republican,* February 10, 1909, The Lincoln Museum, Ft. Wayne, IN; AL, "Second Debate with Stephen A. Douglas at Freeport, Illinois" (August 27, 1858), in *C.W.,* volume three, pp. 44–45, 46–47; "Mr. Lincoln's Opening Speech," in *Lincoln-Douglas Debates,* ed. Holzer, pp. 99–101; "Mr. Lincoln's Speech," in *Lincoln-Douglas Debates,* ed. Sparks, pp. 154–57.

24. Villard, "Douglas and Lincoln—The Second Debate at Freeport, Ill"; *A Hoosier Salad: Recollections of Thomas R. Marshall, Vice-President and Hoosier Philosopher* (Indianapolis: Bobbs-Merrill, 1925), p. 52; "Black Republican Outrages," *Chicago Daily Times,* October 7, 1858; SAD, "Second Debate with Stephen A. Douglas at Freeport, Illinois" (August 27, 1858), in *C.W.,* volume three, pp. 49–50; "Mr. Douglas' Reply," in *Lincoln-Douglas Debates,* ed. Holzer, pp. 103–9; "Mr. Douglas's Reply," in *Lincoln-Douglas Debates,* ed. Sparks, pp. 160–62; Trumbull, "Kansas Affairs" (June 9, 1856), *Congressional Globe,* 34th Congress 1st Session, pp. 1370–71; Daniel Fish, *Legal Phases of the Lincoln and Douglas Debates: Annual Address before the State Bar Association of Minnesota at Minneapolis, July 14, 1909* (Minneapolis, 1909), p. 14; Sheahan, *Life of Stephen A. Douglas,* p. 144; O. M. Dickerson, "Stephen A. Douglas and the Split in the Democratic Party," *Proceedings of the Mississippi Valley Historical Association for the Year 1913–14* (Cedar Rapids, IA: Torch Press, 1914), pp. 201–3; Wells, *Stephen Douglas: The Last Years,* p. 123.

25. "The Discussion of Friday Last," *Freeport Weekly Bulletin,* September 1, 1858; SAD, "Second Debate with Stephen A. Douglas at Freeport, Illinois" (August 27, 1858), in *C.W.,* volume three, pp. 51–53; "Mr. Douglas's Reply," in *Lincoln-Douglas Debates,* ed. Sparks, pp. 163–65; Jaffa, *Crisis of the House Divided,* p. 350.

26. SAD, "Second Debate with Stephen A. Douglas at Freeport, Illinois" (August 27, 1858), in *C.W.,* volume three, pp. 55–56; "Mr. Douglas's Reply," in *Lincoln-Douglas Debates,* ed. Holzer, pp. 110–11; "Mr. Douglas's Reply," in *Lincoln-Douglas Debates,* ed. Sparks, pp. 165–66; "Beauties of Black Republicanism—Lincoln's Friends Endorse Fred Douglas and Negro Equality," *Jacksonville Sentinel,* September 3, 1858.

27. "Dr. Ward Woodbridge Writes His Recollections," *Cedar Rapids Republican,* February 10, 1909; SAD, "Second Debate with Stephen A. Douglas at Freeport, Illinois" (August 27, 1858), in *C.W.,* volume three, pp. 56, 60, 63, 69–70; "Mr. Douglas' Reply," in *Lincoln-Douglas Debates,* ed. Holzer, pp. 115–16, 119, 126; "Mr. Douglas's Reply," in *Lincoln-Douglas Debates,* ed. Sparks, pp. 171, 174, 181; "The Lincoln and Douglas Debate at Freeport," *Alton Weekly Courier,* September 2, 1858.

28. William Bross, in *Recollected Words*, p. 58; AL, "Second Debate with Stephen A. Douglas at Freeport, Illinois" (August 27, 1858), in *C.W.*, volume three, pp. 71–72; "Mr. Lincoln's Rejoinder," in *Lincoln-Douglas Debates*, ed. Holzer, pp. 127–29; "Mr. Lincoln's Rejoinder," in *Lincoln-Douglas Debates*, ed. Sparks, pp. 182–83.

29. AL, "Second Debate with Stephen A. Douglas at Freeport, Illinois" (August 27, 1858), in *C.W.*, volume three, p. 76; "Mr. Lincoln's Rejoinder," in *Lincoln-Douglas Debates*, ed. Holzer, pp. 134–35; "Mr. Douglas's Reply," in *Lincoln-Douglas Debates*, ed. Sparks, pp. 184, 188.

30. "The Great Debate at Freeport," *Weekly Northwestern Gazette*, September 7, 1858; "The Great Gathering at Freeport," *Rockford Republican*, September 2, 1858; "Hon. Owen Lovejoy," *Freeport Weekly Bulletin*, September 2, 1858; Villard, "Developments of the Campaign," *New-Yorker Staats-Zeitung*, September 16, 1858.

31. Zarefsky, "The Lincoln-Douglas Debates Revisited," p. 173; Medill, "A Reminiscence of Lincoln," in *Lincoln-Douglas Debates*, ed. Sparks, p. 204; Holland, *Life of Abraham Lincoln*, p. 189; Beveridge, *Abraham Lincoln*, p. 656; Smith D. Atkins, "The Freeport Debate," in MacChesney, ed., *Abraham Lincoln: The Tribute of a Century, 1809–1909* (Chicago: A. C. McClurg, 1910), p. 141.

32. Medill, "A Reminiscence of Lincoln," p. 203; Medill to AL, August 27, 1858, Abraham Lincoln Papers.

33. AL to Henry Asbury (July 31, 1858), in *C.W.*, volume two, p. 530; Fish, *Legal Phases of the Lincoln and Douglas Debates*, p. 14; S. W. Randall to SAD, August 28, 1858, Stephen A. Douglas Papers; SAD, "The Freeport Debate," in *The Lincoln-Douglas Debates*, ed. Sparks, p. 161; Fehrenbacher, *Prelude to Greatness*, pp. 122–28.

34. Carr, "The So-Called 'Freeport Doctrine,'" in *Stephen A. Douglas*, p. 283; J. H. Sturgeon to Sidney Breese, September 11, 1858, Sidney Breese Papers, ALPLM; Donald, *Lincoln* (New York: Simon & Schuster, 1995), p. 633; Ernest James Wesson, "Debates of Lincoln and Douglas: A Bibliographical Discussion," *Papers of the Bibliographical Society of America* 40 (1946), pp. 101–2.

35. Arnold, *History of Abraham Lincoln and the Overthrow of Slavery*, p. 133; Koerner, *Memoirs*, volume two, p. 65; William H. Herndon to Horace White, August 26, 1890, Horace White Papers, ALPLM; Herndon's account of the Judd interview (October 2, 1890) is in *Herndon's Informants*, pp. 723–24, and Horace White's version in his chapter on the Lincoln-Douglas debates for the 1892 edition of *Herndon's Lincoln* seems to be based on this document (Wilson and Douglas, eds., *Herndon's Lincoln*, p. 399); White, *The Lincoln-Douglas Debates: An Address before the Chicago Historical Society, February 17, 1914* (Chicago: University of Chicago Press, 1914), pp. 22–23; "Wells H. Blodgett's Experience," in Stevens, *A Reporter's Lincoln*, p. 51.

36. AL, "Second Debate with Stephen A. Douglas at Freeport, Illinois" (August 27, 1858), in *C.W.*, volume three, p. 76; "Mr. Lincoln's Rejoinder," in *Lincoln-Douglas Debates*, ed. Sparks, p. 188; Holland, *Life of Abraham Lincoln*, p. 158; Johannsen, *Stephen A. Douglas*, pp. 585–86, 634, 637, 638; Beveridge, *Abraham Lincoln*, vol-

ume two, pp. 556, 558; P. W. Randle to SAD, July 4, 1858, Stephen A. Douglas Papers; Dewey to AL, October 30, 1858, Abraham Lincoln Papers.

37. "The Campaign in Illinois," *Daily Missouri Republican*, September 8, 1858; "Douglas Dodgeth," *Chicago Daily Journal*, September 8, 1858; "Douglas in the Circus," *Chicago Press & Tribune*, September 7, 1858.

38. "Lincoln in Old Tazewell," *Chicago Press & Tribune*, September 2, 1858; "Great Mass Meeting in Clinton," [Clinton] *Central Transcript*, September 3, 1858; "Progress of the Campaign," *Chicago Press & Tribune*, September 3, 1858; "Progress of the Campaign," *Chicago Press & Tribune*, September 6, 1858; AL, "Speech at Tremont, Illinois" (August 30, 1858) and "Speech at Carlinville, Illinois" (August 31, 1858), in *C.W.*, volume three, pp. 76, 78.

39. Norman Judd to Elihu Washburne, August 14, 1858, Elihu Washburne Papers (volume 4), LOC; Ozias Hatch to John C. Bagby, August 31 and September 15, 1858, John C. Bagby Papers, ALPLM; "Mr. Lincoln's Appointments," *Chicago Press & Tribune*, September 1, 1858; "Douglas and Lincoln Face to Face!" *Philadelphia Press*, August 26, 1858; William Ross to Ozias Hatch, August 16, 1858, and Jackson Grimshaw to Ozias Hatch, August 15, 1858, Ozias M. Hatch Papers, ALPLM; Heckman, "Out-of-State Influences and the Lincoln-Douglas Campaign of 1858," p. 47; George Fanning Hill to SAD, September 6, 1858, and E. H. Stainback to SAD, September 2, 1858, Stephen A. Douglas Papers.

40. "Illinois Political Items," *Chicago Daily Journal*, September 13, 1858; Heckman, *Lincoln vs. Douglas*, pp. 1–2, 78; Davidson, *Complete History of Illinois*, pp. 709–10.

41. R. J. Oglesby to AL and Thomas A. Marshall to AL, August 29, 1858, Abraham Lincoln Papers; "Sangamon County Convention," *Illinois State Journal*, August 30, 1858; "Sangamon County Douglas Convention," *Illinois State Journal*, September 6, 1858; Jesse K. Dubois to AL, September 7, 1858, Abraham Lincoln Papers; Sturtevant, in *Recollected Words*, p. 432; "Tazewell County," *Illinois State Register*, September 4, 1858; "Douglas Following a Circus," *Illinois State Journal*, September 4, 1858; Thompson, "Lincoln and Douglas: The Great Freeport Debate," pp. 172–73; Jonathan Birch (Jesse W. Weik interview), in *Herndon's Informants*, p. 728.

42. "Mr. Lincoln," *Weekly Madison Press*, September 15, 1858; "Lincoln at Monticello," *Chicago Daily Journal*, September 9, 1858; "Hon. Abram Lincoln," *Weekly Madison Press*, August 25, 1858; "People's Convention," *Weekly Madison Press*, September 22, 1858; AL, "Speech at Edwardsville, Illinois" (September 11, 1858), in *C.W.*, volume three, p. 94.

43. "Politics on the Wabash," *Quincy Daily Whig & Republican*, September 14, 1858; Horace White, in Wilson and Davis, ed. *Herndon's Lincoln*, p. 404; George W. Smith, *When Lincoln Came Down to Egypt* (Herrin, IL: Trovillion Private Press, 1940), pp. 88–89.

44. "St. Louis Fair," *Chicago Press & Tribune*, September 8, 1858; "Douglas at Jacksonville," *Chicago Daily Journal*, September 9, 1858; "Douglas in Macoupin," *Illinois State Register*, September 10, 1858; "Douglas at Macoupin," *Illinois State Journal*, September 11, 1858; George W. Smith, *A History of Southern Illinois* (Chicago: Lewis Publications, 1912), volume one, pp. 258–59.

45. Daniel McCook to Thomas L. Harris (September 15, 1858) and S. S. Marshall to Charles Lanphier (October 24, 1858), in *Glory to God and the Sucker Democracy*, volume four, pp. 102, 135; O. R. Winters to AL, September 3, 1858, Abraham Lincoln Papers.

46. "Adele Cutts Douglas to Her Mother" (June 24, 1857), in *Letters of Stephen A. Douglas*, p. 384; Smith, *History of Southern Illinois*, volume one, pp. 263–64; "Little Dug Entered at the State Fair," *Chicago Press & Tribune*, September 20, 1858; "Letter from Southern Illinois," *Chicago Daily Journal*, September 16, 1858.

47. William Henry Perrin, *History of Alexander, Union and Pulaski Counties*, Illinois (Chicago: O. L. Baskin, 1883), p. 359; John Y. Simon, "Union County in 1858 and the Lincoln-Douglas Debate," *Journal of the Illinois State Historical Society* 62 (1969), pp. 271–72, 275, 279.

48. Simon, "Union County in 1858 and the Lincoln-Douglas Debate," pp. 281, 283; Amy Davis Winship in Rawleigh, *Freeport's Lincoln*, p. 182; *One Hundred Years of Progress: The Centennial History of Anna, Illinois* (Cape Girardeau, MO: Missourian Printing & Stationery, 1954); "Douglas and Lincoln Debate in Lower Egypt," *Chicago Daily Journal*, September 17, 1858.

49. Smith, *History of Southern Illinois*, volume one, pp. 264–65; "Great Debate Between Lincoln and Douglas at Jonesboro," *Chicago Press & Tribune*, September 17, 1858; "Great Debate between Lincoln and Douglas at Jonesboro," *Illinois State Journal*, September 20, 1858.

50. Dewey, in *Lincoln-Douglas Debates*, ed. Sparks, p. 262; SAD, "Third Debate with Stephen A. Douglas at Jonesboro, Illinois" (September 15, 1858), in *C.W.*, volume three, pp. 103–4; "Mr. Douglas' Opening Speech," in *Lincoln-Douglas Debates*, ed. Holzer, pp. 140–41.

51. SAD, "Third Debate with Stephen A. Douglas at Jonesboro, Illinois" (September 15, 1858), in *C.W.*, volume three, pp. 108–10; "Mr. Douglas' Opening Speech," in *Lincoln-Douglas Debates*, ed. Holzer, pp. 142, 144, 146; "Mr. Douglas's Speech," *Lincoln-Douglas Debates*, in ed. Sparks, pp. 215–16, 218, 220.

52. SAD, "Third Debate with Stephen A. Douglas at Jonesboro, Illinois" (September 15, 1858), in *C.W.*, volume three, pp. 111–13; "Mr. Douglas' Opening Speech," in *Lincoln-Douglas Debates*, ed. Holzer, pp. 149–52; "Mr. Douglas's Speech," in *Lincoln-Douglas Debates*, ed. Sparks, pp. 222, 225–26.

53. AL, "Notes for the Debate at Jonesboro, Illinois" (September 15, 1858), in *C.W.*, volume three, p. 101.

54. AL, "Third Debate with Stephen A. Douglas at Jonesboro, Illinois" (September 15, 1858), in *C.W.*, volume three, pp. 116–17, 118; "Mr. Lincoln's Reply," in *Lincoln-Douglas Debates*, ed. Holzer, pp. 156–57; "Mr. Lincoln's Reply," in *Lincoln-Douglas Debates*, ed. Sparks, pp. 229–30.

55. AL, "Third Debate with Stephen A. Douglas at Jonesboro, Illinois" (September 15, 1858), in *C.W.*, volume three, pp. 120–21; "Mr. Lincoln's Reply," in *Lincoln-Douglas Debates*, ed. Holzer, pp. 159–60; "Mr. Lincoln's Reply," in *Lincoln-Douglas Debates*, ed. Sparks, pp. 234–35.

56. Al, "To Martin P. Sweet" (September 16, 1858) and "Third Debate with Stephen A. Douglas at Jonesboro, Illinois" (September 15, 1858), in *C.W.*, volume three,

pp. 119, 120–21, 125–26; "Mr. Lincoln's Reply," in *Lincoln-Douglas Debates*, ed. Holzer, pp. 161–67; "Mr. Lincoln's Reply," in *Lincoln-Douglas Debates*, ed. Sparks, pp. 235–41.

57. AL, "Third Debate with Stephen A. Douglas at Jonesboro, Illinois" (September 15, 1858), in *C.W.*, volume three, pp. 127–28; "Mr. Lincoln's Reply," in *Lincoln-Douglas Debates*, ed. Holzer, pp. 167–70; "Mr. Lincoln's Reply," in *Lincoln-Douglas Debates*, ed. Sparks, pp. 241–44.

58. AL, "Third Debate with Stephen A. Douglas at Jonesboro, Illinois" (September 15, 1858), in *C.W.*, volume three, p. 132; "Mr. Lincoln's Reply," in *Lincoln-Douglas Debates*, ed. Holzer, p. 172; "Mr. Lincoln's Reply," in *Lincoln-Douglas Debates*, ed. Sparks, pp. 246–47; O. M. Dickerson, "Stephen A. Douglas and the Split in the Democratic Party," p. 204; Trumbull to AL, September 14, 1858, Abraham Lincoln Papers.

59. AL, "Third Debate with Stephen A. Douglas at Jonesboro, Illinois" (September 15, 1858), in *C.W.*, volume three, pp. 137–38; "Mr. Douglas' Rejoinder," in *Lincoln-Douglas Debates*, ed. Holzer, pp. 176–77; "Mr. Douglas's Rejoinder," in *Lincoln-Douglas Debates*, ed. Sparks, pp. 250–51.

60. SAD, "Third Debate with Stephen A. Douglas at Jonesboro, Illinois" (September 15, 1858), in *C.W.*, volume three, pp. 139–40; "Mr. Douglas' Rejoinder," in *Lincoln-Douglas Debates*, ed. Holzer, pp. 179–80; "Mr. Douglas's Rejoinder," in *Lincoln-Douglas Debates*, ed. Sparks, pp. 253–54.

61. SAD, "Third Debate with Stephen A. Douglas at Jonesboro, Illinois" (September 15, 1858), in *C.W.*, volume three, pp. 141–42, 144; "Mr. Douglas' Rejoinder," in *Lincoln-Douglas Debates*, ed. Holzer, pp. 182, 184; "Mr. Douglas's Rejoinder," in *Lincoln-Douglas Debates*, ed. Sparks, pp. 256–57, 258.

62. "The Douglas and Lincoln Debate in Lower Egypt," *Chicago Daily Journal*, September 17, 1858; "Great Debate between Lincoln and Douglas at Jonesboro," *Illinois State Journal*, September 20, 1858.

CHAPTER 5: IN THE FACE OF THE NATION

1. Keith Thomas, *Religion and the Decline of Magic* (New York: Charles Scribner's Sons, 1971), pp. 90, 334, 326, 350; George Clark, *The Seventeenth Century* (New York: Oxford University Press, 1961), pp. 245–46; John Redwood, *Reason, Ridicule and Religion: The Age of Englightenment in England, 1660–1750* (Cambridge, MA: Harvard University Press, 1976), pp. 144–45; Pierre Bayle, *Miscellaneous Reflections, Occasion'd by the Comet which appeared in December 1680* (London, 1708), volume two, p. 421.

2. *American Almanac and Repository of Useful Knowledge for the Year 1859*, p. 369; Browning, diary entry for August 23, 1858, in *Diary of Orville Hickman Browning*, volume one, p. 113; "The Comet," *Illinois State Register*, October 6, 1858; van Deren, in Stevens, *A Reporter's Lincoln*, p. 226; White in Wilson and Davis, eds., *Herndon's Lincoln*, p. 405.

3. Clipping from the *Terre Haute Express* [undated], and Joseph Gillespie to Herndon (December 8, 1866), in *Herndon's Informants*, pp. 505–6, 641; *Memoirs of*

Henry Villard, Journalist and Financier, 1835–1900 (Boston: Houghton Mifflin, 1904), volume one, p. 97; Herndon, in *The Hidden Lincoln*, p. 90; Stuart in *The Lincoln Papers*, ed. David C. Mearns (Garden City, NY: Doubleday, 1948), volume one, p. 159; Eugene F. Miller, "Democratic Statecraft and Technological Advance: Abraham Lincoln's Reflections on 'Discoveries and Inventions'" *Review of Politics*, 63 (Summer 2001), pp. 485–515.

4. "Donati's Comet," *Illinois State Journal*, September 22, 1858; Wilson and Davis, eds., *Herndon's Lincoln*, p. 188.

5. "The Meeting at Centralia," "Little Dug Entered at the State Fair," *Chicago Press & Tribune*, September 18 and 20, 1858.

6. "Douglas and Lincoln at Springfield," *Chicago Press & Tribune*, July 20, 1858; J. R. Vaughan to SAD, August 3, 1858, Stephen A. Douglas Papers; Douglass, "Freedom in the West Indies: An Address Delivered in Poughkeepsie, New York, August 2, 1858," in J. W. Blassingame, ed., *The Frederick Douglass Papers, Series One, Speeches, Debates, and Interviews, Volume 3, 1855–63* (New Haven: Yale University Press, 1985), pp. 233–34; "The Brutal Douglas," *The Liberator*, October 15, 1858; "Douglas at Centralia," *Chicago Press & Tribune*, September 21, 1858.

7. J. Henly Smith to Alexander Stephens, August 3, 1858, Alexander H. Stephens Papers (volume 5), LOC; "Douglas—Lincoln," *Montgomery County Herald*, September 17, 1858; William Lee Miller, *Lincoln's Virtues: An Ethical Biography* (New York: Alfred A. Knopf, 2002), pp. 350–51; Jediah Alexander to AL, August 5, 1858, John M. Palmer to AL, July 19, 1858, and Thomas A. Marshall to AL, July 22, 1858, Abraham Lincoln Papers; Charles H. Coleman, "The Lincoln-Douglas Debate at Charleston, Illinois, September 18, 1858," *Eastern Illinois University Bulletin* 220 (October 1, 1957), pp. 38–39.

8. *Political Textbook for 1860*, p. 220; Ida M. Tarbell, *In the Footsteps of the Lincolns* (New York: Harper & Bros., 1924), pp. 162–63, Kenneth J. Winkle, *The Young Eagle: The Rise of Abraham Lincoln* (Dallas: Taylor, 2001), p. 142; Isaac N. Arnold, *The Life of Abraham Lincoln* (1884; Lincoln: University of Nebraska Press, 1994), p. 147; Chapman to AL, July 24, 1858, Abraham Lincoln Papers.

9. O. Knight to SAD, September 11, 1858, Stephen A. Douglas Papers; "George E. Mason's Account of the Memorable Day" and Jasper Miller, "The Lincoln-Douglas Debate" (May 19, 1930), news clippings in the files of the Lincoln Museum, Fort Wayne, IN; Coleman, "The Lincoln-Douglas Debate at Charleston," pp. 40, 44–45; Simeon E. Thomas, "Lincoln-Douglas Debate: The Fourth Joint Debate between Abraham Lincoln and Stephen A. Douglas, held in Charleston," *Eastern Illinois State Teachers College Bulletin* 86 (October 1, 1924), pp. 5–6; "The Campaign," *Chicago Times*, September 21, 1858; "The Great Triumph of the Campaign," *Chicago Press & Tribune*, September 21, 1858; "Theophilus van Deren," in Stevens, *A Reporter's Lincoln*, p. 224.

10. Coleman, "The Lincoln-Douglas Debate at Charleston," pp. 34–35, 36, 45, 46; Thomas, "Lincoln-Douglas Debate," pp. 5, 7; "Lincoln and Douglas at Charleston," *Chicago Daily Journal*, September 20, 1858.

11. S. E. Thomas, "An Authentic Account of the Great Historical Event," news clipping in the files of the Lincoln Museum, Fort Wayne, IN.

12. Heckman, *Lincoln vs. Douglas*, p. 109; Thomas, "An Authentic Account of the Great Historical Event"; Coleman, "The Lincoln-Douglas Debate at Charleston," pp. 47–48; "Lincoln and Douglas at Charleston," *Chicago Daily Journal*, September 20, 1858; Thomas, "Lincoln-Douglas Debate," p. 8; *Lew Wallace: An Autobiography* (New York: Harper & Bros., 1906), volume one, p. 253.

13. AL, "Fourth Debate with Stephen A. Douglas at Charleston, Illinois" (September 18, 1858), in *C.W.*, volume three, pp. 145–46; "Mr. Lincoln's Speech," in *Lincoln-Douglas Debates*, ed. Sparks, pp. 267–68; "Mr. Lincoln's Opening Speech," in *Lincoln-Douglas Debates*, ed. Holzer, pp. 189–90.

14. Horace White, in Wilson and Davis, eds., *Herndon's Lincoln*, p. 406; Henry C. Whitney to AL, August 26, 1858, and J. H. Jordan to AL, August 24, 1858, Abraham Lincoln Papers.

15. AL, "Fourth Debate with Stephen A. Douglas at Charleston, Illinois" (September 18, 1858), in *C.W.*, volume three, pp. 146, 157–58; "Mr. Lincoln's Speech," in *Lincoln-Douglas Debates*, ed. Sparks, pp. 269, 280–81; "Mr. Lincoln's Opening Speech," in *Lincoln-Douglas Debates*, ed. Holzer, p. 203; Zarefsky, *Lincoln, Douglas and Slavery*, pp. 59–60.

16. "Theophilus van Deren," in Stevens, *A Reporter's Lincoln*, p. 225; SAD, "Fourth Debate with Stephen A. Douglas at Charleston, Illinois" (September 18, 1858), in *C.W.*, volume three, pp. 159–61; "Senator Douglas's Reply," in *Lincoln-Douglas Debates*, ed. Sparks, pp. 281, 283–84; "Mr. Douglas' Reply," in *Lincoln-Douglas Debates*, ed. Holzer, pp. 204, 206–7.

17. SAD, "Fourth Debate with Stephen A. Douglas at Charleston, Illinois" (September 18, 1858), in *C.W.*, volume three, p. 162; "Senator Douglas's Reply," in *Lincoln-Douglas Debates*, ed. Sparks, pp. 285; "Mr. Douglas' Reply," in *Lincoln-Douglas Debates*, ed. Holzer, pp. 207–8.

18. SAD, "Fourth Debate with Stephen A. Douglas at Charleston, Illinois" (September 18, 1858), in *C.W.*, volume three, pp. 169, 171, 174–75; "Senator Douglas's Reply," in *Lincoln-Douglas Debates*, ed. Sparks, pp. 291–93, 298–99; "Mr. Douglas' Reply," in *Lincoln-Douglas Debates*, ed. Holzer, pp. 214–15, 217, 222.

19. SAD, "Fourth Debate with Stephen A. Douglas at Charleston, Illinois" (September 18, 1858), in *C.W.*, volume three, pp. 177–78; "Senator Douglas's Reply," in *Lincoln-Douglas Debates*, ed. Sparks, pp. 301, 302; "Mr. Douglas' Reply," in *Lincoln-Douglas Debates*, ed. Holzer, pp. 223–25.

20. AL, "Fourth Debate with Stephen A. Douglas at Charleston, Illinois" (September 18, 1858), in *C.W.*, volume three, pp. 179, 180, 181; "Mr. Lincoln's Rejoinder," in *Lincoln-Douglas Debates*, ed. Sparks, pp. 303–4, 305; "Mr. Lincoln's Rejoinder," in *Lincoln-Douglas Debates*, ed. Holzer, pp. 226.

21. AL, "Fourth Debate with Stephen A. Douglas at Charleston, Illinois" (September 18, 1858), in *C.W.*, volume three, p. 182; "Mr. Lincoln's Rejoinder," in *Lincoln-Douglas Debates*, ed. Sparks, p. 306; "Mr. Lincoln's Rejoinder," in *Lincoln-Douglas Debates*, ed. Holzer, p. 229; Ford, *A History of Illinois, from its*

Commencement as a State in 1818 to 1847 (New York: Ivison & Phinney, 1854), pp. 305–6, 388; Thomas, "Lincoln-Douglas Debate," p. 10.

22. Joseph G. Cannon, in *Recollected Words*, 77; Ward Hill Lamon, *Recollections of Abraham Lincoln*, ed. D. L. Teillard (1911; Lincoln: University of Nebraska Press, 1994), pp. 23–24; AL, "Fourth Debate with Stephen A. Douglas at Charleston, Illinois" (September 18, 1858), in *C.W.*, volume three, p. 184; "Mr. Lincoln's Rejoinder," in *Lincoln-Douglas Debates*, ed. Sparks, p. 309; "Mr. Lincoln's Rejoinder," in *Lincoln-Douglas Debates*, ed. Holzer, pp. 229–30; "Abraham Lincoln," *Weekly Belleville Advocate*, September 29, 1858.

23. AL, "Fourth Debate with Stephen A. Douglas at Charleston, Illinois" (September 18, 1858), in *C.W.*, volume three, pp. 186; "Mr. Lincoln's Rejoinder," in *Lincoln-Douglas Debates*, ed. Sparks, p. 311; "Mr. Lincoln's Rejoinder," in *Lincoln-Douglas Debates*, ed. Holzer, p. 233; "Lincoln and Douglas at Charleston," *Prairie Beacon News*, September 24, 1858; "Fourth Joint Debate between Lincoln and Douglas," *Rockford Republican*, October 7, 1858; Arnold, *Life of Abraham Lincoln*, p. 148.

24. "Votes on the Cars," *Chicago Daily Journal*, September 24, 1858 (the same poll was published in the *Illinois State Journal* on September 20); Arnold, *Life of Abraham Lincoln*, p. 148; "Abram Lincoln," *Weekly North-Western Gazette*, September 28, 1858; Bissell to Elihu Washburne, September 23, 1858, Elihu B. Washburne Papers, LOC; Richard Carwardine, *Lincoln* (London: Pearson Education, 2003), p. 77; "Serenade to Mr. Lincoln," *Illinois State Journal*, September 27, 1858; David Davis to AL, September 25, 1858, Abraham Lincoln Papers; David Davis to George Davis, September 22, 1858, David Davis Papers, ALPLM.

25. Coleman, "The Lincoln-Douglas Debate at Charleston," p. 49; S. E. Thomas, "Lincoln-Douglas Debate," p. 11.

26. "Prospects of the Campaign," *Chicago Daily Journal*, September 11, 1858.

27. "The Proof Is Here," *Freeport Weekly Bulletin*, October 14, 1858; Villard, "The Electoral Battle in Illinois" and "Outrage in the Republican Camp in Illinois," *New-Yorker Staats-Zeitung*, September 27 and October 13, 1858.

28. "Douglas and the Illinois Central Railroad: Something for the Tax-Payers to Think About," *Central Transcript*, September 3, 1858; Whitney (statement for W. H. Herndon, November, 1866), in *Herndon's Informants*, p. 406; "Response to the Bulletin," *Freeport Weekly Journal*, October 14, 1858; "Letter from Capt. McClellan," *Chicago Daily Press & Tribune*, August 9, 1858; Ethan S. Rafuse, *McClellan's War: The Failure of Moderation in the Struggle for the Union* (Bloomington: Indiana University Press, 2005), pp. 74–80.

29. Johannsen, *Stephen A. Douglas*, p. 310; C. B. Buckner, Chicago, Illinois Central Railroad Company, to SAD, July 30, 1858, Stephen A. Douglas Papers; "The Illinois Central Railroad," *Weekly Madison Press*, September 1, 1858.

30. "Illegal Voting—An Explanation," *Chicago Press & Tribune*, October 29, 1858.

31. Alexander Sympson to John C. Bagby, October 15, 1858, John C. Bagby Papers, Abraham Lincoln Presidential Library & Museum (ALPLM), Springfield, IL; "Mr. Lincoln's Appointments," *Chicago Press & Tribune*, September 1, 1858.

32. David L. Lightner, "Construction Labor on the Illinois Central Railroad," pp. 286–87, 289, 290–91; Mike Matejka, "Beneath the Celtic Cross: Irish Immigrants Who Built the Railroads of Central Illinois," *Labor's Heritage* 11 (Spring–Summer 2001), pp. 6, 7; Thomas J. Craughwell, *Stealing Lincoln's Body* (Cambridge, MA: Harvard University Press, 2007), pp. 58–59; Paul Wallace Gates, *The Illinois Central Railroad and Its Colonization Work* (Cambridge, MA: Harvard University Press, 1934), pp. 189, 199–200.

33. "Political Matters in Lasalle County," *Chicago Press & Tribune*, October 27, 1858; "The Two Despotisms," *Illinois State Journal*, August 30, 1858.

34. "Other Indications of Fraud" and "More Indications of Fraud," *Chicago Press & Tribune*, October 23 and 25, 1858.

35. F. R. Payne to Lyman Trumbull, May 21, 1856, Lyman Trumbull Papers, LOC; Henry Villard, "Douglas and Lincoln" and "Self-Confidence, Independence and Steadiness of German Republicans in Illinois!" *New-Yorker Staats-Zeitung*, January 2 and September 9, 1858; Louis Didies to SAD, August 1858, Stephen A. Douglas Papers; Kenneth J. Winkle, "The Second Party System in Lincoln's Springfield," *Civil War History* 44 (December 1998), p. 283.

36. AL, "To Joshua F. Speed" (August 24, 1855) and "To Norman Judd" (October 20, 1858), in *C.W.*, volume two, p. 323, and volume three, p. 330; Holt, *Rise and Fall of the American Whig Party*, p. 746; R. W. Burton to SAD, August 30, 1858, Stephen A. Douglas Papers; Heckman, *Lincoln vs. Douglas*, p. 60; Joseph Gillespie undated memorandum, Joseph Gillespie Papers, ALPLM.

37. Stephen Hansen and Paul Nygard, "Stephen A. Douglas, the Know-Nothings, and the Democratic Party in Illinois, 1854–1858," *Illinois Historical Journal* 87 (Summer 1994), pp. 110, 116, 121–22, 126, 129; "Who Are Opposed to Foreigners?" *Freeport Weekly Bulletin*, August 26, 1858; "War on the Irish" and "A Genuine Black Republican," *Illinois State Register*, September 2 and September 27, 1858; "Public Address," *Illinois State Journal*, April 29, 1856; "Anti-Slavery Lecture," *Belvidere Standard*, August 17, 1858; H. Ford Douglass to SAD, January 3, 1858, Stephen A. Douglas Papers.

38. "Col. Carpenter on Duty—Democratic Beauties" and "The Happy Family," *Chicago Press & Tribune*, September 29, 1858; Jacob May to Sidney Breese, September 23, 1858, Sidney Breese Papers, Abraham Lincoln Presidential Library & Museum (ALPLM), Springfield, IL; "New Postmaster at Clinton," *Clinton Central Transcript*, June 26, 1858; S. S. Marshall to Charles H. Lanphier, October 9, 1858, Charles H. Lanphier Papers, ALPLM.

39. Dillard C. Donnohue (J. W. Weik interview, February 13, 1887), in *Herndon's Informants*, p. 602; "Oquawka Correspondence," *Chicago Daily Journal*, October 16, 1858; Diary entries for September 24, October 6, and October 9, 1858, in *Diary of Orville Hickman Browning*, volume one, pp. 337–38; "Poor Little Dug!" *Chicago Press & Tribune*, September 28, 1858; Herndon to Parker, October 4, 1858, Herndon-Parker Mss., University of Iowa Library, Iowa City.

40. "The Decency Party," *Freeport Weekly Bulletin*, October 14, 1858; "Republican Demonstrations at Rock Island," *Chicago Press & Tribune*, October 2, 1858; Davidson, *Complete History of Illinois*, pp. 713–14; "Collision Between the

Friends of Douglas and Lincoln," *Jacksonville Sentinel*, October 8, 1858; "The Persecuted Douglasites in Moultrie County," *Chicago Press & Tribune*, October 1, 1858; James G. Wright to AL, October 11, 1858, Abraham Lincoln Papers.

41. Stewart, "The People and the Lincoln-Douglas Campaign of 1858," pp. 290–91; "Progress of the Campaign," *Illinois State Journal*, September 27, 1858.

42. Medill to Elihu Washburne, October 21, 1858, Elihu Washburne Papers (volume 4), LOC; "Serenade to Mr. Lincoln" and "A Grand Demonstration at Jacksonville," *Illinois State Journal*, September 27 and September 28, 1858; "Lincoln at Jacksonville," *Chicago Press & Tribune*, September 30, 1858.

43. Nat Brandt, *The Town That Started the Civil War* (New York: Laurel, 1991), p. 33; *The Memoirs of Charles G. Finney: The Complete Restored Text*, ed. G. M. Rosell and R. A. G. Dupuis (Grand Rapids: Zondervan, 1989), p. 284.

44. Matthew Norman, "From an 'Abolition City' to the Color Line: Galesburg, Knox College, and the Legacy of Antislavery Activism," *Journal of Illinois History* 10 (Spring 2007), 5–6.

45. Gates, *Illinois Central Railroad and Its Colonization Work*, pp. 209–13, 229–30; John S. Winter to AL, September 9, 1858, Abraham Lincoln Papers.

46. Albert Britt, "Lincoln-Douglas Debate at Galesburg Recalled," and "Lincoln at Galesburg," October 5, 1896, The Lincoln Museum, Ft. Wayne, Ind; "Galesburg Debate," *Galesburg Semi-Weekly Democrat*, October 9, 1858.

47. Winter to AL, September 9, 1858, Abraham Lincoln Papers; Joseph F. Evans, "Lincoln at Galesburg," *Journal of the Illinois State Historical Society* 8 (1916), pp. 560–61; "Great Debate between Douglas and Lincoln at Galesburg," *Chicago Press & Tribune*, October 9, 1858; "The Prairie State in Fryer," *Pennsylvania* [Harrisburg] *Daily Telegraph*, September 7, 1858.

48. "Great Debate between Douglas and Lincoln at Galesburg," *Chicago Press & Tribune*, October 9, 1858; Sheahan, *Life of Stephen A. Douglas*, p. 432; Albert Britt, "Lincoln-Douglas Debate at Galesburg Recalled," and "Lincoln at Galesburg," October 5, 1896; Thomas Wakefield Goodspeed, "Lincoln and Douglas: With Some Personal Reminiscences," *Journal of the Illinois State Historical Society* 26 (October 1933), p. 191.

49. Journal entry for October 11, 1858, Samuel Wright's Journal, Knox College Archives; Goodspeed, "Lincoln and Douglas," p. 192; J. H. Dunn, in Rawleigh, *Freeport's Lincoln*, p. 142; SAD, "Fifth Debate with Stephen A. Douglas, at Galesburg, Illinois" (October 7, 1858), in *C.W.*, volume three, pp. 207–8, 209; "Mr. Douglas's Speech," in *Lincoln-Douglas Debates*, ed. Sparks, pp. 335; "Mr. Douglas's Opening Speech," in *Lincoln-Douglas Debates*, ed. Holzer, pp. 238, 240.

50. SAD, "Fifth Debate with Stephen A. Douglas, at Galesburg, Illinois" (October 7, 1858), in *C.W.*, volume three, pp. 211–12, 214, 216; "Mr. Douglas's Speech," in *Lincoln-Douglas Debates*, ed. Sparks, pp. 338, 342; "Mr. Douglas's Opening Speech," in *Lincoln-Douglas Debates*, ed. Holzer, pp. 242, 244, 247.

51. SAD, "Fifth Debate with Stephen A. Douglas, at Galesburg, Illinois" (October 7, 1858), in *C.W.*, volume three, pp. 217, 219; "Mr. Douglas's Speech," in *Lincoln-Douglas Debates*, ed. Sparks, pp. 343, 346; "Mr. Douglas's Opening Speech," in *Lincoln-Douglas Debates*, ed. Holzer, pp. 249, 250.

52. Emma J. Scott, in Rawleigh, *Freeport's Lincoln*, p. 139; Goodspeed, "Lincoln and Douglas," p. 192; Evans, "Lincoln at Galesburg," pp. 560–61; AL, "Fifth Debate with Stephen A. Douglas, at Galesburg, Illinois" (October 7, 1858), in *C.W.*, volume three, pp. 219–20; "Mr. Lincoln's Reply," in *Lincoln-Douglas Debates*, ed. Sparks, p. 346; Mr. Lincoln's Reply," in *Lincoln-Douglas Debates*, ed. Holzer, p. 252.

53. AL, "Fifth Debate with Stephen A. Douglas, at Galesburg, Illinois" (October 7, 1858), in *C.W.*, volume three, pp. 220, 223, 226; "Mr. Lincoln's Reply," in *Lincoln-Douglas Debates*, ed. Sparks, pp. 347, 349, 350, 352–53; "Mr. Lincoln's Reply," p. 346; "Mr. Lincoln's Reply," pp. 253, 254, 257–58; Zarefsky, *Lincoln, Douglas and Slavery*, p. 62.

54. AL, "Fifth Debate with Stephen A. Douglas, at Galesburg, Illinois" (October 7, 1858), in *C.W.*, volume three, pp. 227–30; "Mr. Lincoln's Reply," in *Lincoln-Douglas Debates*, ed. Sparks, p. 354; "Mr. Lincoln's Reply," p. 346; "Mr. Lincoln's Reply," pp. 259–60.

55. AL, "Fifth Debate with Stephen A. Douglas, at Galesburg, Illinois" (October 7, 1858), in *C.W.*, volume three, pp. 230, 231–32, 233; "Mr. Lincoln's Reply," in *Lincoln-Douglas Debates*, ed. Sparks, pp. 357–58, 361; "Mr. Lincoln's Reply," p. 346; "Mr. Lincoln's Reply," pp. 262–63, 265.

56. "October 7, 1858," *Peoria Daily Record*, April 1935; newspaper clipping in the files of The Lincoln Museum, Fort Wayne, IN; Heckman, *Lincoln vs. Douglas*, p. 116; SAD, "Fifth Debate with Stephen A. Douglas, at Galesburg, Illinois" (October 7, 1858), in *C.W.*, volume three, pp. 237–38, 239; "Mr. Douglas's Rejoinder," in *Lincoln-Douglas Debates*, ed. Sparks, pp. 365–66; "Mr. Lincoln's Reply," p. 346; "Mr. Douglas's Rejoinder," in *Lincoln-Douglas Debates*, ed. Holzer, pp. 269, 271.

57. Evans, "Lincoln at Galesburg," p. 563; "Lincoln at Galesburg," clipping; SAD, "Fifth Debate with Stephen A. Douglas, at Galesburg, Illinois" (October 7, 1858), in *C.W.*, volume three, pp. 239–40, 244; "Mr. Douglas's Rejoinder," in *Lincoln-Douglas Debates*, ed. Sparks, pp. 367, 370; "Mr. Douglas's Rejoinder," in *Lincoln-Douglas Debates*, ed. Holzer, pp. 272, 274.

58. "The Galesburgh Debate," *Chicago Daily Journal*, October 8, 1858; AL, "Fourth Debate with Stephen A. Douglas at Charleston, Illinois" (September 18, 1858), "Fifth Debate with Stephen A. Douglas, at Galesburg, Illinois" (October 7, 1858), and "Sixth Debate with Stephen A. Douglas, at Quincy, Illinois" (October 13, 1858), in *C.W.*, volume three, pp. 147, 221, 253; "A Last Appeal," *Illinois State Journal*, November 2, 1858; Emmanuel Hertz, *Abraham Lincoln at the Climax of the Great Lincoln-Douglas Joint debate in Galesburg, Illinois* (n.p., 1928), p. 11.

6: THE SAME TYRANNICAL PRINCIPLE

1. "Progress of the Campaign," *Illinois State Journal*, September 30, 1858; "Public Discussion at Chatham," *Illinois State Journal*, September 29, 1858; "Big Meeting at Richland," *Illinois State Journal*, October 14, 1858; Conkling to Sheldon Root, September 28, 1858, in Alfred Ronald Conkling, *The Life and Letters of*

Roscoe Conkling: Orator, Statesman, Advocate (New York: C. L. Webster, 1889), p. 80; "Letter from Ohio," *Philadelphia Press*, October 22, 1858.

2. "Appointments for the Campaign," *Chicago Daily Journal*, October 22, 1858; "County Meetings," *Illinois State Journal*, September 28, 1858; "The Pennsylvania Election," *Pennsylvania Daily Telegraph*, October 23, 1858; "One Month for Work and Preparation," *Chicago Daily Journal*, October 6, 1858; "The Battle-Cry is Up—Hurrah for Lincoln," *Chicago Daily Journal*, October 27, 1858.

3. Grimes to William Herndon (October 20, 1866), in *Herndon's Informants*, p. 378; "Progress of the Campaign," *Chicago Daily Press & Tribune*, October 15, 1858; AL, "Speech at Monmouth, Illinois" (October 11, 1858), in *C.W.*, volume three, p. 244; Diary entry for October 11, 1858, in *Diary of Orville Hickman Browning*, volume one, p. 339.

4. Nevins, *The Emergence of Lincoln*, pp. 400–401; *Dallas Weekly Herald*, August 14, 1858; "A Political Word or Two," *Houston Weekly Telegraph*, October 6, 1858; "By Midnight Mail," *Philadelphia Press*, October 13, 1858; "Speaker Orr," *Daily Missouri Republican*, August 28, 1858; Wise to John Moore, October 13, 1858, and Vallandigham to John Moore, October 19, 1858, in *Glory to God and the Sucker Democracy*, volume four, pp. 201, 208; Heckman, "Out-of-State Influences and the Lincoln-Douglas Campaign of 1858," pp. 37–39.

5. Diary entry for October 13, 1858, in *Diary of Orville Hickman Browning*, volume one, p. 339; William H. Collins and Cicero F. Perry, *Past and Present of the City of Quincy and Adams County, Illinois* (Chicago: S. J. Clarke, 1905), pp. 163–67; David H. Donald, *We Are Lincoln Men: Abraham Lincoln and His Friends* (New York: Simon & Schuster, 2003), p. 107.

6. Collins and Perry, *Past and Present of the City of Quincy*, pp. 167, 181, 174, 574; *The Census of Adams County, Illinois, for the year 1850 by Township* (Illinois State Genealogical Society, 1972), ALPLM, Springfield, IL.

7. "The Great Debate between Lincoln and Douglas," *Chicago Press & Tribune*, October 15, 1858; Diary entry for October 13, 1858, in *Diary of Orville Hickman Browning*, volume one, p. 339; "Programme," *Quincy Daily Whig and Republican*, October 12, 1858; David F. Wilcox and Lyman McCarl, *Quincy and Adams County: History and Representative Men* (Chicago: Lewis Publishing, 1919), p. 468; Herndon-Weik, Wilson and Davis, eds., *Herndon's Lincoln*, p. 407; Shurz, "Reminiscences of a Long Life," *McClure's Magazine* 28 (January 1907), p. 253.

8. Levi M. Dort reminiscence, Lincoln-Douglas Semi-Centennial Society of Quincy file, October 12, 1908, ALPLM, Springfield, IL; "The Great Discussion of the Canvass," *Quincy Daily Whig & Herald*, October 15, 1858; "Great Debate Between Lincoln and Douglas," *Chicago Press & Tribune*, October 15, 1858; "The Sixth Joint Debate between Lincoln and Douglas," *Chicago Daily Journal*, October 15, 1858.

9. "Sixth Debate with Stephen A. Douglas, at Quincy, Illinois" (October 13, 1858), in *C.W.*, volume three, pp. 246–47, 249, 251, 253; "Mr. Lincoln's Speech," in *Lincoln-Douglas Debates*, ed. Sparks, pp. 396–97, 401; "Mr. Lincoln's Opening Speech," in *Lincoln-Douglas Debates*, ed. Holzer, pp. 282, 284, 287, 289.

10. "Sixth Debate with Stephen A. Douglas, at Quincy, Illinois" (October 13, 1858), in *C.W.*, volume three, pp. 250–51, 254, 255, 256; "Mr. Lincoln's Speech," in *Lincoln-Douglas Debates*, ed. Sparks, pp. 400, 401, 403, 404–5, 406, 407; "Mr. Lincoln's Opening Speech," in *Lincoln-Douglas Debates*, ed. Holzer, pp. 286–87, 289.

11. *Missouri Democrat*, October 15, 1858, in *Lincoln-Douglas Debates*, ed. Sparks, p. 443; Shurz, "Reminiscences of a Long Life," p. 255; White to Jesse W. Weik (December 14, 1913), in Weik, *The Real Lincoln*, ed. Burlingame, p. 382; Charles Hubert Coleman, "The 'Grocery Keeper' and His Customer," *Journal of the Illinois State Historical Society* (Winter 1959), pp. 550–51; "Sixth Debate with Stephen A. Douglas, at Quincy, Illinois" (October 13, 1858), in *C.W.*, volume three, p. 258; "Mr. Douglas's Reply," in *Lincoln-Douglas Debates*, ed. Sparks, pp. 408, 409; "Mr. Douglas's Reply," in *Lincoln-Douglas Debates*, ed. Holzer, pp. 294–95, 297.

12. "Sixth Debate with Stephen A. Douglas, at Quincy, Illinois" (October 13, 1858), in *C.W.*, volume three, pp. 259, 260, 261–62, 263, 264; "Mr. Douglas's Reply," in *Lincoln-Douglas Debates*, ed. Sparks, pp. 410–11, 414, 415; "Mr. Douglas's Reply," in *Lincoln-Douglas Debates*, ed. Holzer, pp. 296–97, 298, 300.

13. "Sixth Debate with Stephen A. Douglas, at Quincy, Illinois" (October 13, 1858), in *C.W.*, volume three, pp. 266, 267; "Mr. Douglas's Reply," in *Lincoln-Douglas Debates*, ed. Sparks, pp. 416–17, 418; "Mr. Douglas's Reply," in *Lincoln-Douglas Debates*, ed. Holzer, pp. 302–3, 304.

14. "Sixth Debate with Stephen A. Douglas, at Quincy, Illinois" (October 13, 1858), in *C.W.*, volume three, pp. 269, 270, 272; "Mr. Douglas's Reply," in *Lincoln-Douglas Debates*, ed. Sparks, pp. 420–21; "Mr. Douglas's Reply," in *Lincoln-Douglas Debates*, ed. Holzer, pp. 306, 307, 310.

15. "Sixth Debate with Stephen A. Douglas, at Quincy, Illinois" (October 13, 1858), in *C.W.*, volume three, pp. 266, 275; "Mr. Douglas's Reply," in *Lincoln-Douglas Debates*, ed. Sparks, pp. 417, 425–26; "Mr. Douglas's Reply," in *Lincoln-Douglas Debates*, ed. Holzer, pp. 303, 310–11.

16. "Mr. Lincoln's Rejoinder," in *Lincoln-Douglas Debates*, ed. Sparks, pp. 428; "Mr. Lincoln's Reply," in *Lincoln-Douglas Debates*, ed. Holzer, pp. 313–14, 316; Seneca Selby reminiscences, Lincoln-Douglas Semi-Centennial Society of Quincy file, October 12, 1908, ALPLM, Springfield, IL; "Sixth Debate with Stephen A. Douglas, at Quincy, Illinois" (October 13, 1858), *C.W.*, volume three, p. 276.

17. "Sixth Debate with Stephen A. Douglas, at Quincy, Illinois" (October 13, 1858), *C.W.*, volume three, p. 279; "Mr. Lincoln's Rejoinder," in *Lincoln-Douglas Debates*, ed. Sparks, p. 431; "Mr. Lincoln's Reply," in *Lincoln-Douglas Debates*, ed. Holzer, p. 316.

18. "Sixth Debate with Stephen A. Douglas, at Quincy, Illinois" (October 13, 1858), in *C.W.*, volume three, pp. 277; "Mr. Lincoln's Rejoinder," in *Lincoln-Douglas Debates*, ed. Sparks, pp. 429–30; "Mr. Lincoln's Reply," in *Lincoln-Douglas Debates*, ed. Holzer, pp. 314–15; Johannsen, *Stephen A. Douglas*, pp. 84–87.

19. "Sixth Debate with Stephen A. Douglas, at Quincy, Illinois" (October 13, 1858),

in *C.W.*, volume three, pp. 280, 282; "Mr. Lincoln's Rejoinder," in *Lincoln-Douglas Debates*, ed. Sparks, pp. 432, 434; "Mr. Lincoln's Reply," in *Lincoln-Douglas Debates*, ed. Holzer, pp. 317–18.

20. "Lincoln and Douglas at Quincy," *Illinois State Journal*, October 18, 1858.

21. Heckman, *Lincoln vs. Douglas*, p. 125; Louis P. Filler, *The Crusade Against Slavery, 1830–1860* (New York: Harper & Row, 1960), pp. 78–81; Sutton, *The Illinois Central Railroad in Peace and War*, p. 40; Henry Mayer, *All on Fire: William Lloyd Garrison and the Abolition of Slavery* (New York: St. Martin's, 1998), pp. 237–38; Evan Carton, *Patriotic Treason: John Brown and the Soul of America* (New York: Free Press, 2006), pp. 82–83.

22. "Democratic Convention," *Weekly Madison Press*, October 6, 1858; Joy Wilson Upton, *Madison County, Illinois, 1860 Census* (Utica, KY: McDonald Publications, 1986), n.p.; "The People's Convention," *Weekly Madison Press*, September 22, 1858; W. T. Norton, *Centennial History of Madison County, Illinois, and Its People, 1812–1912* (Chicago: Lewis Pubs., 1912), p. 236.

23. Upton, *Madison County, Illinois*, n.p.; *Portrait and Biographical Record of Madison County, Illinois* (Chicago: Biographical Publishing, 1894), p. 522; *History of Madison County, Illinois* (Edwardsville, IL: W. R. Brink & Co., 1882), p. 412.

24. Rawleigh, *Freeport's Lincoln*, pp. 187–88; "Seventh and Last Debate between Lincoln and Douglas," *Chicago Press & Tribune*, October 18, 1858; Smith, *When Lincoln Came to Egypt*, p. 101; Daniel M. Grissom reminiscence, in "St. Louis Veteran, 97 Years Old . . . Recalls Meeting of These Two Oratorical Stalwarts," *Washington Post*, February 12, 1928; "Last Joint Debate between Lincoln and Douglas," *Alton Weekly Courier*, October 21, 1858.

25. Beveridge, *Abraham Lincoln*, volume two, p. 690; "They Heard the Final Debate," in Stevens, *A Reporter's Lincoln*, ed. Burlingame, p. 57; "Seventh and Last Debate with Stephen A. Douglas at Alton, Illinois" (October 15, 1858), in *C.W.*, volume three, pp. 283–84; "Senator Douglas's Speech," in *Lincoln-Douglas Debates*, ed. Sparks, p. 451; "Mr. Douglas' Opening Speech," in *Lincoln-Douglas Debates*, ed. Holzer, p. 325; Koerner, *Memoirs*, volume two, pp. 66–67; Rawleigh, *Freeport's Lincoln*, p. 188; Edward Beall, "Recollections of the Lincoln-Douglas Debate, p. 487.

26. "Seventh and Last Debate with Stephen A. Douglas at Alton, Illinois" (October 15, 1858), in *C.W.*, volume three, p. 284; "Senator Douglas's Speech," in *Lincoln-Douglas Debates*, ed. Sparks, pp. 451–52; "Mr. Douglas' Opening Speech," in *Lincoln-Douglas Debates*, ed. Holzer, pp. 325–26.

27. "Seventh and Last Debate with Stephen A. Douglas at Alton, Illinois" (October 15, 1858), in *C.W.*, volume three, pp. 285–86, 287, 289; "Senator Douglas's Speech," in *Lincoln-Douglas Debates*, ed. Sparks, pp. 454–55, 457; "Mr. Douglas' Opening Speech," in *Lincoln-Douglas Debates*, ed. Holzer, pp. 327, 328–29, 330–31.

28. "Seventh and Last Debate with Stephen A. Douglas at Alton, Illinois" (October 15, 1858), in *C.W.*, volume three, p. 293; "Senator Douglas's Speech," in *Lincoln-Douglas Debates*, ed. Sparks, pp. 459, 460, 461; "Mr. Douglas' Opening Speech," in *Lincoln-Douglas Debates*, ed. Holzer, pp. 332–33, 334–35.

29. "Seventh and Last Debate with Stephen A. Douglas at Alton, Illinois" (October 15, 1858), in *C.W.*, volume three, p. 297; "Senator Douglas's Speech," in *Lincoln-Douglas Debates*, ed. Sparks, pp. 463, 464, 466; "Mr. Douglas' Opening Speech," in *Lincoln-Douglas Debates*, ed. Holzer, pp. 337, 338–39. Actually, assuming that a raw-throated Douglas was speaking somewhat more slowly than his normal rate, at about 112 words per minute, he would have finished at exactly sixty minutes.

30. Beall, "Recollections of the Lincoln-Douglas Debate," p. 487.

31. White, *The Lincoln-Douglas Debates*, pp. 7–8; "Seventh and Last Debate with Stephen A. Douglas at Alton, Illinois" (October 15, 1858), in *C.W.*, volume three, p. 298; "Mr. Lincoln's Reply," in *Lincoln-Douglas Debates*, ed. Sparks, pp. 466–67; Koerner, *Memoirs*, volume two, pp. 66–67; "Mr. Lincoln's Reply," in *Lincoln-Douglas Debates*, ed. Holzer, pp. 340–41.

32. "Seventh and Last Debate with Stephen A. Douglas at Alton, Illinois" (October 15, 1858), in *C.W.*, volume three, pp. 302, 303–4; "Mr. Lincoln's Reply," in *Lincoln-Douglas Debates*, ed. Sparks, pp. 470, 471, 472–73; "Mr. Lincoln's Reply," in *Lincoln-Douglas Debates*, ed. Holzer, pp. 344, 347–48.

33. "Seventh and Last Debate with Stephen A. Douglas at Alton, Illinois" (October 15, 1858), in *C.W.*, volume three, pp. 305, 307, 308; "Mr. Lincoln's Reply," in *Lincoln-Douglas Debates*, ed. Sparks, pp. 474, 475, 477; "Mr. Lincoln's Reply," in *Lincoln-Douglas Debates*, ed. Holzer, pp. 349, 350, 352.

34. "Seventh and Last Debate with Stephen A. Douglas at Alton, Illinois" (October 15, 1858), in *C.W.*, volume three, pp. 309, 310, 311, 312; "Mr. Lincoln's Reply," in *Lincoln-Douglas Debates*, ed. Sparks, pp. 478, 479–80, 481; "Mr. Lincoln's Reply," in *Lincoln-Douglas Debates*, ed. Holzer, pp. 353, 354, 356; Rozett, "Racism and Republican Emergence in Illinois," p. 107.

35. "Seventh and Last Debate with Stephen A. Douglas at Alton, Illinois" (October 15, 1858), in *C.W.*, volume three, pp. 312–13, 314, 315; "Mr. Lincoln's Reply," in *Lincoln-Douglas Debates*, ed. Sparks, pp. 482, 483, 484; "Mr. Lincoln's Reply," in *Lincoln-Douglas Debates*, ed. Holzer, pp. 356–57, 358–59.

36. AL, "Speech at Chicago, Illinois" (July 10, 1858) and "Seventh and Last Debate with Stephen A. Douglas at Alton, Illinois" (October 15, 1858), in *C.W.*, volume two, p. 500, and volume three, p. 315; "Mr. Lincoln's Reply," in *Lincoln-Douglas Debates*, ed. Sparks, p. 485; "Mr. Lincoln's Reply," in *Lincoln-Douglas Debates*, ed. Holzer, p. 359.

37. AL, "To Henry L. Pierce and Others" (April 6, 1859) and "Fragment on Free Labor" (September 17, 1859), in *C.W.*, volume three, pp. 375–76, 462.

38. Jonathan Birch interview with Jesse W. Weik (1887), in *Herndon's Informants*, p. 728; "Seventh and Last Debate with Stephen A. Douglas at Alton, Illinois" (October 15, 1858), in *C.W.*, volume three, p. 317; "Mr. Lincoln's Reply," in *Lincoln-Douglas Debates*, ed. Sparks, pp. 486–88; "Mr. Lincoln's Reply," in *Lincoln-Douglas Debates*, ed. Holzer, p. 360.

39. "Seventh and Last Debate with Stephen A. Douglas at Alton, Illinois" (October 15, 1858), in *C.W.*, volume three, pp. 317, 319, 323–24; "Mr. Douglas's Rejoin-

der," in *Lincoln-Douglas Debates*, ed. Sparks, pp. 488–89, 490, 492, 494; "Mr. Douglas' Rejoinder," in *Lincoln-Douglas Debates*, ed. Holzer, pp. 363, 368.

40. "Seventh and Last Debate with Stephen A. Douglas at Alton, Illinois" (October 15, 1858), in *C.W.*, volume three, p. 325; "Mr. Douglas's Rejoinder," in *Lincoln-Douglas Debates*, ed. Sparks, pp. 495–96; "Mr. Douglas' Rejoinder," in *Lincoln-Douglas Debates*, ed. Holzer, pp. 369–70.

41. "They Heard the Final Debate," in Stevens, *A Reporter's Lincoln*, ed. Burlingame, pp. 58–59; J. Rowan Herndon to AL, October 25, 1858, Abraham Lincoln Papers, AL, "To Norman Judd" (October 20, 1858), in *C.W.*, volume three, p. 330; William P. Ramsay to Bagby, October 23, 1858, and Cole Sympson to Bagby, October 23, 1858, John C. Bagby Papers, ALPLM; "More Indications of Fraud," *Chicago Press & Tribune*, October 25, 1858; "Illinois Central Railroad Corruption Scheme," *Peoria Daily Transcript*, October 25, 1858.

42. Stewart, "The People and the Lincoln-Douglas Campaign of 1858," p. 291; Fehrenbacher, *Prelude to Greatness*, p. 102; Alexander Sympson to John C. Bagby, October 26, 1858, in John C. Bagby Papers, ALPLM; Miller, *Lincoln's Virtues*, p. 340; AL, "To James N. Brown" (October 18, 1858), in *C.W.*, volume three, p. 326; Sigelschiffer, *The American Conscience*, pp. 373–75; *Montgomery County Herald* (Hillsboro, IL), October 29, 1858.

43. "The Little Giant Gets Cornered and Loses His Temper," *Chicago Daily Press & Tribune*, October 22, 1858; "Douglas at Gillespie," *Montgomery County Herald*, October 22, 1858; "Douglas' Second 'Trotting Out' at Springfield," *Chicago Daily Press & Tribune*, October 23, 1858; C. R. Parke to Peter D. Brown, October 26, 1858, C. R. Parke Correspondence (SC 1141), ALPLM; "Douglas in Rock Island," *Daily Islander & Argus*, October 30, 1858.

44. AL, "To Richard Yates" (December 10, 1847), "To Usher F. Linder" (March 22, 1848), "To Joshua F. Speed" (February 20, 1849), and "To John J. Crittenden and Thomas Corwin" (September 2, 1850), in *C.W.*, volume one, p. 419, volume two, pp. 28, 93; Paul Findley, *A. Lincoln: The Crucible of Congress* (Jacksonville, IL: Findley Books, 1979), p. 92; Lowell H. Harrison, *Lincoln of Kentucky* (Lexington: University of Kentucky Press, 2000), p. 57; Joshua F. Speed to William Herndon (February 14, 1866), in *Herndon's Informants*, p. 213.

45. W. P. Boyd to Crittenden, July 17, 1858, John Jordan Crittenden Papers (reel 11), LOC; Trumbull to Palmer (June 19, 1858) in "Letters from Lyman Trumbull to John M. Palmer," pp. 38–40; Thomas L. Harris to SAD, July 7, 1858, Stephen A. Douglas Papers; AL to Crittenden (July 7, 1858), in *C.W.*, volume 2, pp. 483–84; Crittenden to AL, July 29, 1858, Abraham Lincoln Papers.

46. J. J. Crittenden to T. Lyle Dickey (August 1, 1858), in Mrs. Chapman Coleman [Anna Mary Crittenden], *The Life of John J. Crittenden* (Philadelphia: J. B. Lippincott, 1871), volume two, pp. 164–65; Harrison, *Lincoln of Kentucky*, p. 107; Johannsen, *Stephen A. Douglas*, pp. 652–53; Beveridge, *Abraham Lincoln*, volume two, p. 639; "Judge Dickey's Speech at Decatur. Letter from John J. Crittenden!" *Illinois State Register*, October 23, 1858; "The Crittenden Letter," *Philadelphia Press*, October 27, 1858; "Douglas' Speech on Saturday Evening," *Peoria Daily Transcript*, October 26, 1858.

47. Sigelschiffer, *The American Conscience*, p. 378; Milton, *Eve of Conflict*, pp. 325–26; Herndon to John J. Crittenden, November 1, 1858, John Jordan Crittenden Papers; "Crittenden on Douglas," *National Era*, November 4, 1858; "A Roorback Spoiled," *Illinois State Journal*, October 26, 1858; "Hon. John J. Crittenden and Douglas," *Chicago Daily Journal*, October 27, 1858; AL, "Speech at Macomb, Illinois" (October 25, 1858) and "To John J. Crittenden" (November 4, 1858), in *C.W.*, volume three, pp. 333, 335; Crittenden to AL, October 27, 1858, Abraham Lincoln Papers; "The Views and Sentiments of Henry Clay and Abe Lincoln," *Illinois State Journal*, October 30, 1858.

48. "Mr. Lincoln at Home," *Illinois State Journal*, November 2, 1858; AL, "Fragment: Last Speech of the Campaign at Springfield, Illinois" (October 30, 1858), in *C.W.*, volume three, p. 334.

49. "Preparing to Colonize," *Chicago Press & Tribune*, September 6, 1858; "How to Vote for Lincoln," *Freeport Weekly Journal*, October 14, 1858.

50. Richard Bensel, "The American Ballot Box: Law, Identity, and the Polling Place in Mid-Nineteenth Century America," *Studies in American Political Development* 17 (Spring 2003), pp. 6–8, 12, 24; William Wayne Smith, "The Whig Party in Maryland, 1826–1856" (unpublished Ph.D. dissertation, University of Maryland, 1967), pp. 47, 85; "The Result in Peoria," *Peoria Daily Transcript*, November 4, 1858; Gienapp, " 'Politics Seem To Enter Into Everything': Political Culture in the North, 1840–1860," in Maizlish and Kushma, eds., *Essays on American Antebellum Politics*, p. 23; Norman Judd to Elihu Washburne, October 22, 1858, in Elihu Washburne Papers (volume 4); LOC; Henry C. Whitney to AL, October 14, 1858, Abraham Lincoln Papers.

51. Diary entry for November 1, 1858, in *Diary of Orville Hickman Browning*, volume one, p. 341; "A Last Appeal," *Illinois State Journal*, November 2, 1858.

EPILOGUE

1. Diary entries for October 25, November 2, and November 9, 1858, in *Diary of Orville Hickman Browning*, volume one, pp. 340–41.

2. Diary entry for November 8, 1864, in *Inside Lincoln's White House: The Complete Civil War Diary of John Hay*, p. 244; "Lincoln's Chances Improving," *Chicago Press & Tribune*, November 4, 1858; "Douglas Sustained!" [Rock Island] *Daily Islander & Argus*, November 5, 1858; "The Late Election," *Chicago Press & Tribune*, November 5, 1858; "Illinois Republicans!" *Quincy Daily Whig & Republican*, November 9, 1858; "The Result," *Jacksonville Sentinel*, November 12, 1858.

3. Illinois Election Returns, State Senate and State House, 1858, Illinois State Archives, 216–19, 220–25 (microfilm roll 30–45); Richard J. Carwardine, *Lincoln* (London: Pearson Education, 2003), p. 85; Stephen Hansen and Paul Nygard, "Stephen A. Douglas, the Know-Nothings, and the Democratic Party in Illinois, 1854–1858," *Illinois Historical Journal* 87 (Summer 1994), p. 129.

4. Stevens, "Life of Stephen Arnold Douglas," p. 588; Arnold, *The History of Abraham Lincoln and the Overthrow of Slavery* (Chicago: Clarke & Co., 1866), p. 134; *Tribune Almanac for 1859*, p. 60; Illinois Election Returns, State Senate and State

House, 1858. It has been argued that although the Republicans gained a majority of the overall vote in 1858, Democrats actually increased their voter turnout from 1856 (see Forest L. Whan, "Stephen A. Douglas," in Crocker, *Analysis of Lincoln and Douglas*, p. 183). The question, however, is *which vote?* If we compare the 1856 state house district votes with the same district votes from 1858, Democrats won a majority of the seats in the state house and increased their turnout from 147,425 to 166,374. But the aggregate numbers of voters also increased by 1858, so that the percentage of Democratic votes rose only from 45.06 percent in 1856 to 45.30 percent in 1858. In the state senate races, Democratic candidates won 71,998 votes (51.17 percent), but because of the senators' staggered terms, the Democratic vote in 1858 in state senate races *fell* to 44,750 (44.82 percent).

5. Heckman, *Lincoln vs. Douglas*, p. 45; Zarefsky, *Lincoln, Douglas and Slavery*, p. 51; *Tribune Almanac for 1858*, pp. 60–61; Bruce Collins, "The Lincoln-Douglas Contest of 1858 and Illinois' Electorate," *Journal of American Studies* 20 (1986), p. 409; Harry E. Pratt, *The Great Debates* (Springfield, Illinois State Historical Society 1956), p. 30; "The Apportionment," *Chicago Press & Tribune*, November 6, 1858; "Illinois Republicans!" *Quincy Daily Whig & Republican*, November 9, 1858; "The Result in Illinois," *Chicago Daily Journal*, November 5, 1858. Based on an argument by Frank Stevens (in his "Life of Stephen Arnold Douglas," p. 589), Don Fehrenbacher (in *Prelude to Greatness*, pp. 118–19) disputes the significance of the apportionment, arguing (a) that even a direct popular vote would have won Lincoln only 44 seats in the state house (instead of the 46 he needed), so malapportionment was not the decisive factor, and (b) that Lyman Trumbull ran twice as a Republican in Illinois and won election to the Senate, despite the apportionment. But Fehrenbacher was using the state office vote, not the actual vote in the districts (which, when taken as a "popular vote," gave Lincoln a much larger margin), and Lyman Trumbull did not run as Republican in 1855—in fact, he did not run at all until he was inserted as a compromise, anti-Nebraska Democrat as the state legislature was conducting its senatorial vote.

6. "Illinois Legislature," *Central Transcript*, January 7, 1859; "Douglas Elected," *Carlinville Free Democrat*, January 6, 1859; Lanphier to SAD, January 4, 1859, and SAD to Lanphier, January 6, 1859, in *Glory to God and the Sucker Democracy*, volume four, p. 296.

7. Miller to AL, November 15, 1858, Abraham Lincoln Papers; David Davis to George Davis, November 7, 1858, David Davis Papers, ALPLM; Rives to Hatch, November 5, 1858, in Ozias M. Hatch Papers, ALPLM; Grimshaw to AL, November 11, 1858, Abraham Lincoln Papers; Fehrenbacher, *Prelude to Greatness*, pp. 114–15; "Illinois Election," *Montgomery County Herald* [Hillsboro], November 12, 1858; Francis Fisher Browne, *The Every-Day Life of Abraham Lincoln* (1886; Lincoln: University of Nebraska Press, 1995), p. 276; David Davis to AL, November 7, 1858, Abraham Lincoln Papers; "The Late Election," *Chicago Press & Tribune*, November 5, 1858; Herndon to Theodore Parker, November 8, 1858, in Joseph Fort Newton, *Lincoln and Herndon* (Cedar Rapids,

IA: Torch Press, 1910), pp. 231–32, 234–35; "The Administration Routed!" *Carlinville Free Democrat*, November 4, 1858; Unknown to Washburne, November 22, 1858, Elihu Washburne Papers (volume 4), LOC.

8. John Tillson to Ozias M. Hatch, November 15, 1858, Ozias M. Hatch Papers, ALPLM; Fehrenbacher, *Chicago Giant*, pp. 161, 176–77; Fehrenbacher, *Lincoln in Text and Context*, pp. 39–40; David Davis to AL, January 1, 1859, Abraham Lincoln Papers; Pratt, *The Great Debates*, p. 30; Thomas C. Sharpe to John C. Bagby, November 4, 1858, John C. Bagby Papers, ALPLM.

9. L. H. Walters to Hatch, November 3, 1858, and Alex B. Morean to Hatch, November 8, 1858, Ozias M. Hatch Papers, ALPLM; Robert Bruce Warden, *A Voter's Version of the Life and Character of Stephen Arnold Douglas* (Cincinnati: Follett & Foster, 1860), p. 106.

10. "Vote of the Principal Cities and Towns of Illinois," *Chicago Press & Tribune*, November 5, 1858; Coleman, "The Lincoln-Douglas Debate at Charleston," p. 49.

11. "From Illinois," *National Era*, November 18, 1858.

12. Heckman, *Lincoln vs. Douglas*, p. 45; Pratt, *The Great Debates of 1858*, pp. 5–9; Johannsen, *Stephen A. Douglas*, p. 658; Wells, *Stephen Douglas: The Last Years*, p. 137; Zarefsky, *Lincoln, Douglas and Slavery*, p. 51; Warden, *Voter's Version of the Life and Character of Stephen Arnold Douglas*, p. 104; "Senator Douglas Speech at Chicago," *Montgomery County Herald* [Hillsboro], November 26, 1858; Ray to Elihu Washburne, November 22, 1858, Elihu Washburne Papers, (volume 4), LOC; Martineau, "The World's Interest in the West," in *Writings on Slavery and the American Civil War*, ed. Deborah Anna Logan (DeKalb: Northern Illinois University Press, 2002), p. 138.

13. Nevins, *The Emergence of Lincoln: Douglas, Buchanan, and Party Chaos, 1857–1859*, pp. 401–3; *Tribune Almanac for 1859*, pp. 18, 55; Hansen, *Making of the Third Party System*, p. 120; Wells, *Stephen Douglas: The Last Years*, pp. 130–31; Heckman, *Lincoln vs. Douglas*, p. 139; "Harris Elected by 2000 maj'y!" *Montgomery County Herald*, November 5, 1858.

14. Sheahan to Charles H. Lanphier, December 31, 1858, Charles H. Lanphier Papers, ALPLM; "Douglas and the Senate," *Cairo Weekly Times & Delta*, November 17, 1858; Sheahan, *Life of Stephen A. Douglas*, p. 434; Heckman, *Lincoln vs. Douglas*, p. 138; Angle, *"Here I Have Lived,"* p. 235; Davidson, *Complete History of Illinois*, p. 715; AL, "To Lyman Trumbull" (December 20, 1858), in *C.W.*, volume three, p. 345.

15. SAD, "To William A. Seaver" (July 17, 1859) and "To Harper Brothers" (September 24, 1859), in *Letters of Stephen A. Douglas*, p. 449; Johannsen, *Stephen A. Douglas*, pp. 682–84; Wells, *Stephen Douglas: The Last Years*, pp. 151–52; SAD, "The Dividing Line Between Federal and Local Authority: Popular Sovereignty in the Territories," *Harper's New Monthly Magazine* 19 (September 1859), pp. 531–32.

16. Davis, "Speech at Vicksburg" (November 27, 1858), in *The Papers of Jefferson Davis*, ed. L. L. Crist and M. S. Dix (Baton Rouge: Louisiana State University Press, 1989), volume six, pp. 228–29; William C. Davis, *Jefferson Davis: The Man*

and His Hour, A Biography (New York: HarperCollins, 1991), p. 268; Davis, "Relations of the States" (February 2, 1860), Congressional Globe, 36th Congress, 1st session, p. 658; Diary entry for January 22, 1858 and January 8, 1859, in The Diary of Edmund Ruffin, ed. W. K. Scarborough (Baton Rouge, LA: Louisiana State University Press, 1972), volume one, pp. 149, 263; Stevens, "Life of Stephen A. Douglas," p. 599; Wells, Stephen Douglas: The Last Years, pp. 156–58; Brown, "Legislative, etc., Appropriation Bill" (February 23, 1859), Congressional Globe, 35th Congress, 2nd session, p. 1242; O. M. Dickerson, "Stephen A. Douglas and the Split in the Democratic Party," Proceedings of the Mississippi Valley Historical Association for the Year 1913–1914 (Cedar Rapids, IA: Torch Press, 1914), volume seven, pp. 205–6.

17. Benjamin, Defence of the National Democracy against the Attack of Judge Douglas (Washington: L. Towers, 1860), pp. 13–14; Robert W. Johannsen, "Stephen A. Douglas, Harper's Magazine, and Popular Sovereignty," in The Frontier, the Union, and Stephen A. Douglas (Chicago: University of Illinois Press, 1980), p. 135; Ernest James Wesson, "Debates of Lincoln and Douglas: A Bibliographical Discussion," Papers of the Bibliographical Society of America 40 (2nd quarter, 1946), pp. 101–2.

18. Zarefsky, Lincoln, Douglas and Slavery, p. 51; AL, "To Samuel C. Davis and Company" (November 17, 1858) and "To Norman B. Judd" (November 15, 1858), in C.W., volume three, pp. 336, 338; Diary entry for November 8, 1864, in Inside Lincoln's White House, 244; Michael Burlingame, The Inner World of Abraham Lincoln (Urbana, IL: 1994), 248; Rankin, Intimate Character Sketches of Abraham Lincoln (Philadelphia: J.B. Lippincott, 1924), pp. 117–18.

19. Wendt, Chicago Tribune, p. 104; Norman B. Judd to AL, November 15, 1858, Abraham Lincoln Papers; Recollected Words, p. 5; Hannah interview with William H. Herndon (1865–66), in Herndon's Informants, p. 459; AL, "To Norman B. Judd" (November 16, 1858) and "To Newton Bateman" (November 20, 1858), in C.W., volume three, pp. 337, 341; Beveridge, Abraham Lincoln, volume two, p. 696.

20. Rankin, Intimate Character Sketches, p. 118; AL, "To Samuel C. Davis and Company (November 30, 1858) and "To William McNeely" (November 30, 1858), in C.W., volume three, p. 342; AL, "To Norman B. Judd" (November 16, 1858), "To Henry Asbury" (November 19, 1858), and "To Charles H. Ray" (November 20, 1858), in C.W., volume three, pp. 337, 339, 341; Joshua Wolf Shenk, Lincoln's Melancholy: How Depression Challenged a President and Fueled His Greatness (Boston: Houghton Mifflin, 2005), p. 150; Charles S. Zane, "Lincoln As I Knew Him," Journal of the Illinois State Historical Society 14 (1921–22), pp. 79–80.

21. Zane, in Recollected Words, p. 510; AL, "To Anson G. Henry" (November 19, 1858), in C.W., volume three, p. 339; AL, "To Norman B. Judd" (November 15, 1858), in C.W., volume three, p. 336–37; "To Lyman Trumbull" (December 11, 1858), in C.W. Supplement (Westport, CT: Greenwood Press, 1974), p. 34. The new state legislature actually did write a new apportionment bill when it met in January 1859, but with a Democratic majority in both houses, not very much changed, and Republican governor William Bissell vetoed it, the veto

message being ghostwritten by Lincoln (AL, "Veto Message of Apportionment Bill Written for Governor William H. Bissell" [February 22, 1859], in *C.W.*, volume three, p. 364).

22. Hanna to AL, November 5, 1858, Dewey to AL, October 30, 1858, and Bromwell to AL, November 5, 1858, Abraham Lincoln Papers; Rives to Hatch, November 5, 1858, and J. M. Lucas to Hatch, November 20, 1858, in Ozias M. Hatch Papers, ALPLM; Baringer, "Campaign Technique in Illinois in 1860," pp. 206–7; White to AL, November 5, 1858, and Lundy to AL, November 22, 1858, Abraham Lincoln Papers; Beveridge, *Abraham Lincoln*, volume two, p. 700; Fehrenbacher, *Prelude to Greatness*, pp. 143, 145–46; Heckman, *Lincoln vs. Douglas*, p. 141; Tarbell, *Life of Abraham Lincoln*, volume one, p. 322.

23. Villard, in *Recollected Words*, ed. Fehrenbacher, p. 455; AL, "To Thomas J. Pickett" (April 16, 1859) and "Speech at Columbus, Ohio" in *C.W.*, volume three, pp. 377, 426; Donald, *Lincoln*, 233–34.

24. AL, "To Charles H. Ray" (November 20, 1858), "To Henry C. Whitney" (November 30, 1858 and December 25, 1858), "To W. H. Wells" (January 8, 1859), and "To William A. Ross" (March 26, 1859), in *C.W.*, volume three, pp. 341, 343, 346, 347, 372–73; Heckman, *Lincoln vs. Douglas*, p. 143.

25. AL, "To George M. Parsons and Others" (December 19, 1859), in *C.W.*, volume three, p. 510; Lionel Crocker, *An Analysis of Lincoln and Douglas as Public Speakers and Debaters* (Springfield: C. C. Thomas, 1968), x; "Introduction," in *Lincoln-Douglas Debates*, ed. Holzer, pp. 29–32; Wesson, "Debates of Lincoln and Douglas," pp. 93–94, 99–100; Heckman, *Lincoln vs. Douglas*, p. 144.

26. SAD, "To Follett and Foster Company" (June 9, 1860), in *Letters of Stephen A. Douglas*, pp. 489–90; Douglas L. Wilson, "The Lincoln-Douglas Debates: An Unfinished Text," in *Lincoln Before Washington: New Perspectives on the Illinois Years* (Chicago: University of Illinois Press, 1997), pp. 161–62; E. Earle Sparks, "Editions of the Debates," *Lincoln-Douglas Debates*, pp. 591–95.

27. SAD, "Last Speech in Congress—Final Plea for the Union" (January 3, 1861), in Carr, *Stephen A. Douglas*, pp. 130, 135, 136–38; 262, 269, 270–71; SAD, "Statement" (April 14, 1861), in *Letters of Stephen A. Douglas*, pp. 509–10; Jacob Dolson Cox, "War Preparations in the North," in *Battles and Leaders of the Civil War*, ed. R. U. Johnson and C. C. Buel (New York: Thomas Yoseloff, 1956), volume one, p. 87; Diary entry for April 26, 1861, in *Diary of Orville Hickman Browning*, volume one, p. 466; "Douglas's Farewell Words," in Edward McPherson, ed., *The Political History of the United States of America, During the Great Rebellion* (Washington: Philip & Solomons, 1864), p. 392; Johannsen, *Stephen A. Douglas*, p. 843. On the hat incident at the inauguration, see Carr, *Stephen A. Douglas*, p. 123, Holland, *Life of Abraham Lincoln*, p. 278, Arnold, *History of Abraham Lincoln*, p. 174, and Merrill D. Peterson, *Lincoln in American Memory* (New York: Oxford University Press, 1994), p. 90.

28. SAD, "To Virgil Hickox" (May 10, 1861), in *Letters of Stephen A. Douglas*, pp. 512–13; Johannsen, *Stephen A. Douglas*, pp. 871–72; Stevens, "Life of Stephen Arnold Douglas," p. 633.

29. Clark E. Carr, "Speech at Quincy," Lincoln-Douglas Semi-Centennial Society of

Quincy file, October 13, 1903, ALPLM; B. C. Corrigan, *Tailgating the Lincoln-Douglas Debates* (Jacksonville, IL: ADS Press, 1984), pp. 28–29, 39, 49, 51, 59; *Freeport's Lincoln*, pp. 41, 42–43; W. T. Norton, *Centennial History of Madison County, Illinois, and Its People, 1812–1912* (Chicago: Lewis Pubs., 1912), pp. 237–38.

30. Whitney to Herndon, in *The Hidden Lincoln*, p. 10; Whitney to Herndon, July 18, 1887, in *Herndon's Informants*, p. 622; Robert H. Browne, *Abraham Lincoln and the Men of His Time* (Cincinnati: Jennings & Pye, 1901), volume one, p. 257; Burlingame, *Inner World*, p. 248; Heckman, *Lincoln vs. Douglas*, p. 180; Church, *History of the Republican Party in Illinois, 1854–1912*, p. 71; Medill and Greeley, in *Lincoln-Douglas Debates*, ed. Sparks, p. 583.

31. Cullom, *Fifty Years of Public Service*, 34; Judd to Lincoln, November 15, 1858, and Ray to Lincoln, July 27, 1858, Abraham Lincoln Papers; Baringer, "Campaign Technique in Illinois in 1860," pp. 206–7; Morehead, in *Recollected Words*, p. 334.

32. Parker, in Newton, *Lincoln and Herndon*, p. 239; Eliot, "Choruses from the Rock," in *The Complete Poems and Plays, 1909–1950* (New York: Harcourt, Brace, 1952), p. 106; Sandel, *Democracy's Discontents*, pp. 7–8; Berman, *Terror and Liberalism*, pp. 164–65; Francis Fukuyama, "The End of History?" *The National Interest* 16 (Summer 1989) pp. 3–18, and *The End of History and the Last Man* (New York: Free Press, 1992), p. 4.

33. Berman, *Terror and Liberalism*, pp. 169–71; David F. Ericson, *The Shaping of American Liberalism: The Debates over Ratification, Nullification, and Slavery* (Chicago: University of Chicago Press, 1993), p. 173.

34. *Speech of the Hon. Robert T. Lincoln made at the Celebration of the Thirty-eighth Anniversary of the Lincoln-Douglas Debate, Galesburg, Ill., October 7, 1858* (Hancock, NY: Herald Print, 1921), p. 2.

ACKNOWLEDGMENTS

T HERE IS NO vanity which quite matches the vanity of authorship, something which is only compounded when the author is an academic, where a very specialized and bizarre form of vanity is the coin of the realm. That can sometimes make the offer of acknowledgments a grudging business, since it involves the frequently reluctant concession that no author is an island, and much of any author's work is dependent on others. It is in no grudging spirit, however, that I cheerfully admit to an open-armed dependence on the goodwill and assistance of a vast number of people in this project, many of them drawn from that most remarkable fraternity of what my fellow Philadelphian George Boker called "Lincoln-lovers." This admission begins with Michael Burlingame, the preeminent Lincolnite of our times, whose generosity in sharing materials on Lincoln and Douglas (including the manuscript of two chapters of his forthcoming multivolume biography of Lincoln) breaks all the known rules on sharing. Rodney Davis and Douglas Wilson (Lincoln Studies Center at Knox College) were hardly less reckless in their generosity, not only for providing a transcript of William D. Pierce's "Reminiscence of Lincoln" from the Library of Congress but also for an advance version (on CD-ROM) of their own forthcoming edition of the texts of the Lincoln-Douglas debates.

Libraries and archives are the meat and drink of a scholar's life, and I have feasted well at a variety of such tables, starting with the Abraham Lincoln Presidential Library and Museum in Springfield, IL, where Thomas Schwartz provided his lively and genteel entrée to the priceless collections now enjoying sparkling new housing. Bryon Andreason and Kathryn Harris, also of the ALPLM, happily unearthed resources on topics as arcane as Hezekiah Ford Douglass and opened doors to the state vote ledgers in the Illinois secretary of state's office in Springfield. Beyond Springfield, John Sellers, as always, made work in the manuscripts of the Library of Congress easy and delightful; Sara Gabbard and the research staff of the Lincoln Museum in Fort Wayne, Indiana, turned up dozens of personal accounts of the debates which had been collected by the museum's founding director; Jane Westerfeld provided items from the Ida Tarbell Papers at Allegheny College's Pelletier Library; and the staff of the Musselman Library at Gettysburg College handled my seemingly endless requests for interlibrary loans of microfilm of obscure Illinois newspapers.

On a more personal note, Richard and Ann Hart, and Jim and Anne Patton, all of Springfield, welcomed this weary academic traveler as almost a member of their families. Richard, in his capacity as president of the Abraham Lincoln Association, arranged for a preliminary talk on this project at the Elijah Iles House in Springfield in July 2006; the Pattons crowned their hospitality with a five-volume set of the photocopied papers of Jim's ancestor Charles Lanphier, the editor of Springfield's *Illinois State Register,* one of the two major supports of Stephen Douglas's political life. Charles Doty of the Lincoln Group of the District of Columbia arranged for me to present yet another portion of this research to the group in May 2007. Matthew Norman came to Gettysburg College from the Lincoln Studies Center at Knox College for a two-year stint as a visiting professor and provided a living link to sources and materials in Illinois history. George Buss, of the Lincoln-

Douglas Society of Freeport, Illinois, has been a constant encourager of this project. A word of editorial thanks goes deservedly to the *Journal of American History* for permission to use portions of my "Houses Divided: Lincoln, Douglas, and the Political Landscape of Illinois in 1858," which appeared in the September 2007 issue. Virginia Tinkler-Moor (of the Special Microfilm Office at the Van Pelt Library at the University of Pennsylvania) rescued me from certain disaster at the levers of the Van Pelt's microfilm readers. She will not remember me, but she may remember the mess I nearly made.

Speaking of messes I created, I have nothing but praise for the way Cathy Bain, my administrative assistant in the Civil War Era Studies program at Gettysburg College, so often stepped in to cover day-to-day matters while I was busy gathering wool over Lincoln and Douglas; and for my three student workers, Leah Briner, Brandon Roos, and Brian M. Jordan, who transcribed my collection of raw research material onto four-by-six cards, my favorite medium of record.

Finally, there are the thanks—as if that single syllable suffices to bear the weight I'm about to put on it—I must, by commingled desire and necessity, give to my loving, patient, and radiant wife, Debra, and our three children (all now grown and flown), Jerusha Mast (and her husband Jon), Alexandra Fanucci (and her husband, Jonah), and Lance-Corporal Jonathan E. Guelzo, 2nd Battalion, 3rd Marine Regiment. They are, beyond any debate—including Lincoln and Douglas—my treasure.

INDEX

abolitionist movement, 16, 32–33, 141, 174, 218, 226, 246, 303
  Galesburg as center of, 218–19
  Harpers Ferry raid and, 298
  Lovejoy killing and, 254–55
  Republican Party and, 36, 38–39, 42, 43, 47, 71, 72–73, 83, 107, 109–10, 117–20, 125, 153, 156, 157–58, 173, 178–80, 186–87, 195, 196–97, 222–23, 243, 247–48, 261, 272, 273
Abraham Lincoln: 1809–1858 (Beveridge), xxi
Abraham Lincoln Association, xxiii
Abzug, Bella, 310
Adams, John Quincy, 101
Addams, Jane, 146
Addams, John H., 145–46, 278
"Almanac Trial," 110
Alton, Ill., 93, 237, 254–71, 290–91
  audience for debate at, 257–58
  commemoration of debate in, 309
  Douglas's closing speech at, 267–68
  Douglas's opening speech at, 258–61
  Hope's interruption of Douglas at, 258–59
  joint arrangements committee of, 255–57
  key points of debate at, 269

  Lincoln's speech at, 261–67
  as major rail center, 254
Alton & Terre Haute Railroad, 254, 257
Altschuler, Glenn, xvii–xviii
American Almanac, The, xix
American Conscience (Sigelschiffer), xxii, xxiii
American Debater (McElligott), 94
American Orator (Cooke), 95, 103
American (Know-Nothing) Party, 38, 39, 42, 45, 168, 187, 208, 209, 210, 211, 274
"American System," 26
"Appeal of the Independent Democrats, An" (Chase), 16
Aristotle, xx
Arkansas territory, 2
Armstrong, Duff, 110
Arnold, Isaac, xiii, 61, 163, 285
Arthur, James, 240
Associated Press, xxii, 97, 115
Auchampaugh, Philip G., 65
Augustana Lutheran Synod, 218
Aurora resolutions, 132, 153, 178–79, 227, 230, 243, 247, 252, 262

Bagby, John C., 165, 207, 270
Baker, Edward, 98

Baker, Samuel, 289
Bane, Moses, 243
Bank of the United States, Second, 5, 252
Barnum, P. T., xvii
Barrett, John T., 219
Barrett, Joseph, xiii
Basler, Roy P., xxiii
Bateman, Newton, 56, 285
Bayle, Pierre, 183
Beatty, George, xvii, 96, 100, 101
Beckwith, Hiram, 127
Bell, John, 299
Benjamin, Judah P., 298
Bennett, James Gordon, 97
Benson, Lee, xvii
Benton, Thomas Hart, xii, 7
Berman, Paul, xxi, 312–13
Bernard, John, 241
Bertschanger, Otto, 241
Beveridge, Albert, xvi, xxi
Bigler, William, 142
Billings, Henry W., 255, 256, 258, 267
Bingham, Caleb, 95
Bingham, Kinsley, 16
Binmore, Henry, 117, 133, 134, 232, 306
Birkbeck, Morris, 218
Bissell, William, 42, 202
Blair, Frank P., 138, 215
Blair, Hugh, 103
Blair, Montgomery, 138
Blanchard, Jonathan, 93–94
Blumin, Stuart, xvii–xviii
Bond, George, 240, 241
border ruffians, 20
Boston Ledger, 166
Botts, John Minor, 16
Bowles, Samuel, 48, 62
Breckinridge, John C., 137, 298, 307
Breese, Sidney, 50, 136, 162, 174, 197, 212, 295
Brewster, John K., 147
Bright, Hiram, 133
Bright, Jesse, 10
Broderick, David, 25
Bromwell, Henry, 188, 302
Brooks, Austin S., 66, 242
Bross, William "Deacon," 98
Brown, Albert Gallatin, 297
Brown, Jacob, 137

Brown, James, 199
Brown, James N., 271
Brown, John, 141, 255, 298
Browning, Orville Hickman, 6, 143, 184, 213–14, 308
    Illinois Republican convention and, 42, 56
    Lincoln campaign and, 73–74, 138
    Lincoln-Douglas debates and, 93, 238, 240, 242
Bryant, William Cullen, 116
Buchanan, James, 58, 60, 71, 124, 126, 142, 157, 158, 247, 298, 310
    Douglas's conflict with, 10, 22–25, 47, 48, 60, 64–70, 75, 91, 134–38, 184, 219, 222, 239, 260, 262, 268, 274, 293, 294–98
    election of 1856 and, 42, 44, 45, 46, 146, 170, 187, 240
Buckmaster, Samuel, 257
Burleigh, Joseph Bartlett, 94
Burns, Robert, 28
Bushnell, Nehemiah, 74

California, 3, 256
Campbell, Alexander, 94, 95
Campbell, Thompson, 177, 179
Carlin, Thomas, 6, 252
Carlin, William H., 251
Carlinville Free Democrat, 272
Carpenter, Richard B., 66, 68, 135–36, 185
Carr, Clark, 162
Carroll, Anna Ella, 17
Cass, Lewis, 13
Chambers, Robert, 185
Chapman, Augustus H., 188, 202
Chapman, Harriet, 188, 202
Charleston, Ill., xxv, xxvi, 187–204, 290–91
    debate museum in, 309
    Douglas's speech at, 194–98
    key points of debate at, 203
    Lincoln and Douglas's arrival in, 188–90
    Lincoln's closing speech at, 198–201
    Lincoln's opening speech at, 191–94
    straw polls on winner of debate in, 201–2

Chase, Salmon P., 16, 124, 138
    Lincoln's campaigning for, 304
Chicago, Burlington & Quincy Railroad,
    218, 219
Chicago & Alton Railroad, 257
Chicago and Rock Island Railroad, 113,
    114
Chicago Democratic Union, 98
Chicago Journal, 55, 79, 105, 111, 115,
    133–34, 141, 144, 151–52, 187, 213,
    232, 236–37, 276, 286, 289
Chicago Press & Tribune, xxii, xxiii, 98
Chicago Times, xxii, xxiii, 49, 67, 78, 79,
    91, 97, 106, 109, 117, 127, 128,
    133–34, 149, 204, 211, 275, 305,
    307, 310
Chicago Tribune, 44, 49, 62, 68, 79, 90, 115,
    116–17, 128, 130, 132, 133–34, 160,
    172, 202, 205, 209, 240, 282, 292, 300,
    303, 305, 306, 310
Chicago Union, 98
Church, Frederick Edwin, 185
Cincinnati Weekly Gazette, 53
civil rights, 83–84, 122, 165, 168, 191–93,
    206
civil rights movement, xvii
Civil War, U.S., xiii, xxv, xxvi, 254, 307–9,
    314
Clay, Henry, 12, 13–14, 72, 94, 187, 237,
    273
    Compromise of 1850 and, 13–14, 196,
        249, 261
    Douglas as successor to, 14, 109, 189,
        237, 244, 245, 261
    Lincoln as successor to, 190
    as Lincoln's model, 25–28, 29, 104, 124,
        125, 190, 252, 263–64, 276
    Missouri Compromise and, 12, 262
    raccoon as campaign emblem of, 242
    reason over passion as aim of, 104
    slavery issue and, 263–64
Cold War, xvi, xvii
Colfax, Schuyler, 48, 138
Collected Works of Abraham Lincoln, xxiii
*Collections of the Illinois State Historical
    Library*, xxiii
Columbian Orator (Bingham), 95, 103
comets, xii, 183–85, 232
communism, xx, 312

Compromise of 1850, 13–14, 15, 17, 21,
    196, 198, 247, 249, 261
Congregational Herald, 204
Congress, U.S.:
    Compromise of 1850 and, 13–14, 15
    Kansas-Nebraska Act and, 1–2, 14–19,
        298
    Kansas statehood issue and, 19–25
    Lecompton constitution and, 22–25
    slavery issue and, 10–19, 20, 21, 22–25,
        259, 297–98
    see also House of Representatives, U.S.;
        Senate, U.S.
Conkling, James Cook, 59, 216, 217
Conkling, Roscoe, 236
Conley, Philip, 65
Constitution, U.S., 53, 201, 268
    admission of states and, 2
    Jackson and, 252
    popular sovereignty and, 34, 221
    slavery issue and, 33–34, 80–81, 245,
        249, 250–51, 260, 261, 264, 267, 297
Constitutional Union Party, 299, 307
convention system, 51–53
Cook, Burton C., 36, 37, 39, 113
Cook, Isaac, 65, 66, 67, 68, 98, 138, 294,
    295
Cooke, Increase, 95
Cooper Institute, xxvi, xxvii
Corcoran, W. W., 7
Corwin, Norman, 309
Corwin, Thomas, 138, 216
cotton gin, 250
Craddock, William, 190
Crisis of the House Divided (Jaffa), xix–xx,
    xxii, xxiii
Crittenden, John J., 273–76, 277, 288
Crunelle, Leonard, 309
C-Span, 310
Cullom, Shelby, 9, 30, 57, 236, 311
Cunningham, Joseph, 130
Cuomo, Mario, 310
Curtis, George William, 99

Daley, Richard J., 310
Dallas Weekly Herald, 239
Danites, 135, 137, 162, 167, 170, 172, 174,
    177, 185–86, 211–15, 251, 256, 257,
    258, 285, 294–96

Davidson, James, 66, 219, 220

Davis, David, 42, 72–73, 103, 113, 127, 143, 202, 287, 288

Davis, Jacob, 135, 251

Davis, James, 108

Davis, Jefferson, 261, 297

Davis, John A., 146–47, 278

Dayton, William L., 43

debating, history of, 93–95

Declaration of Independence (1776), 32, 81–84, 112, 120, 122, 125, 165, 168, 197, 220, 223, 225, 229, 252, 261, 263

Delahay, Mark, 69

democracy, xix–xxi, xxvi–xxvii, 311–14

Democracy's Discontent (Sandel), xxi

Democratic Party, 117

   Clay's "National Republican" faction in, 27

   Danite faction in, 135, 137, 162, 167, 170, 172, 174, 177, 185–86, 211–15, 251, 256, 257, 258, 285, 294–96

   Douglas and, 9–10, 67–68, 196, 294–96

   election of 1858 and, 282–87, 294–96

   election of 1860 and, 286–87, 294, 298–99, 307

   immigrant voters and, 208, 211–12, 287–88

   oratorical style and, 103–4

   race baiting as tactic of, 271, 288

   slavery issue and, 10–12, 245, 255, 271

   Southern split from, 296–99, 307

Democratic Review, 53, 64

Depression, Great, xvi

Dewey, Chester P., 116, 149, 164, 166, 173, 302

Dewey, John, xxvii

Dickey, Theophilus Lyle, 109–10, 273, 274, 275, 288, 295

District of Columbia, slavery in, 118, 119, 150–51, 173–74, 245

"Dividing Line Between Federal and Local Authority" (Douglas), xxvii, 296–97

Donald, David, 162

Donati, Giovanni, 183

Donati's comet, xii, 183–85, 232

Dougherty, John, 68, 69, 170, 174, 181–82, 197

Douglas, Adele Cutts, 8, 75, 106, 147, 170, 171, 188, 202, 272, 296, 308

Douglas, Martha Martin, 8

Douglas, Robert D., 309

Douglas, Stephen A.:

   background of, 3–4

   biographies of, xvi, xxvii

   book publication of debates and, 306–7

   Buchanan's conflict with, 10, 22–25, 47, 48, 60, 64–70, 75, 91, 134–38, 184, 219, 222, 239, 260, 262, 268, 274, 293, 294–98

   campaign (1858) of, *see* election of 1858

   Civil War and, 307–9

   as Clay's successor, 14, 109, 189, 237, 244, 245, 261

   Compromise of 1850 and, 13–14, 15, 247, 249, 261

   as congressman, 6

   Crittenden's endorsement of, 273–76, 277, 288

   death of, xxvii, 308

   Dred Scott decision and, 85, 121, 124, 129, 152, 162, 178, 223–24, 230, 244, 247–48, 251, 297–98, 310

   drinking of, 167, 170, 213, 214, 246, 248, 267

   Eastern Republican establishment and, 288

   education of, 3, 4

   election of 1860 and, 286–87, 294, 298–99, 307

   Havana trip of, 296

   homes and properties of, 8, 136, 294

   Illinois Central Railroad and, 7–8, 106, 164, 204–9, 213, 270, 287

   as Illinois legislator and justice, 5–6, 252

   illnesses of, 17, 214, 221, 308

   internal improvements doctrine and, 7, 8

   Kansas-Nebraska Act and, 1–2, 14–19, 35, 47, 124, 126, 158, 176, 193–94, 200, 212, 221, 262, 298

   Kansas statehood issue and, 19–25, 154, 260

   Lanphier's victory telegram to, 287

   as lawyer, 4–5

   Lecompton constitution and, 23–25, 47, 51, 60, 107, 121, 124, 138, 142, 154, 158, 163, 222, 260, 274, 275, 294, 298

   Lincoln compared with, 25

Lincoln's dislike of, 29–30, 304
Lincoln's inauguration and, 307
"Little Giant" nickname of, 9
marriages of, 8
Ohio campaigning of, 304, 307
oratorical skills of, 5, 101–2, 104
physical appearance of, 7, 8
political philosophy of, xx, xxi,
    xxvi–xxvii, 6–7
popular sovereignty and, xxi, xxvii,
    13–14, 15, 18, 19, 20–22, 24, 35,
    57–58, 80, 85, 107, 108, 121, 125–26,
    129, 142, 152, 153, 155, 160, 162, 164,
    175, 176, 180, 193–94, 200, 201,
    220–21, 244, 249–50, 251, 260, 261,
    266, 286, 296–98, 304, 310–11
race baiting of, xxv, 77–78, 84, 85, 107,
    113, 120–21, 125, 155–57, 167,
    186–87, 192, 193, 219
real estate speculation of, 7–8
rehabilitation of reputation of, 309–10
Republican Party and, 47–62, 138–39,
    158, 163–64, 216, 288
senatorial election of, 6
senatorial reelection of, 301
slavery issue and, 10–12, 13–14, 61,
    63, 120–21, 201, 222, 223–24, 225,
    226–27, 245, 246, 249, 260, 266,
    296–98, 313
Southern Democrats' repudiation of,
    296–99
Toombs amendment and, 141–43,
    193–96, 200, 220, 272
victory speech of, 293
see also election of 1858; Lincoln-
    Douglas debates (1858)
Douglass, Frederick, 33, 49, 155–56, 186,
    247
Douglass, Hezekiah Ford, 212
Dred Scott v. Sanford, 20–22, 46–47, 58, 60,
    61, 77, 80, 85, 121, 123–24, 129,
    144–45, 151, 152, 153, 155, 162, 164,
    178, 197, 210, 223–24, 227–28, 230,
    244, 247–48, 251, 252, 259, 262–63,
    267, 297–98, 310
Dubois, Jesse, 42, 49, 50, 59, 69

Edwards, Cyrus, 258
Edwards, Jonathan, 217

Edwards, Ninian, 30
election of 1858, xii, xix, xxi–xxvi, 70
aftermath of, 299–314
balloting and vote count in, 277–79,
    281–86, 289, 290–91
Douglas as technical loser of, 285–87
fifth phase of Lincoln-Douglas
    campaigns in, map of, 238
first phase of Lincoln-Douglas
    campaigns in, map of, 105
fourth phase of Lincoln-Douglas
    campaigns in, map of, 216
Illinois Central Railroad and, 7–8, 106,
    164, 204–9, 213, 270, 287
Illinois reapportionment as factor in,
    44–45, 286, 287, 302
immigrant vote in, 206–12, 240, 241,
    270, 287–88, 289
Lincoln's recognition of his loss in, 282,
    299
in Northeast states, 294
popular vote in, 285, 287
press coverage of, 236–37, 239,
    271–72, 275, 276, 277, 279, 282,
    295, 303
reasons for Lincoln's loss in, 285–90
ruffianism and violence in, 214
second phase of Lincoln-Douglas
    campaigns in, map of, 146
third phase of Lincoln-Douglas
    campaigns in, map of, 169
voter fraud feared by Republicans in,
    206–9, 210, 270, 278, 289
weather as factor in, 213–14, 220–21,
    237, 238, 241, 276, 278–79, 281–82,
    289, 306
Whig Belt vote as critical in, 71–72,
    109–10, 182, 187, 206, 209, 236–37,
    275–76, 282–84, 286, 288, 289
see also Lincoln-Douglas debates
    (1858)
elections:
of 1838, 29
of 1840, 29, 241
of 1846, 30
of 1848, 31
of 1850, 177
of 1852, 10, 170, 210, 254
of 1854, 19, 35–38, 254

elections (*cont.*)
    of 1856, 10, 22, 42–46, 70–72, 73, 113,
        146–47, 170, 172, 187, 211, 236, 240,
        254, 282, 283, 284
    of 1860, xiii, xxvi, 160–62, 286–87, 294,
        298–99, 303, 307, 311, 314
Electoral College, 287
Eliot, T. S., 311–12
Elwell, George, 219
Emerson, John, 20–21
Emerson, Ralph Waldo, 104
English, William, 25
Epler, Cyrus, 282
Everett, Edward, 18
Ewing, Thomas, 17

Fehrenbacher, Don E., xix
Fell, Jesse, 54, 94, 303
Ficklin, Orlando Bell, 189, 199–200, 202
Field, Alexander, 252
Fillmore, Millard, 39, 42, 44, 45, 70–71, 72,
    146, 187, 211, 236, 254, 273, 283, 284
Finney, Charles Grandison, 218
Flack, Ferdinand, 241
Florville, Varveel, 218
Follett, Oran, 306
Follett & Foster, 305–7, 310
Fondey, William B., 68, 285
Foote, Henry Stuart, 16
Ford, Thomas, 199
Formisano, Ronald, xvii
Forney, John W., 66, 75, 114, 116
Forth, Robert, 213
Fort Madison, 218
Fort Sumter, S.C., 307, 308
Fouke, Philip B., 136
Francis, Simeon, 98
Freeport, Ill., xix, 93, 145–65, 253, 290–91
    commemorations of debate in, 309–10
    description of, 145–47
    Douglas's arrival in, 147
    Douglas's speech at, 154–57, 298
    key points of debate in, 159
    Lincoln's arrival in, 147–48
    Lincoln's closing address at, 157–58
    Lincoln's "Freeport Question" at, xix,
        xxiv, 160–64, 165, 292, 296, 297–98
    Lincoln's opening address at, 149–53
Freeport Weekly Bulletin, 84–85

Freeport Weekly Journal, 277
freethinkers, 218
Frémont, John Charles, 42, 44, 45, 46, 47,
    70–71, 72, 113, 146, 170, 172, 187,
    211, 236, 283, 284
French, Augustus C., 68, 285
Fry, Jacob, 65
Fugitive Slave Law (1850), 118, 119, 149,
    151, 157, 173

Gabel, Martin, 309
Gale, George Washington, 217, 218
Galena & Chicago Union Railroad, 147
Galesburg, Ill., xiv, 93, 215, 217–33,
        290–91
    as antislavery center, 218–19
    commemoration of debate in, 309, 314
    Douglas's arrival in, 219
    Douglas's closing speech at, 229–31
    Douglas's opening speech at, 221–24
    history of, 217–18
    key points of debate at, 231
    Knox College in, 218, 221
    Lincoln's arrival in, 219–20
    Lincoln's speech in, 224–29
    weather conditions at, 220–21
Galloway, Samuel, 216
Garrison, William Lloyd, xii, 33, 223, 247
German immigrants, 207, 209–12, 241
Gillespie, Joseph, 35, 37, 100, 168, 184,
        197, 211
Glover, Joseph, 116, 126
Gold Rush, 256
Great Awakening, xi, 217
Great Awakening, Second, 217–18
Great Western Railroad, 110, 216, 241
Greeley, Horace, xi, 47, 48, 51, 55, 62, 78,
        90, 310
    Associated Press and, 97
    election of 1858 vote count by, 285
    Lincoln's betrayal by, 288
Grimes, James W., 237
Grimshaw, Jackson, 54, 74, 166, 235–36,
        254
Gross, William L., 99–100

Halley, Edmund, 183
Halstead, Murat, 298
Hanna, William H., 300–301, 303

Harding, Warren G., xvi
Harpers Ferry, Va. raid (1859), 298
Harper's New Monthly Magazine, xxvii, 296–97
Harris, Thomas L., 19, 38, 132, 133, 170, 227, 230, 254, 274, 303
Harrison, William Henry, 29, 241, 273
Hatch, Ozias Mather, 42, 49, 143, 165, 287, 288–89, 301, 303
Hawthorne, Nathaniel, 183–84
Hayne, Robert, 59, 93
Heckman, Richard, xxi
Henderson, Thomas, 219
Hennepin Tribune, 303
Henry, Anson G., 302
Herndon, Elliott, 134–35
Herndon, Rowan, 270
Herndon, William Henry, 75, 100–101, 163, 184, 185, 288, 311
  Douglas and, 49, 50
  Lincoln campaign and, 70, 100–101, 102, 161, 211–12, 275
  Lincoln's "House Divided" speech and, 59–60
  as Lincoln's law partner, 31, 36, 49, 299
Hesing, Anton, 210
Historical and Critical Dictionary (Bayle), 183
History of Abraham Lincoln and the Overthrow of Slavery, The (Arnold), xiii, 163, 285
History of Illinois (Ford), 199
Hitler, Adolf, 312
Hitt, Elisha, 282
Hitt, Robert R., 116–17, 130, 131–32, 133, 172, 201, 232, 309
Hoe, Robert, 96
Holbrook, Josiah, 99
Holmes, Oliver Wendell, xxvii
Holzer, Harold, 310
Hope, Thomas M., 257
House of Representatives, U.S.:
  election of 1858 and, 294
  "gag rule" in, 11
  Kansas-Nebraska Act and, 18, 19
  Lecompton constitution and, 25
  Lincoln in, 30, 31–32, 120, 123, 273, 300
  slavery issue and, 11, 25

Toombs amendment and, 142
  see also Congress, U.S.; Senate, U.S.
Houston Telegraph, 239
Hurlbut, Stephen, 141

Illinois:
  congressional districts in, 92
  Democratic convention (1858) in, 67–68, 69–70, 295
  Douglas's political position in, 9–10, 294–96
  political regions of, 70–72
  reapportionment in, 44–45, 286, 287, 302
  recession in, xi
  Republican state platform in, 118, 122, 131–33, 153, 158, 177, 178–79, 227, 243, 247, 252
  revival movement in, 217–18
  Whig belt in, 71–72, 104, 106–10, 143, 164, 167–68, 182, 187, 206, 209, 215, 236–37, 240, 249, 254, 282–84, 286, 288, 289, 307
Illinois and Michigan Canal, 113
Illinois Central Railroad, xi, 7–8, 9, 106, 136, 147, 148, 164, 171, 182, 188, 204–9, 213, 254, 270, 287
Illinois Political Canvass of 1858, The, 305
Illinois State Journal, 93, 98, 128, 134, 202, 208, 279
Illinois State Register, 55, 62, 64, 65, 67, 78, 84, 86, 97, 106, 113, 127, 132, 184, 211–12, 275
immigrants, immigration, 206–12, 240, 241, 270, 287–88, 289
Impending Crisis, The (Potter), xviii
Indiana, 44, 236, 239, 304
internal improvements, 7, 8, 26, 28, 30
Iowa, 44, 237
Iowa territory, 2
Irish immigrants, 206–12, 240, 270, 287–88, 289
Islam, 312

Jackson, Andrew, 4–5, 23, 25, 26, 28, 104, 189, 252, 261
Jacksonian Democrats, 5, 26–28
Jacksonville Sentinel, 45, 133
Jaffa, Harry V., xix–xx, xxii, xxiii, 155

James, William, xxvii

Janson, Eric, 218

Jayne, William, 236

Jefferson, Thomas, 2, 4, 83, 225

Jeffersonians, 4

Job, Zephaniah, 256–57

Jones, George W., 50

Jonesboro, Ill., 93, 167, 171–82, 290–91
    Douglas's opening speech at, 173–75
    key points of debate in, 181
    Lincoln's closing speech at, 178–81
    Lincoln's speech at, 175–78

Juarez, Benito, xii

Judd, Norman Buel, 43, 98
    as anti-Douglas Democrat, 36, 37
    Douglas convention and, 69, 70
    Illinois apportionment issue and, 302
    Lincoln campaign and, 72, 75, 87, 140,
        143–45, 165, 210, 270, 275, 278, 289,
        290, 299–300, 301
    Lincoln-Douglas debates and, 90–91,
        93, 111, 161, 163
    Lincoln senatorial nomination and, 53,
        54–55, 56, 61, 63
    Republican Party joined by, 39
    Trumbull and, 140

Kansas, 118, 121
    civil war in, 46, 58, 61
    statehood issue for, 19–25, 141–43, 154,
        177, 180, 193–94, 247, 260

Kansas-Nebraska Act (1854), 1–2, 14–19,
        21, 32–36, 47, 51, 57, 60–61, 94, 98,
        124, 126, 153, 158, 176, 193–94, 200,
        212, 221, 226, 262, 298

Kellogg, Hiram H., 218

Kellogg, William Pitt, 49, 57, 69, 92, 101,
        219

Kennedy, John F., xiv–xv

Kinear, A. R., 213

Knox, James, 229

Knox, John, 218

Knox College, 218, 221

Koerner, Gustave, 72, 163, 210, 259, 262

Kune, Julian, 33

Lamon, Ward Hill, 30, 52

Lanphier, Charles, 65, 67, 78, 84, 93, 106,
        113, 132, 137, 212, 213, 227, 230, 287

Lecompton constitution, 19–25, 47, 51, 58,
        60, 107, 121, 124, 138, 142, 154, 158,
        163, 198, 222, 260, 274, 275, 294, 298

Lectures on Elocution (Scott), 103

Lectures on Rhetoric (Blair), 103

Legislative Guide (Burleigh), 94

Leib, Charles, 68, 69–70

liberal democracy, xx–xxi, xxvi–xxvii,
        311–14

Life of Abraham Lincoln (Tarbell), xiii

Lincoln, Abraham:
    abolitionist movement and, 32–33,
        38–39, 73, 107, 109–10, 153, 157–58,
        178–80, 195, 196–97, 243, 247–48,
        272, 303
    ambition of, 31, 37–38, 305
    appearance of, 99
    background of, 25, 26–27, 28
    biographies of, xiii, xxi, xxiii, 160, 163
    book publication of debates and, 292,
        305–7, 310
    campaign (1858) of, see election of 1858
    Chase's support for, 304
    Clay as model for, 25–28, 29, 104, 124,
        125, 190, 252, 263–64, 276
    Collected Works of, xxiii
    as congressman, 30, 31–32, 120, 123,
        273, 300
    Cooper Institute address of, xxvi, xxvii
    Crittenden and, 273–74, 276, 277, 288
    Douglas compared with, 25
    Douglas convention and, 69–70
    Douglas disliked by, 29–30, 304
    Dred Scott decision and, 46–47, 58, 60,
        61, 77, 80, 85–86, 123–24, 151, 164,
        175, 197, 198, 227–28, 230, 244,
        247–48, 251, 252, 259, 262–63, 267
    election of 1860 and, xxvi, 160–62,
        286–87, 299, 303–4, 307, 311, 314
    equality of blacks issue and, 82–85,
        191–93, 195, 197, 223, 225, 229, 244,
        247, 259, 261–62, 288
    finances of, 300–301
    first senatorial bid of, 35–38, 42, 43, 139,
        141, 300
    "House Divided" speech of, xxiv, 57–64,
        80, 85–86, 107, 108, 109, 110–11, 129,
        174, 198, 247, 259, 264, 288, 308, 309
    as Illinois legislator, 25, 28, 30

inauguration of, 307
Kansas-Nebraska Act and, 32–36, 57,
    60–61, 94, 124, 176, 226
Know-Nothings and, 210
as lawyer, 28–29, 30, 31, 32, 110,
    187–88, 299, 301
Lovejoy killing and, 255
Mexican War and, 31, 120, 123, 156,
    199–200, 230, 247, 273
natural rights and, 81–84, 122–23, 165,
    191, 198, 201, 206, 210, 225–26, 263,
    266, 304
Ohio campaigning of, 304, 305
as orator, 99–101, 102–3
political philosophy of, xx–xxi,
    xxvi–xxvii
popular sovereignty and, 34, 35–36,
    46–47, 57–58, 80, 85, 123–24, 125,
    129, 151, 165, 198, 226–28, 244, 251,
    264–65, 267, 304
religious views of, 184
Republican Party and, 38–39, 43, 70–74,
    87, 90–91, 138, 288–89, 303–4, 305–6
Republican senatorial nomination and,
    50–61
scientific interests of, 184–85
Shields's duel with, 35, 258
slavery issue and, xxi, xxv, 32–39,
    57–61, 77, 80–84, 123–24, 129–30,
    142, 149–51, 165, 168, 175–76,
    193–94, 198–99, 201, 225–29,
    244–45, 246, 249, 260, 262–67,
    276–77, 310, 313
Trumbull as rival of, 43, 139–43, 310
Whig Party and, 28–30, 35, 38, 123,
    165, 168, 179, 301–2
see also election of 1858; elections;
    Lincoln-Douglas debates (1858)
Lincoln, Douglas and Slavery (Zarefsky),
    xxii
Lincoln, Mary Todd, 29, 30, 98, 257
Lincoln, Robert Todd, 257, 309, 314
Lincoln, Sarah Bush, 188
Lincoln, Thomas, 26–27, 188
Lincoln-Douglas debates (1858):
    first, xvii, 93, 113–30, 260, 290–91
    second, xix, 93, 145–65, 253, 290–91,
        292, 296, 297–98, 309–10
    third, 93, 167, 171–82, 290–91

fourth, xxv, xxvi, 187–204, 290–91,
    309
fifth, xiv, 93, 215, 217–33, 290–91, 314
sixth, xiv, 93, 237, 239, 240–54, 265,
    290–91, 307, 309
seventh, 93, 237, 254–71, 290–91, 309
arrangements for, 91–93
book publication of, 292, 305–7, 310
candidates' differing perceptions of,
    292
commemorations and reenactments of,
    309–10
debates inspired by, 235–36
as defining moment for liberal
    democracy, xix–xxi, xxvi–xxvii,
    311–14
as entertainment, xv, xvii–xviii
first suggestions for, 89–90
format of, 93
Freeport Question in, xix, xxiv, 160–64,
    165, 292, 296, 297–98
as literary oratory, xv
Nixon-Kennedy debates compared with,
    xiv–xv
press coverage of, 116–17, 127–28, 130,
    131–34, 149, 151–52, 166, 202, 204,
    220, 232–33, 236, 237, 246, 256, 292,
    293, 302, 305, 306–7, 310
schedule of, 93
Trumbull and, 127, 131, 178, 193–96,
    256, 270
Lincoln-Douglas Society, 309
Lincoln vs. Douglas (Heckman), xxi
Linder, Usher F., 38, 137–38, 171, 181,
    186, 188, 190, 202–3
Logan, John A., 166, 171
Logan, Mary Cunningham, 103
Logan, Stephen A., 28–29, 30
Lombard University, 219
London Spectator, 293
Longfellow, Henry Wadsworth, 99
Louisiana Purchase (1803), 2, 16, 21
Lovejoy, Elijah, 72, 254–55
Lovejoy, Owen, 43, 72–73, 92, 109, 113,
    114, 127, 138, 155, 158–59, 180, 223,
    247, 254, 255
Lundy, Benjamin, 303
lyceums, 99
Lyell, Charles, 185

McClellan, George B., 205, 206
McConnell, George Murray, 7
McCormick, Richard, xvii
McElligott, James, 94
McMichael, Morton, 48
McPike, Henry Guest, 256, 258, 309
Magoffin, Beriah, 137
Maine, election of 1858 and, 294
manufacturing, 26, 28
Marble Faun, The (Hawthorne), 184
Marshall, Samuel S., 170, 171, 213
Marshall, Thomas, 187, 188, 190, 202,
    203
Marshall, Thomas R., 154
Martineau, Harriet, 293
Massachusetts, 294
Massey, Raymond, 309
Mather, Cotton, 139
Mathers, John, 86
Matteson, Joel, 38
Medill, Joseph, 45, 49, 55, 62, 98, 128, 134,
    139, 144, 145, 160, 161, 162, 209, 216,
    286, 288, 310
Meerse, David, 65
Merrick, Richard, 206
Mexican War, xii, 109, 210
    Lincoln and, 31, 120, 123, 156, 199–200,
        230, 247, 273
    Polk and, 2–3, 31, 123, 200
Mexico, xii, 12–13
Michigan, 36, 44, 71
    election of 1858 and, 294
    revival movement in, 217
Michigan Central Railroad, xi
Miles, Rufus, 137
Military Road, 218
Miller, Anson, xii, 287
Miller, James, 56, 285
Minnesota territory, 2
Mississippi Valley Historical Association,
    xvi
Missouri, 20
Missouri Compromise (1820), 12, 14–16,
    18, 21, 34, 36, 46, 262, 277
Missouri Daily Republican, 275
Missouri Democrat, 246
Missouri territory, 2, 12
Mitchell, James, 148
Montgomery County Herald, 271–72, 295

Moore, John, 67, 137, 295
Morehead, Charles, 311
Morgan, Edwin D., 294
Mormons, 218
Morris, Buckner, 211
Morris, Isaac, 135, 235–36

Napier steam press, 96
National Era, 16, 102, 139
nativism, 208, 209, 210, 289
    see also American (Know-Nothing) Party
natural rights, 81–84, 122–23, 165, 191,
    198, 201, 206, 210, 225–26, 263, 266,
    304
Nebraska, 118, 260
Neely, Mark, xviii
neoconservatism, xx
Nevins, Allan, xix
New England:
    as Republican stronghold, 294
    revival movement and, 217–18
New Jersey, election of 1858 and, 294
newspapers, political coverage by, xii,
    xxii–xxiii, 84, 86–87, 89–90, 95–99,
    105, 106, 109–10, 113, 114, 115,
    116–17, 127–28, 131–34, 141,
    149, 151–52, 166, 202, 204, 209,
    211–12, 220, 232–33, 236–37, 239,
    246, 256, 271–72, 275, 276, 277,
    279, 282, 288, 292–93, 295, 302, 303,
    305–7, 310
    see also election of 1858; Lincoln-
        Douglas Debates (1858); *specific*
        newspapers
New York, 44
    election of 1858 and, 294
    revival movement and, 217
New-Yorker Staats-Zeitung, xii, 90, 106, 204
New York Evening Post, 116, 149, 302
New York Herald, 97
New York Sun, 86–87
New York Times, 86
New-York Tribune, xi, 47, 51, 78, 90, 288
Niagara (Church), 185
Nichols, Roy F., 65
Nicolay, John G., 161
Nixon, Richard M., xiv–xv
Northern Cross Railroad, 218
Northwest Ordinance (1787), 264

Oberlin, Ohio, 217–18
Oberlin Collegiate Institute, 218
Oglesby, Richard, 138, 190, 203
Ohio, 36, 44, 71
    Douglas's stumping in, 304, 307
    election of 1858 and, 236, 239
    Lincoln's campaigning for Chase in, 304,
        305
    Republican Party in, 304, 305–6
    revival movement in, 217–18
Ohio State Journal, 306
Olmsted, Charles, 94
Oregon territory, 2, 31
Organization of American Historians,
    xvi
Orr, James L., xii, 239, 261
Ottawa, Ill., 93, 113–30, 260, 290–91,
    292
    description of, 113–14, 115
    Douglas's closing address at, 125–26
    Douglas's opening address at, 117–21
    key points of debate in, 128–29
    Lincoln's speech at, 122–25
    press coverage of debate in, 166
Owen, Robert, 94

Paine, Thomas, 28
Palmer, John M., 36, 42, 138, 139, 187
Parker, Theodore, 311
Parsons, George, 305
Pearson, John, 66
Peck, Ebenezer, 50, 144–45, 161
Pennsylvania, 44, 236, 239
People's Party, 168, 197
Peoria and Oquawka Railroad, 217, 218,
    229
Perry, Matthew, xii
Philadelphia North American, 48
Philadelphia Press, 114, 116, 128, 236
Phillips, David L., 172, 175
Phillips, Wendell, 172, 247, 255
Pickett, Thomas J., 304
Pierce, Franklin, 10, 16, 18, 58, 60, 126,
    142, 157, 170
Pietists, 218
Pinkham, N., 242
Pinkney, William, 93
Pitman, Benn, 116
Pitman, Isaac, 116

Plato, xx
Political Debates Between Hon. Abraham
    Lincoln and Hon. Stephen A. Douglas in
    the Celebrated Campaign of 1858, in
    Illinois (Follett & Foster) 306–7
Polk, James K., 2–3, 31
popular sovereignty:
    Douglas and, xxi, xxvii, 13–14, 15, 18,
        19, 20–22, 24, 35, 57–58, 80, 85, 107,
        108, 121, 125–26, 129, 142, 152, 153,
        155, 160, 162, 164, 175, 176, 180,
        193–94, 200, 201, 220–21, 244,
        249–50, 251, 260, 261, 266, 286,
        296–98, 304, 310–11
    Lincoln and, 34, 35–36, 46–47, 57–58,
        80, 85, 123–24, 125, 129, 151, 165,
        198, 226–28, 244, 251, 264–65, 267,
        304
Postman, Neil, xv
Pottawatomie massacre (1856), 141
Potter, David, xviii
Powell, John G., 135
Powell, Lazarus, 137
Prentiss, Benjamin M., 254
Principles of Geology (Lyell), 185
printing presses, 96
Progressive movement, xvi
Protestants, Protestantism, 28, 208
Provincial Freeman, 212
Purcell, Jean Baptiste, 94
Putnam, Azro, 114
Putnam's Magazine, 99

Quincy, Ill., xiv, 93, 237, 239, 240–54, 265,
    290, 307
    commemorations of debate in, 309
    as Douglas political base, 240
    Douglas's arrival in, 241
    Douglas's speech at, 245–50
    election of 1856 and, 240
    key points in debate at, 253
    Lincoln-Douglas monument in, 309
    Lincoln's arrival in, 241
    Lincoln's closing speech at, 250–53
    Lincoln's opening speech at, 243–45
    platform accident at, 242–43
    Republican arrangements committee in,
        240–41
    welcoming parades in, 241–42

Quincy Herald, 66
Quitman, John A., xii

railroads, xi, 136, 147, 171, 188, 216, 217,
    218
  Alton as major terminal for, 254
  Douglas and, 7–8, 9, 106, 164, 204–9,
    213, 270, 287
  election of 1858 and, 106, 164, 182,
    204–9, 213, 270, 276, 287
  Lincoln and, 110, 182, 276
  Lincoln-Douglas debates and, xxii, 113,
    114, 148, 219, 229, 241, 257
  straw polls taken on, 201–2
  see also specific company names
Randall, James Garfield, xvi, xix
Raney, George, 98
Rankin, Henry, 299, 301
Ray, Charles H., 44, 49, 50, 68, 69, 98, 128,
    134, 144, 209, 275, 293, 301, 304, 305
Republican Party:
  abolitionist movement and, 36, 38–39,
    42, 43, 47, 71, 72–73, 83, 107, 109–10,
    117–20, 125, 153, 156, 157–58, 173,
    178–80, 186–87, 195, 196–97,
    222–23, 226, 243, 247–48, 261, 272,
    273
  anti-Nebraska Democrats in, 42
  Douglas and, 47–62, 138–39, 158,
    163–64, 216, 288
  East Coast faction of, 47, 288
  formation of, 36
  Illinois state platform of, 118, 122,
    131–33, 153, 158, 177, 178–79, 227,
    243, 247, 252
  immigrant voters and, 209–11, 287–88,
    289
  Know-Nothings and, 209, 210, 274
  Lincoln and, 38–39, 43, 70–74, 87,
    90–91, 138, 288–89, 303–4, 305–6
  in Northeast states, 294
  in Ohio, 304, 305–6
  oratorical style and, 103–4
  Whigs and, 41–44, 45, 70–74, 103–4,
    179, 275–76, 288–89
  see also election of 1858; elections
revival movement, 217–18
Reynolds, John, 68, 135, 174, 185–86, 197
Rice, Joel, 241

Rice, Nathan L., 94
Richardson, William A., 19, 73–74, 138,
    240
Richmond South, xii
Rivals, The (Corwin), 309
Rives, George, 287, 303
Robertson, George, 59
Robinson, James, 190
Rock Island Weekly Register, 304
Rogers, Timothy, 241
Roman Catholics, Roman Catholicism, 94,
    208, 211, 240
Roosevelt, Theodore, 309
Rude Republic (Altschuler and Blumin),
    xvii–xviii
Ruffin, Edmund, 297
Rutherford, Friend S., 256, 258

St. Louis, Alton & Chicago Railroad,
    254
St. Louis, Mo., 254
St. Louis Observer, 255
Sandel, Michael, xxi, xxvi, 313
Sanderson, Henry, 220
Sargent, Epes, 103
Schurz, Carl, xi, 101–2, 138, 139,
    210
  Lincoln-Douglas debates and, 241, 246,
    254
Scott, Dred, 20–21, 138, 310
Scott, William, 103
Scott, Winfield, 170, 210
Scripps, John Locke, 63, 98, 132, 160,
    163
secession, 307
Selby, Seneca, 250–51
Senate, U.S.:
  Chase amendment and, 153, 193
  Civil War and, 307
  Committee on Territories of, 142, 196,
    297
  Crittenden's career in, 273
  Douglas in, 1–2, 6–7, 8, 18, 23–25, 140,
    141–43, 153, 195–96, 297–98
  election of 1858 and, 294
  election of members of, 53
  Kansas-Nebraska Act and, 1–2, 18,
    298
  Lecompton constitution and, 23–25

Toombs amendment and, 141–43,
193–96
see also Congress, U.S.; House of
Representatives, U.S.
September 11, 2001 terrorist attacks, xxi,
312
Seventeenth Amendment (1913), 33
Seward, William Henry, 16, 47, 48–49,
138, 288, 303
Sheahan, James W., 49, 67, 78, 91, 106, 133,
134, 296
Sheridan, James B., 116–17, 133, 306
Shields, James, 19, 35, 37–38, 258
Shiloh, Battle of (1862), 254
Sigelschiffer, Saul, xxi–xxii
slavery, xxi, xxv, 10–19, 26
Clay's condemnation of, 263–64
Congress and, 10–19, 20, 21, 22–25,
259, 297–98
Constitution and, 33–34, 80–81, 245,
249, 250–51, 260, 261, 264, 267, 297
Democratic Party and, 10–12, 245,
296–99
in District of Columbia, 118, 119,
150–51, 173–74, 245
Douglas and, 10–12, 13–14, 61, 63,
120–21, 201, 222, 223–24, 225,
226–27, 245, 246, 249, 260, 266,
296–98, 313
Dred Scott decision and, 20–22, 46–47,
58, 60, 61, 77, 80, 85–86, 121, 123–24,
129, 144–45, 155, 162, 164, 174–75,
178, 197, 198, 210, 223–24, 227–28,
230, 244, 247–48, 251, 252, 259,
262–63, 267, 297–98, 310
Jefferson and, 225
Lecompton constitution and territorial
extension of, 19–25, 47, 51, 58, 60,
107, 121, 124, 138, 142, 154, 158, 163,
198, 222, 260, 274, 275, 294, 298
Lincoln and, xxi, xxv, 32–39, 57–61, 77,
80–84, 123–24, 129–30, 142, 149–51,
165, 168, 175–76, 193–94, 198–99,
201, 225–29, 244–45, 246, 249, 260,
262–67, 276–77, 310, 313
Supreme Court and, 20–22, 46, 60, 61,
77, 144–45, 152, 153, 155, 174–75,
178, 198, 227–28, 230, 244, 245,
247–48, 252, 259, 268

"unfriendly legislation" strategy for
blocking of, 22, 46, 61, 80, 145, 162,
178, 224, 227–28, 244, 248–49, 251,
267, 296–97
slave trade, 123, 174, 250, 264
Slidell, John, 10, 136, 294
Smith, Caleb Blood, 138, 216
Smith, James, 94
Smith, Persifor, xii
Soviet Union, 312
Sparks, Edwin Earle, xxiii
Springfield Republican, 48, 62
Stalin, Joseph, 312
Standard Speaker (Sargent), 103
Stephen A. Douglas Association, 310
Stowe, Harriet Beecher, 101
Strauss, Leo, xix–xx
straw polls, 201–2
Stuart, Charles, 25
Stuart, John Todd, 6, 29, 30, 108, 185
Sturtevant, Julian, 167
Sumner, Charles, 16
Supreme Court, U.S., slavery issue and,
20–22, 46, 60, 61, 77, 144–45, 152,
153, 155, 174–75, 178, 198, 227–28,
230, 244, 245, 247–48, 252, 259, 268
Swarthout, Alonzo, 241
Sweat, Peter, 66
Swedish immigrants, 207
Swett, Leonard, 43, 63, 73, 288

Taft, Lorado, 309
Taney, Roger Brooke, 20–21, 60, 61, 80,
121, 126, 142, 157, 198, 223, 227–28,
247, 248, 263
Tarbell, Ida, xiii, 115, 130
Taylor, Nathaniel William, xii
Taylor, Zachary, 31, 273
telegraph, xii, 97
television, xiv, xv
Terpnitz, Joseph, 171, 172
Terror and Liberalism (Berman), xxi,
312–13
Texas, 3, 12–13
Thomas, John H., 93
Thompson, Seymour, 100
Tilden, Josiah, 219
Tillson, John, 242
Toombs, Robert, 141–42, 193, 194, 220

Toombs amendment, 141–43, 193–96, 200, 220, 272

Toulon Prairie Advocate, 98

Tribble (Alton lawyer), 256

Tribune Almanac (Greeley), 285

Trumbull, John, 140

Trumbull, Lyman, 39, 47, 56, 69, 70, 71, 98, 209, 236

　Crittenden and, 274

　Douglas Republican overtures and, 48–49, 50, 51

　Douglas's charge of conspiracy between Lincoln and, 117–18, 122, 154, 157, 169, 173–74, 179, 195–97, 199, 200, 244, 262

　election of 1854 and, 36, 37, 38

　Kansas issue and, 141–42, 154

　Lincoln-Douglas debates and, 127, 131, 178, 193–96, 256, 270

　as Lincoln's rival, 43, 139–43, 310

　slavery issue and, 83, 131

Turner, Thomas J., 147, 148

Twain, Mark, 258

Urbana Union, 130

Usher, John P., 190

Vallandigham, Clement Laird, 239

Vanderbilt, Cornelius, 75

Vanderen, Cyrus, 217

van Deren, Theophilus, 184, 189

van Doom, Joseph, 241

Vermont, election of 1858 and, 294

Vestiges of the Natural History of Creation (Chambers), 185

Villard, Henry, xii, 76, 89–90, 99, 100, 106, 116, 151, 159, 184, 204, 304

Volk, Leonard, 106

voting rights, 206

Wade, Benjamin F., 138, 216

Wagley, William C., 251

Wallace, Lew, 191

War of 1812, 5, 25–26

Washburne, Elihu, 48, 92, 145, 161, 177, 202, 288

Washington Union, 78, 86

Wead, Hezekiah, 9, 17

Webster, Daniel, 59, 93, 104, 245, 273

Weekly North-Western Gazette, 202

Weik, Jesse, 246

Wells, David, 185

Wentworth, John, 36, 37, 39, 43, 54–55, 138, 174, 179, 289, 295

Western Reserve, 217

Wheeler, John, 240–41

Whig Party, Whig voters, 27–30, 35, 38–39, 41–44, 45, 46, 70–74, 103–4, 117, 123, 165, 179, 187, 196–97, 245, 252, 254, 261, 307

　election of 1858 and, 71–72, 109–10, 167–68, 182, 187, 206, 209, 236–37, 275–76, 282–84, 286, 288–89, 299, 301–2

White, Horace, 115, 116, 160, 163, 172, 184, 200, 201, 246, 272, 303, 309

Whitefield, George, 217

Whitney, Henry Clay, 127, 205, 206, 278, 299, 305

Wiley, Benjamin, 166

Williams, Archibald, 301

Wilson, Charles, 55, 56, 79, 105, 111, 144, 151–52, 276, 288, 289

Wilson, Harold, 271

Wilson, Henry, 47, 48–49

Wilson, I. T., 243

Wisconsin, 36, 44, 71, 304

Wise, Henry, 239

World's Antislavery Convention (1843), 218

World War I, xxvii

World War II, xvii

Worley, Harvey, 190

Yates, Richard, 254

Zane, Charles, 102, 301

Zarefsky, David, xix, xxii, xxiii

ILLUSTRATION CREDITS